MCDST:
Microsoft® Certified
Desktop Support Technician
Study Guide
Deluxe Edition

MCDST:
Microsoft® Certified
Desktop Support Technician
Study Guide
Deluxe Edition

Bill Ferguson

Brad Causey

Wiley Publishing, Inc.

Acquisitions and Development Editor: Maureen Adams
Technical Editor: Craig Vazquez
Production Editor: Daria Meoli
Copy Editor: Judy Flynn
Production Manager: Tim Tate
Vice President and Executive Group Publisher:
    Richard Swadley
Vice President and Executive Publisher: Joseph B. Wikert
Vice President and Publisher: Neil Edde
Media Development Specialist: Angie Denny
Book Designer: Judy Fung
Illustrator: Jeffrey Wilson, Happenstance Type-O-Rama
Compositor: Jeffrey Wilson, Happenstance Type-O-Rama
Proofreader: Jennifer Larsen, Word One
Indexer: Ted Laux
Cover Designer: Archer Design

Sybex®
An Imprint of
WILEY

To Our Valued Readers:

Thank you for looking to Sybex for your Microsoft exam prep needs. The Sybex team is proud of its reputation for providing certification candidates with the practical knowledge and skills needed to succeed in the highly competitive IT marketplace. Just as Microsoft is committed to establishing measurable standards for certifying individuals who will support Windows systems worldwide, Sybex is committed to providing those individuals with the skills needed to meet those standards.

The authors and editors have worked hard to ensure that the Study Guide that you hold in your hands is comprehensive, in-depth, and pedagogically sound. We're confident that this book will exceed the demanding standards of the certification marketplace and help you, the MCDST certification candidate, succeed in your endeavors.

As always, your feedback is important to us. If you believe you've identified an error in the book, please visit the Customer Support section of the Wiley web site. And if you have general comments or suggestions, feel free to drop me a line directly at nedde@wiley.com. At Sybex we're continually striving to meet the needs of individuals preparing for certification exams.

Good luck in pursuit of your MCDST certification!

Neil Edde
Vice President and Publisher
Sybex, an Imprint of John Wiley & Sons

Wiley Publishing, Inc., End-User License Agreement

To my father, who has always been a source of encouragement in regard to my career, and has also given me a great amount of practical experience troubleshooting his computer! Thanks Dad! :-)
—Bill Ferguson

To my wife and two daughters, who have been the reason for everything I do and continue to support me in my endeavors. I love you.
—Brad Causey

Acknowledgments

First, I'd like to thank Brad Causey for assisting me in re-writing the Deluxe Edition of this book. Brad forced us to take a look at some topics from a different angle and thereby added even more usability and realism to the book. This makes it easier to read and easier to remember, which will result in more people passing the tests. Thanks, Brad, for the late night hours that you spent re-writing and proofing this important tool.

My thanks also go to Maureen Adams, who set us up with the right resources to get the book off to a strong start and then kept us on track throughout the entire project. Kudos to Daria Meoli for her adept project editing. Special appreciation to my Technical Editor, Craig Vazquez, whose attention to even the finest detail is absolutely amazing. To all of the copyeditors, compositors, and proofreaders...Thank you for a job well done!

Finally I'd like to acknowledge the encouragement and prayers of my family and friends and the students in my technical classes and Sunday School classes. In Him, all things are possible!

Contents at a Glance

Contents

Introduction

Microsoft's new Microsoft Certified Desktop Support Technician (MCDST) certification is designed to help get you started on your career by ensuring that you have the skills to troubleshoot desktop environments running on the Windows operating system.

This book has been developed to give you the critical skills and knowledge that you need to prepare for the two exams that you are required to pass to become an MCDST. These exams are MS 70-271 (Supporting Users and Troubleshooting a Microsoft Windows XP Operating System) and MS 70-272 (Supporting Users and Troubleshooting Desktop Applications on a Microsoft Windows XP Operating System).

This Deluxe Edition contains even more information about troubleshooting the Windows XP operating system and recovering it from failure than the original version of this book contained. We feel sure that this book will assist you in passing the certification exams and give you the knowledge to be a well-rounded Windows XP troubleshooter. We have mapped the content of this book in direct relation to Microsoft's stated objectives for these exams. You can read the objectives at www.microsoft.com/mcdst.

Why Become Certified as an MCDST?

As the computer network industry grows in both size and complexity, the need for *proven* ability is increasing. Companies rely on certifications to verify the skills of prospective employees and contractors. Whether you are just getting started or are ready to move ahead in the computer industry, the knowledge, skills, and credentials you have are your most valuable assets.

Microsoft has developed its Microsoft Certified Professional program to give you credentials that verify your ability to troubleshoot the user's desktop, including the operating systems and the applications that they use most. In addition, you will learn how to communicate with users to assist them and ensure their continued productivity to the organization.

Over the next few years, thousands of companies around the world will be searching for IT professionals who can help improve their user productivity by quickly troubleshooting and repairing issues related to their desktop operating systems and the applications that they use most often. They will turn to people who can prove that they have the ability to work with computers and with the users in the network. Your certification will be proof that you understand not only the technical aspects of troubleshooting the problem but also how to work with end users to ensure their continued productivity for their organization. The MCDST certification will give you an advantage over your competition for the same job.

Is This Book for You?

If you want to acquire a solid foundation in troubleshooting the latest desktop operating systems and working with the end users of a network, this book is for you. You'll find clear explanations of the fundamental concepts you need to grasp.

If your goal is to prepare for the exam by learning how Microsoft wants you to communicate with users and troubleshoot their issues, this book is for you. It will help you to achieve the high level of professional competency you need to succeed in this field.

If you want to become certified as an MCDST, this book is definitely for you. However, if you just want to attempt to pass the exam without really understanding the role of an MCDST, this book is *not* for you. This book is written for those who want to acquire hands-on skills and in-depth knowledge of the Microsoft Certified Desktop Support Technician certification and its role in an organization.

What Does This Book Cover?

Think of this book as your complete guide to troubleshooting Windows XP and the most common operating systems utilized by users in a Microsoft Windows environment. It begins by covering basic concepts, such as installing the Windows operating system and managing access to resources. Each chapter teaches you how to perform important tasks, including the following:

- Configuring and troubleshooting hardware devices and drivers
- Configuring and troubleshooting desktop user environments
- Troubleshooting network protocols and services
- Configuring and troubleshooting connectivity for applications

Throughout the book, you will be provided with technical information and practical experience for each exam objective. At the end of each chapter, you'll find a summary of the topics covered in the chapter. Each chapter will incorporate key terms indicated in *italic* type. The key terms represent not only the terminology that you should recognize but also the underlying concepts that you should understand to pass the exam. All of the key terms are defined in the glossary at the back of the study guide.

Finally, each chapter concludes with 20 review questions that test your knowledge of the information covered and provides thorough explanations of the answers. Four bonus exams, as well as multimedia demonstrations of the hands-on exercises, are included on the CD that accompanies this book, as explained in the section "What's on the CD?" later in this introduction.

The topics covered in this book map directly to Microsoft's official exam objectives. Each exam objective is covered completely.

How Do You Become an MCDST?

Attaining MCDST certification is a challenge. Prospective MCDSTs will need to complete a course of study that provides not only detailed knowledge of a wide range of topics but true skills derived from working with Windows XP and related software products. If you are willing to dedicate time and effort with Windows XP and the desktop applications, you can prepare for the exams by using the proper tools. If you work through this book, you should meet the exam requirements successfully.

This book is a part of a complete series of MCDST, MCSA, and MCSE Study Guides, published by Sybex, that covers the core and elective requirements you need to obtain these Microsoft certifications. Titles include the following:

- *MCSA/MCSE: Windows Server 2003 Environment Management and Maintenance Study Guide (70-290)*

- *MCSA/MCSE: Windows Server 2003 Network Infrastructure Implementation, Management, and Maintenance Study Guide (70-291)*

- *MCSE: Windows Server 2003 Network Infrastructure Planning and Maintenance Study Guide (70-293)*

- *MCSE: Windows Server 2003 Active Directory Planning, Implementation, and Maintenance Study Guide (70-294)*

- *MCSA/MCSE: Windows 2000 Professional Study Guide, Second Edition (70-210)*

- *MCSA/MCSE: Windows XP Professional Study Guide, Second Edition (70-270)*

- *MCSA/MCSE: Windows Server 2003 Upgrade Study Guide (70-292 and 70-296)*

Types of Exam Questions on the MCDST Exams

Microsoft has introduced some new exam elements on many of its certification exams. You will not know in advance which type of format you will see on your exam. These innovations make the exams more challenging, and they make it much more difficult for someone to pass an exam after simply "cramming" for it.

> **NOTE** Microsoft will be accomplishing its goal of protecting the exams by regularly adding and removing exam questions, limiting the number of questions that any individual sees in a beta exam, and adding new exam elements.

Exam questions come in many forms in the new MCDST exams, so let's examine these forms now.

Active Screen

The active screen question, seen in Figure 1, tests your working knowledge of the product by presenting you with a dialog box and requiring you to configure or change one or more options in order to successfully answer the question. You may need to select or deselect options, use drop-down menus, or drag text elements into text areas within the dialog box to meet the requirements of the question. Note that not every element you see in the dialog box will be active for you to interact with—use this to your advantage in weeding out actions that you do not need to perform.

Build List and Reorder

The build list and reorder question type, seen in Figure 2, has been used in MCP exams for quite some time but has been refined a bit for the new exams. When presented with a build list and reorder type of question, you will be required to create a list, in the correct order, that represents the steps required to complete the stated problem.

FIGURE 1   The active screen question format

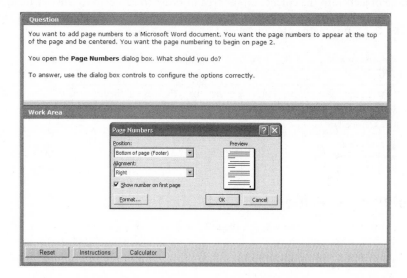

FIGURE 2   The build list and reorder question format

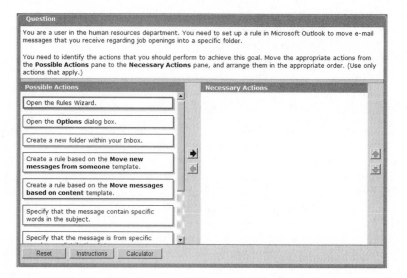

Create a Tree

When presented with a create a tree question, as seen in Figure 3, you are being asked to drag source nodes into the answer tree area in their correct location in order to successfully answer the question.

Drag and Drop

One of the new question types, the drag and drop question, seen in Figure 4, requires you to drag source objects into the correct target area in order to successfully answer the question.

FIGURE 3   The create a tree question format

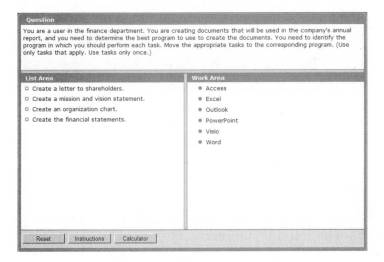

FIGURE 4   The drag and drop question format

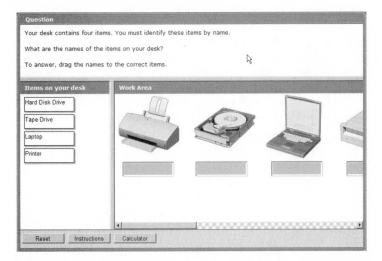

Hot Area

The hot area question type, seen in Figure 5, asks you to select one or more areas of a graphic to correctly answer the question. You will be able to easily see where selectable options exist within the graphic.

FIGURE 5   The hot area question format

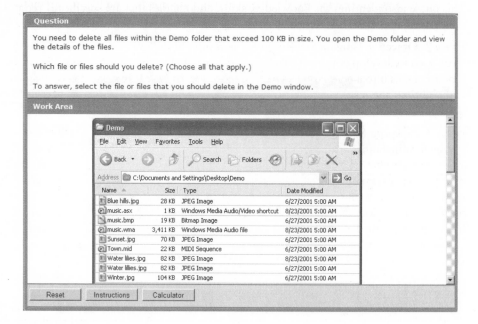

Multiple Choice

The multiple-choice question is the old standby when it comes to certification exams. Not much has changed with this question type. You can expect questions that require one correct answer or multiple correct answers. In some instances you will be told specifically how many choices to make; in others you will not. Microsoft has made this question more difficult, however, by increasing the amount of information that you must sift through in order to success-fully answer the question correctly.

The questions throughout this study guide and on the accompanying CD are presented in the same multiple-choice format that you will see on the exam.

Exam Question Development

Microsoft follows an exam-development process consisting of eight mandatory phases. The process takes an average of seven months and involves more than 150 specific steps. The MCP exam development consists of the following phases:

Phase 1: Job Analysis   Phase 1 is an analysis of all of the tasks that make up a specific job function based on tasks performed by people who are currently performing that job function. This phase also identifies the knowledge, skills, and abilities that are specifically required in the performance area to be certified.

Phase 2: Objective Domain Definition   The results of the job analysis provide the framework used to develop objectives. The development of objectives involves translating the job-function tasks into a comprehensive set of more specific and measurable knowledge, skills, and abilities. The resulting list of objectives—the *objective domain*—is the basis for the development of both the certification exams and the training materials.

Phase 3: Blueprint Survey   The final objective domain is transformed into a blueprint survey in which contributors are asked to rate each objective. Contributors may be past MCP candidates, appropriately skilled exam-development volunteers, or Microsoft employees. Based on the contributors' input, the objectives are prioritized and weighted. The actual exam items are written according to the prioritized objectives. Contributors are queried about how they spend their time on the job. If a contributor doesn't spend an adequate amount of time actually performing the specified job function, the data from that contributor is eliminated from the analysis. The blueprint survey phase helps determine which objectives to measure, as well as the appropriate number and types of items to include on the exam.

Phase 4: Item Development   A pool of items is developed to measure the blueprinted objective domain. The number and types of items to be written are based on the results of the blueprint survey.

Phase 5: Alpha Review and Item Revision   During this phase, a panel of technical and job-function experts reviews each item for technical accuracy and then answers each item, reaching a consensus on all technical issues. Once the items have been verified as technically accurate, they are edited to ensure that they are expressed in the clearest language possible.

Phase 6: Beta Exam   The reviewed and edited items are collected into beta exams. Based on the responses of all beta participants, Microsoft performs a statistical analysis to verify the validity of the exam items and to determine which items will be used in the certification exam. Once the analysis has been completed, the items are distributed into multiple parallel forms, or *versions*, of the final certification exam.

Phase 7: Item Selection and Cut-Score Setting   The results of the beta exams are analyzed to determine which items should be included in the certification exam based on many factors, including item difficulty and relevance. During this phase, a panel of job-function experts determines the *cut score* (minimum passing score) for the exams. The cut score differs from exam to exam because it is based on an item-by-item determination of the percentage of candidates who answered the item correctly and who would be expected to answer the item correctly.

Phase 8: Live Exam   As the final phase, the exams are given to candidates. MCP exams are administered by Sylvan Prometric and Virtual University Enterprises (VUE).

Microsoft will regularly add and remove questions from the exams. This is called item *seeding*. It is part of the effort to make it more difficult for individuals to merely memorize exam questions passed along by previous test-takers.

Tips for Taking the MCDST Exams

Here are some general tips for taking the exam successfully:

- Arrive early at the exam center so you can relax and review your study materials. During your final review, you can look over tables and lists of exam-related information.

- Read the questions carefully. Don't be tempted to jump to an early conclusion. Make sure you know *exactly* what the question is asking.

- Answer all questions.

- Use a process of elimination to get rid of the obviously incorrect answers first on questions that you're not sure about. This method will improve your odds of selecting the correct answer if you need to make an educated guess.

Exam Registration

You may take the exams at any of more than 1,000 Authorized Prometric Testing Centers (APTCs) and VUE Testing Centers around the world. For the location of a testing center near you, call Sylvan Prometric at (800) 755-EXAM (755-3926), or call VUE at (888) 837-8616. Outside the United States and Canada, contact your local Sylvan Prometric or VUE registration center.

You should determine the number of the exam you want to take and then register with the Sylvan Prometric or VUE registration center nearest to you. At this point, you will be asked for advance payment for the exam. The exams are $125 each. Exams must be taken within one year of payment. You can schedule exams up to six weeks in advance or as late as one working day prior to the date of the exam. You can cancel or reschedule your exam if you contact the center at least two working days prior to the exam. Same-day registration is available in some locations, subject to space availability. Where same-day registration is available, you must register a minimum of two hours before test time.

 You may also register for your exams online at www.2test.com or www.vue.com.

When you schedule the exam, you will be provided with instructions regarding appointment and cancellation procedures, ID requirements, and information about the testing center location. In addition, you will receive a registration and payment confirmation letter from Sylvan Prometric or VUE.

Microsoft requires certification candidates to accept the terms of a nondisclosure agreement before taking certification exams.

What's on the CD?

With this new book in our best-selling MCDST, MCSA, and MCSE Study Guide series, we are including quite an array of training resources. On the CD are numerous simulations, practice exams, and flashcards to help you study for the exam. Also included are the entire contents of the book. These resources are described in the following sections.

The Sybex E-book for MCDST Exams

Many people like the convenience of being able to carry their whole study guide on a CD. They also like being able to search the text to find specific information quickly and easily. For these reasons, we have included the entire contents of this study guide on the CD, in PDF format. We've also included Adobe Acrobat Reader, which provides the interface for the contents as well as the search capabilities.

The Sybex MCDST Test Engine

This is a collection of multiple-choice questions that will help you prepare for your exam. There are three sets of questions:

- Four bonus exams designed to simulate the actual live exam.

- All the questions from the study guide, presented in a test engine for your review. You can review questions by objective or take a random test.

- The assessment test.

Here is a sample screen from the Sybex MCDST Test Engine:

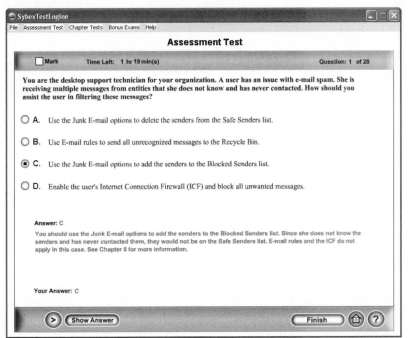

Sybex MCDST Flashcards for PCs and Palm Devices

The "flashcard" style of question offers an effective way to quickly and efficiently test your understanding of the fundamental concepts covered in the MCDST exams. The Sybex MCDST Flashcards set consists of approximately 350 questions presented in a special engine developed specifically for this Study Guide series. Here's what the Sybex MCDST Flashcards interface looks like:

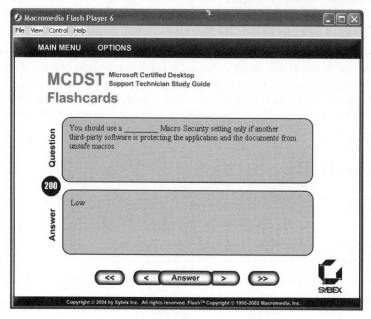

How Do You Use This Book?

This book can provide a solid foundation for the serious effort of preparing for the MCDST exams. To best benefit from this book, you may wish to use the following study method:

1. Study each chapter carefully. Do your best to fully understand the information.

2. Complete all hands-on exercises in the chapter, referring back to the text as necessary so that you understand each step you take.

3. Answer the review questions at the end of each chapter. If you would prefer to answer the questions in a timed and graded format, install the Sybex Test Engine from the CD that accompanies this book and answer the chapter questions there instead of in the book.

4. Note the questions you did not understand, and study the corresponding sections of the book again.

5. Make sure you complete the entire book.

6. Before taking the exam, go through the training resources included on the CD that accompanies this book. Try the adaptive version that is included with the Sybex Test Engine. Review and sharpen your knowledge with the MCDST Flashcards.

In order to complete the exercises in this book, you'll need to have access to at least one machine running Windows XP and preferably two such machines networked together. You will also need access to Microsoft Office; you can order a trial version through Microsoft. Some exercises may require you to have administrative access or to be part of an Active Directory domain.

 To learn all of the material covered in this book, you will need to study regularly and with discipline. Try to set aside the same time every day to study, and select a comfortable and quiet place in which to do it. If you work hard, you will be surprised at how quickly you learn this material. Good luck!

Contacts and Resources

To find out more about Microsoft Education and Certification materials and programs, to register with Sylvan Prometric or VUE, or to get other useful information, check the following resources.

Microsoft Learning Home Page   `www.microsoft.com/learning`

This website provides information about the MCDST program and exams. You can also get information on related Microsoft products.

Prometric   `www.2test.com`

(800) 755-EXAM

Contact Sylvan Prometric to register to take an MCDST exam at any of more than 800 Prometric Testing Centers around the world.

Virtual University Enterprises (VUE)   `www.vue.com`

(888) 837-8616

Contact the VUE registration center to register to take an MCDST exam at one of the VUE Testing Centers.

Assessment Test

1. You are the desktop support technician for your organization. A user has an issue with email spam. She is receiving multiple messages from entities that she does not know and has never contacted. How should you assist the user in filtering these messages?

    A. Use the Junk E-mail Options dialog box to delete the senders from the Safe Senders list.

    B. Use email rules to send all unrecognized messages to the Recycle Bin.

    C. Use the Junk E-mail options to add the senders to the Blocked Senders list.

    D. Enable the user's Internet Connection Firewall (ICF) and block all unwanted messages.

2. You are the desktop support technician for your organization. A group of Japanese users needs to have the latest Windows XP operating system software with Japanese language menus and Help menus. Your organization currently has only the English version of Windows XP. Which of the following are valid options to assist the Japanese users? (Choose two.)

    A. Install the Japanese language in the Regional and Language Options tools of the Windows XP English version.

    B. Purchase and install the MUI version of the Windows XP software; select the Japanese language.

    C. Purchase and install the Japanese version of the Windows XP software.

    D. Add the Japanese fonts to the menus and Help menus of the English version of Windows XP.

3. You are the desktop support technician for your organization. The user requests your assistance in configuring the AutoComplete feature in his Internet Explorer application. Which tab in Internet Options contains these settings?

    A. General

    B. Security

    C. Privacy

    D. Content

4. You are the desktop support technician for your organization. You are assisting in troubleshooting name resolution problems on a client computer. The application that the user is utilizing requires hostname resolution. Which of the following services or files are directly related to hostname resolution? (Choose all that apply.)

    A. WINS

    B. DNS

    C. LMHOSTS file

    D. Hosts file

5. You are the desktop support technician for your organization. An Outlook Express user has received an email that has unique stationery. She asks you how she can save the stationery so she can use it on future email. To which menu of Outlook Express settings should you direct her?

   A. Message

   B. File

   C. View

   D. Tools

6. You are the desktop support technician for your organization. A user has some older computers on which he wants to install Windows XP operating system software. Which of the following would cause a Windows XP installation to fail? (Choose all that apply.)

   A. Pentium III 350MHz processor

   B. 32MB RAM

   C. 16X CD-ROM drive

   D. VGA resolution

7. You are the desktop support technician for your company. A user is having problems with Microsoft Word 2003. You want to ensure that the user's computer contains the latest security updates for this application. Which of the following are valid methods to start the process of obtaining these updates? (Choose all that apply.)

   A. Choose Help and then choose Check for Updates.

   B. Use the browser to connect to the Windows Update website.

   C. Use the browser to connect to the Office Update website.

   D. Choose File and then choose Check for Updates.

8. You are the desktop support technician for your organization. The user is experiencing general connectivity issues on a client computer. You want to determine the IP address of the computer as well as the IP addresses of all of the name resolution servers configured for the computer. Which of the following should you type on a command prompt?

   A. `ipconfig`

   B. `nbtstat -n`

   C. `arp -a`

   D. `ipconfig /all`

9. You are the desktop support technician for your organization. You're setting up NTFS permissions on a local computer. You want a user to be able to read files in a folder and create new files within the folder but not be able to delete the folder. Which NTFS folder permissions should you assign to the user?

   A. Write, Read and Execute, List Folder Contents

   B. Modify, Read and Execute, List Folder Contents

   C. Read and Execute, List Folder Contents

   D. Read and Execute, Modify

10. You are the desktop support technician for your company. A user is experiencing problems with an application that utilizes DirectX. You want to troubleshoot the problem and determine whether DirectX is functioning properly on the computer. Which of the following is a valid method of beginning to access the DirectX Diagnostic tool? (Choose all that apply.)

   A. Type `msinfo32` on the command prompt.

   B. Choose System Information in Control Panel.

   C. Type `msinfo32` on the Run line.

   D. Choose System Information from System Tools in Accessories.

11. You are the desktop support technician for your organization. A user has been working on an Excel spreadsheet in Excel 2003 for many hours. She saved the spreadsheet earlier in the day, but she has not performed any subsequent save operations. Your organization experiences a power failure and her computer suddenly loses all power. Which feature in Office 2003 might assist her in preserving most, if not all, of her spreadsheet changes?

   A. AutoComplete

   B. Microsoft Application Recovery Tool

   C. AutoCorrect

   D. AutoRecover

12. You are the desktop support technician for your company. A user is experiencing a general connectivity issue. She can connect to resources within her own subnet, but she cannot connect to any resources outside her subnet. Which of the following elements of her IP configuration should you examine first?

   A. Default gateway

   B. IP address of her computer

   C. Subnet mask

   D. IP address of the DNS server

13. You are the desktop support technician for your organization. One of your users makes many presentations during the day using her laptop. She asks you if there is a way to store the presentation already loaded on the laptop when she carries the laptop inside its carrying case between locations. Which power option of Windows XP should the user utilize?

   A. Standby

   B. Power schemes

   C. UPS

   D. Hibernation

14. You are the desktop support technician for your organization. In an effort to tighten security, management has decided to disallow password caching in Internet Explorer 6.0 on all of the computers in your department. Your supervisor has asked you to check each of the client computers and make sure that password caching is not allowed. Which tab in Internet Options contains the correct settings?

A. General

B. Security

C. Content

D. Advanced

15. You are the desktop support technician for your company. A user is having general connectivity problems with a client computer. You ask the user to type ipconfig on a command line and then read the resulting IP address. The IP address that the user reads is 169.254.1.4. Which of the following network services is most likely associated with this problem?

A. WINS

B. DNS

C. RAS

D. DHCP

16. You are the desktop support technician for your organization. A user is having problems with his Windows XP software. You want to make sure that the user has the latest security updates. You click the Automatic Updates tab within System Properties, but you find that it is preset and that the settings are grayed out so that you can't change them. Which of the following should you suspect first?

A. A virus

B. A macro

C. A corrupted file

D. A group policy

17. You are the desktop support technician for your company. A user asks you for assistance in setting up print options within Internet Explorer. In particular, he wants to find the Page Setup option. To which Internet Explorer menu should you direct him?

A. File

B. Edit

C. View

D. Tools

18. You are the desktop support technician for your organization. A user is experiencing security issues with a computer that is a member of a domain. You want to determine which group policies are affecting the computer and the user. Which command-line tool should you use?

    A. `ipconfig`

    B. `ipconfig /all`

    C. `nbtstat -n`

    D. `gpresult`

19. You are the desktop support technician for your company. You control a hierarchy of files and folders on a user's computer. You have decided to move and copy some of these files and folders, all of which have NTFS permissions applied to them. You are moving and copying them into folders that are located on a different NTFS volume. Which of the following statements are true? (Choose two.)

    A. All files that are copied will inherit the permissions of the folder into which they are copied.

    B. All files that are moved will retain the permissions from which they were moved.

    C. All files that are moved will inherit the permissions of the folder to which they are moved.

    D. All files that are copied will retain the permissions of the folder from which they were copied.

20. You are the desktop support technician for your organization. You want to capture the configuration settings of a computer that is a member of a domain so that you can load the settings onto other computers that are also members of a domain. Which tool will allow you to perform this task?

    A. Loadstate

    B. File and Settings Transfer Wizard

    C. Scanstate

    D. Upgrade Advisor

Answers to Assessment Test

1. C. You should use the Junk E-mail Options dialog box to add the senders to the Blocked Senders list. Since she does not know the senders and has never contacted them, they would not be on the Safe Senders list. E-mail rules and the ICF do not apply in this case. See Chapter 7 for more information.

2. B, C. You should purchase and install either the Japanese version or the Multilanguage User Interface (MUI) version of the Windows XP software. The Regional and Language options will not change the menus and Help menus of the operating system software. You cannot just install a new font in the English version of Windows XP. See Chapter 4 for more information.

3. D. The Content tab within Internet Options in the Tools menu contains the settings for Auto-Complete. The other options are valid tabs, but they do not contain the settings required. See Chapter 6 for more information.

4. B, D. The elements that might affect hostname resolution are Domain Name System (DNS) services and the Hosts file. Windows Internet Name Services (WINS) and the LMHOSTS file are not directly related to hostname resolution; instead, they are related to NetBIOS name resolution. See Chapter 9 for more information.

5. B. You should direct her to the File menu and then to Save As Stationery. The other options are valid tabs in Outlook Express but they do not contain the required setting. See Chapter 7 for more information.

6. B, D. Windows XP requires at least 64MB of RAM and a Super VGA resolution video adapter. It also requires only a Pentium 233MHz processor and any CD-ROM; therefore, a Pentium III 350MHz processor and a 16X CD-ROM drive would not cause the installation to fail. See Chapter 1 for more information.

7. A, C. Either you should choose Help from the Word 2003 application and then choose Check for Updates or you should use the browser to connect to the Microsoft Office Update website. The Windows Update website does not contain the latest security updates for Word 2003. The File menu does not contain the Check for Updates option. See Chapter 11 for more information.

8. D. You should type `ipconfig /all` to obtain the IP address of the computer as well as the IP addresses of all of the name resolution servers configured for the computer. The `ipconfig` command will display only the IP address of the computer. The `arp -a` command will display the Address Resolution Protocol (ARP) cache. The `nbtstat -n` command will display the list of NetBIOS names used by the computer. See Chapter 6 for more information.

9. A. You should assign Write, Read and Execute, and List Folder Contents to the folder. Assigning Modify permissions would allow the user to delete the folder. Assigning only Read and Execute and List Folder Contents would not allow the user to add files and folders to the folder. See Chapter 2 for more information.

10. C, D.   You should either type **msinfo32** on the Run line or choose System Information from the System Tools in the Accessories menu. Typing **msinfo32** on a command prompt is not a valid option. System Information is not contained in Control Panel by default. See Chapter 3 for more information.

11. D.   The AutoRecover feature of Office 2003 automatically saves a user's document at regular intervals. The user can select the recovered document in the case of a power failure. AutoComplete is a feature included with IE 6.0, not Office 2003. The Microsoft Application Recovery Tool can be used to close hung applications without losing data. The AutoCorrect feature is used to correct common spelling errors or substitute typed words with other words or phrases. See Chapter 7 for more information about AutoRecover.

12. A.   You should first examine the default gateway configured for her computer. An incorrectly configured default gateway will cause this problem. Since she can connect to resources within her own subnet, her IP address and subnet mask must be correct. Since she cannot connect to any resources outside her own subnet, the problem is more than just an incorrectly configured IP address for her DNS server. See Chapter 10 for more information.

13. D.   The user should utilize hibernation, provided that she has enough hard drive space available on her laptop to hold the amount of RAM installed in the laptop. Hibernation will ensure that the laptop is completely shut down when she places it into its carrying case. She can then resume her presentation at the next location. The other power options do not address the problem of completely shutting down the laptop while holding the presentation. See Chapter 3 for more information.

14. C.   You should use the Content tab in Internet Options to access AutoComplete within the Personal Information section. You can configure password caching, and even clear previous passwords, using the AutoComplete tool. The other options are all valid tabs in Internet Options, but they do not contain the correct setting. See Chapter 6 for more information.

15. D.   The Dynamic Host Configuration Protocol (DHCP) service is most likely associated with this problem. The client is very likely configured to obtain an IP address automatically, and it could not find a DHCP server when it was last started. The other options are valid network services, but they are not likely associated with this problem. See Chapter 6 for more information.

16. D.   You should first suspect that an administrator is controlling automatic updates using Group Policy. The other options are also possible, but they are much less likely. See Chapter 11 for more information.

17. A.   You should direct him to the File menu to find Page Setup. The other options are all valid menus in Internet Explorer, but they do not contain Page Setup. See Chapter 7 for more information.

18. D.   You should use the gpresult tool to determine which group policies are affecting the computer and the user. Ipconfig and ipconfig /all can be used to troubleshoot problems with connectivity. Nbtstat -n displays a list of NetBIOS names for the computer. See Chapter 4 for more information.

19. A, C.   The key to this scenario is the fact that all of the files are being moved or copied to a different NTFS volume. For this reason, whether they are moved or copied, they will inherit the permissions of their new folder. See Chapter 2 for more information.

20. C.   You should use the `scanstate` tool in the User State Migration Tool to capture the settings on a computer that is part of a domain. You can then use the `loadstate` tool to configure other computers with those settings. You cannot use the File and Settings Transfer Wizard on computers that are members of a domain. The Upgrade Advisor is not the appropriate tool for this action. See Chapter 1 for more information.

User Support and Troubleshooting a Microsoft Windows XP Operating System

Chapter

1

Installing a Windows Desktop Operating System

MICROSOFT EXAM OBJECTIVES COVERED IN THIS CHAPTER:

✓ **Perform and troubleshoot an attended installation of a Windows XP operating system.**

- Answer end-user questions related to performing an attended installation of a Windows XP operating system.

- Troubleshoot and complete installations in which an installation does not start. Tasks include configuring the device boot order and ascertaining probable cause of the failure to start.

- Troubleshoot and complete installations in which an installation fails to complete. Tasks include reviewing setup log files and providing needed files.

- Perform postinstallation configuration. Tasks include customizing installations for individual users and applying service packs.

✓ **Perform and troubleshoot an unattended installation of a Windows desktop operating system.**

- Answer end-user questions related to performing an unattended installation of a Windows XP operating system. Tasks include starting an installation, answering questions asked by an end user during an installation, and performing postinstallation tasks.

- Configure a PC to boot to a network device and start installation of a Windows XP operating system. Tasks include configuring PXE-compliant network cards.

- Perform an installation by using unattended installation files.

✓ **Upgrade from a previous version of Windows.**

- Answer end-user questions related to upgrading from a previous version of Windows. Considerations include available upgrade paths and methods for transferring user state data.

- Verify hardware compatibility for upgrade. Considerations include minimum hardware and system resource requirements.

- Verify application compatibility for upgrade. Tasks include ascertaining which applications can and cannot run and using the application compatibility tools.

- Migrate user state data from an existing PC to a new PC.

- Install a second instance of an operating system on a computer.

Understanding how an operating system is installed is the first step toward understanding how to troubleshoot a failed installation. Therefore, a desktop support technician must have expert knowledge of the hardware and software components involved in installing an operating system and of how they work together at each stage of the installation process. Your ability to quickly troubleshoot and repair a failed installation will be a key to keeping your customer (the end user) productive and happy.

In this chapter, we will discuss the major types of operating system installations, the components involved in each of them, and how to quickly troubleshoot and repair a failed installation. There are four main types of operating system installations:

Attended An *attended installation* consists of a user or an administrator acquiring the operating system software from a CD/DVD or a shared network source. In this case, the user or administrator begins the installation and monitors the entire process, answering questions and filling in information where appropriate. This is sometimes referred to as "baby-sitting" the installation. This method takes a tremendous amount of time and may not be the best alternative when many installations must be performed.

Unattended One type of *unattended installation* makes use of special files called *answer files* and *uniqueness database files (UDFs)* to automate the process. Although it takes time and effort to create these files, it's well worth it in the long run if you are installing an operating system on many computers. This method not only saves time, it can also increase the consistency of the options and settings that are applied to the computers because the answer file provides the answers to each of the computers. The relationship of the answer files to the uniqueness database files is a key element in this type of installation.

Another type of unattended installation involves a *Remote Installation Services (RIS)* server that is installed and configured by the network administrator. With a properly configured RIS server, you can install new client operating systems through the network with the push of a button.

Upgrade An *upgrade installation* is performed on a computer that currently has a Windows operating system installed and functional. The purpose of the upgrade is generally to take advantage of new features and functionality that the newer operating system offers by replacing the older operating system with the newer one. A chief concern in an upgrade installation is the compatibility of the current hardware and application software with the proposed new operating system. Users are also primarily concerned that their settings and documents will be left intact. One disadvantage of an upgrade versus a new installation is that an upgrade might inadvertently bring in software bugs that would have been fixed completely with a new installation. You should consider this issue when you are deciding whether to upgrade or perform a complete new installation.

Multiboot   Like an upgrade, a *multiboot installation* is also performed on a computer that currently has a Windows operating system installed and functional. The difference between a multiboot and an upgrade is that the purpose of a multiboot installation is to create other functional Windows operating systems on the same computer. Once a multiboot installation is successfully performed, a user will be able to choose which operating system to boot to at startup. The keys to creating a successful multiboot installation are the order in which the operating systems are installed and the capability to install the second operating system without disturbing the first operating system.

The rest of this chapter is about the procedures and components involved with each major type of installation and their relation to troubleshooting a failed installation.

Performing and Troubleshooting an Attended Installation of Windows XP

A successful installation of Windows XP requires some up-front planning and preparation. When you are responsible for troubleshooting a failed installation, it is essential that you know what should have been done to prepare for the installation. By knowing what should have been done, you can ask the right questions to determine the problem. You can then isolate what needs to be done to provide a solution. The steps involved in a successful installation of Windows XP are discussed in the following sections.

Verifying that Hardware Meets the Minimum Requirements

Before you begin an installation of Windows XP, you should ensure that the computer on which you are installing the operating system meets at least the minimum requirements for the installation. You should also be aware that the minimum requirements will ensure only that the operating system will function, not that it will function with acceptable speed. In addition, you should realize that the minimum hard drive requirements pertain only to the operating system running efficiently and do not include the space to contain applications. The following list represents the minimum hardware specifications from Microsoft's website:

- 233MHz processor from the Pentium/Celeron family or the AMD K6/Athlon/Duron family
- 64MB of RAM
- 1.5GB of available hard disk space
- Super VGA (800 × 600) resolution
- CD-ROM or DVD drive
- Keyboard and Microsoft mouse or compatible pointing device

Checking Hardware and Software Compatibility

Just because a computer meets the minimum hardware requirements does not mean that all of the hardware and software on the computer is compatible with the Windows XP operating system. You should ensure that all of hardware is compatible prior to installing the operating system. You can ensure that the hardware is compatible using the methods described in the following sections.

Use the Windows XP CD to Check System Compatibility

You can use the Windows XP operating system installation CD to verify a computer's compatibility with Windows XP just prior to installing the operating system. It is not necessary to have an operating system installed on the computer to check the system compatibility. You should have a hard drive installed and formatted with at least one partition. Exercise 1.1 outlines the steps that you can use to check a computer's compatibility with the Windows XP operating system before continuing to install the operating system. Later in this chapter, we will discuss the steps that you might take prior to installing the operating system and what you might do with a failed installation. For this exercise, we are just letting the operating system examine the computer prior to installing the software normally. You can use a Windows XP Home Edition or Windows XP Professional CD for this exercise. If you encounter any errors during the installation, read further into this chapter to get clues about troubleshooting your own system.

EXERCISE 1.1

Using the Windows XP CD to Check System Compatibility

1. Set the boot order in the computer's BIOS settings to recognize the CD-ROM drive before the hard drives.

2. Insert the Windows XP CD into the CD-ROM drive.

3. Restart the computer.

4. When you see "Press any key to boot to the CD" on the screen, press a key.

5. The computer will then copy files from the CD-ROM to the hard drive and examine the configuration of the computer. At this point, you will be informed if any hardware fails the compatibility test.

6. If all of your hardware is compatible, you can proceed with the installation of the operating system.

Check the Windows Catalog on the Web

You can use the Windows Catalog located on the Web at www.microsoft.com/windows/catalog to find hardware and software that is designed to work with the Windows XP operating system. The Windows Catalog is shown in Figures 1.1 and 1.2. It contains hardware and software in two main categories:

- Designed for Windows XP
- Compatible with Windows XP

FIGURE 1.1 The Windows Catalog home page

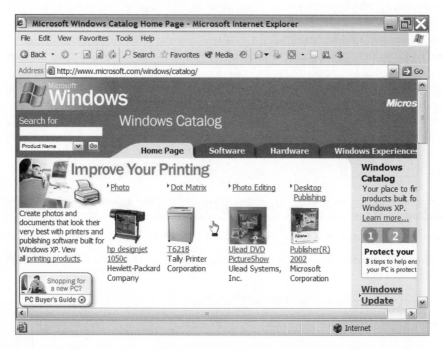

Hardware and software that carries the Designed for Windows XP logo is specifically designed for use with Windows XP. The use of this hardware and software will reduce the number of problems and frustrations associated with using the Windows XP product. If your hardware or software is listed as Compatible with Windows XP, then it has not met all of the requirements of the Windows Logo Program but has been deemed compatible by Microsoft and/or the manufacturer of the software.

The Hardware Compatibility List (HCL) was absorbed by the Windows Catalog. It is still maintained and may have useful information for additional operating systems, such as Windows Server 2003 and Windows 2000. The HCL is shown in Figure 1.3 and can be found at www.microsoft.com/whdc/hcl.

FIGURE 1.2   Designed for Windows XP and Compatible with Windows XP listings

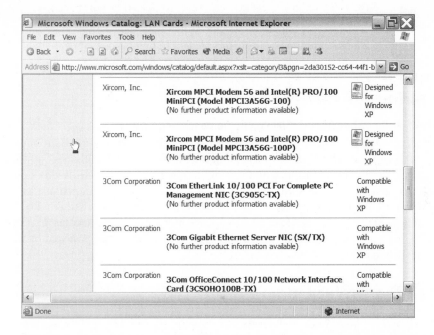

FIGURE 1.3   The Windows Hardware Compatibility List home page

If your hardware or software is not listed, this does not always mean that it will not work with Windows XP. In this case, you should check with the manufacturer of the hardware or software to determine compatibility.

Preparing the BIOS

The *basic input/output system (BIOS)* is the most basic intelligence of a computer. The BIOS is a set of software that tests hardware at startup, starts the operating system, and supports the transfer of data, including date and time, among hardware devices. If a BIOS is out-of-date for the software and hardware installed on the computer, it can cause problems with power management, peripheral configuration, disk partitioning, and other crucial functions. You should check with the computer or motherboard manufacturer to determine whether a BIOS update is available. You can often download a BIOS update and perform an electronic *flash* to update the BIOS of a computer. You should carefully follow the instructions provided by the manufacturer when updating a computer's BIOS.

Obtaining Driver Updates

A *driver* is software that allows hardware to communicate with the operating system. Consequently, drivers are usually very specific to an operating system. You should therefore make sure that you have obtained the necessary drivers for the hardware that is installed on your computer prior to installing the operating system. If your computer is equipped with *Plug-and-Play* (and most new computers are), it will ask for the drivers at the end portion of the setup. The Windows XP CD contains a cache that includes many of the most common drivers for network interface cards, video cards, sound cards, and other computer hardware. You can also obtain drivers from the website of the manufacturer of the hardware.

Preparing the Hard Disk for Installation

Since the operating system will be installed on a hard disk, it's important to understand the organization of a hard disk in a computer and the file systems from which you can choose. You should also be familiar with the tools that you can use to prepare the hard disk for installation and to begin to install the system. In this section, we will discuss the key terms relating to hard disks, the tools used to prepare the installation, and the order of their use.

Partitions

When you purchase a new hard disk or buy a computer without an operating system installed, the only formatting on the hard disk is a *low-level format* from the factory. This low-level format is the basis on which you can begin to build a working hard disk and install an operating system. The first step that you should take to begin to prepare a hard disk is to *partition* it. Partitioning the disk is logically setting aside a portion of it. A partition is sometimes referred to as a *volume*, but a partition is actually one area limited to one physical hard disk, whereas a volume can contain multiple partitions on the same disk or even on multiple disks.

There are three critical partition types you should be aware of as a desktop support technician: active, system, and boot.

Active Partition

The *active partition* on a disk is the partition from which an x86-based computer boots. It is the partition that contains the files required to boot the operating system that is designated as the default operating system in the computer. The active partition must always be on the first hard disk attached to the computer. This disk is referred to as *Disk 0*.

System Partition

The *system partition* is the partition that contains the bootstrap files that are required to display the boot menu and start the operating system. On most client computers, this is the first primary partition on Disk 0. The following bootstrap files must be on the system partition on a computer running the Windows XP operating system:

- `Ntldr`: This is a hidden file.
- `Ntdetect.com`: This is hidden file.
- `Boot.ini`: This is a hidden file.
- `Bootsect.dos`: This file is for dual configurations only.
- `Ntbootdd.sys`: This file is for system partitions located on Small Computer System Interface (SCSI) drives only.

Boot Partition

The boot partition is the partition that contains the Windows system files. The folder in which the files are located is referred to as the *systemroot* folder. The files are by default located in a folder within the `systemroot` folder named the *systemroot/system32* folder. On most client computers, this partition is the same as the system partition. Typically this is the C: drive. On client computers with *multiboot* configuration, the boot partition may be assigned a different drive letter.

WARNING   Logically speaking, the names of the system and boot partitions seem backward based on what they contain and what they do. This naming was established long ago with the first PCs. The best way to remember this is that they are backward!

Formatting and File Systems

After you have created a partition on a disk, you must *format* the partition to prepare it to hold data or, as in this case, an operating system. When you format the partition, you are creating a *file system* on which files can be stored and managed. File systems have evolved over time, and some file systems offer significant advantages over others. Table 1.1 illustrates the features of file systems and the Microsoft clients that can use each type.

You should be familiar with the advantages and disadvantages of each file system. The NTFS file system allows you to enable encryption, compression, and security features, as seen in Figures 1.4, 1.5, and 1.6. Operating systems such as Windows Me and Windows 98 do not support or understand these features.

F I G U R E   1 . 4   Enabling NTFS compression

F I G U R E   1 . 5   Enabling NTFS encryption

FIGURE 1.6   Examining NTFS permissions

There are many variations of the NTFS file system. When verifying compatibility between operating systems, be sure to use the most recent version unless you must support an older version of Windows, such as Windows NT prior to Service Pack 4.

TABLE 1.1   File System Features

Feature	FAT	FAT32	NTFS
Microsoft clients that support the file system	Windows 95 OSR1, Windows 95 OSR2, Windows 98, Windows Me, Windows NT Workstation, Windows 2000 Professional, Windows XP Home Edition, Windows XP Professional	Windows 98, Windows Me, Windows 2000 Professional, Windows XP Home Edition, Windows XP Professional	Windows NT Workstation, Windows 2000 Professional, Windows XP Home Edition, Windows XP Professional
Maximum partition size	4GB	32GB	2TB (terabytes)
Sector size	16KB to 64KB	As low as 4KB	As low as 4KB
Security	File attributes	File attributes	File, folder, and encryption attributes
Compression	None	None	Files

You should use the NTFS file system for all partitions on a computer with the Windows XP operating system installed. This takes advantage of the additional security and stability of the file system. The only exception is when you are multibooting the computer with an operating system that does not support NTFS, such as Windows 95, Windows 98, and Windows Me.

Tools for Hard Disk Preparation

There are many tools that you can use to prepare a hard disk. In this section, we will focus on the tools that are inherent to Microsoft clients. These tools can be used to partition the disk and then format the partitions with the various file systems. They have evolved over time and have become easier to use with the latest operating systems, such as Windows XP. The tools that you can use create partitions and format them are described in the following sections.

Fdisk

The *fdisk tool* is an MS-DOS-based tool that you can use to partition a hard disk. You can use the fdisk tool to create, change, delete, or display the current partitions on a hard disk. You can create primary partitions and extended partitions. You can then create logical drives on the extended partitions.

Format

After you create partitions with the fdisk tool, you can format them with the *format tool*. As mentioned earlier, the format tool places on the disk a file system on which data can be stored and managed. You can use the format tool to apply FAT, FAT32, and NTFS file systems.

The Windows XP CD

Another method of creating partitions is to use the Windows XP CD itself. You can create and format partitions just prior to installing Windows XP using only the Windows XP CD. Exercise 1.2 outlines the steps involved in this process.

EXERCISE 1.2

Creating and Formatting Partitions with the Windows XP CD

1. Set the boot order in the computer's BIOS settings to recognize the CD-ROM drive before the hard drives.

2. Insert the Windows XP CD into the CD-ROM drive.

3. Restart the computer.

4. When you see "Press any key to boot to the CD" on the screen, press a key.

OBJECTIVE	CHAPTER
Configure and troubleshoot display devices.	3
Answer end-user questions related to configuring desktop display settings. Configure display devices and display settings. Troubleshoot display device settings.	3
Configure and troubleshoot Advanced Configuration and Power Interface (ACPI).	3
Answer end-user questions related to configuring ACPI settings. Configure and troubleshoot operating system power settings. Configure and troubleshoot system standby and hibernate settings.	3
Configure and troubleshoot I/O devices.	3
Answer end-user questions related to configuring I/O devices. Configure and troubleshoot device settings. Configure and troubleshoot device drivers for I/O devices. Configure and troubleshoot hardware profiles.	3
Configure and troubleshoot storage devices.	3
Answer end-user questions related to configuring hard disks and partitions or volumes. Manage and troubleshoot disk partitioning. Answer end-user questions related to optical drives such as CD-ROM, CD-RW, DVD, and DVD-R. Configure and troubleshoot removable storage devices such as pen drives, flash drives, and memory cards.	3
Configure and troubleshoot display devices.	3
Answer end-user questions related to configuring desktop display settings. Configure display devices and display settings. Troubleshoot display device settings.	3
Configure and troubleshoot Advanced Configuration and Power Interface (ACPI).	3
Answer end-user questions related to configuring ACPI settings. Configure and troubleshoot operating system power settings. Configure and troubleshoot system standby and hibernate settings.	3
Configure and troubleshoot I/O devices.	3
Answer end-user questions related to configuring I/O devices. Configure and troubleshoot device settings. Configure and troubleshoot device drivers for I/O devices. Configure and troubleshoot hardware profiles.	3

Configuring and Troubleshooting the Desktop and User Environments

Configure the user environment.	4
Answer end-user questions related to configuring the desktop and user environment. Configure and troubleshoot Taskbar and toolbar settings. Configure and troubleshoot accessibility options. Configure and troubleshoot pointing device settings. Configure and troubleshoot Fast User Switching.	4
Configure support for multiple languages or multiple locations.	4
Answer end-user questions related to regional settings. Configure and troubleshoot regional settings. Answer end-user questions related to language settings. Configure and troubleshoot language settings.	4
Troubleshoot security settings and local security policy.	4
Answer end-user questions related to security settings. Identify end-user issues caused by local security policies such as Local Security Settings and Security Configuration and Analysis. Identify end-user issues caused by network security policies such as Resultant Set of Policy (RSoP) and Group Policy.	4
Configure and troubleshoot local user and group accounts.	4
Answer end-user questions related to user accounts. Configure and troubleshoot local user accounts. Answer end-user questions related to local group accounts. Configure and troubleshoot local group accounts. Considerations include rights and permissions.	4
Troubleshoot system startup and user logon problems.	4
Answer end-user questions related to system startup issues. Troubleshoot system startup problems. Answer end-user questions related to user logon issues. Troubleshoot local user logon issues. Troubleshoot domain user logon issues.	4

Exam objectives are subject to change at any time without prior notice and at Microsoft's sole discretion. Please visit Microsoft's Training & Certification Web site (www.microsoft.com/trainingandservices) for the most current listing of exam objectives.

Sybex®
An Imprint of
WILEY

Exam 70-272: Supporting Users and Troubleshooting Desktop Applications on a Microsoft Windows XP Operating System

Sybex®
An Imprint of
WILEY

Exam objectives are subject to change at any time without prior notice and at Microsoft's sole discretion. Please visit Microsoft's Training & Certification Web site (www.microsoft.com/trainingandservices) for the most current listing of exam objectives.

Sybex®
An Imprint of
WILEY

Microsoft Certified Desktop Support Technician (MCDST) Study Guide

Exam 70-271: Supporting Users and Troubleshooting a Microsoft Windows XP Operating System

OBJECTIVE	CHAPTER
Installing a Windows Desktop Operating System	
Perform and troubleshoot an attended installation of a Windows XP operating system.	1
Answer end-user questions related to performing an attended installation of a Windows XP operating system; troubleshoot and complete installations in which an installation does not start. Tasks include configuring the device boot order and ascertaining probable cause of the failure to start. Troubleshoot and complete installations in which an installation fails to complete. Tasks include reviewing setup log files and providing needed files. Perform postinstallation configuration. Tasks include customizing installations for individual users and applying service packs.	1
Perform and troubleshoot an unattended installation of a Windows desktop operating system.	1
Answer end-user questions related to performing an unattended installation of a Windows XP operating system. Tasks include starting an installation, answering questions asked by an end user during an installation, and performing postinstallation tasks. Configure a PC to boot to a network device and start installation of a Windows XP operating system. Tasks include configuring PXE-compliant network cards. Perform an installation by using unattended installation files.	1
Upgrade from a previous version of Windows.	1
Answer end-user questions related to upgrading from a previous version of Windows. Considerations include available upgrade paths and methods for transferring user state data. Verify hardware compatibility for upgrade. Considerations include minimum hardware and system resource requirements. Verify application compatibility for upgrade. Tasks include ascertaining which applications can and cannot run and using the application compatibility tools. Migrate user state data from an existing PC to a new PC. Install a second instance of an operating system on a computer.	1
Managing and Troubleshooting Access to Resources	
Monitor, manage, and troubleshoot access to files and folders.	2
Answer end-user questions related to managing and troubleshooting access to files and folders. Monitor, manage, and troubleshoot NTFS file permissions. Manage and troubleshoot simple file sharing. Manage and troubleshoot file encryption.	2
Manage and troubleshoot access to shared folders.	2
Answer end-user questions related to managing and troubleshooting access to shared folders. Create shared folders. Configure access permission for shared folders on NTFS partitions. Troubleshoot and interpret Access Denied messages.	2
Connect to local and network print devices.	2
Answer end-user questions related to printing locally. Configure and manage local printing. Answer end-user questions related to network-based printing. Connect to and manage printing to a network-based printer.	2
Manage and troubleshoot access to and synchronization of offline files.	2
Answer end-user questions related to configuring and synchronizing offline files. Configure and troubleshoot offline files. Configure and troubleshoot offline file synchronization.	2
Configuring and Troubleshooting Hardware Devices and Drivers	
Configure and troubleshoot storage devices.	3
Answer end-user questions related to configuring hard disks and partitions or volumes. Manage and troubleshoot disk partitioning. Answer end-user questions related to optical drives such as CD-ROM, CD-RW, DVD, and DVD-R. Configure and troubleshoot removable storage devices such as pen drives, flash drives, and memory cards.	3

Sybex®
An Imprint of

WILEY

5. The computer will then copy files from the CD-ROM to the hard drive and examine the configuration of the computer.

6. At the Welcome to Setup page, press the Enter key to continue.

7. Press F8 to accept the Windows XP Licensing Agreement.

8. If another Windows XP installation is detected, you will be prompted to repair it. Press Esc. Do not repair.

9. All existing partitions and unallocated space on the hard disk will now be listed. Use the arrow keys to select a partition or unallocated space where you want to create a partition.

10. Press D to delete an existing partition or C to create a new partition using unallocated space. If you press D, then you must press L to confirm that you want to delete a partition.

11. After pressing C to create a new partition, type the size in megabytes that you want to use for the partition and press Enter, or just press Enter to create the partition using the maximum available size.

12. Repeat steps 10 and 11 to create additional partitions.

13. Select the format option that you want to use for the partition, and press Enter.

14. After the setup program formats the partition, you can follow the instructions to continue installing the operating system.

Installing the Windows XP Operating System

Once all of the preparation is done, you are ready to install the operating system. Installing the operating system includes running the setup program, configuring the options for networking, choosing a Windows Update option, and activating the software. We will now discuss each of these steps in greater detail, examining potential problem areas and the methods that you can use to troubleshoot the problems.

Running the Setup Program

The setup program installs the operating system in four basic steps:

1. File Copy: Windows Setup files are copied to a temporary folder on the partition where they can be run when you restart the system.

2. Text Mode: In this step you select the partition to use to install the operating system. You should press F6 at this step to load any custom drivers. If you have custom hardware for which Windows does not have drivers and you do not press F6 at this step, then you may experience a *stop error*. If this happens, restart and press F6 when prompted.

3. GUI Mode: This is the graphical portion of Windows Setup, which is also known as the Setup Wizard. In this step, you can select regional settings, such as language and time zone, and enter details, such as the product key, computer name, and administrator password.

4. Windows Welcome: This is the final portion of Setup, when you have the option to create user accounts and activate Windows. Sometimes manufacturers use this step to customize the installation, adding their own logos, custom registration screens, and other features.

In a successful installation, Setup will progress through each of these steps and the operating system will basically install itself. However, if Setup detects any hardware for which it does not have appropriate drivers, it may ask you for some help. If you have a custom piece of hardware in your system, you should look for a prompt during the text mode portion of Setup and press F6 when prompted. You can then install the custom drivers. If you do not press F6, the installation may terminate with a stop error.

Installing Network Components

If the Windows XP operating system that you have just installed detects the presence of network hardware on your system, the Installing Network Components window will appear automatically. You should select either Typical Settings or Custom Settings. Your choice is determined by how you are planning to use the computer. We will now discuss the guidelines for each setting.

Typical Settings

When Typical Settings is selected, the system will configure the computer to obtain its Internet Protocol (IP) address and its Domain Name System (DNS) server address from the Dynamic Host Configuration Protocol (DHCP) server. This setting should be used only if you know that that a DHCP server is available in your organization or through your Internet service provider (ISP).

Custom Settings

When Custom Settings is selected, Setup displays screens to allow the user to enter the IP address and DNS server address manually. If you choose this setting, then you should obtain a proper IP address from your network administrator. If the IP address is not properly configured, the computer will not be able to communicate on the network and could potentially affect the communication of other computers on the network.

Customizing the Installation of Windows XP

During the many installs you will most likely be required to do, there will be situations in which a default or standard install just won't do. There are many features and options available to customize Windows XP.

Upgrade Installation Switches

If you already have an operating system installed, you might decide to start the installation from inside the existing setup. This provides various advantages, especially with the available switches for the upgrade installation executable, `Winnt32.exe`.

/S:sourcepath   This will allow you to choose the installation source, which is extremely valuable for network and unattended installs.

/tempdrive:drive letter   You can use this switch to choose an alternate drive letter to store your temporary files during the installation.

/Unattend   This allows you to use an answer file and automate the installation of Windows XP.

/copydir:directory   This allows you to have an alternate driver cache to automatically install device drivers during the setup of Windows XP.

/cmd:command   You can choose to have *command* executed directly after the successful installation of Windows XP. This is usually used in conjunction with USMT and Sysprep.

/udf:id, UD file   This allows you to select a Uniqueness Database file for customization and automation of your installation.

/syspart:drive letter   You can choose to have the setup files copied to your hard drive, mark that disk active, and install it into another computer. Starting the target computer will then resume the installation. This is especially useful if you are attempting to distribute the same installation to many systems that do not have similar hardware. You must have a previous installation of an older version of the Windows operating system, such as NT or 2000.

You must also use the `/tempdrive` switch in conjunction with `syspart`.

/checkupgradeonly   This will only check to see if an upgrade is possible. (We would have never guessed!)

/cmdcons   This will install the recovery console.

There are many more Installation switches. The switches in the preceding list are the most commonly used. To obtain more information, simply type `Winnt32.exe /?`.

Options Available during Setup

During the text mode phase of Setup, you will see "Press F6 if you have to install a third-party SCSI or RAID driver" appear at the bottom of the screen. This will provide many more options than just alternate drivers. If you press the F5 key, you have the option to choose your computer type. Pressing F6 will allow you to choose an alternate or additional hardware RAID or SCSI device driver. Pressing F7 will bypass the installation and use of Advanced Configuration and Power Interface, or ACPI. Although Windows Setup can usually automatically detect these options, there may be an instance in which specialized hardware will not install properly, and these options can allow you to select the proper hardware compatibility. Now let's visit some of the alternate computer hardware types that are available when you press F6:

ACPI Multiprocessor PC   Applies to a multiple-processor ACPI computer. This would basically be a workstation that has multiple processors. Most likely you will use this option only if you are using a server with two or more processors.

ACPI Uniprocessor PC   Applies to an ACPI multiple-processor board but with a single processor installed.

Advanced Configuration and Power Interface (ACPI) PC   Applies to a single processor motherboard with single processor. This will be the default configuration chosen by the installation.

Compaq SystemPro Multiprocessor or 100% Compatible   Applies to a Compaq SystemPro computer.

MPS Uniprocessor PC   Applies to non-ACPI computers that have a dual-processor motherboard with a single processor installed.

MPS Multiprocessor PC   Applies to non-ACPI computers with dual processors.

Standard PC   Applies to any standard PC (non-ACPI or non-MPS). The CPU may be a 386, a 486, a Pentium, a Pentium II, or a Pentium III.

Standard PC with C-Step i486   Applies only to C-Step i486 machines.

Other   Any computers that don't meet the preceding criteria.

Customizing the Installation Source

Regardless of the source from which you choose to install, there may be hardware driver problems when Windows Setup loads a driver from its default cache. This is normally a result of Setup incorrectly recognizing a device. Usually it tries to load the closest driver it can find, often resulting in an undesired error. You can see options for installation customization in Exercise 1.3.

You can easily resolve this by adding your driver into the `$WIN_NT$.~BT` directory in the installation source. This should overwrite the driver that Setup is trying to use and replace it with your correct driver. If you are installing from CD, then you will have to burn a new copy with the customized driver file.

Setting Windows Update

Once you have your operating system installed and a network connection established, the next step is to protect the operating system from unwanted intrusion. Periodically, Microsoft discovers a security threat to the operating system and publishes a patch on its website, making it available for download. The best way to keep up with all of the available patches is with the help of the *Windows Update* feature of Windows XP. Exercise 1.4 illustrates the steps to set up the Windows Update feature.

EXERCISE 1.3

Using Custom Settings during the Install of Windows XP

1. Set the boot order in the computer's BIOS settings to recognize the CD-ROM drive before the hard drives.

2. Insert the Windows XP CD into the CD-ROM drive.

3. Restart the computer.

4. When you see "Press any key to boot to the CD" on the screen, press a key.

5. After starting the installation, during the text mode phase, choose one of the following:

    a. Press F6 if you have to install a third-party SCSI or RAID driver. Use this option for OEM drivers that are not automatically loaded during setup or do not function properly.

    b. Press the F5 button. This will allow you to choose from various computer hardware types, also known as "configuring an alternate Hardware Abstraction Layer."

    c. Press the F7 button. This option will bypass the configuration of the ACPI.

    Note that most often you will perform the preceding steps only after an install has failed with errors such as "Setup did not find any hard disk drives installed in your system" or "Inaccessible_boot_device."

6. Once you have reached the GUI phase of the setup process, you will be prompted to customize your regional and language options. Choose one of the following:

    a. Choose Customize to configure your regional options. Your regional options allow you to choose how dates and currency will appear when you're reading or typing. These settings can also be configured after Setup has completed.

    b. Choose Details to configure your text input options. This will allow you to choose how Windows reacts to keystrokes. Various geographical locations have alternate keyboard layouts.

7. Type your name and organization into the Personalize Your Software dialog box.

8. Type your product key in the Your Product Key wizard screen.

9. Type the appropriate information into the Computer Name and Administrator Password dialog box.

10. Enter the proper information in the Date and Time Settings dialog box.

11. Choose one of the following in the Network Settings dialog box:

    a. Typical Settings. This will configure your computer for DHCP.

    b. Custom Settings. This will allow you manually configure network settings such as IP address, DNS server, and WINS server.

EXERCISE 1.3 *(continued)*

12. Choose one of the following in the Workgroup or Computer Domain dialog box:

    a. This Computer Is Not Part of a Network, or Is Part of a Workgroup. This option is usually used in small office or Home networks that don't have a domain controller, or for testing purposes. You will rarely use this option in a corporate environment unless you intend to join a domain after the installation.

    b. Make This Computer a Member of the Following Domain. This will allow you to join your corporate domain environment. Choosing this option has many benefits, including centralized management and ease of administration.

13. Depending on the type of Windows XP source, you may have additional options, but most likely you will now proceed to registration and activation, and create an account.

Windows Automatic Update retrieves only the critical updates. To view, download, and install other Windows updates and newly released drivers, you should visit the Windows Update site at http://windowsupdate.microsoft.com.

Activating Windows XP

A new feature has been added to Windows XP to combat software piracy and casual copying. In addition to entering the 25-character product key during the setup process (as with previous versions of Windows), you must also *activate* the software within 30 days of installation. This new feature is referred to as *Windows Product Activation (WPA)*.

In most cases, activation of the software is automatic. After the installation has completed successfully and you have established a network connection, Windows XP will ask you if you would like to activate the software. The system will use your Internet connection to connect to Microsoft to activate the software. The whole process takes only a few seconds to complete. You can also activate the software by calling Microsoft, giving the automated system the product key that came with the software, and following the instructions that you are given.

Activation and registration are very different. Activation does not require you to divulge your name or any personal information. Your choice to register the software is completely separate from your choice to activate it. The registration process does ask for some personal information.

EXERCISE 1.4

Setting Windows Update

1. Open the System applet in Control Panel.

2. Click the Automatic Updates tab.

3. Select the Keep My Computer Up To Date check box.

4. Choose from the following options:

   a. Notify Me Before Downloading Any Updates and Notify Me Again Before Installing Them on My Computer

   You should choose this option if you are using a dial-up connection and you do not want to tie up the connection with the downloads.

   b. Download the Updates Automatically and Notify Me When They Are Ready to Be Installed

   You should choose this option if you are using a high-speed, always-on connection such as a cable modem or digital subscriber line (DSL) connection. An alert bubble will pop up from the system tray area to let you know when the download has arrived. You can accept or reject any download.

c. Automatically Download the Updates, and Install Them on the Schedule That I Specify

You should choose this option when you want to specify the time that Windows Update runs. The default time is 3:00 a.m. every day. Windows Update will download and install each critical update that is available when it runs.

As part of the activation process, Microsoft examines and registers key hardware components in your computer system. Because of this, if you decide to reinstall the operating system on the same computer, you can reinstall it without activating it again. However, if you upgrade your hardware or replace your computer completely and then reinstall the operating system, you might have to reactivate the Windows XP operating system as well. In this case, the activation will not be automatic and you will need to call your Microsoft *customer representative* at the telephone number listed on the software in the Activation Wizard. You will need to explain the situation to the Microsoft customer representative and then follow the directions they give you.

There are some cases in which you may not need to activate the Windows XP operating system software:

- The manufacturer of the computer has activated the software: In this case, the software is likely to be associated only with the computer BIOS. You can therefore reinstall the operating system and upgrade the hardware as many times as you want as long as you don't change the BIOS of the computer.

- Volume license agreements: Businesses that purchase multiple copies of operating system software might receive software and a product key from Microsoft that allows them to install the software without requiring activation.

Using Log Files to Troubleshoot Installations

Windows XP automatically generates log files that can help you determine the cause of a failed installation. These files are automatically created in the folder that you designated as the *systemroot*, usually the `Windows` folder. Depending on how far the installation progressed, you can view these files on the computer on which you are installing the operating system or copy them to another computer and view them there. You should open the files with Notepad and examine them for clues as to what may have gone wrong in the installation process. The following are log files created by the installation and a brief description of the clues that they may contain:

- `Setuplog.txt`: Describes the tasks performed during setup.
- `Setupapi.log`: Lists hardware and driver detection and installation issues.
- `Setuperr.log`: Created if errors occur during setup.
- `Setupapt.log`: Records actions that are taken during setup.
- `PNPlog.txt`: Lists Plug-and-Play hardware and driver detection issues.

Additional Tips for Installation Problems

There are various steps to take once you have run into a problem during an installation of Windows XP. Most early problems are related to hardware or configuration issues. Be sure to verify hardware compatibly through Microsoft's online process. You might also try manipulating the default diver cache or installation source.

If you find that your hardware is not supported by Microsoft, you should be sure to contact the manufacturer. Most manufacturers will have drivers available either via technical support or on their download page on their website.

You should also be wary of the installation directory. You can usually choose the installation location on the hard drive. If you have another operating system installed, such as Windows NT, you might face conflicts when accepting defaults. Sometimes the installation will attempt to create another WINNT directory when the original still exists, resulting in an installation directory named WINNT.001. This should be a clue that Windows XP didn't perform an upgrade; it performed a multiboot installation on the same partition. This is usually not the desired result!

Performing and Troubleshooting an Unattended Installation of Windows XP

If you install client operating systems infrequently, then you might be completely satisfied with the attended installation method. On the other hand, if you are responsible for installing many client operating systems, you might like to know of ways to further automate that process and answer the questions that the system asks on every installation.

Administrators who are responsible for many installations of operating systems might use the *Setup Manager Wizard* or *text editor* to create special files called *answer files* and *uniqueness database files (UDFs)*. As a desktop support technician, you should be aware of how these files are used in the installation of the operating system.

Another tool that administrators might use to install many client operating systems is Remote Installation Services (RIS). In this case, the administrator might create and test a client computer and then image that client computer into a server so that it can be installed on future client computers. This method requires specific hardware and configuration to function properly.

We will now discuss each of the tools used for unattended installation in greater detail.

Answer Files

An *answer file* is a text file that provides configuration settings that would otherwise be entered by the administrator during setup. The answer file provides answers that are common to all of the computers on which it will be used. Each entry in the answer file is divided into two parts, the *section title* and the *settings*. Figure 1.7 shows an answer file that was created using the Setup Manager Wizard, and in the following sections, we'll discuss the parts of this file in more detail.

FIGURE 1.7 Example of unattend.txt file

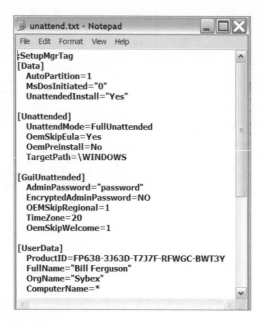

Section Title

A *section title* indicates the category of the settings that follow it. Section titles in an answer file might include Userdata, Identification, and Networking. The more complex the file, the more section titles will be included in it. Each section title can contain many settings.

Settings

Within each section title, the configuration settings are created using *keys* and *values*. These take the form of *Key=Value*, where the key represents the parameter and the value represents the actual configuration setting for the computer. For example, Computer Name=Sybex1 is a setting. As mentioned earlier, each section title can have many settings.

Uniqueness Database Files

Whenever more than one computer name is entered into an answer file created by the Setup Manager Wizard, a UDF named `unattend.udb` is automatically created. The *uniqueness database file (UDF)* provides computer settings that are unique to each computer. It is created with syntax that is very similar to that used for an answer file.

A UDF is divided into two sections. The first section, named UniqueIDs, provides the computer names and the sections of data to be replaced or merged with the answer file for each individual computer. Figure 1.8 is an example of the first section of a UDF.

FIGURE 1.8   Example of the first section of an unattend.udb file

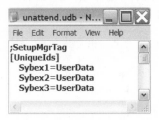

The second section contains the actual values that Setup will use for these *Keys*. Figure 1.9 shows the settings in the second section of a UDF. Initially, the UDF contains only the computer names to be used, but it can be modified to contain other settings that can be individually configured during setup.

FIGURE 1.9   Example of the second section of an unattend.udb file

In most cases, the values in the UDF will be used instead of the values in the answer file for the same computer. The only time that a value will be used from the answer file is when there is no corresponding value in the UDF. In some cases, if there is a key specified but no value specified in a UDF, then no value will be automatically set and the user will be prompted to input the information. If the UDF has an entire section that the answer file does not have, then Setup will use that section and its keys and values. Table 1.2 illustrates the priority that Setup gives answer files and UDFs.

TABLE 1.2   Priority and Use of Answer Files and UDFs

Answer File	UDF	Result
Key and value specified	Key not specified	Value in answer file used
Key not specified	Key and value specified	Value in UDF used

TABLE 1.2   Priority and Use of Answer Files and UDFs *(continued)*

Answer File	UDF	Result
Key and value specified	Key and value specified	Value in UDF used
Key not specified	Key specified without value	No value set; user may be prompted for input
Section and/or key not specified	Key and value specified	Section and/or key created and used by Setup

The process for creating a set of unattended installation files is pretty straightforward. There a few requirements and modifications that need to be made on the files after creation, as seen in Exercise 1.5.

EXERCISE 1.5

Creating an Unattended Answer File

1. Insert the Windows XP CD into a computer that already has Windows XP installed.

2. Close the splash screen and browse to the root of the CD drive.

3. Browse to x:\Support\Tools\.

4. Copy the Deploy.cab file to your local hard drive and extract the files from it.

5. Start the Setupmgr.exe program and follow the screens to create your answer file.

    You should explore the many available options here.

Be sure to rename the unattend.txt file Winnt.sif and rename the unattend.bat file Winnt.bat. Otherwise, your install will fail.

Remote Installation Services

Remote Installation Services (RIS) allows network administrators who are in charge of many computer installations to more easily deploy those installations through the network. The only clients that can use RIS are Windows 2000 Professional and Windows XP Professional. As a desktop support technician, you are responsible for understanding only the client portion of the RIS setup. Since RIS requires significant setup on the server and the network as well, many issues related to RIS will be escalated to the network administrator.

In order for computers to use RIS, they must have at least one of the following three components:

- A Net PC-compliant motherboard; therefore, a RIS-compliant network interface card must be built into the motherboard of the computer.
- A PXE-enabled network interface card installed in the computer. (PXE stands for preboot execution environment.)
- A network interface card that is compliant with the software but not PXE compliant *and* the special RIS boot disk created by the network administrator. The RIS boot disk must be in the floppy drive of the client computer on which the software will be installed.

Once the computer has met one of these conditions and the network administrator has prepared the image and made the connections to the computer, the client software can be installed through the network as follows:

1. The user or administrator restarts the computer and presses F12 to perform a network boot.
2. The computer broadcasts on the network for the presence of a Dynamic Host Configuration Protocol (DHCP) server.
3. The DHCP server responds with the address of the RIS server.
4. The computer connects to the RIS server, and the user or administrator is presented with a selection of operating systems from which to install. These can be in a user-friendly format, such as "Windows XP for 3rd Floor Accounting."
5. The user or administrator selects the appropriate image, and the installation proceeds automatically.

 Since RIS requires that the DHCP server, DNS, Active Directory, and all physical connections be correct, many issues related to its installation will be escalated to the network administrator. As an MCDST, you should be familiar with what is required for the system to operate properly so you know when to escalate the issue.

Performing and Troubleshooting an Upgrade Installation of Windows XP

If a user currently has a working installation of Windows but wishes to upgrade the client software to Windows XP, they can begin the upgrade by simply placing the Windows XP CD into the CD-ROM drive and closing it. The computer will likely detect the Windows XP CD and offer to run the upgrade. As a desktop support technician, you should be aware that what seemed to start out very simply can get much more complicated very quickly. Whether the computer can be successfully upgraded to Windows XP will depend upon the hardware installed in the computer. How well the upgrade will work will further be determined by the drivers and other software that are to be upgraded. All client computers with Windows 98 or later operating systems can be upgraded to Windows XP.

If a user is upgrading both the computer and operating system (changing computers), then the task is further complicated because they may want to make sure they retain the settings and configurations from the current operating system. These can be very important to some users.

You can use the Upgrade Advisor to run a test and create a report that you can examine for any inconsistencies with the Windows XP operating system. In this way, you can ensure that the upgrade installation will go smoothly, without any surprises. In addition, if the user is changing computers, you can use the User State Migration Tool (USMT) and/or Files and Settings Transfer (FAST) Wizard to transfer configuration settings and files from the current computer to the new one. We will discuss these tools and their use in greater detail in the following sections.

Using the Upgrade Advisor

The *Upgrade Advisor* is software built into the Windows XP operating system disk and/or available from Microsoft's website at www.microsoft.com/windowsxp/pro/howtobuy/upgrading/advisor.asp. The software checks a computer for compatibility and automatically creates a report listing problems that you might encounter during the upgrade process. The report might even direct you to install a service pack or patch before continuing the installation. When you're upgrading from Windows 98 or Millennium Edition, the system may even suggest that you uninstall some programs before continuing and then reinstall them after the installation is complete. Exercise 1.6 outlines the steps for using the Upgrade Advisor. This exercise can be performed on a computer running Windows 98, Windows Millennium Edition, Windows 2000 Professional, Windows XP Home Edition, or even Windows XP Professional.

EXERCISE 1.6

Using the Upgrade Advisor for Windows XP

1. Insert the Windows XP CD into the CD-ROM drive and close it.

2. The system will recognize the CD and you will see "Welcome to Microsoft Windows XP" on the screen. If you do not see this screen, browse the disk and click the setup.exe file to access the Welcome screen.

3. Click Check System Compatibility.

4. Click Check My System Automatically.

5. The system will run an abbreviated version of Setup and produce a report that lists problems that you might encounter regarding hardware and software. The report might contain instructions to download upgrade packs or temporarily uninstall some software. You should follow the instructions in the report.

Using the User State Migration Tool

The term *user state* refers to the configuration settings applied to a user's computer. These could include settings such as background, screensaver, font, and resolution. In a large organization, administrators might want to standardize and record these settings so that they can be reproduced on computers throughout the organization. Administrators use the *User State Migration Tool (USMT)* built into Windows XP to record and distribute a user state to multiple computers. The USMT is located on the Windows XP CD in the VALUEADD\MSFT\USMT folder. You can also copy the entire USMT folder to your computer to use the tools it contains.

The USMT consists of two main commands, each with multiple switches. We will discuss the two main commands in the User State Migration Tool in the following sections.

Scanstate

Scanstate is used to create an "electronic recording" of the settings in a computer. You can use `scanstate` to record the settings on all Microsoft clients later than Windows 98. Using the switches provided by the USMT, you can further configure `scanstate` to record Registry settings or give more or less output. To see the syntax and switches for `scanstate`, you can type `scanstate /?` on the command prompt in the folder that contains the USMT files.

Loadstate

Loadstate is used to configure a computer or computers with the settings that were recorded with `scanstate`. You can use `loadstate` with all clients later than Windows 95. Using the switches provided by the USMT, you can configure `loadstate` to migrate Registry settings, log errors, and load only specified files. To see the syntax and switches for `loadstate`, you can type `loadstate /?` on the command prompt in the folder that contains the USMT files.

Remember that scanstate gathers the information from the source computer and loadstate configures the information to the destination computer.

Using the Files and Settings Transfer Wizard

The *Files and Settings Transfer (FAST) Wizard* can be used only on a computer that is not a member of a domain. On stand-alone computers or computers that are part of a workgroup, the FAST Wizard can be used to make it easier to copy files and settings from an old computer to a newer one. To locate the FAST Wizard, choose Accessories from the All Programs menu and then choose System Tools.

The FAST Wizard refers to the two computers involved in the transfer as the old computer and the new computer. On the old computer, the wizard walks the user through the process of choosing whether to transfer files, settings, or both. The user can even create a custom list of files that they want transferred from the old computer to the new computer. The files and settings are then stored on a shared drive or removable media or are sent to the computer through a direct transfer. Figure 1.10 shows the options available in the FAST Wizard. The computer that will receive the files must be configured with the FAST Wizard as the new computer. Similar configuration settings are required for the old computer. The user chooses where the files and information will be read from and how the computer will be configured. They can configure to read the shared drive, use removable media, or use direct transfer to receive the data.

FIGURE 1.10 The Select a Transfer Method screen in the FAST Wizard

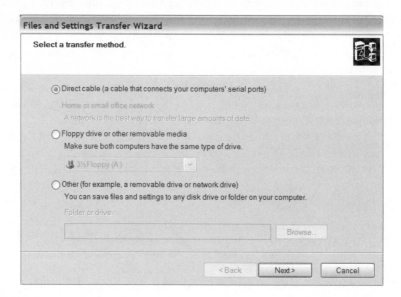

 The FAST Wizard transfers only data files to the new computers. You still have to install the applications that run the data files.

 You should be familiar with the basic workings of the Files and Settings Transfer Wizard. You should also know that you are unlikely to have to troubleshoot this tool in a corporate environment because it cannot be used on computers that are members of a domain.

Uninstalling Windows XP

If you have chosen to upgrade your operating system to Windows XP, you may find that some of the hardware or applications do not function properly. If you decide to reverse your upgrade, given the right circumstances, you can uninstall Windows XP.

In order to qualify for this, you must have upgraded from Windows 98, 98 SE, or Windows Me. Exercise 1.7 walks you through uninstalling Windows XP.

EXERCISE 1.7

Uninstalling Windows XP

1. Reboot your computer into safe mode by pressing F8 during the boot process after the BIOS has loaded.

2. On the text mode screen in the boot options, choose Safe Mode.

3. Log into your machine using administrative credentials.

4. Use Control Panel to access the Add or Remove Programs applet.

5. Choose Windows XP from the programs list.

6. Accept the confirmation dialog.

Performing and Troubleshooting a Multiboot Installation of Windows XP

If the computer that you are using already has a Windows 32-bit (Windows 95 or later) operating system and you have at least two partitions defined, you can install a clean copy of Windows XP without disturbing your current installation or any of the applications that it uses. If you do this properly, the system will automatically change the boot.ini file and you will be prompted to choose the operating system that you wish to boot to at each new startup. You can use this multiboot installation method to run multiple and different Windows operating systems on the same computer. You can also use this method to install multiple instances of Windows XP on the same computer. In this way, you could use one instance for experimentation and troubleshooting and another for your main operating system.

> To run multiple virtual operating systems within one operating system, you can also use virtual operating system software such as VMWare or Microsoft's Virtual PC.

If you are troubleshooting a multiboot installation that was attempted by a user, then you should be aware of the following:

- The operating systems should be installed in hierarchical order with the oldest first. For example, if a user wants to multiboot Windows 98 and Windows XP Professional, then they should install Windows 98 first.

- Each operating system must be installed on its own partition. Microsoft recommends that you install each operating system on a primary partition.

- The active partition will contain the boot.ini file and must be formatted with a file system that is common to both operating systems. For example, if you are dual-booting Windows 98 and Windows XP Professional, then the active partition must be formatted with FAT or FAT32.

- The boot.ini file will bring up the operating system selection screen when the computer is booted. You can choose the operating system to boot to or let a 30-second timer run down and accept the default.

- You can change the operating system selection and time-out value in the Startup and Recovery Settings within the Advanced tab of System Properties.

 Real World Scenario

Creating Your Own Test Environment

One thing that has been invaluable to us is the hands-on experience that we've received through network administration, consulting, and setting up classrooms. Even if you don't get the chance to work with a large number of computer installations, you can still benefit greatly from the experience of setting up a multiboot computer test environment. If you have an old desktop that is at least a PII 233 with 64MB of RAM, it will do just fine. If you have an old laptop, that might be even better.

Start out by obtaining as many types of operating system software as you can find. You can often get free evaluation software by attending a Microsoft class or by browsing the Microsoft website at www.microsoft.com/technet/downloads. Get a trial copy of some client and server operating systems.

After you have the software in hand, completely format and repartition the computer that will be your test computer. Of course, you should make sure that you have a backup of anything that was on the computer and that you might need later. Create partitions that are about 4GB in size, and create as many as you can on your disk.

Next, begin installing the operating systems that you have obtained in order of their hierarchy from lowest to highest. As you install each system, you will test yourself on display drivers, network card drivers, USB drivers, and perhaps printer drivers. See if you can make everything functional on one operating system before moving on to the next one. See how many operating systems you can get working on one computer!

You will learn a tremendous amount from setting up a computer in this fashion. In addition, you will then have a tool that you can use to test drivers and applications. Finally, you can also load your certification study material on the computer and study for the test in the operating system that you are learning. If you don't know the answer to a question, you can often just Alt+Tab out of the study material and find the answer within the operating system software. If you find the answers that way, you are much more likely to retain the information for the test and for real life.

Case Study: Widgets Incorporated: Windows XP Professional Rollout.

Widgets Incorporated is a medium-sized corporate organization. It manufactures sprockets for automobile manufacturers throughout the world. There are approximately 1,200 PCs throughout the United States, all running either Windows 95 or Windows 98. Widgets requires that all of its PCs are upgraded to Windows XP Professional. It has a custom application named Engine 3 Pro that is used to engineer its sprockets for new automobiles. It also has a custom application named HM Enterprise that is used to interface with the machines that create the sprockets. It is using Server 2003 to host its Active Directory domain, widgets.inc, and DHCP is used in each of the 10 locations for network configuration. Each location will have a file server for users' data.

The company is requiring that all of the PCs be upgraded to Windows XP Professional over a single weekend. There are only three different types of PC hardware. Type 1 is a standard clone PC with standard hardware. Type 2 is specialized computer with custom-built components, a SCSI CD-ROM, and a pair of Jinseguz Xtrate SCSI hard drives. The Type 3 computers are using standard hardware except for the IBM Ultrastar SCSI hard drives.

Type 1 computers are using only Windows 95 and are the computers used by the engineers to interact with Engine 3 Pro. There is no other software running on the Type 1 computers. There are 500 Type 1 computers.

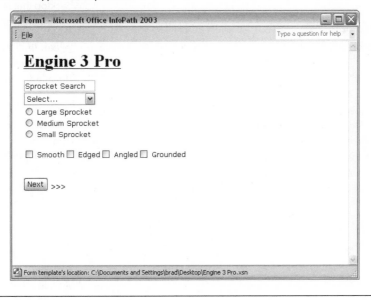

Type 2 computers are running only Windows 98 and are used to control the sprocket machines. They have specialized software and drivers that allow connections using the parallel port of the computer to a parallel port on the machine. The machine software requires that the operating system be installed using a certain path, D:\OS\Windows\. The Type 2 computers also host the HM Enterprises application that allows the machine specialists to import the settings from the engineers' designs in Engine 3 Pro. There are 500 Type 2 computers.

The Type 3 computers are used for the managers and executive-level personnel. The operating system can be either 95 or 98 and runs only Microsoft Office. The users store their data on file servers. There are only 200 Type 3 computers.

Widgets Inc. requires that all of the PCs are upgraded using an automated solution and that all users are able to resume their normal activities on the Monday following the upgrade.

We should develop a solution that is unique for each of our computer types.

Type 1 Solution:

Because the Type 1 computers are all running Windows 95, we will have two choices to get Windows XP installed.

First, we could upgrade the operating system to Windows 98 or Windows 2000 followed by an upgrade to Windows XP. This is a pretty inefficient method, but it is our only choice for upgrading Windows 95. Alternatively, there is only one major application running on these machines, so we could simply perform an unattended clean install of Windows XP. We should be sure to verify the compatibility of the application, Engine 3 Pro. Most likely you will want to run the application in compatibility mode. We can use the USMT to export the users' settings to the local file server. The upgrade of the Type 1 computers should go very smoothly.

Type 2 Solution:

There are quite a few potential problems with our Type 2 computers. We will need to contact the vendor that is responsible for the drivers and application that allow parallel access to the machines. It is likely that the drivers will not function with Windows 98. This can often be overcome by choosing to perform an upgrade instead of a clean install. By upgrading, Windows XP will keep the existing drivers and adapt them to the new environment. Because we will perform an upgrade, Windows XP system files will end up in the proper directory, D:\OS\Windows. We will also need to verify compatibility for HM Enterprise. Our unique hardware might also cause us a problem; it's a safe bet that we won't find the Jinseguz Xtrate hard drives on the HCL or Windows Catalog. Nor will we find any of the other unique hardware. We can test-upgrade to see if the drivers convert over to Windows XP or contact the manufacturer for driver updates. We will still perform an automated installation using unattend files and UDF files.

Type 3 Solution:

Type 3 might require a little bit more flexibility. Because we are using both Windows 95 and Windows 98, we should decide if we would like to create two different solutions. We could upgrade the Windows 98 computers and perform a clean install of the Windows 95 computers. Because the computers are running only Microsoft Office and the users are storing their data on network drives, we will most likely perform an automated clean installation. Having simple applications and users' data on networked environments makes our job much easier as an MCDST.

In Review:

Even though Widgets was faced with the daunting task of upgrading over 1,000 computers with various hardware and software hurdles, a properly trained MCDST can overcome those to provide solutions. By being familiar with hardware compatibility and options available to you for dealing with unique device drivers and software, you can bring most any hardware setup up to standard for running Windows XP. Although software is usually much easier to deal with, it can often mean the difference between a successful migration and nonfunctioning workstations.

Summary

It's important that you understand how operating systems should be installed so that you can troubleshoot failed installations. There are four main types of operating system installation:

- Attended
- Unattended
- Upgrade
- Multiboot

An attended installation is the most time consuming to perform because the user or administrator has to "baby-sit" the installation and respond to all of the prompts and questions. The main concern with an attended installation is the preparation before the installation. Compatibility issues with hardware and software can cause an installation to fail. You can reduce failures and troubleshoot failed installations using the Windows Catalog and the hardware manufacturers' websites to obtain the latest information regarding compatibility.

For an unattended installation, either an answer file or Remote Installation Services (RIS) is used. In the case of an answer file, you should know how to examine the file for obvious errors and then escalate the problem to the network administrator who created it. If you use Remote Installation Services, you should be familiar with the client portion of the remote installation. The client requires connectivity to the network and some type of network boot provided by a Net PC-or a PXE-compliant card. You can also use a Windows XP-compliant card and a *RIS* boot disk on the client.

An upgrade installation is an attempt to gain greater benefits from the new operating system features without losing anything else. The main concern regarding an upgrade installation is the compatibility of the currently working hardware and software with the new operating system. Users will also be concerned about losing data and/or functionality as a result of the upgrade.

A multiboot installation means adding another operating system to a computer that is already functioning with one or more. The trick is to keep both of the operating systems functional. You should install operating systems in hierarchical order with the oldest first. The system will automatically change the boot.ini file to accommodate the new operating systems. You can use these new systems for fault tolerance and for testing and experimental purposes.

Exam Essentials

Know the minimum requirements to install Windows XP.   Although you will probably never install Windows XP on a computer that meets only the minimum requirements, it is still important to know these specifications for the test. You may need to define which components will need to be upgraded to install the operating system.

Understand the differences between file systems.   You should understand the advantages and disadvantages of the main file systems that Microsoft clients use. You should also know which clients can use which file systems. Multiboot scenarios might require this knowledge.

Understand how answer files and UDFs operate.   You don't need to be an expert on the syntax in answer files, but you do need to know what happens if a setting in a UDF conflicts with a setting in an answer file. You should also know what will happen if there is a section in a UDF that does not exist in an answer file for the same computer.

Know how to use the Upgrade Advisor.   You should know how to use the Upgrade Advisor by inserting the Windows XP CD and selecting the options to check compatibility. You should also know the location of the file on the Windows CD and on the Internet.

Know what is required to create a successful multiboot.   You should know the basics of what is required to create a successful multiboot, such as, for example, the order of installation of multiple operating systems and your options for file systems on the system partition. You should be familiar with the fact that the boot.ini file will be changed automatically by the operating system when you create a multiboot installation.

Review Questions

1. You are the desktop support technician for a large company. Management is considering upgrading some older Windows 98 clients to Windows XP Professional. The client computers have PII 233MHz processors with 16MB of RAM. They all have at least 2GB of free disk space. In addition, they have 8X CD-ROM drives and SVGA display adapters. Which component(s) will require upgrading before installation can begin?

    A. Processor

    B. RAM

    C. CD-ROM

    D. Free disk space

2. You are the desktop support technician for your organization. One of the users is attempting to install Windows XP and is encountering stop errors. You suspect that some of the hardware in the computer is not compatible with Windows XP. You obtain a list of the hardware installed in the computer. Which of the following resources should you use to determine the compatibility of the hardware? (Choose two.)

    A. The Windows Update website

    B. Windows Catalog

    C. The website of the manufacturer of the hardware

    D. Microsoft TechNet

3. You are the desktop support technician for a large company. You are called in to assist on a failed Windows XP installation. You want to make sure that the correct bootstrap files are on the system partition. Which of the following files must be on the system partition in order for Windows XP to load and start? (Choose three.)

    A. `autoexec.bat`

    B. `ntldr`

    C. `boot.ini`

    D. `ntoskrnl.exe`

    E. `config.sys`

4. You are the desktop support technician for your company. You want to multiboot a computer with Windows 98 and Windows XP Professional. Which of the following file systems could you use for the system partition of the computer? (Choose all that apply.)

    A. FAT

    B. NTFS

    C. FAT32

    D. None of the above

5. You are the desktop support technician for your company. You have installed a new (out of the box) hard drive on a computer and you want to begin setting it up to store data. Which of the following should be your first step?

    A. Format the hard drive to create the partitions.

    B. Ensure that the boot order in your setup reads the hard disk first.

    C. Use fdisk to create the partitions on the drive.

    D. Delete the low-level format installed at the factory.

6. You are the desktop support technician for your company. You are troubleshooting a failed unattended installation. Upon examination of the answer file and UDF used for the installation, you discover that there is a section in the UDF that is not mentioned at all in the answer file. Which of the following should occur during installation?

    A. The section and its keys will be created and used by Setup.

    B. The installation should fail because the answer file is incomplete.

    C. Setup should prompt the user for a response.

    D. The section and its keys should be ignored by Setup.

7. You are the desktop support technician of a large company. You want to create a standard for settings such as background, screensaver, and font size. You have configured the computer settings on your test computer connected to your domain. You would like to save the settings to a file and load them to other computers on your domain. Which tool should you use to capture and save the configuration settings?

    A. `loadstate.exe`

    B. Files and Settings Transfer (FAST) Wizard

    C. `fdisk.exe`

    D. `scanstate.exe`

8. You are the desktop support technician for your company. You are troubleshooting a failed RIS installation. You suspect that the computer was unable to obtain an IP address. You wish to escalate the problem to the network administrator. Which type of server should have assigned the computer an IP address during the installation?

    A. Domain controller

    B. DHCP server

    C. DNS server

    D. RIS server

9. You are the desktop support technician for a large company. You are troubleshooting a failed installation using the log files created by the installation. Which file describes all of the tasks performed during startup, whether they succeeded or not?

    A. `setuplog.txt`

    B. `PNPlog.txt`

    C. `setuperr.log`

    D. `setupapi.log`

10. You are the desktop support technician for your company. Security is always a key concern in your organization. You are creating a multiboot installation with Windows 2000 Professional and Windows XP Professional on the same computer. Which of the following file systems should you use for the system partition?

    A. FAT

    B. NTFS

    C. FAT32

    D. All file systems are equal in this case.

11. You are the desktop support technician for your organization. You have been asked to perform a manual installation of Windows XP Professional on a new workstation. The manufacturer's documentation states that the BIOS and hardware do not support ACPI. When you begin the installation, you receive errors. What can you do to avoid errors during the installation of Windows XP?

    A. Load custom device drivers from the manufacturer's CD.

    B. Press F6 during the text mode phase of Setup.

    C. Press F5 during the text mode phase of Setup.

    D. Press F7 during the text mode phase of Setup.

12. You are the help desk support technician for your company. Your company has designated Windows XP as the operating system of choice. Your company has ordered a new shipment of 50 computers for distribution throughout the company. Before they can be distributed, you must install Windows XP Professional. Your company is replacing all of the hard drives with SCSI hard drives for reliability purposes. During your initial test installation, you receive the following error: "Setup did not find any hard disk drives installed on your system." What do you need?

    A. Bootable floppy disk

    B. Windows XP CD

    C. OEM device driver

    D. Server 2003 Resource Kit

13. You are the help desk technician for your company. You are required to install Windows XP onto a no-name computer purchased by your company. You need to verify that this computer will work with Windows XP before you begin the installation. What should you do?

    A. Check the Hardware Compatibility List.

    B. Check the Software Compatibility List.

    C. Check the System Compatibility List.

    D. Check the Manufacturer Compatibility Resource.

14. You are the help desk support technician for your organization. You are installing Windows XP using the command line. You want Setup to copy all the necessary boot files and temporary setup files to a drive and mark the partition active. What switch should you use?

    A. /syspart

    B. /sysset

    C. /drive

    D. /local

15. You are the lead support technician in your company. You have recently completed a company-wide rollout of Windows XP. Your previous operating systems included Windows 98, Windows 2000, and Windows 95. You receive a call from a user who is responsible for a PC that is running a mission-critical application. The user states that since the upgrade, he cannot run the application because it is only compatible with Windows 98 SE. You need to provide the user with a solution immediately. What should you do?

    A. Restore the workstation from a previous backup.

    B. Revert to Windows 2000.

    C. Perform a clean installation of Windows 98.

    D. Uninstall Windows XP from Add or Remove Programs.

16. You are the help desk technician for your organization. Your company is moving toward Windows XP as its primary operating system. You are currently running Windows NT 4.0 and wish to dual-boot with Windows XP. Your hard drive is currently formatted with NTFS and you want to be sure that your installation of Windows XP will be compatible. What precautions can you take?

    A. Patch Windows NT to Service Pack 3.

    B. Patch Windows NT to Service Pack 4.

    C. NTFS will be compatible with Windows XP.

    D. Upgrade Windows XP to Service Pack 1a.

17. You are the lead desktop support technician for your company. You have been instructed to install Windows XP on all laptops in your company. The users of the laptops plan to store confidential company information on the drives of the system. You are responsible for ensuring the security of the company's confidential data. You have decided to use file encryption to protect data in the event a laptop is stolen. What must you do to ensure that encryption is available to company users?

   A. During the installation, format at least one partition with FAT32.

   B. Request that money in the budget be reserved for encryption software.

   C. During the installation, format your hard drive with NTFS.

   D. Request that an administrator enable EFS on your laptops.

18. You are a desktop support technician for your organization. Your supervisor gives you a file named `standardunattend.txt` to use for the unattended installation for the company's computers. You insert the Windows XP CD and the floppy disk with the `standardunattend.txt` file. When you start the installation, you are prompted for configuration information. What can you do to ensure an unattended installation?

   A. Set the computer's BIOS to boot from the floppy disk.

   B. Change the name of the answer file to `Install.txt`.

   C. Change the name of the answer file to `Install.sif`.

   D. Change the name of the answer file to `Winnt.sif`.

19. You are the desktop support technician for your company. You have been volunteered to perform a network install on a Windows NT 4.0 workstation. You wish to use a network share to install Windows XP. After booting to a network boot disk, you start the installation. During the early stages, you receive an error that requests the Windows XP files. What switch should use with `Winnt32.exe` to ensure that Setup is looking on the correct network share?

   A. `/source`

   B. `/S`

   C. `/Network Share`

   D. `/boot`

20. You are the primary desktop support technician in your company. You have been asked to prepare files that allow other desktop support technicians to perform unattended installations of Windows XP on various workstations. What file must you use from the `deploy.cab` file to accomplish this?

   A. `setupmanager.exe`

   B. `unattend.exe`

   C. `winnt32.exe`

   D. `setupmgr.exe`

Answers to Review Questions

1. B. The minimum RAM requirement for installing Windows XP is 64MB. The installation will fail if the client computer does not have at least the minimum requirement. The processor should probably be upgraded as well, as it barely meets the minimum requirement. The 8X CD-ROM (or any CD-ROM) meets the requirement. The minimum requirement for free disk space is 1.5GB, so the client computers exceed the minimum requirement.

2. B, C. The Windows Catalog contains a list of hardware that is designed for and/or compatible with Windows XP. You should check the catalog first. If you do not find the hardware listed in the Windows Catalog, then you can also check the website of the manufacturer of the hardware. The Windows Update and TechNet websites do not contain information about hardware compatibility.

3. B, C, D. The system partition contains the files that are required to boot the Windows XP operating system. The files that must be in the system partition in order for Windows XP to load and start are `ntldr`, `boot.ini`, and `ntoskrnl.exe`. The `autoexec.bat` and `config.sys` files are configuration files for Windows *9x* operating systems, not for Windows XP.

4. A, C. You must format the system partition with a file system that is common to both operating systems. Windows 98 cannot use the NTFS file system, but Windows XP can use all three of the file systems; therefore, you should format the system partition with FAT or FAT32.

5. C. If you have a new hard drive from the factory, then the only formatting on it is low-level formatting. Your first step should be to use the fdisk tool or the Windows XP CD to create partitions. Formatting does not create partitions; you can format a partition only after you have created it. You should not delete the low-level format installed at the factory.

6. A. When a section and/or key is mentioned in the UDF but not in the answer file for the same computer, the section and/or key will be created and used by Setup. If this does not happen, then you should escalate the issue to the network administrator or the creator of the files. The installation should not fail because of this occurrence. Setup will not prompt the user for a response. The section and/or key should not be ignored by Setup.

7. D. You should use the `scanstate` tool from a command prompt to capture configuration settings of a computer that is a member of a domain. You should use `loadstate.exe` to distribute the settings to the other computers in the domain. You can use the Files and Settings Transfer (FAST) Wizard only for stand-alone computers or for computers that are part of a workgroup. `Fdisk.exe` is not the correct tool to use to collect computer settings.

8. B. In order for a Remote Installation Services (RIS) installation to succeed, the computer must obtain an address from the Dynamic Host Configuration Protocol (DHCP) server. Domain controllers, DNS servers, and RIS servers are all involved in the process of a RIS installation, but they do not assign IP addresses to the client.

9. A. The `setuplog.txt` file records all of the events in a startup. You can examine it to see what occurred just prior to the failure of the installation. The `PNPlog.txt` file and `setupapi.log` file record the detection of devices and drivers. The `setuperr.log` file is created only when errors occur and records only the errors.

10. B. Since security is always a key concern in your organization, you should use the file system that is the most secure and is common to both of the operating systems that you are installing. In this case, since both Windows 2000 Professional and Windows XP Professional can use NTFS and since NTFS has much greater security, you should use NTFS. All file systems are not equal; FAT and FAT32 do not offer the security features that NTFS offers.

11. D. During the text mode phase of Setup you will see "Press F6 if you have to install a third-party SCSI or RAID driver" on the screen. You should press F7, which will allow you to bypass loading ACPI. You can also choose F6 for drivers or F5 for HAL type. Pay close attention to the manufacturer's guidelines for setup.

12. C. When installing Windows XP, Setup may not detect your SCSI drives. You will have a chance to load the OEM driver during the text mode phase of the setup by pressing F6. There can also be scenarios in which Windows will misunderstand what your device is. For example, Windows could load the driver for an IBM Travelstar 70 IDE hard drive when it is in fact an IBM Ultrastar 70 SCSI drive. This will cause Setup to look for the wrong drive during the later phases.

13. A. The hardware compatibility list is maintained by Microsoft to show that computer hardware is known to function with certain hardware. You should always check the HCL before installing Windows onto any computer to ensure compatibility. The HCL can be found at `www.microsoft.com/whdc/hcl/default.mspx`.

14. A. During a command-line installation of Windows XP, you usually use the `Winnt32.exe` file to kick off the install. You can use various switches to accomplish different tasks. The `/syspart` switch will allow you to copy your setup files into a temp drive and mark it active. This will allow you to simply turn the system on and proceed into the setup process without a CD.

15. D. After upgrading Windows 98, Windows 98 SE, or Windows Me, you have the option to uninstall an upgrade to Windows XP using the Add or Remove Programs Applet in Control Panel. This should revert the user's machine back to its previous state and allow the user to utilize his application.

16. B. The version of NTFS that comes with Windows NT 4.0 is not compatible with Windows XP. In order to achieve compatibility with Windows NT 4.0 and Windows XP, you must patch Windows NT up to Service Pack 4.

17. C. You must use the NTFS file system to enable the use of EFS, or Encryption File System. You can create the NTFS file system either during the installation of Windows XP or afterward using the Convert utility.

18. D. When performing a local unattended installation from the Windows XP CD, you must rename the answer file to `Winnt.sif` so that Setup will recognize it. Always be sure to properly name and perform a virus scan on your answer files and installation source before attempting an unattended installation of Windows XP.

19. B. There are various switches available to ensure that your installation of Windows XP takes place properly. We choose to boot from a network disk so that we can load the network card drivers and access the network shared source files. We will then use the `/S:path` command to ensure that Setup looks in the proper directory.

20. D. In order to create the needed files for an unattended installation, you can use the Setup Manager Wizard. The Setup Manager Wizard is located inside the `deploy.cab` on the Windows XP installation CD inside the `\Support\Tools` directory.

Chapter 2

Managing and Troubleshooting Access to Resources

MICROSOFT EXAM OBJECTIVES COVERED IN THIS CHAPTER:

✓ **Monitor, manage, and troubleshoot access to files and folders.**

- Answer end-user questions related to managing and troubleshooting access to files and folders.
- Monitor, manage, and troubleshoot NTFS file permissions.
- Manage and troubleshoot simple file sharing.
- Manage and troubleshoot file encryption.

✓ **Manage and troubleshoot access to shared folders.**

- Answer end-user questions related to managing and troubleshooting access to shared folders.
- Create shared folders.
- Configure access permission for shared folders on NTFS partitions.
- Troubleshoot and interpret Access Denied messages.

✓ **Connect to local and network print devices.**

- Answer end-user questions related to printing locally.
- Configure and manage local printing.
- Answer end-user questions related to network-based printing.
- Connect to and manage printing to a network-based printer.

✓ **Manage and troubleshoot access to and synchronization of offline files.**

- Answer end-user questions related to configuring and synchronizing offline files.
- Configure and troubleshoot offline files.
- Configure and troubleshoot offline file synchronization.

The main reason that we create a network is to share resources. The resources that we can share on a network include hardware, such as computers, printers, and fax machines, and software, such as files, folders, and applications. When a resource is shared, more than one person can benefit from it, often simultaneously. Resource sharing provides many benefits to the organization as well. For example, the ability to share a color printer with many users can save an organization a tremendous amount of money. In addition, the ability to share files, folders, and applications aids in the collaborative effort of teams within an organization.

The challenge to you as a desktop support technician is to understand how resource sharing operates within a network and how the various forms of permissions that can be assigned to resources will affect the end user. In this chapter, we will focus on managing and troubleshooting access to files, folders, and printers. We will focus on the four main types of resource access:

Files and folders   A user stores important data on the computer in the form of files and folders. Some folders may contain important and/or confidential files. When a user logs on to a Windows XP computer, the *access token* generated by the operating system gives them access to all of the files and folders to which they have NTFS permissions. It's important to understand how this access is granted and what can affect a user's access to a file or folder.

Shared folders   While file and folder permissions in NTFS control the local access to a resource, share permissions control the access to *shared folders* on a network. When a resource is shared, users can gain access to the resource through the network from other computers on the network. It's important to understand how shared permissions operate and how they combine with file and folder permissions.

Printers   Print permissions are specific to software on the network called *printers*. Printers are used to control the hardware that actually makes the hard copy, which is called a *print device*. Users should be able to use the printers that they need in a transparent fashion. They should also be prevented from using printers that are set aside for special users or groups. You should understand how print permissions operate and what can affect a user's ability to print to a specific print device.

Offline files and folders   Many users now work at home or while traveling on business. When they are in the office, they connect their laptop computer to the network to synchronize files and folders with files and folders on the network server so they can work on the files while they are away from the office. When they return to the office, they synchronize any changes that they have made while they were not connected. You should be aware of the additional challenges of managing and troubleshooting these *offline files and folders*.

The rest of this chapter discusses the management and troubleshooting of these four types of resource access.

Files and Folders

The primary benefit of the NTFS file system is its ability to control access to specific files and folders. This is accomplished by assigning *NTFS permissions* for the files and folders. NTFS permissions are characteristics that can be assigned to any file or folder and control who may access that resource and what tasks they can perform after accessing it. NTFS permissions provide security for files and folders whether they are accessed by local logon or connected to through a network share. Only the NTFS file system supports file- and folder-level permissions. Other file systems used by Windows operating systems, such as FAT and FAT32, do not support them.

NTFS permissions can be assigned to a user directly or inherited based on their member in a security group. Microsoft recommends assigning permissions to security groups and then placing the user account in the appropriate security group to give the permissions. This practice enables administrators to more efficiently manage permissions to resources by only having to assign them to groups; users are then added to and removed from these groups as needed. NTFS permissions are divided into two main categories: file permissions and folder permissions. For the most part, the permissions that can be assigned to a file or the permissions that can be assigned to a folder are very similar, although there are some important differences. You can't, for example, execute a folder as you can a file, but you can open a folder and read its contents with the appropriate permissions. As a desktop support technician, you must understand how these permissions are assigned and how they affect the end user.

Normally, only an individual who has the Full Control permission to an object can assign permissions to other users or groups. Usually, this is someone with administrator permissions, the creator-owner of the object, or someone who has been explicitly assigned the Full Control permission. You can access and control the NTFS permissions for any file or folder on a partition formatted with NTFS by right-clicking the file or folder in Windows Explorer or My Computer and clicking the Security tab. We will discuss the two main categories of NTFS permissions, verifying permission settings, and some special permission considerations in the following sections.

NTFS File Permissions

NTFS file permissions can be assigned to each file within a folder and are specific to the file to which they are assigned. Different files within the same folder can have different NTFS permissions assigned to them. In this way, you can control a user's access to resources in a very granular fashion. This can also create a troubleshooting problem for a user who does not understand how these permissions operate. Table 2.1 shows the available standard NTFS file permissions. Notice that the permission levels increase as you read down the table; each permission enables the user to perform a specific task in addition to the tasks allowed with the permission listed above it, except for Write permission, which will implicitly give Read permission.

TABLE 2.1   Standard NTFS File Permissions

NTFS File Permission	Enables User To
Read	View the file, open the file, right-click the file, and choose Properties to view its attributes and ownership
Read and Execute	Perform all tasks described above plus double-click the file to open the application that can be used to view it
Write	Perform all tasks described above plus change the file
Modify	Perform all tasks described above plus delete the file
Full Control	Perform all tasks described above plus take ownership and thereby give other users permission for the file

NTFS Folder Permissions

NTFS folder permissions can be assigned to each folder in a folder hierarchy and are specific to the folder. In addition, folders within other folders can be assigned different NTFS permissions. This allows you to create, for example, a hierarchy of folders that are accessible at the root (top) by administrators or managers but within the hierarchy by only a specific user for each folder. This type of granular control can also lead to confusion for a user who is unaware of how it operates. You should make sure that users have transparent access to the folders they need to use and that they cannot even view those they do not need to use, but you should also ensure that people have access to the resources needed to do their jobs. Table 2.2 shows the available standard NTFS folder permissions.

TABLE 2.2   NTFS Folder Permissions

NTFS Folder Permission	Enables User To
List Folder Contents	View the folder, click the folder, and view the files and folders within the folder
Read	Perform all tasks described above plus right-click the folder and view its permissions, attributes, and ownership
Read and Execute	Perform all tasks described above plus double-click the folders within the folder to view their contents (traverse the folders)
Write	Perform all tasks described above plus create new files and folders within the folder and change the folder's attributes

TABLE 2.2   NTFS Folder Permissions *(continued)*

NTFS Folder Permission	Enables User To
Modify	Perform all tasks described above plus delete the folder
Full Control	Perform all tasks described above plus take ownership of the folder and thereby give other users permissions for the folder

Verifying NTFS File and Folder Permissions

If a user cannot view a file or folder or cannot perform the actions they need to perform, then verifying their NTFS permission settings should be your first step to troubleshooting the problem. If they can at least view the file or folder, then you might be able to help them verify their own permissions. If they cannot even view the resource, then you or someone with the appropriate level of permissions will have to get involved.

Verifying NTFS permissions can be accomplished by looking at the properties of the file. Exercise 2.1 walks you through the steps to verify permissions for a user.

EXERCISE 2.1

Verifying NTFS Permissions

1. Click Start, and then choose My Computer.

2. Locate the file or folder that you want to verify, in this case Folder A.

3. Right-click the file or folder, choose Properties, and then click the Security tab.

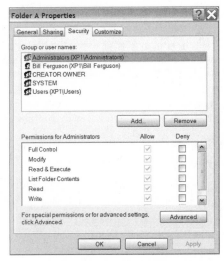

4. In the Group or User Names box, select the user or the security group of which the user is a member, in this case Bill Ferguson.

5. View the permissions assigned in the Permissions For box.

6. Adjust the permissions based on the minimum needs of the user.

7. To add a user or group, click Add and then type the name of the user or group that you want to add.

8. Adjust the permissions needed based upon the requirements of the new user or group.

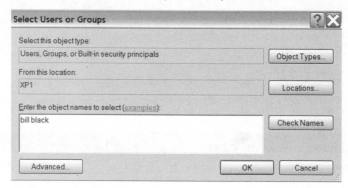

9. To remove a user or group, select the user or group in the Group or User Names box and click Remove.

If the Security tab is not available, either the file or folder is not in an NTFS volume or simple file sharing is enabled. If you are using a FAT or FAT32 volume, you must run the CONVERT command from a command prompt to convert the file system from FAT to NTFS to access the Security tab. If simple file sharing is enabled, you can disable it on the View tab in the Folder Options dialog box accessible from the Tools menu in My Documents or Windows Explorer.

Using the NTFS Effective Permissions Tool

When a user is a member of multiple security groups, it may not be as easy to determine their effective permissions by just reviewing the permissions of all of the groups of which they are a member. For this reason, Windows XP and Windows Server 2003 have a new feature called the *Effective Permissions tool*. You should be aware that this tool calculates only the effective NTFS permissions and does not factor in share permissions or encrypted files and folders, which we will discuss later in this chapter. The Effective Permissions tool can be seen in Figure 2.1.

The Effective Permissions tool is located in the Advanced Security settings for each file or folder. Exercise 2.2 walks you through the steps to determine a user's effective NTFS permissions using the Effective Permissions tool.

FIGURE 2.1   The Effective Permissions tool

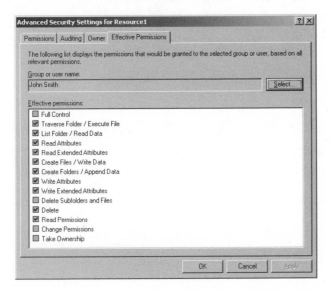

EXERCISE 2.2

Using the Effective Permissions Tool

1. Click Start, and then choose My Computer.

2. Locate the file or folder that you want to verify.

3. Right-click the file or folder and click the Security tab.

4. Click the Advanced button.

5. In the Advanced Security Settings dialog box, click the Effective Permissions tab.

6. Click Select.

EXERCISE 2.2 *(continued)*

7. In the Enter the Object Name to Select box, type the name of the user for whom you want to verify NTFS permissions, in this case Bill Black.

8. The check boxes that are selected indicate the effective NTFS permissions for that user.

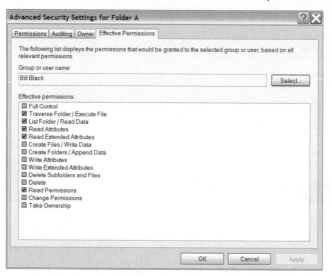

 You should be aware that the Effective Permissions tool calculates only the effective NTFS permissions to a file or folder and does not factor in share permissions or encrypted files and folders.

Special Considerations with Managing and Troubleshooting NTFS Permissions

In a completely static environment with very few users, permissions are relatively easy to manage and troubleshoot. It gets a bit more complicated when there are many (or hundreds) of users and many resources to manage as well. Also, users have the nasty habit of not staying in the same job; therefore, their security group memberships and their file and folder needs are likely to change with their job.

In this section, we will discuss the special considerations that make managing permissions a little trickier than just understanding standard file and folder permissions. In particular, we will discuss managing permissions inheritance, using Deny permissions, copying and moving files and folders, managing special permissions, and dealing with special troubleshooting issues.

Managing Permissions Inheritance

NTFS permissions follow rules of inheritance. Inheritance means that, by default, a child object (a file or folder) will inherit the permissions of its parent object. When you apply permissions to a folder, the permissions are inherited by all of the files and folders that are in that folder. If you create a new file or folder within that folder, the new file or folder will also inherit the permissions of the folder in which it is contained, referred to as its *parent folder*.

If you do not want the files and folders to inherit permissions, then you must clear the default setting in the Advanced Security Settings dialog box. Exercise 2.3 walks you through the process of preventing NTFS permissions inheritance.

Using Deny Permissions

You may have noticed that there are two columns for each type of permission for a resource, namely Allow and Deny. So you might be thinking, "What's the difference between a permission box that is just not checked Allow and a permission box that is explicitly checked Deny?" We're glad you asked.

EXERCISE 2.3

Preventing NTFS Permissions Inheritance

1. Click Start, and then choose My Computer.

2. Locate the file or folder you want to prevent from inheriting permissions.

3. Right-click the file or folder and click the Security tab.

4. Click the Advanced button.

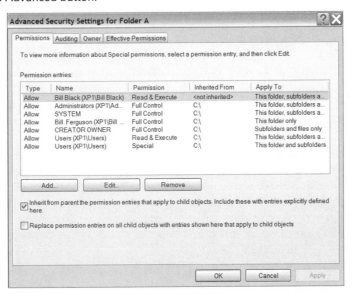

5. Clear the check box that's labeled Inherit from Parent the Permissions Entries That Apply to Child Objects.

6. Select to copy the current permissions and make changes by clicking the Edit button, or to remove all permissions and set your own, click the Remove button.

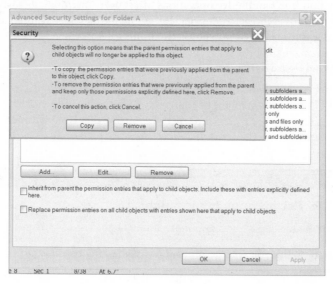

Simply not granting permissions to a user or group is called an *implicit deny*. This has the effect of not granting a person permission to a resource, but it does not prevent them from getting permissions to that resource if they later become part of a group that does have permissions. An *explicit deny*, on the other hand, is assigned to a user when the administrator wants to ensure that they will *never* get those particular permissions to the resource, even if they are later put into a group that has them. A Deny permission will override an Allow permission. This means that if a user is a member of multiple groups and some of the groups are granted Allow Read on a resource but one of them is explicitly set to Deny Read, then the user will not be able to view the resource. The Deny permission on one group will override all of the other Allow permissions. You should avoid assigning the Deny permission for any reason other than an emergency. Setting the Deny permission can cause complications when troubleshooting access for users on critical network resources. If you deny a small group of users that happens to include a user that needs access to a resource, you will have to manually go through and audit each group that the user is a member of. Using the Effective Permissions tool can ease this process, but it can still be a lot of work. If you don't want a user to have access to a resource, just don't give them permissions!

Managing Permissions When Copying and Moving Files and Folders

So far, we have discussed permissions that are applied to files and folders in their original locations. Unfortunately, real life isn't always that "neat and clean." Files and folders are often copied or moved from one hierarchy to another with cut-and-paste operations in Explorer and My Computer or commands entered on the command line. As a desktop support technician, you need to know how copy and move operations affect users' permissions to a resource.

There are only two possibilities to consider. Either the file or folder will retain the permissions it had before it was moved or it will inherit all of its permissions from its new parent folder. This depends on whether the file is copied or moved and whether it is moved within the same volume or to another volume. Fortunately, it's all of one or all of the other; there is no in-between or mix to consider. Table 2.3 illustrates the consequences when files and folders with NTFS permissions are copied or moved.

TABLE 2.3 Consequences When Files and Folders with NTFS Permissions Are Moved or Copied

Action	NTFS Permissions Consequence
Copying a file or folder to an NTFS drive on the same volume as the original	The new copy of the file or folder inherits the permissions of the destination folder.
Copying a file or folder to an NTFS drive on a different volume than the original	The new copy of the file or folder inherits the permissions of the destination folder.
Moving a file or folder within a single NTFS volume	The moved file or folder retains the permissions that it had before it was moved.
Moving a file or folder from one NTFS volume to another	The moved file or folder inherits the permissions of the destination folder.
Copying or moving a file or folder from a FAT32 partition to an NTFS volume	The newly created folder inherits the permissions of the destination folder.
Copying or moving a file or folder from an NTFS volume to a FAT32 partition	The moved or copied file in the new destination loses all NTFS permissions.

Managing Special Permissions

So far, we have discussed only standard NTFS permissions. There are actually two major categories of NTFS permissions, standard and special. In this section we will examine special NTFS permissions.

Special permissions are basically just the standard permissions further broken down. For example, the Read standard permission actually consists of three special permissions: Read

Data, Read Attributes, and Read Extended Attributes. You would assign special permissions only if you desire to get to a finer level of granularity and control. For example, you may want a user to be able to read a file but not read its extended attributes. This would be accomplished by setting the special permissions. You can set special permissions by accessing the Advanced Security options of a file or folder. Exercise 2.4 walks you through viewing and configuring special NTFS permissions for files and folders.

EXERCISE 2.4

Viewing and Configuring Special NTFS Permissions for Files and Folders

1. Click Start, and then choose My Computer.

2. Locate the file or folder.

3. Right-click the file or folder and click the Security tab.

4. Click the Advanced button.

5. Select the user or group for which you wish to define special permissions.

6. Click the Edit button.

7. The checked boxes indicate the granular settings of NTFS standard permissions assigned to the user or group. Any change to the standard settings check boxes will create special permissions.

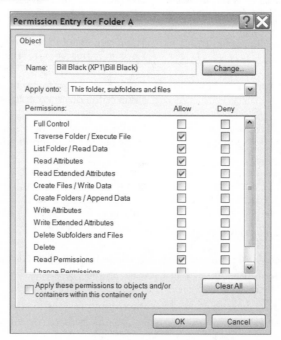

8.   Clear any checked boxes except Full Control, and then click OK.

9.   Note that the Permission entry has changed to Special for the user or group that you selected.

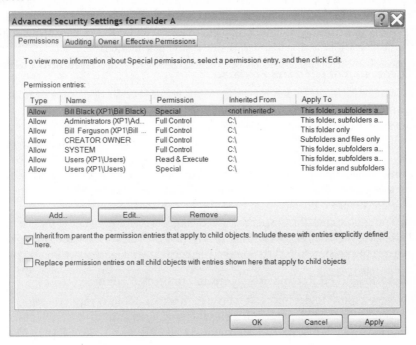

Special Considerations When Troubleshooting NTFS Permissions

It may seem as if we have covered everything there is to know about file and folder access and NTFS permissions. Actually, though, there are a few situations that require you to "think outside the box" that are worth mentioning at this point. For example, what happens if you change a user's permissions to a resource while the user is logged on? Also, what if the person who created a file makes sure that they are the only one who has permissions for it and then leaves the company? Finally, what about files that are encrypted as well as protected by NTFS?

In this section, we will fill in the gaps in regard to NTFS file and folder permissions. In particular, we will discuss access token generation, taking ownership of files and folders, and troubleshooting encrypted files versus files protected by NTFS.

Access Token Generation

When a user logs on to a domain, the domain controller examines the permissions assigned to the user and to the groups of which the user is a member. The domain controller then gives this information to the client computer, which uses it to create an access token that will be used to gain access to resources on the network. The user's access token is not changed until they log off and log back on, even if the permissions for the user are changed while they are logged on. For this reason, if a user complains that they cannot access a resource for which they have just been given permissions, you should ask them to log off and then log back on again so that a new access token with the updated permissions will be generated.

Taking Ownership of Files and Folders

When a user creates a file or folder, they become the *creator owner* of that file or folder. This means that they have Full Control permissions and nobody else has any permissions at all. If the person leaves the company, the easiest thing to do is to change the name of their account so the new user has access to the files and folders; but what if the user is promoted instead? In that case, the new person will not have access to the file or folder and may not even be able to view the file or folder, that is, unless the original user or the administrator gives the new user the right to *take ownership* of the file or folder and assign the permissions to use the file or folder. The right to take ownership can be set in the Advanced Security settings for each file and folder. You should click the Owner tab and then select the new owner of the file from the users and groups in the Change Owner To box. The new user must be assigned the special permission of Take Ownership to be listed in the Change Owner To box.

Troubleshooting NTFS Permissions versus Encrypted Files

If a user can view a file or folder but cannot open it, they may not have the permissions to open it or the file or folder may be encrypted so that only certain users can open it. As a desktop support technician, you should be able to determine which of these problems is occurring. The clue that will allow you to determine the problem is in the error message itself.

If a user is denied access to a file or folder due to insufficient NTFS permissions, they will receive an "Access is denied" error message with the folder name that is not accessible like the one in Figure 2.2. If, on the other hand, the user is denied access because the file or folder is encrypted, then the message will be a simple "Access is denied" message, like the one in Figure 2.3. Determining the true nature of the problem will allow you to fix it yourself or escalate it to a network administrator.

FIGURE 2.2   "Access is denied" message caused by insufficient NTFS permissions

FIGURE 2.3 "Access is denied" message caused by encryption

Managing Encrypted Files

You can manage the encryption of a file or folder using the Advanced button in the General tab of its Properties dialog box. File and folder encryption is a feature of the NTFS file system only. Computers using FAT or FAT32 cannot support encryption. In most cases, you should encrypt folders and then place files into them. You should know that files placed into an encrypted folder will become encrypted. You can encrypt only the root folder or the entire folder hierarchy based on your needs. Once files are encrypted, only the user who encrypted the files, and therefore possesses the private key, will be able to use the files normally. In most organizations, the administrator is also designated as a recovery agent who can decrypt the files if the user's private key should become corrupt.

Shared Folders

Actually, no matter how you set the NTFS permissions on a file or folder, if the file or folder is not shared, then it will be available only locally on the computer where it exists. Sharing folders is like opening the main gate that allows access to the folder from other computers on the network. Note that only folders are shared and have share permissions; files are not explicitly shared. Any file you wish users across the network to have access to must be placed in a shared folder. The permissions that you assign to the share will combine with the NTFS permissions assigned to the resource to create a result called the *effective permissions* to the resource.

Keep in mind that the true effective permissions to the resource are not just the permissions obtained by the Effective Permissions tool that we discussed earlier. The Effective Permissions tool provides only the effective NTFS permissions. Determining the true effective permissions requires a little more work on your part. In this section, we will discuss creating and troubleshooting shared folders and determining the effective permissions of a user to a shared folder.

In Windows XP, there are basically two types of file and folder sharing. We will discuss each type and its relation to troubleshooting effective permissions.

Simple File Sharing

Simple file sharing is enabled by default in Windows XP Home Edition. It is available on Windows XP Professional only if the computer is not in a domain. It is not available to any computer that is running Windows XP on a domain. For this reason, you are unlikely to have to troubleshoot simple file sharing, but it still bears mentioning since you might run into it on a stand-alone computer or one that is in a workgroup.

Simple file sharing enables you to share a resource on the network by selecting a single check box. Through the Guest account, Windows XP automatically makes the resource available to everyone and sets the appropriate NTFS permissions on the object as well. You cannot control the NTFS permissions directly when using simple file sharing; in fact, there isn't even a Security tab in the folder's Properties dialog box. Figure 2.4 shows the user interface on a computer that is configured for simple file sharing.

FIGURE 2.4 Simple file sharing on Windows XP

Classic Sharing

Classic sharing is the type of sharing that is used in domains and therefore in most organizations. With classic sharing, you can control access to a resource by user and/or group. When resources are shared, Windows XP automatically searches the network for the shares that are available to the user that is currently logged on. Users can locate these shares through their My Network Places tool, as shown in Figure 2.5. My Network Places is located on the Start menu in Windows XP.

FIGURE 2.5   My Network Places in Windows XP

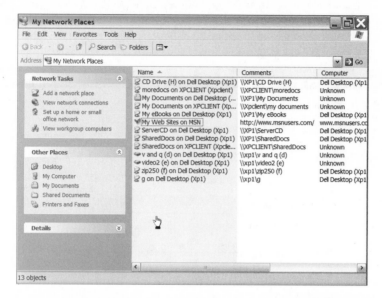

Access is controlled by share permissions that you can set. These share permissions will then combine with the NTFS permissions to create the effective permissions for the share. In the following sections, we will examine share permissions and effective permissions in greater depth.

Share Permissions

Share permissions can be assigned individually to each folder in a hierarchy of folders. In addition, share permissions are inherited by default through a folder hierarchy. You can assign share permissions for a folder specifically to users and groups. Table 2.4 illustrates the type of share permissions available and what they enable a user to do.

TABLE 2.4   Shared Folder Permissions

Shared Folder Permission	Enables User To
Read	View filenames and subfolder names, traverse to subfolders, view data in files, run program files
Change	Perform all tasks described above plus add files and subfolders, change data in files, delete subfolders and files
Full Control	Perform all tasks described above plus change NTFS permissions, take ownership and thereby give other users permissions for the resource

You can set the share permissions for a folder within the Properties dialog box for the folder. In addition, you can control how many users can connect to the share simultaneously. This can be useful if there are limited resources such as processor or memory to support the share. Exercise 2.5 walks you through the steps to create and configure a share with classic sharing.

EXERCISE 2.5

Creating and Configuring a Share

1. Click Start, and then choose My Computer.

2. Locate the folder that you want to share.

3. Right-click the folder and choose Sharing and Security.

4. Select the Share This Folder option, and type the share name that you would like to use or accept the default (the folder name).

5. Accept the Maximum Allowed option or select Allow This Number of Users and enter the number of users that you want to able to use the share simultaneously.

6. Click the Permissions button to configure the permissions for the users and groups.

7. Click Add to configure permissions for users and groups that are not yet listed

8. Type the name of the user or group in the Enter the Object Names to Select box, and press Enter. Repeat to add permissions for additional users and groups.

Administrative Shares

In addition to folders that you explicitly share, there are a few default administrative shares used for various purposes by the operating system. These shares are a mixed blessing. It is nice to be able to use the shares to gain access to key system directories, but they can also create a security hole in the operating system. The administrative shares are accessed using a $ sign on the end of the path. There are three administrative shares by default, as seen in Table 2.5. Each one has it own purpose; you should only disable them if you are sure that they are not used on your network. There are many systems that use the administrative shares for management purposes. These shares are rarely disabled in a corporate network because of their usefulness to management. Disabling them can cause serious problems with Microsoft applications. You will use the Disk Management tool in Computer Management to work with both user-created shares and administrative shares, as seen in Figure 2.6.

FIGURE 2.6   Viewing the administrative shares in Disk Management

TABLE 2.5   Administrative Shares

Administrative Share Name	Purpose
C$	Default share for accessing the root of the system drive
IPC$	Remote management and remote authentication
ADMIN$	System directory access

Accessing Network Shares

You have learned that file-system-based resources can be very valuable, allowing you to share information and even remotely authenticate and manage PCs. One question has yet to be answered: How do you use these wonderful things called shares? There are many different methods to access networking resources such as shares. Probably the most common method is to use the UNC, or Universal Naming Convention. The syntax is very simple: *computer name**share name*. For example, if I wanted to access the Important Documents share shown in Figure 2.7, I would simply type in the computer name followed by the name of the share. You can see, in Figure 2.8, that once the computer recognizes the path you are typing in, it will even attempt to show you the contents of the shared directory.

FIGURE 2.7 The shared folder, Important Documents

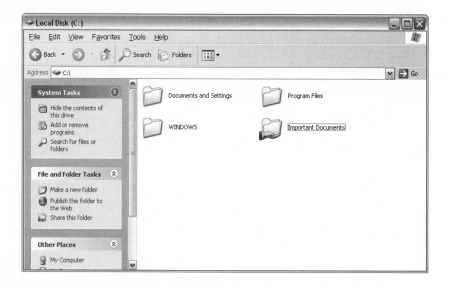

FIGURE 2.8 Accessing a network share using the UNC

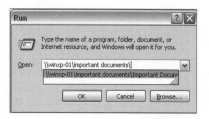

One of the problems with using the UNC for resource access is that you must know the computer name and resource name before you can use it. You can also use My Network

Places. You should use the UNC method when possible, but using My Network Places is much easier. You can find resources such as printers, shares, and faxes by browsing the tree within My Network Places. Windows XP will automatically attempt to find network resources and display them when you first open My Network Places, as shown in Figure 2.9; these are called "Network Places."

FIGURE 2.9 Network places available on a local network

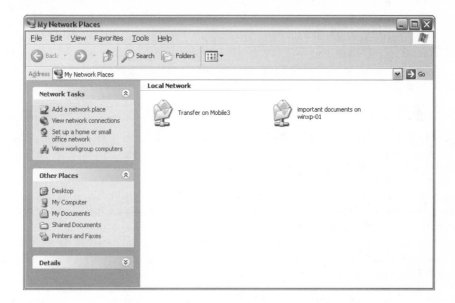

Effective Permissions When Combining Shares and NTFS

If a folder located on a drive that is formatted with NTFS is shared on a network and a user is accessing that folder through the share, then the effective permissions of the user are a combination of the user's share permissions and the user's NTFS permissions. As a desktop support technician, you should know how to combine these permissions to determine the effective permissions for the user.

To determine the user's effective permissions to a folder, follow this three-step method:

1. Determine the effective permissions for the share.

This is accomplished by determining the maximum shared permissions that are assigned to the user or to a group of which the user is a member. For example, if a user has Allow Change permissions from one group and Allow Read from another, then the effective share permissions would be Allow Change.

You should also remember that Deny overrides all other permissions. For example, if a user has Allow Change permission in one group and Deny Change in another group, then the effective share permissions would be Deny Change, which would include Deny Read and therefore would block all access to the resource.

2. Determine the effective NTFS permissions.

    This can be accomplished by determining the maximum NTFS permissions that are assigned to a user or group, keeping in mind that Deny permissions always override Allow permissions unless the Allow permissions are explicit and the Deny permissions are inherited.

    An easier method would be to use the Effective Permissions tool described earlier in this chapter. Using the Effective Permissions tool will allow you to determine the effective NTFS permissions of a user to a resource.

3. Compare the effective share permissions with the effective NTFS permissions. The more restrictive of the two will be the true effective permissions to the share. For example, if the combination of share permissions creates an effective share permission of Allow Full Control but the combination of NTFS permissions creates an effective NTFS permission of Allow Change, then the true effective permission for the user to the resource is Allow Change.

 Real World Scenario

Setting Up Permissions—Backwards!

Some things are easier when you do them backwards! If you were suddenly in charge of setting permissions in a large organization with many users and groups, it could be a little overwhelming. You might ask yourself, "What if I don't get everything set just right and there are problems?" As a desktop support technician, you may or may not have the rights to set permissions, but you should still know a little about the methodology so that you understand how the file and folder permission settings may have ended up the way they are.

A good technique when configuring permissions is to think about it in reverse. In other words, ask yourself, "Which files and folders do I want to make sure only a few users or groups can get access to or even view?" Configure the NTFS permissions and shared folder permissions for those resources first, and then you can put on the next layer of permissions that are a little less-restrictive and continue to add layers until you get to the layer that includes just about everybody.

At each layer, you can check to make sure that you do not change anything that puts the previous layers at risk. In this way, you can gradually make sure that the most important files and folders are protected but that users can access the files and folders that they need. It will still require some research and thought on your part, but doing it backwards will make the whole process a lot smoother.

Another common practice for setting permissions on resources that use both share permissions and NTFS permissions is to give the Everyone group full control permissions on the share. This might sound crazy at first, but because of the nature of the "most restrictive" policy between share and NTFS permissions, you can use NTFS to restrict access. For example, assign the Everyone group Full Control on the share and assign the actual security group Read Only permissions at the NTFS level. This will effectively allow only Read access to the selected security group. Be very careful when using this practice; if you accidentally assign the Everyone group full control at the NTFS level, you will allow anyone and everyone to manipulate your files, even unauthorized users!

Although the preferred method for accessing network shares is to use UNC paths, this requires knowing the proper name and spelling of the resource. This is often not possible, so we are forced to search or browse for the required resource. Exercise 2.6 walks you through this process.

EXERCISE 2.6

Using My Network Places to Find Resources

1. Open My Network Places.

2. Click View Workgroup Computers in the task pane at the left of the window. Note that if you are in a domain environment, the button will appear as Entire Network.

3. Double-click one of the computers listed.

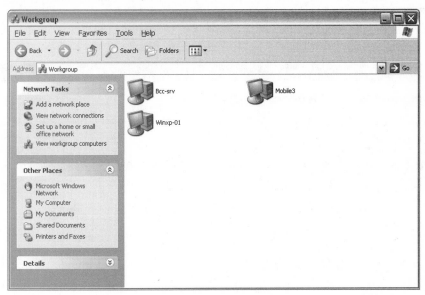

4. Double-click one of the resource groups offered by the computer.

Printers

As we try to develop a "paperless society," we seem to be using more and more paper. In fact, rumor has it that the document that was circulated through Congress about how to use less paper was about 500 pages long! Since people must have their "hard copy," you have to know how to keep their printers operational.

The term *printers* is often misunderstood by users. Actually, a printer is software that is installed in a computer and drives the print operation that sends the *print job* to the print device that makes the hard copy. There are basically two different types of printers: local and network. In the following sections, we will discuss how to install, configure permissions for, and troubleshoot these two types of printers.

Local Printers

A printer is considered local when the computer communicates directly with the printer without having to go through another computer. *Local printers* are usually physically attached to the computer itself through a cable. They can be installed and shared on any computer in the network. Installing and sharing a printer on a computer in a network creates a print server. Users can connect to the print server to use the shared printers.

You can install printers by using the software on the CD that came with the printer or by using the Printers and Faxes tool in Windows XP. Exercise 2.7 walks you through the steps of installing and sharing a local printer in Windows XP.

EXERCISE 2.7

Installing and Sharing a Local Printer

1. Physically attach the print device to the computer using a parallel cable, USB cable, or network cable.

2. Click Start, choose Control Panel, and then choose Printers and Faxes.

3. Choose Add a Printer to start the Add Printer Wizard.

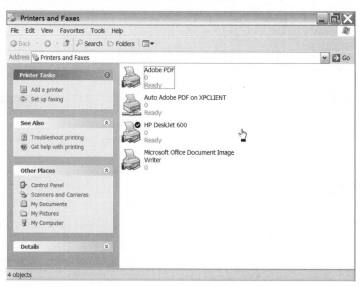

4. Click Next.

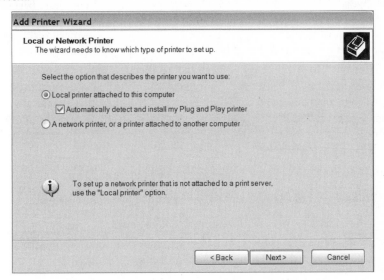

5. Select Local Printer Attached to This Computer and verify that the Automatically Detect and Install My Plug and Play Printer check box is selected.

6. Click Next.

7. Follow the instructions in the wizard to finish setting up the printer.

Removing a local printer is just as easy as installing one. Exercise 2.8 walks you through removing a local printer and removing the printer driver.

EXERCISE 2.8

Removing a Local Printer

1. Shut down the computer and physically remove the print device connection.

2. Restart the Windows XP operating system, click Start, choose Control Panel, and open Printers and Faxes.

3. Right-click the printer that you want to remove, and select Delete.

4. Choose File in the File menu, and then select Server Properties.

5. Click the Drivers tab, select the driver for the printer that you deleted, and click Remove.

Network Printers

When printers are installed and shared on a network, a user can connect to and install the printer through the network. These types of installed printers are referred to as *network printers*. You should know how to install and troubleshoot them.

Installing a network printer is very similar to installing a local printer except that there is no physical installation required. The print device has already been installed and shared as a local printer and you are just connecting to a device that already exists. Exercise 2.9 walks you through the steps to install a network printer on Windows XP in a domain.

EXERCISE 2.9

Installing a Network Printer

1. Click Start, choose Control Panel, and then choose Printers and Faxes.

2. Choose Add a Printer to start the Add Printer Wizard, and then click Next.

3. Select the A Network Printer, or a Printer Attached to Another Computer radio button, and then click Next.

4. Select Find a Printer in the Directory, and then click Next.

5. Define your search parameters (name, location, model), and then click Find Now.

6. Select the printer that you want to install, and then click OK.

Printers that use USB or infrared connections may be automatically detected and installed by the Found New Hardware Wizard. The Found New Hardware Wizard may ask for the CD that came with the printer if the drivers are not found in the operating system's driver cache.

Installing a network printer in a workgroup without the benefit of Active Directory requires a few more steps because Active Directory cannot be used to search for the printer. In this case, you should use the Universal Naming Convention (UNC) command of *server**printer* to locate and install the printer.

Uninstalling a network printer is also very similar to uninstalling a local printer, except that there is no need to physically uninstall the print device. In fact, you might be uninstalling the network printer on only one computer while other computers may continue to use the printer. Exercise 2.10 walks you through the steps to uninstall a network printer in Windows XP.

EXERCISE 2.10

Uninstalling a Network Printer

1. In Printers and Faxes, right-click the icon for the printer that you want to remove, and then select Delete.

2. To delete the printer driver, choose File in the File menu, and then choose Server Properties.

3. Click the Drivers tab, select the driver for the printer that you deleted, and then click Remove.

Printer Permissions

Users should have transparent access to printers they need to use to do their job. At the same time, you may need to restrict access to some printers to only specific users and groups. This is accomplished using *printer permissions*.

In some ways, printer permissions are similar to shared folder permissions in that there are two categories: Allow and Deny. In other ways, printer permissions are completely different. Table 2.6 illustrates the printer permissions that are available and what actions they enable a user to perform.

You should note that a user who has Manage Documents permission but not Print permission for a printer will not be able to send documents to the printer.

TABLE 2.6   Shared Folder Permissions

Printer Permission	Enables User To
Print	Connect and send documents to a printer and delete the documents from the print queue.
Manage Documents	Pause, resume, restart, and cancel the print job and rearrange the order of documents

TABLE 2.6   Shared Folder Permissions *(continued)*

Printer Permission	Enables User To
Manage Printers	Perform all tasks described above plus have complete administrative control over the printer.
Deny	Perform no tasks. User cannot use or manage the printer or adjust permissions.

You can configure printer permissions on the Security tab in the printer's Properties dialog box. Exercise 2.11 walks you through setting permissions on a printer.

EXERCISE 2.11

Configuring Printer Permissions in Windows XP

1. Click Start, choose Control Panel, and then choose Printers and Faxes.

2. Right-click the printer for which you want to set permissions.

3. Choose Properties, and then click the Security tab.

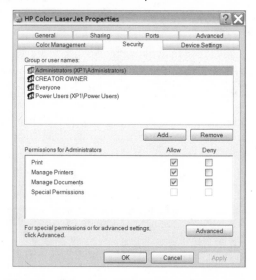

4. Select the user or group for which you wish to set permissions, or click Add to add a new user or group to the list.

5. To remove permissions from a user or group, select the user or group and click Remove.

You should know how to properly install and repair printer drivers when necessary. Exercise 2.12 walks you through installing a new printer driver on a print server.

EXERCISE 2.12

Installing a Printer Driver in Windows XP

1. Click Start, choose Control Panel, and then choose Printers and Faxes.

2. On the menu bar, at the top of the screen, choose File then Server Properties.

3. If there are multiple printers, select the appropriate printer. Otherwise move ahead to Step 4.

4. Select Server Properties, click the Drivers tab, and then click Add.

5. Complete the Add Printer Driver Wizard by selecting the manufacturer and model of the printer and the operating system.

Troubleshooting Printers

It's important that users be able to get their hard copy to create their reports, presentations, letters, memos, and the like. Therefore, a desktop support technician must be able to quickly troubleshoot printers when needed. In the following sections, we will discuss the four areas of printer troubleshooting that are most common in business environments: drivers, the print spooler, connectivity issues, and redirecting print jobs.

In order to properly troubleshoot printer issues, you must understand how printers and their associated components work together. The print process can seem a bit complex, but it is in fact intuitive. It can be broken down into three sections: the client-side processes, the spooler processes, and the physical printer processes. The print process is shown in Figure 2.10.

FIGURE 2.10 The Windows print process

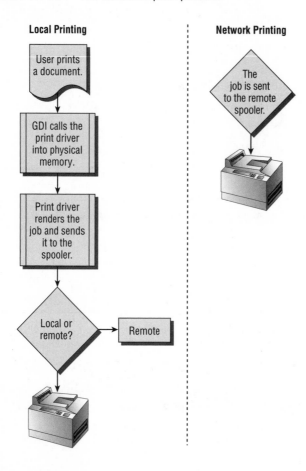

Client Processes

The client processes are as follows:

- A user sends a print job from an application. The application calls the graphics device interface (GDI).

- The GDI calls the printer driver into RAM.

- The GDI sends the job to the print spooler.

Spooler Processes

The Spooler provides the following steps:

- The client-side spooler calls the server-side spooler.
- The job is sent to the print router.
- The router sends the print job to the local print provider or the remote print server if the job is being sent to a network printer.
- The print job is then sent to the print processor, which reformats it to make it print properly.
- The print processor sends the job to the page separator. A separator page is added if required.
- The job is sent to the appropriate port.

Printer Processes

The physical printer continues with the following:

- The printer receives the print job from the print spooler.
- The print job exits the physical printer.

Printer Drivers

A *printer driver* is a software program that enables the operating system and programs that it runs to communicate with a particular printer. Many printing problems are the result of an improper installation of a printer driver or using the wrong printer driver. If a print job has illegible characters or only a few characters per printed page, this is an indication of an improper driver. Another indication of an improper driver is the inability to change the properties of a printer.

From time to time, manufacturers update their printer drivers to provide for more functionality or better-quality printing. Often you can download a program from the manufacturer's website that installs and configures the new driver; however, there may be instances when you must update drivers manually. It's important that you understand how to update printer drivers in all circumstances. Exercise 2.13 walks you through the steps of updating a printer driver manually in Windows XP.

EXERCISE 2.13

Updating Printer Drivers in Windows XP

1. Click Start, choose Control Panel, and then choose Printers and Faxes.

2. Right-click the printer icon that you want to update, and then choose Properties.

3. On the Advanced tab, choose New Driver to start the Add Printer Driver Wizard. Click Next, and then choose Have Disk.

4. Browse for the correct driver on the disk and select it, and then finish the wizard installation by following the prompts.

The Print Spooler

The print spooler is a service that receives a print job into a print server and holds it there until the print device is ready to print. The print spooler folder is located by default in Windows XP at C:\Windows\System32\spool\Printers. There may be instances, such as when the disk space in C: becomes full, when you need to move the location of the print spooler folder. Exercise 2.14 walks you through the steps to move the print spooler folder in Windows XP.

EXERCISE 2.14

Resetting the Print Spooler Folder

1. Click Start, choose Control Panel, and then choose Printers and Faxes.

2. From the File menu, choose Server Properties, and then click the Advanced tab.

3. In the Spool Folder box, type the path that you want to use, and then click OK.

You may also need to restart the Print Spooler service from time to time to clear the print queue and resume normal printing. You should know that users will have to resend their documents if you have to restart the print spooler. Exercise 2.15 walks you through the steps to restart the Print Spooler service in Windows XP.

EXERCISE 2.15

Restarting the Print Spooler Service

1. Click Start, and then choose Run.

2. Type `services.msc`, and then click OK.

3. Right-click the Print Spooler service, and then select Restart.

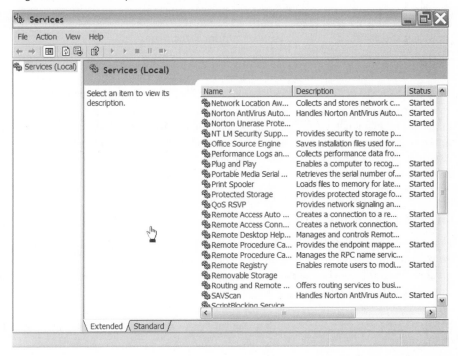

Note: Restarting the Print Spooler service will clear the print queue of all documents. Users will have to resend their documents to the printer.

Troubleshooting Printer Connectivity

When a user cannot print to a print device, you may be called in to troubleshoot the problem. Your first step in troubleshooting should be to isolate the problem to the printer, the connection, or the user's application. You can do this with the help of the user if you are on the phone or on your own if you are physically at the location.

The tools that you will use to isolate the problem are located in the print device and in the operating system software. You should begin by printing a local test page at the print device itself. If the test page will print, then you know that the print device is not the problem. If the test page will not print, then the problem is in the print device itself.

Once you can successfully print a test page on the print device, you should print a test page from the Windows software. Exercise 2.16 walks you through the steps to print a test page from Windows XP.

EXERCISE 2.16

Printing a Test Page from Windows XP

1. Click Start, choose Control Panel, and then choose Printers and Faxes.

2. Right-click the printer on which you wish to print a test page.

3. Choose Properties, and then choose Print Test Page on the General tab.

If you can print a test page from Windows XP but the user cannot print a test page from their application, then you have isolated the problem to the application. If, on the other hand, you cannot print a test page from Windows XP but you were able to print the test page at the print device itself, then you have isolated the problem to the operating system. If the problem is with the operating system, then it is likely that the driver is at fault and that you should reinstall the printer driver.

Redirecting Print Jobs

If you have print devices that are the same or at least use the same driver, you can redirect print jobs from one printer to another. This might be necessary when a print device is very busy or if a print device should fail with many print jobs in the queue. Exercise 2.17 walks you through the steps to redirect print jobs.

EXERCISE 2.17

Redirecting Print Jobs

1. Click Start, choose Control Panel, and then choose Printers and Faxes.

2. Choose Add a Printer to start the Add Printer Wizard, and then click Next.

3. Select Local Printer, and then click Next.

4. Select Create a New Port, select Local Port from the Type box, and then click Next.

5. Type a share name for the port: \ '.

6. Continue with the wizard and install the appropriate driver for the device.

To successfully redirect print jobs to another printer, the two printers must use the same or a very similar and compatible driver.

Offline Files and Folders

Since many users work on laptop computers while outside of the office, the newer Windows client operating systems, such as Windows XP Professional, have a feature named *Offline Files and Folders*. With Offline Files and Folders properly configured, a user can have the best of both worlds, in and out of the office. Offline Files and Folders allows a user to cache the files they are working on when connected to the network. The original file may be contained on a network file server, but a cached copy of the file, the folder, and even the drive can be created on the user's laptop for easy continued use out of the office. When the user returns the laptop to the office and connects it to the network again, they can synchronize the files and folders from their laptop to the file server. As a desktop support technician, you need to understand how to configure and troubleshoot offline file settings and synchronization settings.

Offline File Settings

Before you can take advantage of the Offline Files feature, you have to enable it. Once you enable Offline Files, you can then decide how and when you want to synchronize the files on the laptop with those on the server. Actually, configuring offline file settings involves these three settings:

- Configuring the client computer to use offline files
- Configuring offline files and folders on the client
- Configuring file and folder caching on the server

In the following sections, we will discuss each of these three settings in greater depth.

Configuring the Client Computer to Use Offline Files

You can configure each Windows XP Professional computer to use offline files or to not use them. By default, Windows XP Professional is configured to not use offline files. Exercise 2.18 walks you through the steps to configure a computer to use offline files.

Fast User Switching, enabled on Windows XP computers by default, is not compatible with offline files, as seen in Figure 2.11. To use offline files, you must turn off Fast User Switching. To change your Fast User Switching settings, open User Accounts in Control Panel and select Change the Way Users Log On or Off.

FIGURE 2.11   Fast User Switching settings conflict

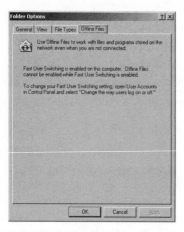

Configuring Windows XP Professional for Offline Files

1. Click Start, and then choose My Computer.

2. From the Tools menu, choose Folder Options.

3. Click the Offline Files tab, and then select the Enable Offline Files check box.

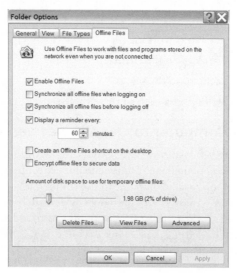

4. Click OK.

After Offline Files and Folders has been configured, a user will be able to cache files that are shared on the network servers as long as the network administrator has made them available for caching. Exercise 2.19 walks you through the process of making files and folders available offline while users are working on them.

EXERCISE 2.19

Making Files and Folders Available Offline

1. Browse to the file or folder on the network server, right-click the file or folder, and then select Make Available Offline.

2. In the Offline Files Wizard, click Next.

3. Select the Automatically Synchronize the Offline Files When I Log On and Log Off My Computer check box, and then click Next.

4. If you wish to create a shortcut on your desktop, select the Create a Shortcut to Offline Files Folder on My Desktop check box.

5. Click Finish.

Users can cache files and folders from network servers only if they are available for caching. File caching is used both to enhance network performance and as part of Offline Files and Folders. To troubleshoot a user's ability to cache a file or folder, you must understand the options that can be set on the computer where the file or folder resides. There are three options available for cache settings, as follows:

Manual Caching of Documents   Manual caching of documents provides caching only to those files that users specifically identify for offline use. Manual caching is the default setting when you create a share. This option is ideal for a shared folder that contains files that may be cached and modified by several users.

Automatic Caching of Documents   With this setting, every file that is opened through a share is automatically cached to the client computer. When you open a cached copy of the share, the cached copy on the computer is used but the original folder is also opened to prevent other users from changing the file while you have it open.

Automatic Caching of Programs and Documents   This setting provides automatic, read-only caching of files from the share. This is ideal for shares that contain static configuration files for network-based applications.

You may not have the permissions to adjust the settings for the caching of shared folders on another computer or server. You should, however, understand what is involved in case you need to adjust the settings or escalate the issue to the network administrator. Exercise 2.20 walks you through the steps involved in configuring the caching settings on a shared folder.

EXERCISE 2.20

Configuring Caching Settings

1. Right-click the shared folder in My Computer or Windows Explorer, and then choose Properties.

2. Click the Sharing tab, and then choose Caching.

3. Select the appropriate caching setting based on your use of the shared folder, and then click OK.

Note: You can also disable file caching for a share by clearing the Allow Caching of Files in This Shared Folder check box in the Caching Settings dialog.

Synchronization

Synchronization is the process of ensuring that shared folders and the offline copies of the folders have the same content. This process takes place automatically when someone using a computer containing offline content logs on to or off of a network. You can also configure the synchronization to take place at scheduled times or based on an interval.

Most of the time, synchronization should be automatic, but users might have an issue if the shared resource changes while the computer containing the offline content is disconnected from the network. During synchronization, the operating system compares the two copies of the folder and, depending on the states of the two copies, makes a decision itself or gives the option to the user. You should always instruct users to retain a file if they are not sure what to do. Table 2.7 illustrates the decision process for synchronization.

TABLE 2.7   Offline File Synchronization

Offline File State	Shared Copy State	Result
Changed	Not Changed	OS updates the shared copy with the offline copy.
Not Changed	Changed	OS updates the offline copy to reflect the changes.
Changed	Changed	User can choose to keep either copy or both.
Deleted	Not Changed	OS deletes the file.
Deleted	Changed	User can choose to delete the shared copy or replace the offline file with the shared copy.
Not Changed	Deleted	OS deletes the offline file.
Changed	Deleted	User can choose to save the file or delete it.

Case Study: ABC Corporation Resource Permissions

Bobby is an IT administrator for the ABC Corporation. He is setting up a new file server that will house multiple directories and files for use by the various departments within the company. There are several different departments, and each department has special security requirements for the resources it will have stored on the new server.

Case A

The sales department has the need for a shared folder on the server that all members of its traveling sales force can access. Members of the Sales group should be able to read and write documents to this folder, and other employees of the company should be allowed read capability to the folder if they have a valid user account on the company's network. How should permissions be configured for the Sales folder?

Solution A

The Sales group should have Modify NTFS permissions and Change share permissions. This will enable them to read and write to the folder. The Authenticated Users group should be assigned both Read NTFS and Read Share permissions.

Case B

The engineering department requires a folder called TechData on the server. Normally, only members of the Engineering group require access to this data, but frequently other users in the Research and Development, Sales, and Managers groups may sometimes require short-term access to these files. Therefore, the Engineering group wants the ability to assign permissions to others. A waiver has been granted to the company security policy that will allow this only in this specific instance. How will Bobby ensure that the Engineering group has the ability to assign permissions to this resource?

Solution B

The Engineering group should be assigned both Full Control NTFS and Full Control share permissions to this resource because that is the only permission level that will allow them to further assign permissions to others. No other permissions should be explicitly assigned or denied to any other group.

Case C

The human resources department requires that the HRData folder on the server, which contains many subfolders and files, be accessible only to the HR group, both across the network and locally at the server. The HR manager wants no one else to have access to the folder, with the exception of the manager's group, which requires read and write access only to selected folders within the HR shared folder but not to the parent folder or other folders. How can the permissions be set to meet these requirements?

Solution C

The HR group should be assigned Modify NTFS and Change share permissions to this resource. No other group or users should be assigned any access at the parent folder level. Any subfolders or files that require access by the Manager's group should have these permissions added at the necessary child folder or file level so they are granted access only to specific resources.

Case D

The Administrators group has a folder called Admin on the server that contains server configuration data, IP address lists, network diagrams, and related information. They do not want anyone accessing the folder across the network and will require administrators to physically sit down at the server in order to access this data. What NTFS and shared folder permissions does the Admin folder require?

Solution D

Only the Administrators group should have any access at all to this folder, so NTFS permissions should be set at Full Control. Since there is a requirement for the folder to be restricted from access over the network, the folder should not be shared or reside in a folder that is shared and no one should be granted any share permissions. This will limit access to the folder to the person logging on interactively at the server itself.

Summary

Networks are created to share resources and thereby increase productivity within an organization. A desktop support technician must understand how resources are shared and how permissions affect a user's ability to use them. Resources that can be shared include files, folders, and printers.

Permissions can be assigned directly to files and folders on NTFS partitions using NTFS permissions. These permissions can be used to allow or deny access to a resource for a user or a group of users based on security group memberships. Permissions assigned to a folder are automatically inherited by the files and folders within that folder, but you can control this inheritance using advanced security options. The main goal is to give transparent access to resources for users who need access while at the same time preventing access to those who are not authorized. You may be called in to troubleshoot a situation in which this goal has not been achieved.

File and folder permissions are only one piece of the puzzle that makes up the true effective permissions for a user to a resource. Another piece of the puzzle is shared folder permissions. NTFS file and folder permissions control a user's access to a resource from a local logon or through the network, but shared folder permissions control a user's access to a resource only through the network from another computer on the network. True effective permissions for a user to a resource are a combination of NTFS permissions and shared folder permissions. You should also remember that Deny permissions override Allow permissions unless the Allow permissions are assigned directly to the resource and the Deny permissions are inherited through a folder hierarchy.

Another resource that users share on a network is a printer. A printer is actually software that controls the print drivers that send a print job to the print device. Since a printer is software, access to a printer can be controlled using permissions. Printer permissions can be assigned directly to a printer through the Printers and Faxes tool in Windows XP. Printer permissions are not inherited. Users should be able to use the printers that they need in a transparent fashion. Some printers may be restricted for use by only specific users and groups. As a desktop support technician, you should know how to redirect a printer and its queue to another port and thereby another print device. In addition, you should know how to stop and restart the print spooler. Your understanding of printer permissions and printer troubleshooting is essential to ensure user productivity.

In today's business world, many users work from outside the office, in their homes or from a hotel "on the road." While they are in the office, they may synchronize their laptops with files and folders from the servers, caching the information onto their hard drives. When they leave the office, they will use these cached files and folders as if they were still connected to the servers. When they return to the office, they will resynchronize the files and folders on their laptop with those on the servers. If both of the copies of the files have been changed, the user will be asked to make a decision as to which one to keep. While this may seem simple, it can bring up some interesting situations that could potentially result in data loss if you are not careful. You should understand how to set up file caching for offline files and folders and how to troubleshoot their use when necessary.

Exam Essentials

Understand NTFS permissions.   You should understand NTFS permissions for files and folders. Your understanding should include standard and special permissions, as well as permission inheritance. You should also be familiar with the new Effective Permissions tool in Windows XP. Be aware that this tool calculates only the effective NTFS permissions of a user or group to a resource.

Understand shared folder permissions.   You should understand shared folder permissions in Windows XP. This includes simple file sharing and classic file sharing. You should know when each type of file sharing is appropriate and when simple file sharing cannot be used. In addition, you should be aware of how shared folders are created and configured in Windows XP.

Know how to determine effective permissions.   You should understand how NTFS file and folder permissions combine with shared folder permissions to create the true effective permissions of a user or group to a resource. You might be asked to determine the effective permissions given a combination of permissions assigned to a user and to groups of which the user is a member.

Understand printers.   You should understand what printers are, how they are installed and configured, and how to troubleshoot them. Your understanding should include printer permissions, printer drivers, and the process for troubleshooting printers. You should be able to redirect a printer to another port and restart the print spooler when necessary.

Understand Offline Files and Folders.   You should know how to configure Offline Files and Folders on the client software and how to troubleshoot the settings when necessary. Your understanding should include file caching, encryption, and permissions of Offline Files and Folders.

Review Questions

1. You are the desktop support technician for a large company. A user named Joe is having a problem accessing a folder and the files within the folder. Joe tells you that he has just been promoted this morning and that the network administrator assured him that he has changed the permissions on Joe's account so that he has access to the folders that he needs. Joe says that he doesn't notice a bit of difference between now and when he received the promotion this morning. What should you do first?

    A. Contact the network administrator and ask him to verify all of Joe's permission settings and make sure that he has removed Joe from his previous groups.

    B. Place a request to change Joe's username so that he can access the resources.

    C. Contact Human Resources to see if Joe's promotion is effective.

    D. Tell Joe to log off and then log back on again.

2. You are the desktop support technician for a large company. A user named Tara has recently been moved from the sales department to the marketing department. She is having a problem accessing the folders that she needs for her new job. She has logged off and back on again, and you have determined that Tara is a member of the Marketing group and that the Marketing group has the appropriate permissions for the folders. After some research, you are able to determine that, for security reasons, all sales personnel are explicitly denied access to the marketing department files. What should you do next?

    A. Tell Tara to log off again and log back on again.

    B. Ask the network administrator to double-check the membership of the Sales group.

    C. Remove Tara from the Marketing group and assign the permissions directly to her account.

    D. Restart the marketing department servers.

3. You are the desktop support technician for a large company. A user named Sam complains that he cannot access a file in a shared folder that he was able to access yesterday. To his knowledge, nothing has changed about his account. He is able to access all other files as normal, including other files in the same folder as the file that he cannot access. He says that he is receiving a simple error message that says, "Access is denied." What should you do first?

    A. Contact the network administrator and ask about any changes in NTFS permissions to the folder hierarchy that the user is accessing.

    B. Tell Sam to log off and log back on again.

    C. Escalate the issue to the network administrator and tell him that you suspect that the file has been encrypted by another user.

    D. Tell Sam to restart his computer and then log back on and try again.

4. You are the desktop support technician for your organization. A user complains that he can view files in a shared folder on a server through the network but that he cannot change the files. You view the user's permissions using the Effective Permissions tool and find that he has NTFS effective permissions of Allow Write for the folder and its files. What should you do next?

   A. Ask the network administrator to change the NTFS permissions to Allow Modify.

   B. Tell the user to try to access the resource from another client computer.

   C. Determine the effective shared folder permissions for the resource.

   D. Ask the network administrator to change the NTFS permissions to Allow Change.

5. You are the desktop support technician for a large corporation. A user named Darla complains that she cannot access a shared folder on a Windows XP client computer logged on to a domain. You suspect that NTFS permissions might be involved. You access the shared folder, but when you right-click the folder, there is no Security tab. Which of the following could be true? (Choose all that apply.)

   A. The computer is using simple file sharing.

   B. The share permissions are overriding the NTFS permissions so that you cannot see them.

   C. The computer needs to be restarted.

   D. The partition that contains the shared folder is formatted with FAT32.

6. You are the desktop support technician for a large organization. A user named Sally complains that she cannot print to a printer that she is in charge of maintaining. She can pause and resume the printer and she can control documents sent by other users, but she cannot send a document to the printer herself. You want to make sure that Sally can print to the printer but that she cannot adjust the properties of the printer. What should you do next?

   A. Ask Sally to try to print to another printer.

   B. Ask the network administrator to add Print to Sally's permissions for the printer.

   C. Ask the network administrator to add Manage Printers to Sally's permissions for the printer.

   D. Restart the print spooler.

7. You are the desktop support technician for your organization. A user reports that when he prints to a network printer, the printout has illegible characters and there are only a few characters per page but there are many pages. What do you suspect is causing the problem?

   A. The network connection to the printer is damaged.

   B. The user's computer does not have enough RAM.

   C. The driver for the printer is incorrect or corrupt.

   D. The print spooler has run out of space.

8. You are the desktop support technician for your company. A user named Donna reports that she cannot print from the application that she is using. You walk her through printing a test page from the Windows XP software on her computer, and it prints normally. Which of the following should you do next?

   A. Tell her to go to the print device and walk her through printing a test page on the print device itself.

   B. Reinstall the Windows XP operating system software on her computer.

   C. Reinstall the printer on her computer.

   D. Reinstall the application on her computer.

9. You are the desktop support technician for your company. A user named Hal complains that he cannot get some shared folders and files that he is using to cache onto the hard drive of his laptop, which is configured to use offline files and folders. Other folders and files cache normally. What should you suspect?

   A. Hal does not have permission to use the share.

   B. Hal's computer is not properly configured.

   C. The network administrator has prevented some files and folders from being cached.

   D. The files and folders are encrypted by another user.

10. You are the desktop support technician for your company. A user suspects that Offline Files and Folders is not working properly. She asks you what should happen if a file that she has cached on her laptop is changed on the server while she is out of the office. What should you tell her? (Choose all that apply.)

    A. It depends on whether you have changed your cached copy of that file or not.

    B. The file on the server will always take precedence over the cached copy.

    C. You will get a choice if you have changed your copy as well; otherwise, the new server copy will replace your cached copy.

    D. The file that was changed last will always take precedence.

11. Sally is a member of both the Sales and Marketing groups. There is a shared folder on the network that allows access to both groups but with different permissions. The Sales group has the Allow Modify NTFS permission and the Allow Read share permission assigned. The Marketing group has Full Control NTFS permission and Allow Change share permissions. Assuming Sally is not explicitly assigned any other permissions to her user account, what are her cumulative NTFS and share permissions and what are her effective permissions?

    A. Full Control NTFS permission and Allow Change share permission, making her effective permissions Allow Change

    B. Allow Modify NTFS permission and Allow Read share permission, making her effective permissions Allow Modify

    C. Full Control NTFS permission and Allow Read share permission, making her effective permissions Full Control

    D. Allow Modify NTFS permission and Allow Read share permission, making her effective permissions Allow Read

12. Bob, a new section supervisor, has been assigned Manage Documents permission for a networked shared printer. He later reports that he is able to cancel and restart documents but he cannot print to the printer. What should you do first to troubleshoot this problem?

    A. Check to make sure Bob has the correct share permissions to the printer.

    B. Ensure that Bob has Print permission to the print device assigned to his user account.

    C. Add Bob to the local administrators group on the print server.

    D. Direct Bob to log off and back on again to receive an updated access token with the new permissions.

13. Your Windows XP workstation has two hard disk drives: the C: drive is a 40GB drive formatted as NTFS and the D: drive is a 30GB drive formatted as FAT32. Under what circumstances can you use the Encrypting File System (EFS)? (Choose all that apply.)

    A. After converting the C: drive to FAT32

    B. After converting the D: drive to NTFS

    C. On the D: drive with no changes in file system

    D. On the C: drive with no changes in file system

14. You are the desktop support technician for the ABC Corporation. Barbara, a user in the marketing department, reports to you that she cannot encrypt sensitive files on her Windows XP Professional computer. You sit down at her computer, and after some preliminary checking, you discover that her hard disk is using the FAT32 file system. What should you do to enable the use of EFS on Sally's computer?

    A. Reformat her hard disk with the NTFS file system.

    B. Put Barbara's user account in the local administrators group.

    C. Run the CONVERT command to convert her hard disk to the NTFS file system.

    D. Enable EFS in the computer's local security policy.

15. You are the desktop support technician for the XYZ Company. A Windows 2000 server named Resource1 has caching enabled for all shared folders. A user named Shelly stores personal files on Resource1 and needs to make them available offline for use on her laptop computer. Shelly calls you and tells you that she cannot make her files available offline. What should you do to ensure that Shelly can make her files available for offline use?

    A. Ensure that the Everyone group has full control over the shared folder.

    B. On Resource1, increase the amount of disk space available for offline files.

    C. Select the Notify Me and Begin Working Offline check box for offline files on Shelly's laptop.

    D. Add Shelly's user account to the Administrators group on Resource1.

16. Bob, an administrator in the IT department of your company, is concerned about excessive access to a shared folder on one of the company's servers. To ensure that only authorized users have access to the shared resource, he adds the appropriate groups and gives them the access levels they need. To keep all others from accessing the share, he explicitly denies the Everyone group the Full Control permission to the share. Very soon after that, authorized users report they get an "Access denied" message when they try to open the shared folder. What should you do to ensure that authorized users can access this resource on the server?

   A. Assign the Full Control Share permission to all users requiring access to the share.

   B. Set the NTFS permissions on the resource to allow the Administrators group full control of the folder, and then add all authorized users to the local Administrators group.

   C. Change the Deny Full Control permission for the Everyone group to Allow Full Control. Then change all the Allow permissions for the other groups to Deny Full Control.

   D. Remove the Deny Full Control permission from the Everyone group and then remove the Everyone group from the permissions list.

17. Mike has installed a new color laser printer on the network and needs to assign permissions for users to print to it and administer it. The Sales group needs to be able to print documents, the Engineering group needs to be able to use the printer and manage all documents, and the IT group needs to be able to completely administer the printer. How will you assign the permissions to the printer?

   A. Assign the Sales group Print permission, the Engineering group Manage Documents permission, and the IT group Manage Printer permission.

   B. Assign the Sales group and the Engineering group Print permission, the Engineering group Manage Documents permission, and the IT group Manage Printer permission.

   C. Assign all groups the Manage Documents permission.

   D. Assign all groups the Manage Printer permission.

18. You manage shared printers in your organization. You install a new shared print device on the network and have two groups of users that need to use the device. They have different permissions and printing priority requirements for the print device. How should you set the printer up for these two groups?

   A. Create two printer devices.

   B. Create two printers.

   C. Set up a printer pool.

   D. Create a print queue.

19. A user with a Windows XP Professional computer cannot use offline files with her computer. You ensure that everything is configured correctly on the server and that she has the correct permissions to the shared folders. You examine her computer and determine that the options for offline files is not available. Which of the following could cause this problem?

    A. She is not a member of the local administrators group on her computer.

    B. Her computer does not have Service Pack 2 loaded on it.

    C. She has Fast User Switching enabled.

    D. She does not have Full Control NTFS permissions to the shared folder.

20. Three users in the Marketing group all use a Windows XP Professional computer with two hard disks, one formatted as FAT32 and one formatted as NTFS. They all log in using the same user account. One user complains that when he copies files from one disk to the other, the files are accessed by others who also use the computer, regardless of what permissions he sets or even if he encrypts the files. What two things need to be done to ensure that his files are kept secure? (Choose two.)

    A. Convert the disk using the FAT32 file system to NTFS using the `Convert.exe` command.

    B. Set file permissions for each user on the FAT32 drive.

    C. Create separate local user accounts for each user on the computer.

    D. Enable Fast User Switching on the computer.

Answers to Review Questions

1. D. Joe was evidently logged on when the network administrator changed the permissions that affect his account. He will need to log off and then log back on to receive his new access token. If logging off and then back on again does not fix the problem, you may want to escalate it to the network administrator, but this should not be your first step. Joe's promotion being effective at Human Resources has nothing to do with his effective permissions to the resources.

2. B. The Sales group is explicitly denied access to the marketing department files; therefore, if Tara is still in the Sales group as well as the Marketing group, the explicit Deny will override all of the Allow permissions that she has from the Marketing group. You should politely ask the network administrator to double-check and make sure that he removed Tara from the Sales group. Tara will have to log off and log back on again once the permissions are fixed, but this should not be the first step. Removing Tara from the Marketing group will not fix the problem. Restarting the marketing department servers will not fix the problem.

3. C. Since the error message reads, "Access is denied" and has no other information, such as the name of the folder or file that Sam was attempting to access, you should suspect that the file has been encrypted by another user and escalate the issue to the network administrator. Based on the error message and the fact that Sam can access all other files and folders normally, this is probably not an NTFS issue. Restarting the computer or logging off and then back on again will not fix this problem.

4. C. The true effective permissions of the user to the shared folder are the most restrictive permissions of the effective NTFS permissions and the effective shared folder permissions. In this case, the effective shared folder permission is probably only Allow Read, which would explain why he can view the files in the folder but cannot change them. Changing the user's NTFS permissions to Allow Modify will not affect the shared folder permissions and therefore will not affect the true effective permissions. Trying to access the resource from another computer will not fix the problem. Allow Change is a shared folder permission and not an NTFS permission.

5. A, D. If you right-click the folder and there is no Security tab, then one of two things is true: either the computer is using simple file sharing or the partition is not formatted with NTFS. In this case, however, the computer is logged on to a domain and therefore cannot use simple file sharing. The share permissions cannot prevent you from seeing NTFS permissions. Restarting the computer would have no effect.

6. B. Since Sally has only Manage Documents permission for the printer, she cannot print to the printer; therefore, you should ask the network administrator to add Print permission to Sally's permissions for the printer. Adding the Manage Printers permission would allow Sally to change the properties of the printer itself; therefore, you should not add the Manage Printers permission. Restarting the print spooler will not affect Sally's permissions for the printer.

7. C. When a user's printout has illegible characters and only a few characters per page, you should suspect the printer driver first. A damaged network connection would not cause this symptom, nor would a computer's not having enough RAM. A print spooler that has run out of space would not create this symptom.

8. D. Since the test page from the Windows XP software printed normally, you can exclude the Windows XP operating system, the printer, and the print device itself from being part of problem. This isolates the problem to the application. You should save her documents and reinstall the application on her computer.

9. C. The network administrator must have cleared the check box setting that allows those folders and files to be cached. Since Hal is currently using the folders and files, you know that he has permission to use them and that they are not encrypted by another user. Since he can cache some folders and files normally, his computer is configured properly.

10. A, C. If a cached copy of a file is not changed but the original shared file is changed, then the new shared file original will be updated to the cache when the user performs a synchronization. If both the original shared file and the cached copy are changed while the client is offline, then the operating system will display a dialog box giving the user a choice of which file to keep or even to keep both files on their next synchronization.

11. A. Since Sally is a member of two groups having access to the resource, her NTFS and share permissions must be sorted out before determining her effective permissions. Sally has the following NTFS permissions from her group membership: Allow Modify and Full Control. Since NTFS permissions are cumulative, she has Full Control NTFS permissions. Her share permissions are Allow Read and Allow Change. Once again, since the permissions are cumulative, her share permissions are overall Allow Change. When the two sets of permissions are then compared, the most restrictive permission is her effective permission—in this case Allow Change.

12. B. Although Manage Documents is a permission that will allow Bob the ability to perform certain administrative functions with the printer, such as restarting and canceling documents, his user account still has to be assigned the Print permission for him to be able to use the printer. Adding Bob to the local administrators group on the print server will not solve the problem, but it will give him an excessive amount of permissions. Directing Bob to log off and on will not work in this scenario because he still will not have the proper permission to print to the device. Bob already has share permissions to the printer; otherwise, he would not be able to manage its documents.

13. B, D. Only NTFS partitions support the Encrypting File System (EFS). FAT partitions do not support EFS. Since the C: drive is already formatted as NTFS, it can support EFS. If the D: drive is converted to NTFS using the CONVERT command, it can also support EFS. NTFS drives cannot be converted to the FAT file system.

14. C. Reformatting Barbara's hard disk is not necessary. The Convert.exe utility, run at the command prompt, will convert the file system from FAT32 to NTFS. Placing Barbara's user account in the local administrators group will not solve the problem, and it will give her more permissions than she requires. By default, EFS is enabled on Windows XP Professional computers, so changes to the local security policy are also not necessary.

15. C. The Everyone group does not need any permissions over this folder for offline caching to be enabled. The space allocated to offline files on Resource1 has nothing to do with the ability of Shelly to access these offline files on her laptop. Shelly does not need to be a member of the Administrators group on Resource1 to be able to use offline files. She should check the Notify Me and Begin Working Offline check box on her laptop.

16. D. Removing the Deny Full Control permission from the Everyone group and then removing the Everyone group from the permissions list is the best answer. Bob essentially denied everyone, even authorized users who had explicit permissions set for the resource, by denying the Everyone group Full Control. An explicit deny is not required in this case because anyone who does not have permissions won't be able to access the resource. Assigning Full Control Share permissions to all users won't negate the Deny permissions, and users still will not be able to access the share. Setting the NTFS permissions on the resource to allow the Administrators group full control of the folder, and then adding all authorized users to the local Administrators group won't fix the problem, but it will give users more permissions than they should have. Likewise, changing the Deny Full Control permission for the Everyone group to Allow Full Control and then changing all the Allow permissions for the other groups to Deny Full Control will only keep denying permissions to authorized users.

17. B. This is the only set of permissions you can assign to achieve the levels of access your users require. Granting all users Manage Documents permission will give the Sales group excessive permissions and the IT group not enough permissions, and additionally, no group would be able to print to the device. Granting all users Manage Printers permission definitely gives the Sales and Engineering groups excessive permissions. Not specifically assigning the Engineering group Print permissions, as in choice A, prevents them from printing to the printer.

18. B. Create two printers, one for each group, and assign the required permissions and priorities for each group. Both printers will use the same print device, but each group will have different settings for it. Creating two print devices is not the answer because those are the physical printer devices themselves. A printer pool uses many devices and one printer so that jobs can be sent to any free device, so this is not the answer. A print queue is used to process the jobs as they are sent to the print device but has nothing to so with permissions or priorities, so this is also incorrect.

19. C. The computer is using Fast User Switching, which cannot be used with offline files caching. You must disable Fast User Switching for her to be able to use offline files. She does not need to be a member of the local administrators group to cache offline files. Service Pack 2 is not necessary for offline file use. She already has appropriate permissions to the resource because the configuration on the server was checked first and determined to be correct.

20. A, C. The first thing that must be done is to use the Convert.exe utility to convert the disk using the FAT32 file system to the NTFS files system, because FAT32 cannot support file permissions or EFS. The second thing that must be done is to create a separate user account for each user rather than have them log in using the same account. Even if the drive supports file permissions and EFS, if they are all using the same account, they can still access each other's files. File permissions cannot be set on a drive formatted with the FAT32 file system, and Fast User Switching has nothing to do with the problem described in the question.

Chapter
3

Configuring and Troubleshooting Hardware Devices and Drivers

MICROSOFT EXAM OBJECTIVES COVERED IN THIS CHAPTER:

✓ **Configure and troubleshoot storage devices.**

- Answer end-user questions related to configuring hard disks and partitions or volumes.
- Manage and troubleshoot disk partitioning.
- Answer end-user questions related to optical drives such as CD-ROM, CD-RW, DVD, and DVD-R.
- Configure and troubleshoot removable storage devices such as pen drives, flash drives, and memory cards.

✓ **Configure and troubleshoot display devices.**

- Answer end-user questions related to configuring desktop display settings.
- Configure display devices and display settings.
- Troubleshoot display device settings.

✓ **Configure and troubleshoot Advanced Configuration and Power Interface (ACPI).**

- Answer end-user questions related to configuring ACPI settings.
- Configure and troubleshoot operating system power settings.
- Configure and troubleshoot system standby and hibernate settings.

✓ **Configure and troubleshoot I/O devices.**

- Answer end-user questions related to configuring I/O devices.

- Configure and troubleshoot device settings.

- Configure and troubleshoot device drivers for I/O devices.

- Configure and troubleshoot hardware profiles.

There are many components in a typical computer that have little to do with the actual computations that the computer performs. The purpose of these components is to make it possible for us to store information on and communicate with the computer and to make it possible for the computer to communicate with us. These components include hard drives, CD-ROM drives, monitors, and input/output devices such as keyboards and mice.

Each of these components typically has a hardware element and a software element. The hardware element is either installed in or connected to the computer for an express purpose. The software element is in the form of a driver that allows the hardware to communicate with the operating system. As a desktop support technician, you should understand how to configure and troubleshoot these devices and their drivers. You should also be able to answer questions from end users regarding these devices. Hardware devices can be divided into four categories:

Storage devices   A *storage device* is any device that is installed in or connected to a computer for the purpose of storing data. There are two main types of storage devices: fixed and removable. Hard disks that are installed in a computer are considered to be fixed storage devices. All others are considered to be removable storage devices. You should be able to configure and troubleshoot both types of storage devices.

Display devices   A *display device* produces visual output that a user can see and interpret. This output can be in the form of text, menus, or images on a screen. This visual output provides a way for the computer to communicate with the user and is also a large part of the *graphical user interface (GUI)* that the user controls to communicate with the computer. Display devices have evolved over time. A typical organization has many types of display devices. You should be able to recognize, configure, and troubleshoot the most common.

Advanced Configuration and Power Interface (ACPI)   *Advanced Configuration and Power Interface (ACPI)* is an open industry specification that defines a flexible method of controlling power to components on a system board. ACPI is installed automatically with Window XP as long as all of the components in the computer can function with it. ACPI can also be used with some earlier operating systems, such as Windows 2000 Professional. While ACPI can provide a useful service (especially for a laptop user), it can also be the source of a troubleshooting headache when the computer has legacy components that do not support it. You should know how to configure ACPI for a user and answer user questions regarding ACPI. You should also be able to recognize a problem caused by ACPI and troubleshoot the problem appropriately.

Input/output (I/O) devices   An *input/output (I/O) device* is any device that can send and receive data to and from a computer. I/O devices have evolved over time and now come in many different forms depending on their purpose. An I/O device can be something as simple as a mouse or a keyboard or something much more complex, such as an infrared port on a laptop. You should be able to configure and troubleshoot the most common I/O devices and their drivers.

The rest of this chapter will focus on configuring and troubleshooting the four main categories of hardware devices and their drivers.

Storage Devices

The computers that we use are capable of processing tremendous amounts of data. After the data is processed, it is then stored in some format so that we can view and use it. Any device that stores the data for a computer is called a storage device. A computer may have many different types of storage devices, depending on the type of computer and its use.

We can divide all storage devices into two categories: fixed and removable.

Fixed Storage Devices

Hard drives installed in a computer are commonly recognized as *fixed storage devices*. The word *recognized* is important here because many client computers and servers actually have removable hard drives. Even if a hard drive is removable, Microsoft still refers to it as a fixed storage device.

Hard disk storage can also be divided into two categories: basic and dynamic. Basic disks have been around since the earliest operating systems, while dynamic disks were new with Windows 2000 operating systems. We will now discuss the difference between *basic disks* and *dynamic disks*, how to configure dynamic disks, and how to troubleshoot dynamic disk configurations. You can see an example of removable storage in Figure 3.1.

 You can view information about the devices recognized as fixed storage and removable storage by opening the Disk Management console.

Basic Disks

Basic disks started with the earliest Microsoft operating systems. When you first install any operating system, including Windows XP, it is installed on a basic disk. When you install a new disk into a computer, it is, by default, a basic disk.

Basic disks have limitations that dynamic disks do not have. For example, you must divide a basic disk into primary partitions and extended partitions. Extended partitions can further be divided into logical drives. Both the primary partitions and the extended partitions must be represented with a letter in the alphabet (A–Z). This would limit the number of logical divisions on a computer to 26 (the number of letters in the alphabet); however, it's even worse than that! The letter *A* is universally considered to be the 3.5-inch floppy drive of the system, while the letter *B* is considered to be the 5.25-inch floppy drive or a second 3.5-inch floppy, neither of which often actually exists on the computer. Therefore, if you use only basic disks, you can have only 24 logical divisions (primary partitions or logical drives on the extended partition) no matter how many drives you have or how much drive space you have. While this might not seem like much of a limitation to most client computers, it can be a significant limitation to servers and specialized client computers that need many drives.

FIGURE 3.1   Removable storage in Computer Management

Another major limitation of basic disks is that their partitions cannot be extended (made larger) using the operating system software. This means that even if you have a large amount of unallocated space that is contiguous to a partition, you cannot extend the basic disk's partition into that space using the operating system software. It also means that you might not get the best efficiency from a disk using only the operating system tools. Finally, you cannot join basic partitions to form larger volumes as you can with dynamic volumes on dynamic disks. Exercise 3.1 walks you through formatting a hard drive using fdisk in DOS.

It is possible to extend basic partitions using third-party software such as PowerQuest's Partition Magic.

EXERCISE 3.1

Booting to a MS-DOS Boot Disk

Some of Microsoft's CDs, such as Volume License editions, are often not bootable. This will force you to find an alternate method to format your basic disks. You will also have to have a way to kick off the installation. You can often solve these problems with an MS-DOS boot disk.

1. Once you have inserted the floppy disk, you can boot the system and wait for MS-DOS to start up.

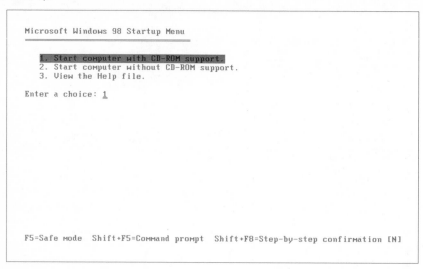

```
Microsoft Windows 98 Startup Menu
=================================================

   1. Start computer with CD-ROM support.
   2. Start computer without CD-ROM support.
   3. View the Help file.

Enter a choice: 1




F5=Safe mode   Shift+F5=Command prompt   Shift+F8=Step-by-step confirmation [N]
```

2. Once you have reached the A: prompt, type **fdisk** to start the fdisk program. This will allow you to create the partitions on your disk.

```
This may take a few minutes. Please wait...

Windows 98 has detected that drive C does not contain a valid FAT or
FAT32 partition. There are several possible causes.

1.   The drive may need to be partitioned. To create a partition on the drive,
run FDISK from the MS-DOS command prompt.

2.   You may be using third-party disk-partitioning software. If you are using
this type of software, remove the Emergency Boot Disk and restart your
computer. Then, follow the on-screen instructions to start your computer from
a floppy disk.
.
3.   Some viruses also cause your drive C to not register. You can use a virus
scanning program to check your computer for viruses.

The diagnostic tools were successfully loaded to drive C.

MSCDEX Version 2.25
Copyright (C) Microsoft Corp. 1986-1995. All rights reserved.
        Drive D: = Driver MSCD001 unit 0

To get help, type HELP and press ENTER.

A:\>fdisk_
```

3. You will be prompted to enable large disk support. Choose Y to enable it and N to disable it.

```
    Your computer has a disk larger than 512 MB. This version of Windows
    includes improved support for large disks, resulting in more efficient
    use of disk space on large drives, and allowing disks over 2 GB to be
    formatted as a single drive.

    IMPORTANT: If you enable large disk support and create any new drives on this
    disk, you will not be able to access the new drive(s) using other operating
    systems, including some versions of Windows 95 and Windows NT, as well as
    earlier versions of Windows and MS-DOS. In addition, disk utilities that
    were not designed explicitly for the FAT32 file system will not be able
    to work with this disk. If you need to access this disk with other operating
    systems or older disk utilities, do not enable large drive support.

    Do you wish to enable large disk support (Y/N)...........? [Y]
```

4. Note that in DOS, large disk support allows the operating system to understand the FAT32 file system. If you choose not to use large disk support, DOS will default to FAT16. If you have already partitioned your disk using NTFS, you will receive a message asking you if you wish to treat the NTFS partitions as large.

```
    Your computer has NTFS partitions which may require large drive
    support. If you are using another operating system, such as
    Windows NT, which supports large drives you should enable treating
    these partitions as large. NOTE: If you answer Y and the
    partition display looks incorrect or a hang or crash occurs
    do nothing, run FDISK again, and answer N to this question.

    Should NTFS partitions on all drives be treated as large (Y/N)? [Y]
```

EXERCISE 3.1 *(continued)*

5. Finally, you will be at the fdisk screen. You have several options to configure your basic disks.

```
                    Microsoft Windows 98
                   Fixed Disk Setup Program
              (C)Copyright Microsoft Corp. 1983 - 1998

                         FDISK Options

        Current fixed disk drive: 1

        Choose one of the following:

        1. Create DOS partition or Logical DOS Drive
        2. Set active partition
        3. Delete partition or Logical DOS Drive
        4. Display partition information



        Enter choice: [1]




        Press Esc to exit FDISK
```

a. Option 1 allows you to create both primary and logical partitions, as well as dynamic disks.

```
              Create DOS Partition or Logical DOS Drive

        Current fixed disk drive: 1

        Choose one of the following:

        1. Create Primary DOS Partition
        2. Create Extended DOS Partition
        3. Create Logical DOS Drive(s) in the Extended DOS Partition



        Enter choice: [1]




        Press Esc to return to FDISK Options
```

b. Option 2 allows you to set any partition as active.

c. Option 3 allows you to delete any partitions on the physical disk.

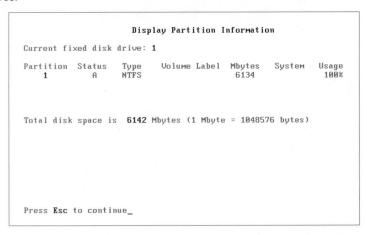

```
                    Delete DOS Partition or Logical DOS Drive

Current fixed disk drive: 1

Choose one of the following:

1.  Delete Primary DOS Partition
2.  Delete Extended DOS Partition
3.  Delete Logical DOS Drive(s) in the Extended DOS Partition
4.  Delete Non-DOS Partition



Enter choice: [_]




Press Esc to return to FDISK Options
```

Note that when deleting partitions, you must follow the order in which they are created. You must first delete all of the logical drives that exist within the extended partition. You can then delete the extended partition followed by the primary partition.

d. Option 4 verifies your configuration by displaying any existing partitions or logical drives.

```
                    Display Partition Information

Current fixed disk drive: 1

Partition  Status    Type    Volume Label   Mbytes   System   Usage
    1        A       NTFS                     6134              100%




Total disk space is  6142 Mbytes (1 Mbyte = 1048576 bytes)





Press Esc to continue_
```

Always remember that you must create the primary partition first, followed by the extended partition, and finally the logic drives within the extended partition.

Dynamic Disks

A dynamic disk is a hard disk that contains dynamic volumes. Now you might ask how the volumes become dynamic. You convert the disk to a dynamic disk using the Disk Management tool, shown in Figure 3.2, included with all operating systems later than Windows 2000. Exercise 3.2 walks you through the steps to convert a disk from basic to dynamic.

FIGURE 3.2   The Disk Management tool

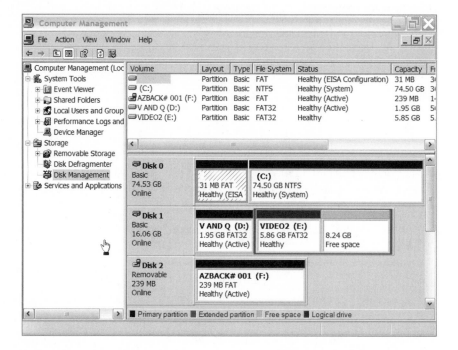

You might also ask why you would want to convert your disks from basic to dynamic. Well, you might not want to convert them at all, but if you do convert them, you will receive the following benefits:

- You can name the volumes anything that you wish and have as many volumes as your disks will hold.

- You can extend any dynamic volume that was originally formatted with NTFS as long as it is not a system volume or a boot volume.

- You can configure other special types of volumes that combine dynamic volumes for specific purposes. These include striped volumes, spanned volumes, and mirrored volumes.

EXERCISE 3.2

Converting a Disk from Basic to Dynamic

1. From the Windows XP Desktop, right-click My Computer, and then choose Manage.

2. In the Computer Management MMC, expand Storage, and then choose Disk Management.

3. After the disk configuration has loaded, right-click the disk that you wish to convert. Note that the disks are labeled toward the left side of the tool.

4. Choose Convert to Dynamic Disk.

5. If you have more than one disk, you can select to convert multiple disks at once. Select all the disks that you want to convert and click OK.

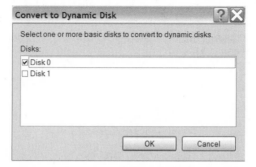

6. Follow the remaining directions of the wizard; you may need to restart your computer twice to complete the process.

Configuring Dynamic Disks

The types of dynamic volumes that you configure on your dynamic disks will depend on your specific use for the disk. Some dynamic volumes improve input/output (I/O) performance, while others provide fault tolerance. There are five types of dynamic volumes that you can configure on a dynamic disk. In this section, we will describe each type of dynamic volume and discuss its use.

Simple   A *simple volume* consists of a single region on a hard disk or multiple regions that are linked together on the same hard disk. Simple volumes are not fault tolerant within themselves, but they can be mirrored with other simple volumes.

Spanned   A *spanned volume* consists of disk space on more than one hard disk. The size of the spanned volume has been increased by extending it onto additional dynamic disks. Spanned volumes are not fault tolerant. When spanned volumes are filled with data, the first disk is completely filled before data is written to the second disk and so on.

Striped   *Striped volumes* are composed of "stripes" of data of equal size that are written across all of the disks in the volume. Striped volumes write to all disks in the volume at the same time, alternating between the disks as they stripe the information across the volume. Therefore, striped volumes improve disk drive I/O performance because I/O requests can be distributed across multiple hard disks. Striped volumes do not offer any fault tolerance.

Mirrored   A *mirrored volume* is a fault-tolerant volume that duplicates data on two separate hard disks. All data is written twice, once to each hard disk. If one of the disks should fail, the other disk will still contain the needed data. Mirrored volumes are sometimes used to create fault tolerance for the operating system files themselves.

RAID-5   *RAID* stands for *Redundant Array of Inexpensive Disks*. A *(RAID-5) volume* is a special type of striped volume that creates fault tolerance as it stripes the data. The additional data coupled with the parity information to rebuild the disk is striped across all of the disks in a RAID-5 volume. *Parity data* is striped across the disks based on a mathematical calculation such that if one (and *only* one) disk fails, the parity data that is on the other disks can be used to keep the system running and to eventually rebuild the information on the disk when it is replaced with a new disk. RAID-5 volumes are generally used to store large amounts of data that is essential for an organization. Software RAID-5 is supported by Windows XP Professional and by all Microsoft server operating systems. Hardware RAID-5 solutions are also available from third-party manufacturers.

Troubleshooting Fixed Storage Devices

Most client computers have only one hard disk installed. When the disk fails or becomes corrupted, the computer will not start. Sometimes the system will report an error that you can interpret. At other times, it may show a stop error screen, referred to as a "blue screen of death." Some client computers and most servers have multiple disks that may be dynamic or basic. You should know how to troubleshoot the most common errors for all types of storage devices, including startup errors, stop errors, and errors related to dynamic disks. In the following sections, we will describe each type of error that you might encounter with Windows XP client computers and discuss how to troubleshoot each one.

Startup Errors

If the computer is unable to locate the active partition or the boot sector volume that contains the operating system files, the user could receive one of these *startup error* messages:

- Invalid partition table
- Missing operating system
- Error loading operating system

If the computer cannot locate and load the NT Loader (NTLDR), the user could receive one of the following startup error messages:

- A disk read error occurred.
- NTLDR is missing.
- NTLDR is compressed.

Both of these issues might be resolved by using the Recovery Console that is included with the Windows XP operating system. Exercise 3.3 walks you through the steps to use the Recovery Console.

EXERCISE 3.3

Troubleshooting with the Recovery Console

1.   Assure that the BIOS boot sequence is configured to recognize the CD-ROM before the hard drive.

2.   Start or restart the computer with the Windows XP CD in the CD-ROM drive.

3.   At the Welcome to Setup screen, press R (for repair) to start the Recovery Console.

4.   Type **fixboot** to replace the boot partition or **fixmbr** to replace the master boot record.

5.   Follow the prompts to complete the fix.

6.   You can also type **help** to see all of the commands available from the Recovery Console.

Stop Errors

Sometimes Windows detects an error from which it cannot recover. This may be at startup or even while the computer is running. Windows reports this error in a full blue-screen non-windowed text mode. These "blue screens of death" sometimes provide information that is specific to the problem that caused the *stop error*. You should read the screen carefully and then search the Microsoft Knowledge Base at microsoft.com/support or Microsoft Technet at microsoft.com/technet. You should enter as much information as you can about the error to obtain the best results.

Dynamic Disk Errors

You can troubleshoot most errors regarding dynamic disks using the Disk Management tool included with Windows XP. The Disk Management tool reports the status of each disk in a computer. Based on the status of the disk, you should be able to resolve the problem. The following is a list of possible statuses for a disk, their cause, and their resolution:

Foreign   This status occurs when you install a new disk or a disk from another computer. Since the computer does not recognize the disk as one of its own, it is considered foreign. You should right-click the disk and then choose Import Foreign Disks.

Missing/Offline   This status occurs whenever a dynamic disk becomes inaccessible. Missing means that the system has recognized the disk before but can't find it now. Offline may mean that the disk was not available on the last startup. To bring a disk with a status of Missing or Offline back online, you should do the following: (1) Repair any hard disk, controller, or cable problems and confirm the physical status of the disk. (2) In Disk Management, right-click the disk and then choose Reactivate Disk. (3) If the disk does not come back online, then you will need to replace the disk and import the new foreign disk.

Not Initialized   This status indicates that the disk does not contain a valid signature in the master boot record (MBR) or a valid disk globally unique identifier (GUID) in the GUID partition table. You should right-click the disk and choose Initialize Disk.

Online (Errors)   This status indicates that I/O errors have been detected on the disk. You may be able to repair the errors by right-clicking the disk and choosing Reactivate Disk.

Unreadable   This status occurs when the system can see the disk but the disk is encountering errors that make it inaccessible. This situation can happen for many reasons, including a corruption in the disk, a hardware failure, or I/O errors. You should attempt to resolve this issue by rescanning the disk. Open the Disk Management tool, choose Action, and then choose Rescan Disks.

Software Errors   You will find that as you move hardware around, or even reinstall operating systems, your logical drive letters can be incorrect. Most often this happens when you add additional hardware. Most applications remember their installation source so that they may reuse it when necessary. Some software also requires the source to be present when you initialize the application. This can cause problems if your drive letters suddenly change. You can easily change the drive letter of a disk inside Disk Management, as seen in Figure 3.3.

FIGURE 3.3   Changing the drive letter on a fixed disk

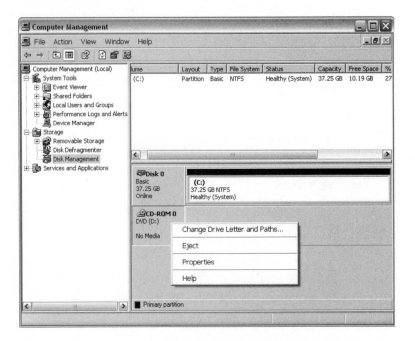

Removable Storage Devices

Removable storage devices include all types of storage devices except hard drives. There are many different types of removable storage devices, including floppy drives, CD-ROMs, DVDs, tape drives, and flash drives. Most of these types of drives are maintenance free and rarely require troubleshooting of any kind. However, if any drive is powered by a *Universal Serial Bus (USB)* port, you should make sure that the device has enough power to operate. If the device that is malfunctioning is connected to a hub, then you should consider moving its connection to the computer to give it more access to power.

A USB device that works well on its own but does not work well when other devices are used simultaneously could be an indication of a lack of adequate power. In this circumstance, you can either rearrange devices or provide another powered hub.

Display Devices

Display devices have evolved over time and with changes in technology, but the old ones and the new ones all do the same things: they let us know what the computer is "thinking" and they give us a way of communicating with the computer. There are several types of display devices in most organizations. In the following sections, we will discuss the most common display devices that can be used with Windows XP. In addition, we will discuss configuring and troubleshooting the display settings in Windows XP.

Types of Display Devices

The following are types of display devices that you might encounter in your network:

CRT monitor   *Cathode ray tube (CRT) monitors* are based on the same technology most of today's televisions are based on. They are the most common type today, but they will probably be superseded by other types of monitors in the future. An advantage of CRTs is that they are inexpensive compared to other monitors. Disadvantages include the fact that they are large and bulky and that they create heat.

Flat-panel monitor   *Flat-panel monitors* are growing in popularity. These are typically liquid crystal displays (LCDs) or plasma gas displays. Flat-panel monitors are not as bulky as CRTs and they do not create heat. While the price of flat-panel monitors is dropping, they are still considerably more expensive than CRTs.

Multimonitor   Windows XP can support up to 10 monitors at one time. While you are unlikely to use 10 monitors on Windows XP, it is sometimes useful to have a second monitor that can be used in tandem with the first. You can drag and drop images from one monitor to the other to create the desktop arrangement that you need.

Tablet PC   Tablet PCs typically feature a touch-sensitive LCD screen that can be rotated for landscape and portrait views. They are becoming more popular for users who need a very mobile device. Tablet PCs generally incorporate handwriting recognition so that the user can enter information with a special pen.

Smart displays   Smart displays are wireless touch-screen monitors that enable you to access your computer from anywhere within your wireless range. All of the actual computing is done on the computer with which the smart display communicates.

Display Settings

Users can configure display settings in Windows XP to customize the look of their computer. As a desktop support technician, you should be able to recognize an errant display setting and reset the computer for the user. You should also be able to troubleshoot display problems using VGA mode. Finally, you should be able to recognize and troubleshoot problems related to DirectX. In the following sections, we will discuss the types of display settings found on Windows XP and how to troubleshoot them. We will also define Windows DirectX and discuss specific troubleshooting scenarios with DirectX.

Types of Display Settings

Using the tools provided by Windows XP, users can customize their display so that it is comfortable for them. Most of the time, this is a good thing; however, if a user applies the wrong settings and then doesn't know how to reverse the process, you may be called in to troubleshoot the problem. The following display settings may have been changed by the user:

- Background: This setting changes the Desktop's background color, pattern, and image. You can also use this setting to apply an active Desktop and use an HTML document for the background.

- Screen Saver. This setting is used to save a monitor from "burnout" by automatically running a pattern or program on the monitor when the keyboard and mouse have not been used for a specified period of time. These are only necessary for CRTs because LCDs do not have a problem with "burnout."

- Appearance: This setting adjusts the color, text, and icon spacing for windows and menus.

- Screen Resolution: This setting controls the size and display of the screen, which is measured in pixels.

- Color Depth: This setting controls the number of colors that can be displayed on the screen. A higher color depth makes a more realistic picture.

- Themes: This setting defines many aspects at once, including background image, icons, sounds, mouse pointers, and other elements that personalize the Desktop for the user.

- Refresh Rate: This setting controls the frequency with which the screen is completely retraced. A higher refresh rate can reduce monitor "flicker" and make the monitor more comfortable to use. You should ensure that the hardware can support the refresh rate that is set.

Troubleshooting Display Settings

Most of the display settings that a user might inadvertently change are located in the same area. To obtain access to the display settings, you should right-click the Desktop and then choose Properties. If a user has made a change that is affecting their display, you will likely be able to correct the problem by examining the settings on each of the tabs in the Display Properties dialog box, shown in Figure 3.4. You can begin to develop more informed users by telling them that they can right-click a setting button and then choose What's This? to view more information about that setting.

FIGURE 3.4   The Display Properties dialog box

Troubleshooting in VGA Mode

Sometimes just knowing where you would change the display settings does you no good at all because when you start the computer, there is no Windows display and therefore no way to find any display settings. This problem can be caused by a screen resolution setting that the monitor cannot handle or by an improper driver. This issue can often be resolved by restarting the computer in VGA mode to make the necessary changes. Exercise 3.4 walks you through the steps to troubleshoot a system that has no Windows display.

EXERCISE 3.4

Troubleshooting a System with No Windows Display

1.   Ensure that the monitor has power and that the video cable is attached to the computer.

2.   Ensure that the Brightness and Contrast settings are in their center position.

3.   Restart the computer, pressing F8 after the computer finishes the startup messages but before Windows starts up.

4.   Select Enable VGA Mode.

5.   Examine the Screen Resolution setting and reduce it to 800 by 600 if necessary.

6.   Attempt to restart the computer normally.

7.   If the Windows display still does not return, you will need to reinstall the video driver. Follow the manufacturer's recommendations to uninstall and reinstall the video driver.

Troubleshooting Microsoft DirectX

Microsoft DirectX is an advanced suite of multimedia application programming interfaces built into Microsoft Windows operating systems. Introduced in 1995, it provides a standard development platform for Windows computer programming for specific tasks such as three-dimensional (3D) graphics, video acceleration, joystick controls, and sound cards. Yes, as you may have guessed, it's mostly for games, but it might also be used in some business applications such as interactive video programs for training.

As a desktop support technician, you might have to troubleshoot an application that will not install properly and indicates an error relating to DirectX. You should know how to determine the version of DirectX that is installed in the computer. You should also know how to troubleshoot the system, either eliminating DirectX as the real cause of the problem or identifying the problem within DirectX.

EXERCISE 3.5

Troubleshooting with the DirectX Diagnostic Tool

1. On the Windows XP Desktop, click Start and then choose Run.

2. On the Run menu, type `msinfo32.exe`, and then click OK.

3. On the System Information menu bar, click Tools, and select DirectX Diagnostic Tool.

4. On the System tab, view the system information to determine the DirectX version.

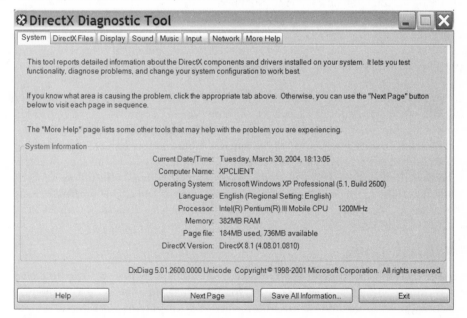

5. Select the DirectX Files tab to determine the DirectX files installed on the computer and any problems with the files.

6. Use the Display, Sound, Music, Input, and Network tabs to test and control DirectX.

7. Use the More Help tab to find additional troubleshooting information specific to DirectX.

Fortunately, DirectX comes with its own diagnostic tool. You can use the DirectX Diagnostic tool to test video, sounds, joystick control, and communication. Using the DirectX Diagnostic tool, you can isolate the problem within DirectX or eliminate DirectX as a possible source of the problem. Exercise 3.5 walks you through the steps to use the DirectX Diagnostic tool to troubleshoot a system.

Advanced Configuration and Power Interface (ACPI)

All of the components of a computer consume electricity to perform their functions. Processors, RAM chips, and electric motors are just a few examples of hardware that consume power. In large organizations, it's important to conserve power on desktop computers because the savings are multiplied over many computers. Controlling computer power usage can also have an indirect effect on the costs in an organization; for example, turning off CRTs reduces heat, which could save on air conditioning costs in the summer.

Laptop computers create another challenge in regard to power consumption. If you charge a laptop and then use it where you don't have access to electrical power, you want the battery to last for as long as possible. In this case, you need to have individual control of all of the major components that consume power, such as the display, hard drives, network interface cards, and so on.

Advanced Configuration and Power Interface (ACPI) is an open industry specification that allows a manufacturer to develop hardware with power interfaces that can be controlled by software. This allows computer manufacturers to create computers that can "sleep" while you are not working on them but "wake" at the touch of a button. It is a great feature, as long as all of the components in a computer are compatible with it. If some of the components are incompatible, then problems can arise that require troubleshooting. In the following sections, we will discuss how to use ACPI to configure power schemes and enable hibernation and standby features. We will also discuss troubleshooting problems associated with ACPI.

Power Schemes

A *power scheme* is a collection of power management settings that allow a user to conveniently configure power management options for individual components on a computer. The options that can be configured vary based on whether a computer is a desktop or a laptop computer. You can create and save power schemes that customize the power consumption of devices on your computer.

When the computer hardware is ACPI compliant and the operating system is ACPI enabled, as is Windows XP, the user can make changes to power management settings through the various tabs in Power Options Properties in Control Panel, as shown in Figure 3.5.

FIGURE 3.5   Power Options Properties in Control Panel

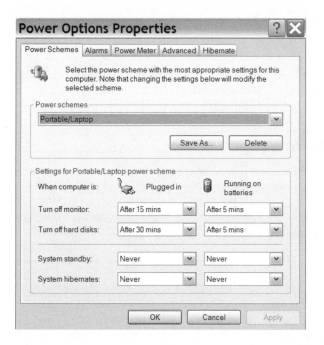

The settings available in the Power Schemes tab in Power Options Properties are as follows:

- Turn Off Monitor: This setting specifies the amount of time the computer can be idle (no keyboard or mouse activity) before the monitor automatically shuts off. This can be used to save energy in desktops and save battery life in laptops.

- Turn Off Hard Disks: This setting specifies the amount of time the computer can be idle before the hard disks will automatically turn off. This is primarily used with laptops to save battery power. It can also provide a quieter laptop for a sales presentation.

- System Standby: This setting specifies the amount of time the computer can be idle before going into Standby mode (falling asleep electronically, as discussed in detail in the next section).

- System Hibernates: This setting specifies the period of time that the computer will remain on before it automatically goes into hibernation. You can define a period of minutes or hours for both the plugged-in state and the battery-powered state on most laptops. This setting applies only if hibernation is enabled.

The remaining tabs in the Power Options Properties dialog box control various other attributes:

- Alarms: This tab lets you define when a laptop user will be warned about low battery power.

- Power Meter: This tab allows you to show the power meter icon in the notification area and display the current power status.

- Advanced: This tab allows a user to set the default options for power buttons on a computer.

- Hibernate: This tab enables hibernation (discussed in detail later in this chapter) and allows the user to confirm whether there is enough disk space.

 You can click and hold the power icon in the notification area to quickly change between power schemes.

Standby vs. Hibernate

Although both Standby and Hibernate can be used to conserve power, there is a huge difference between these two power management options. As a desktop support technician, you should understand the differences between Standby and Hibernate and know how to configure a computer for both power management options. In the following sections, we will contrast Standby and Hibernate and discuss how to configure each for a user.

Standby

Standby is an ACPI feature that can switch the entire computer to a low-power state after a set period of time. When a computer enters Standby mode, devices such as the monitor and hard disks turn off and the computer then uses less power. Standby settings override the individual settings for the monitor and hard disk. You can "wake" the computer simply by pressing any key on the keyboard or moving the mouse.

Standby is typically used with laptops to conserve battery power, but it can also be used for desktops to conserve power usage. You can configure System Standby in the Power Options Properties of Control Panel on the Power Schemes tab. You should know that Standby does not save the Desktop to the hard disk, so a power loss during Standby could result in a loss of any unsaved data.

Hibernate

When you use the Hibernate feature, the computer saves everything that is in memory to the hard disk and then completely shuts down. When you restart your computer, the system is restored to the same Desktop, exactly as you left it. Hibernate takes longer to restore a Desktop for a user, but it protects the data and completely conserves power.

Since the Hibernate feature uses hard disk space to store the information that is in RAM, you must have at least as much hard disk available as you have RAM in your computer in order to configure hibernation. You can configure a computer for hibernation on the Hibernate tab in the Power Options Properties of Control Panel. Exercise 3.6 walks you through the steps to enable and configure Hibernate in Windows XP.

EXERCISE 3.6

Enabling and Configuring Hibernation in Windows XP

1. Click Start, choose Control Panel, and then select Power Options.

2. Select the Hibernate tab, and then click the Enable Hibernation check box.

3. The system will confirm whether you have enough free disk space and either configure your computer for hibernation or advise that you do not have enough disk space.

4. Once hibernation is enabled, select the Power Schemes tab to configure the amount of time before your computer automatically hibernates.

5. You will now have the Hibernate option whenever you click Start and choose Turn Off Computer.

Troubleshooting ACPI

ACPI features should be available automatically as long as the Windows XP operating system detects a compatible BIOS and compatible hardware and device drivers. Most often, ACPI-related problems have to do with the compatibility of computers that are being upgraded. Common ACPI-related problems include the following:

- An inability to shut down the computer
- Standby and Hibernate options not being available

- Problems resuming from standby or hibernation
- Monitor not resuming after being powered off by ACPI

You should first determine whether the operating system has detected that the computer is ACPI compliant. You can determine this by examining the Computer properties in Device Manager. Exercise 3.7 will demonstrate checking for ACPI compliance within Windows XP.

 Real World Scenario

What You Should Not Do with a Laptop!

One day a user brought us a laptop that was hot to the touch! It would not start properly but instead would begin to start and then restart itself, over and over. There was smell of burning plastic or rubber in the air around it! We asked him what happened to it and he said, "It was that way when I took it out of the carrying case." He said this had never happened to him before and that he didn't think he had done anything wrong.

We asked him if the computer might have been on Standby and not turned off completely when he put it in the case. He admitted, "That's possible because I really just threw it in and didn't pay it a lot of attention." He asked if we thought the thing was "toast." We told him that we would give it about 15 minutes to cool off and then try again and hope for the best.

The next 15 minutes were longer for him than they were for us. We left the laptop turned completely off, by way of the 3-second power switch. The smell of burned wires gradually dissipated.

When we turned it back on after 15 minutes, it started up and ran normally! As far as we know, it still runs. He was really lucky that he opened that case when he did. In retrospect, it was probably just an overheating processor that made it keep restarting. Once it cooled off it was okay, although there must be some cooked wire insulation in there somewhere!

Anyway, it's not something that we would recommend users try! You should instruct users to make sure their laptop is either off or fully hibernated before they put it in the carrying case. That way, they won't have to experience those "long 15 minutes" as he did.

I/O Devices

Input/output (I/O) devices provide for communication to and from a computer. There are many ways to connect to and communicate with a computer. Methods of communication have evolved over time and with advances in technology. Depending on how you use a computer, you may require more or fewer of these types of devices. The Windows XP operating system allows you to control which devices are active depending on how a computer is being used. In the following sections, we will discuss the major types of I/O devices and how they provide communication to and from a computer. We will also discuss how to create hardware profiles to control the use of specific I/O devices. In addition, we will examine troubleshooting scenarios related to I/O devices.

EXERCISE 3.7

Determining ACPI Compliance in Windows XP

1. On the Windows XP Desktop, right-click My Computer and choose Properties.

2. On the Hardware tab, select Device Manager.

3. Expand the entry called Computer.

4. Examine the expanded entry. If there is a subentry that identifies ACPI, then ACPI is installed on the computer. If the subentry says Standard PC, then Windows XP did not detect that the computer was ACPI compatible.

5. If your computer was not detected as ACPI compatible, examine the Power section of your computer's BIOS to determine ACPI capability or contact the computer manufacturer.

6. If your computer was detected as ACPI compatible but you are still having problems related to ACPI, make sure you have the latest drivers for the components installed in your computer and confirm that the latest Windows XP service pack is installed.

Types of I/O Devices

The following are types of I/O devices that you might encounter as a desktop support technician.

Serial devices   *Serial communication* is the sequential exchange of information between computers and peripheral devices a bit at a time over a single channel. Serial ports on a computer are sometimes used for pointing devices or for data exchange with personal digital assistants (PDAs). Devices that connect through a serial port are generally not Plug and Play compatible.

Parallel devices *Parallel communication* sends multiple data bits and control bits simultaneously over parallel wires. It is typically used with printers, scanners, plotters, and some external storage devices. Devices use a 25-pin connector called a DB-25 to connect to the parallel port of the computer. Devices that conform to the IEEE 1284 standard are Plug and Play compatible.

Universal Serial Bus (USB) Universal Serial Bus (USB) is an external bus that supports Plug and Play installation. Devices can be connected and disconnected without shutting down the computer or even powering down a port. You can "daisy chain" many types of devices on a USB connection, including printers, scanners, mice, joysticks, tape drives, keyboards, and cameras. A single USB port can support up to 127 devices as long as there are enough powered hubs to provide adequate power for all of the devices.

There are two versions of USB: 1.1 and 2.0. The major difference between the two is that version 2.0 provides for higher bandwidth and therefore greater speed. USB version 2.0 is backward compatible with version 1.1.

You should know that the most common error in regard to USB-type devices is having too many devices on a hub to support the power requirements for the devices. This can cause intermittent failure of devices.

IEEE 1394 devices *IEEE 1394* is an external high-speed serial bus that supports Plug and Play installation. Also referred to as FireWire, IEEE 1394 is typically used to transfer data from high-end video and audio equipment. Other devices such as hard disks, printers, scanners, and DVD drives might also use IEEE 1394.

Modems The term *modem* comes from the words *modulator* and *demodulator*, which refer to converting electronic signals into sounds and vice versa. A modem is a device that allows computers to communicate over a standard telephone line. Modems typically use an RJ-11 jack, just like the ones on the walls of most houses.

Infrared (IR) devices *Infrared (IR)* devices use infrared (below red) light to communicate signals and transfer data. Infrared communication is point-to-point and line-of-sight communication between devices. Devices that have an IR port can use Infrared Data Association (IrDA) standards to communicate. IR ports can often be found on printers, PDAs, laptops, and cellular phones.

Radio frequency (RF) wireless devices *Radio frequency (RF)* wireless devices are a new standard that is growing in popularity. RF devices have an advantage over IR devices in that they use radio waves instead of light and therefore do not require line-of-sight communication. RF capabilities can currently be found in laptops, printers, PDAs, pointing devices, and cellular phones.

Hardware Profiles

You might be thinking, "With all of these I/O options available on a computer, how can I control which ones the computer will use and when?" Well, Windows uses *hardware profiles* to control which devices are used when the computer is started. Windows creates a default hardware profile called Profile 1, which enables every device on the computer. You can modify Profile 1, but the recommended method is to copy the Profile 1 settings to another profile with a different name and then change the settings to whatever you need. Exercise 3.8 walks you through the steps to create and configure a hardware profile in Windows XP.

EXERCISE 3.8

Creating and Configuring a Hardware Profile

1. On the Windows XP Desktop, right-click My Computer and then choose Properties.

2. On the Hardware tab, choose Hardware Profiles.

3. Assure that Profile 1 is selected, and click Copy.

4. Type the name for the new profile that you want to create, and click OK.

5. Close all windows and restart the computer.

6. At the Hardware Profile/Configuration Recovery menu screen, select the name of your new profile. Your computer should now boot into the new profile.

7. Right-click on the Desktop, and choose Properties.

8. On the Hardware tab, choose Device Manager.

9. Locate a device that you want to disable for this profile, right-click the device, and select Properties.

10. In the properties for the device, select Do Not Use This Device in This Profile.

11. Repeat steps 9 and 10 for each device that you want to configure.

Troubleshooting I/O Devices

Most I/O devices are Plug and Play, so they rarely require troubleshooting. If an I/O device is not functioning properly, the problem could be hardware related, software related, or both. You can isolate the problem by performing some or all of the following actions:

- Check all power cabling and connections related to the device.
- Check for power and connection indicators on the device itself.
- Check that the device is compatible with the Windows XP operating system.
- Make sure that you have the correct drivers installed for the device.
- For IR devices, make sure that the device and computer are within range and are not in bright sunlight.
- For RF devices, make sure that there are no other RF devices in the area that are blocking or interrupting the signal.

Drivers

Drivers are specialized software programs that allow hardware to communicate with the operating system. Every device that is installed in or connected to a computer requires a driver. They usually come packaged with the device but can also be obtained through the manufacturer's website.

Windows XP has new features that ensure that drivers are compatible with the operating system and make troubleshooting drivers much easier. You can update to a better driver without fear of losing the driver that you currently have installed. In the following sections, we will discuss updating and rolling back drivers in Windows XP. We will also discuss how Windows XP can assure compatible drivers with driver signing.

Updating Drivers

Microsoft and other companies frequently publish updates for device drivers. Some updates provide new functionality, while others fix problems associated with the current driver. They may come from the manufacturer on a CD-ROM that installs the driver automatically. You might also obtain the new driver from the manufacturer's website and manually install it through Device Manager. In addition, some manufacturers post their new drivers on Microsoft's *Windows Update website* so that you can download them from Microsoft. In the following sections, we will discuss these three main methods of updating a driver.

Updating Drivers Using a CD from the Manufacturer

This is the simplest form of update. Simply place the CD into the CD-ROM drive and follow the instructions from the manufacturer. Note that USB devices should typically be disconnected before you attempt to update their drivers.

Updating Drivers Using Windows Update

To check for updates from the Windows Update website, you can use tools built into Windows XP. Exercise 3.9 walks you through the steps to update drivers through Windows Update.

EXERCISE 3.9

Updating Drivers Using Windows Update

1. Ensure that your computer has a connection to the Internet.

2. Click Start, choose All Programs, and then choose Windows Update.

3. On the Windows Update site, click Scan for Updates. The system will scan your computer and suggest the appropriate updates.

4. To select drivers, choose Driver Updates and click Add. You can review each of the driver updates and select them individually.

5. When you are ready to install the updates, choose Review and Install Updates, and then click Install Now.

Be wary of using Windows Update for your device drivers. Microsoft develops operating systems and software, not hardware. You should always check with the manufacturer for the most recent drivers and look toward Windows Update as a last resort. You should not update device drivers just for kicks. Think of the old saying "If it's not broken, don't fix it." Tampering with drivers that already work definitely won't help your system run better, but it can cause your system to stop functioning.

Updating Drivers Manually with Device Manager

If you obtain a new driver that does not come with an installation disk or a program that automatically installs it, you can install it manually using Device Manager. Exercise 3.10 walks you through the steps to update a driver manually using Windows XP Device Manager. When using Device Manager, you will see devices that have associated icons; usually the icon will represent the device type. If there is a problem with the device, you might see a different icon. There are three available icons for devices with problems, as seen in Figure 3.6:

- A yellow exclamation point, which means that the device has a problem.

- A red X, which means the device is disabled.

- A blue i for *information*, which means that the device has forced resource configurations. This icon is seen only in the two resource views.

FIGURE 3.6 Problem drivers in Device Manager

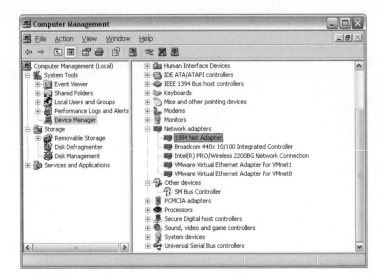

Rolling Back Drivers

If you have ever installed a driver and then wished you had not installed it, you can appreciate the new *Roll Back Driver* feature in Windows XP. The Roll Back Driver feature keeps a cache of the old driver when you update it to a new one. If you then decide that the old driver was actually better, you can select Roll Back Driver and return to the old driver without uninstalling the new driver or reinstalling the old driver. Exercise 3.11 walks you through the steps to roll back a driver.

Remember, if you can't get into the operating system, you can't roll the driver back, so this feature is useful only for noncritical peripheral device drivers.

EXERCISE 3.10

Updating a Driver Using Device Manager

1. On the Windows XP Desktop, right-click My Computer, and then choose Properties.

2. On the Hardware tab, choose Device Manager.

3. Double-click the device whose driver you want to update, and select the Driver tab.

4. Click Update Driver.

5. In the Hardware Update Wizard, select Install From a List or a Specific Location, and then click Next.

6. Select Don't Search. I Will Choose the Driver to Install. Then click Next.

7. Select Have Disk, and then click Browse.

8. Navigate to the folder where the new driver is located, click Open, and then click OK.

9. Select the driver that matches your hardware, click Next, click Next again, and click Finish.

Driver Signing

Microsoft uses *digital signatures* for device drivers to assure users that the drivers are compatible with Windows 2000 Professional and Windows XP Professional operating systems. Digital signatures indicate that the driver has passed the compatibility tests and has not been altered after testing. You can configure computers to use only signed drivers, but you should be aware that your choices of drivers will be more limited. You can also configure the computer to warn you if a driver is not signed but allow the installation if you still choose to install it. Network administrators can configure these options on all of the computers in an organization or on a select group of computers. You should be aware of any unsigned drivers that are allowed to be used by computers in your organization. In the following sections, we will discuss how to configure signed drivers in a single computer. We will also discuss how to identify the signed and unsigned drivers in a single computer.

EXERCISE 3.11

Rolling Back Drivers in Windows XP

1. On the Windows XP Desktop, right-click My Computer, and then choose Properties.

2. On the Hardware tab, select Device Manager.

3. Double-click the device whose driver you want to roll back, and then select the Driver tab.

4. Click Roll Back Driver.

5. After the system is finished rolling back the driver, click OK to close the dialog box and save the settings. You may need to restart your computer to complete the reinstallation of the driver.

Configuring a Computer for Signed Drivers

Windows XP gives you three options in regard to driver signing: Block, Warn, or Ignore. You decide which one to use based on your own experience and on the availability of signed drivers for your devices. Exercise 3.12 walks you through the steps to configure *Driver Signing options* on a single Windows XP computer.

EXERCISE 3.12

Configuring Driver Signing Options for Windows XP

1.   On the Windows XP Desktop, right-click My Computer, and then choose Properties.

2.   Click the Driver Signing button.

3.   Select one of the following options:

>   Ignore: To install unsigned and signed drivers without a warning

>   Warn: To install unsigned drivers after a warning

>   Block: To prevent the installation of unsigned drivers

4.   If you are logged in as an administrator, you can select or clear the Make This Action the System Default check box. If checked, the option applies to all users. If unchecked, it applies only to the current user.

Determining Signed and Unsigned Drivers

If you decide to use only digitally signed drivers from now on, you will receive the benefit of not having to worry about driver compatibility issues. The cost of this decision will be that you are limited in the choices that you can make in regard to drivers. Chances are good that the computers you are using currently have a mixture of signed and unsigned drivers. You can use the *File Signature Verification tool* to determine which drivers in your computer are signed and which are unsigned. Exercise 3.13 walks you through the steps to do so.

EXERCISE 3.13

Using the File Signature Verification Tool

1.   On the Windows XP Desktop, click Start, and then choose Run.

2.   Type **sigverif.exe**, and then click OK.

3.   In the File Signature Verification Wizard, click Start. The system will build a file list and scan the files.

EXERCISE 3.13 *(continued)*

4. When the system has finished the scan, you can view the files that are not signed.

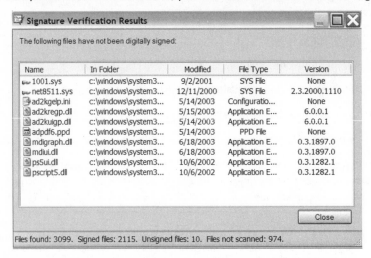

5. You can also use the Advanced options to view the entire log of all files that were scanned.

Case Study: ABC Corporation Help Desk Tickets

Help Desk Case #HD4000027873

Larry, a Microsoft certified desktop support technician, has received a call from Patsy in the human resources department. Patsy states that her workstation no longer works. Larry knows that each problem is mostly likely going to have symptoms. He asks Patsy to describe the problems that she is having.

Patsy: When I came in this morning and tried to turn on my computer, nothing happened.

Larry: Were there any sounds coming from your computer? Did it sound as if it tried to come on?

Patsy: I'm not sure.

Larry: Please verify that all of your components are plugged in. Be sure that there are at least two power cables that lead to the wall outlet from your computer; also verify that all cables beneath your desk are firmly plugged in.

Patsy: Everything looks as if it is plugged in.

Larry: Can you tell if the lights on your computer are lit up? If so, what color are they?

Patsy: There are no lights lit up that I can tell.

Larry: Go ahead and press the power button on the system.

Patsy: It beeped once. Is that good?

Larry: Yes. That means it has passed the power-on self test, or POST. Is there any type of display on your monitor?

Patsy: No.

Larry: There is a light that will most likely be close to the power button on the monitor. Is it on? If not, please press the power button.

Patsy: I have pressed the power button, but the light will not come on.

At this point, it's pretty obvious that the monitor is bad. The video card can be eliminated for two reasons: (1) Usually, if the video card is bad, the workstation will send a series of beeps to alert us. (2) If the video card is bad, the monitor lights would still come on and the monitor would most likely show a test image. The only other viable solution is that monitor is not plugged in. Larry might further verify that this is not the case by asking Patsy to follow the power cable all the way from the monitor to the wall outlet.

That was an easy one. Let's move to a more difficult ticket!

Help Desk Case #HD4000034566

Mary, the senior desktop support technician, has been called into the field to troubleshoot a reported blue screen error.

Charlie's workstation had been acting funny, the Desktop icons were very large, and the colors were very bland. One of Charlie's coworkers suggested that he use Windows Update to download new video drivers. When his downloads were finished, he was prompted to reboot his computer. When the computer rebooted, just before his logon prompt would appear, his screen turned blue with the following error:

```
STOP 0x000000EA, (0x81774538,0x81a8fc78,0x8193e490,0x00000001)
THREAD_STUCK_IN_DEVICE_DRIVER
```

Mary decided to follow the Microsoft recovery recommendations. She first attempted to boot into safe mode but still received the error. That was an indication that the default VGA driver must be corrupt.

Mary knew the default VGA driver was corrupt because that is the driver used when booting into safe mode. You usually boot into safe mode to verify that the current driver is causing any problems you might have. If you can successfully boot into safe mode but not boot into normal mode, that lets you know that your video driver is incompatible or corrupt.

She next tried to evoke the last known good configuration; reverting back to the last configuration that worked. Unfortunately this didn't work either. It seems that the old driver has been overridden or removed. Finally, Mary booted to the Recovery Console and expanded the files to recover the default video drivers.

After rebooting, the system came up with a logon prompt! Charlie was able to log onto the system but his display was the same as before the incident. Mary contacted the device manufacturer and downloaded the proper driver. Charlie's system now works great!

Boot Failure!

Microsoft recommends that you use these tools in this order to recover from boot failure:

1. Last Known Good Configuration

2. Safe mode

3. Recovery Console

4. Automated System Recovery

Summary

A modern computer is a combination of many devices, most of which have little to do with the actual calculations that the computer performs. Each of these devices has a hardware component and a software component called a driver. As a desktop support technician, you should be able to configure and troubleshoot these devices and their drivers.

Storage devices hold data before and after it is used by a computer. Storage devices can be divided into two categories: fixed and removable. Hard disks installed in a computer are considered to be fixed storage devices; all others are removable. Fixed storage devices can be divided into two groups: basic disks and dynamic disks. Basic disks are the standard, default form of storing information on a hard drive. Dynamic disks are new to Windows 2000 Professional and Windows XP, and they enable new benefits such as expanding a volume on a disk using only the operating system software. Dynamic disks are required in Windows XP to create special volumes, such as striped volumes, spanned volumes, and mirrored volumes.

Display devices produce an output that can be viewed and interpreted by the user. They can provide a graphical user interface (GUI) that enables a user to communicate with the computer. Display devices come in many forms, such as CRTs, LCDs, and plasma gas monitors. Windows XP has many settings that allow users to create a custom display based on their preferences. These settings are generally available to the user and therefore may present a troubleshooting issue for a desktop support technician. In addition, new technologies such DirectX are being employed for games and business applications. These new technologies bring their own set of issues and their own set of troubleshooting tools.

Advanced Configuration and Power Interface (ACPI) can help you conserve power and get more life out of the batteries that you use in your laptops. Manufacturers can create hardware and drivers that allow ACPI to control the power of a device. With ACPI, you can configure when and how your monitors, hard drives, and other devices are powered on and powered down. ACPI can also present a troubleshooting issue because some devices are not compatible with it. This will most likely occur when you upgrade the operating system on an existing computer.

Input/output (I/O) devices enable the transfer of data to and from a computer. I/O devices have evolved over time and continue to evolve. Most of the I/O devices that we use today are Plug and Play, which means that they find their own resources and rarely need troubleshooting. I/O devices can use many types of external connections, including serial, parallel, USB, IEEE 1394, and wireless connections. Most of the troubleshooting of I/O devices centers around making sure that the external connections are solid and that you are using the correct driver.

Drivers are special software programs that enable the hardware device to communicate with the operating system. They are specific to each device for each operating system. Windows XP has tools that allow you to update drivers as new drivers become available. You can also use a new tool that enables you to roll back a driver update if you decide that you were better off with the previous driver. In addition, Windows XP provides tools that enable you to ensure the compatibility of drivers in your operating system by identifying and controlling the installation of drivers that are not digitally signed. Digital signatures on drivers indicate that the drivers were tested for compatibility with the operating system and that the drivers have not been altered since they were tested. Using the new tools provided by Windows XP, you can customize your driver signing options based on the needs of your organization.

Exam Essentials

Understand the configuration of fixed and removable storage devices.   You should know the difference between fixed and removable storage devices. In addition, you should know the main differences between basic disks and dynamic disks and the configuration options for each type. Finally, you should be able to troubleshoot startup errors, stop errors, and errors related to dynamic disks.

Know display types, display settings, and DirectX.   You should be familiar with the major types of displays that are in use today and the advantages and disadvantages of each type. In addition, you should know the display settings that users can change to customize the display for their needs. Finally, you should be able to troubleshoot errors related to displays, display settings, and DirectX.

Understand the Advanced Configuration and Power Interface.   You should know how ACPI can be used to control the power consumption of devices in a computer. You should understand that all devices and the operating system must be ACPI compatible in order for

ACPI to operate properly. Finally, you should be able to recognize and troubleshoot problems related to ACPI.

Understand I/O devices.   You should be able to recognize the various types of I/O devices and device connectors, such as serial, parallel, USB, and IEEE 1394. You should know how hardware profiles are used to control the enabled devices at startup and how to create new hardware profiles. Finally, you should understand the general uses of each type of I/O device and how to troubleshoot each type.

Understand drivers.   You should understand what drivers are and how they affect the performance of a device. You should understand that driver compatibility is essential and know how to configure the computer for the various driver signing options. Finally, you should know how to identify the drivers that are in a computer and determine whether they are signed or unsigned.

Review Questions

1. You are the desktop support technician for a large organization. You have installed a second hard disk in a computer running Windows XP Professional on a basic disk. You want to create a mirrored volume. Which of the following must you do to successfully create the mirrored volume?

    A. Format both partitions with the NTFS file system.

    B. Convert both disks to dynamic disks.

    C. Convert only the second disk to a dynamic disk.

    D. Format only the second disk's partition to NTFS.

2. You are the desktop support technician for your organization. A user complains that his computer crashed while he was working on it and he received an error message on a blue screen. Now when he tries to restart the computer he gets the same error message. Which of the following should you do first?

    A. Completely reinstall the operating system as a clean installation.

    B. Start the computer in Windows safe mode and fix the error.

    C. Read the error message and examine the Microsoft Knowledge Base for information.

    D. Start the computer with the Recovery Console and type `fixmbr`.

3. You are the desktop support technician for your company. A user named Susan complains that she can no longer see anything on her monitor. She says that it was okay before and that someone else was using her computer and tried to change the settings, but they "messed it up." Which of the following should you do? (Choose two.)

    A. Remove and reinstall the video drivers.

    B. Ensure that the Brightness and Contrast levels are not all the way down.

    C. Reboot to safe mode and ensure that the Resolution setting is proper for the video card and monitor.

    D. Replace the monitor with one that works.

4. You are the desktop support technician for your company. A user is trying to use a new training application but is getting an error that indicates that she doesn't have the correct version of DirectX installed. You want to determine which version of DirectX is installed on her computer and test the DirectX components. Which of the following should you do? (Choose two. Each answer is a part of the solution.)

    A. Open Device Manager and browse for the DirectX component on her computer.

    B. On the Run line, type `msinfo32.exe`.

    C. In Control Panel, select System Information.

    D. In the System Information tool, select DirectX Diagnostic Tool from the Tools menu.

5. You are the desktop support technician for your organization. A user named Sam says that his laptop "falls asleep" every time that he stops typing on it for a few minutes, even when it is receiving power from the wall socket. What should you do first?

    A. Check the power schemes and power management settings in Power Options on Sam's laptop.

    B. Replace the battery in Sam's laptop.

    C. Replace the power supply in Sam's laptop.

    D. Reinstall the video drivers in Sam's laptop.

6. You are the desktop support technician for your organization. A user named Dave utilizes his laptop for sales presentations outside the office. Dave asks you if there is a way to save his presentation on the Desktop when he turns his computer off. He wants to put the computer into the case to carry it to the next location and then resume with the presentation already on the Desktop. Which of the following should you tell Dave?

    A. There is no way to do what he wants to do.

    B. He can simply put the computer into Standby mode between presentations.

    C. He can use the Hibernate feature as long as he has enough memory.

    D. He can use the Hibernate feature as long as he has enough free hard disk space.

7. You are the desktop support technician for your company. A user complains that a USB-powered network interface card is failing intermittently. The network interface card is plugged into a USB hub that is connected to his computer. The other devices on the hub are working properly. Which of the following should you do first to troubleshoot the problem? (Choose two. Each answer is a part of the solution.)

    A. Disconnect the network interface card from the hub.

    B. Reinstall the software and drivers for the network interface card.

    C. Restart the computer.

    D. Connect the network interface card to the USB port on the computer itself.

8. You are the desktop support technician for your organization. A user has a laptop that she uses in the office as well as out of the office. She says that when she uses the laptop away from the office, she gets a couple of errors at startup that have to do with the computer trying to find the network. She would like to eliminate these errors if possible. What should you do?

    A. Tell her that those errors are unavoidable unless she can connect to the network from home.

    B. Create a user profile that is specifically for use outside the office.

    C. Tell her to always use the Standby feature instead of turning the laptop off.

    D. Create a hardware profile that is specifically for use outside the office.

9. You are the desktop support technician for your company. You want to make sure that some computers can use only drivers that are digitally signed as compatible with the Windows XP operating system. Which of the following should you do? (Choose two. Each answer is a part of the solution.)

   A. Access the Driver tab for each device in Device Manager.

   B. Select Block to prevent unsigned drivers.

   C. Select Allow to permit only signed drivers.

   D. Access the Driver Signing Options from System Properties.

10. You are the desktop support technician for a large organization. You want to determine all of the unsigned drivers on an existing computer. You wish to do this with the least administrative effort. Which of the following should you do? (Choose two. Each answer is a part of the solution.)

   A. Run the File Signature Verification Wizard.

   B. Use the default settings in the wizard.

   C. Use the advanced settings to identify the folders and drives to check.

   D. Use the advanced settings to view the log file created by the scan.

11. You are a desktop support technician for your company. Bill's computer runs Windows XP Professional and is a member of the corporate domain. After Bill plugs in his USB hard drive, he receives a message that requests the drivers for his device. When Bill inserts the driver disk, Windows informs him that his device driver hasn't been signed and won't be installed. How can you ensure that Bill's device will function properly?

   A. Have Bill install the USB driver software before he attempts to install his hardware.

   B. Use Windows Update to obtain the most recent software driver for Bill's hardware.

   C. Use a domain administrator account to force Windows to accept the device driver.

   D. Reinstall the operating system and turn off the Driver Signing feature.

12. You are the senior support technician at your organization. The human resources department computers are configured with dynamic disks in a RAID 1 configuration for redundancy. During routine computer maintenance, a field technician finds that one of the HR computers has a disk that is in Missing/Offline status. You need to be sure that all data on the HR computer is recoverable. What should you do?

   A. Use the Defrag utility to repair the dynamic disk.

   B. Replace the disk and perform an ASR.

   C. Reboot the computer, right-click on the failed disk, and choose Rescan.

   D. Ask an administrator to log onto the computer and delete the failed disk, install a new hard drive, and choose Reactivate Disks from the options in Device Manager.

13. You are the help desk support technician for your company. The security department has created a new security policy that requires that all portable computing devices must have screensavers that come on after 10 minutes of inactivity. They must also require a password to get back to the Desktop. You have been assigned the task of configuring all existing portable devices in this manner. Where can you make the changes on each portable device?

   A. Choose Start ➢ Control Panel ➢ User Accounts ➢ User Accounts, and change the way users log on and off.

   B. Choose Start ➢ Control Panel and open Appearance and Themes ➢ Display ➢ Screen Saver tab.

   C. Right-click on the Desktop and choose Properties ➢ Settings.

   D. Choose Start ➢ Control Panel and open Security ➢ Configuration ➢ Screen Saver Passwords.

14. You are a help desk technician at your organization. A user has recently used Windows Update to update his device drivers. After the update process, the user was prompted to reboot. After rebooting, the user says that he can no longer access the network. Everything else seems to be working fine. You need to ensure that the user can access the network as soon as possible. What should you do?

   A. Restart Windows into VGA mode and revert the video driver.

   B. Use recovery console to revert the network card driver.

   C. In Device Manager, under the properties of the networking device, choose Roll Back Driver.

   D. Instruct the user to reinstall the operating system and rely on the internal update structure in the future.

15. You are the desktop support technician at your company. Shelly, a senior executive in your company, works from home three days a week. She transfers her files using a 1GB flash drive that was given to her by the IT department manager. Her computer recently crashed and her replacement arrived today. She reports that when she plugs her USB flash drive into her USB port on the back of her computer, she receives the message "You have plugged a high speed device into a non-high-speed port." You need to ensure that Shelly does not receive this message and can access her files as usual. What should you do?

   A. Revert Shelly's USB device driver to the original driver.

   B. Use Windows Update to get a newer device driver.

   C. Contact the manufacturer for a device driver that is compatible with Shelly's operating system.

   D. Delete and reinstall Shelly's device in Device Manager.

16. You are the help desk support technician at your company. Bobby uses a laptop computer at his desk as his workstation. The laptop is very old and has recently had a RAM upgrade. He now has a 4GB hard drive with 2GB of RAM. After the RAM upgrade, Bobby has reported that he is receiving message stating that his C: drive is running low on space. Upon investigation, you find a file in the root of the C: drive that is 2,048MB in size. The file is named `Hyberfil.sys`. You need to ensure that Bobby has enough free space on his system to continue normal operations. What should you do? (Choose all that apply.)

   A. Delete the `Hyberfil.sys` file to free up some disk space.

   B. Request that Bobby run the Disk Cleanup Utility to free up some disk space.

   C. Install an operating system that uses less disk space.

   D. Turn off hibernation on Bobby's system.

17. You are the senior help desk technician at your organization. All of your client computers run Windows XP Professional. You receive a call from Sarah, a user in the marketing department. She states that she downloaded an application from the Internet, and after realizing the application was not compatible with Windows XP, she uninstalled it. Her icons are now very large and her Desktop seems to have "shrunk" and she cannot properly read emails and documents. You need to ensure that Sarah can properly read her emails and documents. What should you do?

   A. Use the Recovery Console to revert her video driver back to the OEM driver.

   B. Use the Display Properties dialog box to change the resolution on Sarah's computer.

   C. Use the Device Manager console to roll Sarah's driver back.

   D. Delete any residual files from Sarah's hard drive that might be left from the program's installation.

18. You are a help desk technician at your company. Freddie, a member of the HR group, has recently received a new computer. To save time, the field technician moved Freddie's hard drives from his old computer to his new computer. The users in the HR group have specially configured workstations with specialized hardware. After installing the old hard drives into the new system, the field technician reports that when the system boots up, he receives a stop error that states the video driver has failed. You must instruct the technician on how to get Freddie's computer working as soon as possible. What should you do?

   A. Instruct the field technician to update the drivers to match the new hardware.

   B. Tell the field technician to use the recovery console to repair the damaged driver.

   C. Instruct the field technician to reinstall Freddie's operating system so that it can adapt to the new hardware.

   D. Fire the field technician.

19. You are the help desk technician for your organization. Your company's client computers are running Windows XP Professional. You receive a call from a user who cannot boot his system. He says that when the system begins to boot, he receives an error message that says the NTLDR file is missing or corrupt. You need to repair the user's computer as quickly as possible. What should you do?

    A. Use the Last Known Good Configuration feature.

    B. Use the Recovery Console.

    C. Use safe mode.

    D. Reinstall the operating system.

20. You are the help desk technician at your company. The executives at your company have just been issued PDAs that use infrared (IR) ports to synchronize with the operating system. One of the executives calls your desk and says that her PDA will not synchronize and she has tried many times. Her workstation is beneath her desk, and she has purchased a USB-to-IR adapter to allow for communications. You need to ensure that she can synchronize her desktop files with her PDA. What should you do?

    A. Ensure that the path between her USB-to-IR adapter and her PDA is clear of obstruction.

    B. Reinstall the drivers and software for the PDA.

    C. Return the PDA and adapter as defective.

    D. Reconfigure her PDA to use the USB driver.

Answers to Review Questions

1. B. Dynamic disks are required to create any special volumes such as mirrored volumes. You will need to convert both disks, not just the second disk, to dynamic disks. Dynamic disks can contain volumes formatted with FAT, FAT32, or NTFS, so there is no need to format the partitions.

2. C. The user has encountered a stop error. You should read the message in the blue screen and examine the Microsoft Knowledge Base to determine the solution. You should not reinstall the operating system as a first step. You cannot boot to safe mode because the computer is not getting that far at startup. Since the user's computer initially crashed while he was working on it, the stop error is not likely to have been caused by a problem with the master boot record; therefore, `fixmbr` is not the correct solution.

3. B, C. The problem is likely related to the display settings. You should ensure that the Brightness and Contrast settings are not all the way down and ensure that the Resolution setting is proper for the monitor and video card. You will need to reboot to safe mode to examine and change the Resolution setting. The problem is not likely related to drivers or the monitor itself because the monitor was working fine before the Susan's friend used her computer.

4. B, D. You can use the DirectX Diagnostic tool to determine the current version of DirectX installed on the computer and test the DirectX components. You should type **`msinfo32.exe`** on the Run line and then select the DirectX Diagnostic tool from the Tools menu in System Information.

5. A. The most likely cause of Sam's computer problem is that the power management settings are set to a very low amount of idle time. You should check the power schemes and power management settings in Power Options.

6. D. Dave can use the Hibernate feature as long as he has at least as much free hard disk space as he has RAM in his computer. The Hibernate feature will save his Desktop and turn the computer off completely between presentations. The Standby feature does not completely turn the laptop off, so it could overheat in the case.

7. A, D. Since there are multiple devices on the hub and the problem is intermittent, the issue is likely related to a lack of adequate power for the device. You should disconnect the network interface card from the hub and plug it directly into the computer to determine whether the problem is power related. You should not reinstall the drivers or restart the computer as a first step to troubleshooting this issue.

8. D. You should create a hardware profile that is specifically for use outside the office. The hardware profile that you create should disable the network interface card to eliminate the error that she is experiencing relating to the network. A hardware profile, not a user profile, is used to control which devices are enabled at startup.

9. B, D. You should access the Driver Signing Options tab from System Properties and select Block to prevent unsigned drivers from being installed in the computer. You do not need to identify each device. Allow is not an option in Driver Signing Options.

10. A, B. You should run the File Signature Verification tool with the default settings. The default settings will scan all of the drives and folders in the computer and identify and indicate all unsigned drivers in the computer. You do not need to use the advanced settings in this case.

11. C. There is a group policy that is forcing Windows to deny any attempt to install an unsigned device driver. The only way to force acceptance of this driver is to use an account that has local administrative permissions.

12. C. When a disk goes missing or offline, that means that the operating system did not properly recognize the drive during the last boot process. You can usually fix this problem by rescanning the disk that has errors. Often rebooting the system will fix the problem as well.

13. B. You can configure the screensaver and the "on resume password protect" settings in the Display box on the Screen Saver tab. You can reach it by simply right-clicking on the Desktop and choosing Properties or choosing the appropriate applets in Control Panel.

14. C. Option B will provide access to the network, but not in a timely manner. Option C is the best answer because it allows you to quickly and efficiently revert back to the original, working device driver. You should use Device Manager when possible to work with device drivers.

15. C. Often, Windows will load a device driver that is similar to the device installed in a system. This driver may allow the hardware to function, but with reduced or limited functionality. To ensure proper performance and functionality, you should obtain device drivers from the manufacturer of the hardware. Shelly is currently using the default USB 1.1 device driver for her device; this will allow for only 12MBps data transfer. You could possibly obtain a USB 2.0 driver from Windows Update, but it is recommended that you use the OEM driver from the manufacturer. USB 2.0 can allow for much faster data transfers.

16. B, D. Bobby has experienced a loss of disk space because hibernation creates a file named Hyberfil.sys that is equal to the amount of physical RAM installed in his system. You should not delete this file. To remove the file, simply disable hibernation. You can also run the Disk Cleanup Utility to let Windows find old and unused files.

17. B. Some applications can change the system's resolution to ensure proper display of program components. Some applications will fail to change the resolution back after they are closed, especially applications that aren't compatible, such as the one Sarah installed. You can usually just change the resolution back manually to resolve the problem.

18. C. You usually cannot simply move an operating system from one set of hardware to another unless the hardware is exactly the same. Often the transfer will still not work properly. When you install an operating system, it adapts itself to work with the hardware that it finds during the installation process. There are programs that can "image" a system and allow it to be used on many different computers, but they require extensive configuration and are usually very expensive. The field technician should be familiar with device drivers and operating systems, so although you might be tempted to choose option D, it won't fix the problem!

19. B. When the NTLDR file is not located by Windows during the boot process, the boot process halts, resulting in the error received by the user. Sometimes a simple reboot will fix the problem. Often you will need to boot into the recovery console with the Windows XP CD to repair the NTLDR file.

20. A. Infrared devices require a line of sight in order to communicate properly. Most likely the user is attempting synchronize her device with the adapter plugged into her USB port on the back of her system. This would block the light from making the connection between devices.

Chapter 4

Configuring and Troubleshooting the Desktop and User Environments

---

MICROSOFT EXAM OBJECTIVES COVERED IN THIS CHAPTER:

✓ **Configure the user environment.**

- Answer end-user questions related to configuring the desktop and user environment.
- Configure and troubleshoot task and toolbar settings.
- Configure and troubleshoot accessibility options.
- Configure and troubleshoot pointing device settings.
- Configure and troubleshoot Fast User Switching.

✓ **Configure support for multiple languages or multiple locations.**

- Answer end-user questions related to regional settings.
- Configure and troubleshoot regional settings.
- Answer end-user questions related to language settings.
- Configure and troubleshoot language settings.

✓ **Troubleshoot security settings and local security policy.**

- Answer end-user questions related to security settings.
- Identify end-user issues caused by the local security policies such as Local Security Settings and Security Configuration and Analysis.
- Identify end-user issues caused by network security policies such as Resultant Set of Policy (RSoP) and Group Policy.

✓ **Configure and troubleshoot local user and group accounts.**

- Answer end-user questions related to user accounts.
- Configure and troubleshoot local user accounts.
- Answer end-user questions related to local group accounts.
- Configure and troubleshoot local group accounts. Considerations include rights and permissions.

✓ **Troubleshoot system startup and user logon problems.**

- Answer end-user questions related to system startup issues.
- Troubleshoot system startup problems.
- Answer end-user questions related to user logon issues.
- Troubleshoot local user logon issues.
- Troubleshoot domain user logon issues.

✓ **Monitor and analyze system performance.**

- Answer end-user questions related to system performance.
- Use Help and Support to view and troubleshoot system performance.
- Use Task Manager to view and troubleshoot system performance.
- Use the Performance tool to capture system performance information.

As a desktop support technician, you are responsible for providing and maintaining the tools that keep users productive. Users' productivity increases when they can customize their Desktop for their specific needs. Some users have special needs to address, such as a disability or a second language, while others simply need reliable access to their computer and/or to the domain resources.

A user's access to resources is controlled locally but it's also influenced by many other factors, such as network security and group policies. Depending on how a user is logged on, they can gain access to only a specific set of resources. Their productivity will also be affected by the performance of their computer. Your ability to provide reliable access to computer resources is dependent upon your understanding of the "big picture." In this chapter, we will discuss configuring and troubleshooting the user's Desktop and the user's environment to keep users productive.

Maintaining the productivity of users requires an understanding of six categories of resource configuration and troubleshooting:

User environment   Let's face it; people just do better work when they are comfortable. Windows XP has many tools and settings that are designed to make users more comfortable and therefore more productive. These tools include Taskbar and toolbar settings, accessibility options, pointing device settings, and Fast User Switching. You should be able to configure and troubleshoot these tools and settings.

Multiple languages or multiple locations   Windows XP and Windows 2000 Professional are offered in three distinct variations: English, Localized, and Multilanguage User Interface (MUI). In addition, each variation provides users with the ability to change their input language. You should know the difference between Regional Language options and MUI software. You should also know how to configure and troubleshoot these features.

Security settings and local security policy   When computers are in a workgroup, each computer controls its own security, making security management relatively simple. In a domain environment, many other factors can control the security of a computer, including network security policies and group policies. You should know the factors that can affect security on a computer in each environment. You should also know how to troubleshoot problems and when to escalate the issue to a network administrator.

Local user and group accounts   In order for a user to log on locally to a computer, they must have a user account. User accounts are generally created by the administrator to identify the user and define the actions they can perform. There are only two built-in local user accounts in Windows XP: Administrator and Guest. You should know how to use the User Accounts settings in Control Panel to identify the local accounts in a computer.

System startup and user logon   When a user starts up a computer and logs on to the computer locally, a process of authentication and validation takes place that will determine what the user can see and do after they are successfully logged on. This process is very similar when the user logs on to a domain, but there are some differences. You should understand the logon process and how logging on to a computer is different than logging on to a domain.

System performance   There are four essential resources in most computer systems: processor, memory, disk subsystem, and network subsystem. Each resource performs a specific function, but they also work together with all of the other resources. A weakness in one resource can affect the performance of all of the resources on the computer, creating a bottleneck. You should understand this balance of resources and know how to use the Windows XP Task Manager and Windows Performance tools to identify and troubleshoot bottlenecks and to create a baseline of performance.

The rest of this chapter discusses configuring and troubleshooting these six categories of resources that are essential to the productivity of users.

User Environment

A computer can provide many resources for a user, such as e-mail, word processing, spreadsheets, Web access, and much more. Since users utilize a computer in their own way, each Windows operating system has become more flexible in regard to the way the user can organize and access the tools they need. A user can create their own environment using the Taskbar and toolbar settings included in the Windows XP operating system. Windows XP also has special features to adjust to the needs of a person who has a physical disability. In addition, a user can customize the pointing devices that they use to communicate with the computer. In a workgroup environment, users can even share a computer without the need for either user to log off. In the following sections, we will discuss how to configure and troubleshoot these important elements of a user environment.

Desktop Settings

The Desktop is the central interface from which most user activity is launched or controlled. Because it is important for the user to be able to configure the Desktop to enhance their productivity to the fullest, there are several settings that can be adjusted to suit the user's needs. Desktop items are stored in the user's profile. By default, when Windows XP is first installed, the Desktop contains only the Recycle Bin shortcut. More shortcuts, however, can be added, such as My Computer and My Documents.

Adding Desktop shortcuts is quite simple. You can add them one of two ways. First, you can right-click on the Desktop, select New and then Shortcut, and then follow the Create Shortcut Wizard by locating the file to which you would like to point the shortcut. The second way is to already have the file selected, right-click it and point to Send To, and then click Desktop (Create Shortcut).

In Display Properties in Control Panel, you can change many different categories of settings, such as Themes, Desktop, Screen Saver, Appearance, and Settings. Themes are saved configuration settings consisting of Desktop images, screensavers, cursors, and sounds. The Desktop settings allow you to change the appearance of Desktop items, such as the background and Desktop icons. The Screen Saver settings allow you to change the screensaver and its timing. On the Appearance tab, you can set the Windows dialog box style, color, and font size. The last tab, Settings, allows you to change the screen resolution and color settings. You can view the available settings for the Desktop in Figure 4.1.

FIGURE 4.1   Desktop settings

Taskbar, Start Menu, and Toolbar Settings

Users of Windows XP can customize the look and feel of the Taskbar, Start menu, and toolbar for their own needs. These items allow users to have the tools they use in view while the tools they rarely use are still accessible but not as obvious. As a desktop support technician, you should know how to customize these settings for a user. In the following sections, we will discuss configuring and troubleshooting the Taskbar, the Start menu, and the toolbars in Windows XP.

Taskbar Settings

The Taskbar, which contains the Start button and holds icons indicating programs that a user is currently using, can be customized to hold miniature icons of all types. In addition, the Taskbar can hold the clock and the notification area, which Windows XP uses to report events such as available updates. By default, it appears at the bottom of the screen, but you can customize it to be located on any side of the Desktop. You can also hide it when it's not being used. Exercise 4.1 walks you through the steps to configure the Taskbar in Windows XP.

EXERCISE 4.1

Configuring the Taskbar

1. On the Windows XP Desktop, right-click an empty area of the Taskbar. (Note that the Taskbar is initially located on the bottom of the screen and contains the clock.)

2. Choose Properties.

3. Click the check boxes to select the individual items, such as Show the Clock, Show Quick Launch, and Hide Inactive Icons.

4. Click OK to close the window and save your changes.

Start Menu Settings

The Start button and Start menu are used to access all of the programs and other items you will use in your daily work. The Start menu can be customized to contain the most commonly used program shortcuts and the user's specific frequently accessed items. There are two groups of items on the Start menu: the pinned items list and the frequently used programs. The pinned items list, located above the separator bar, contains the most commonly used menu items, such as Internet Explorer; the user can add to this list. The most frequently used programs list is located below the separator line and contains program shortcuts that are added automatically after they are used several times. Users can also manually add shortcuts to this list. An example of the default Start menu can be seen in Figure 4.2.

FIGURE 4.2   The Start menu

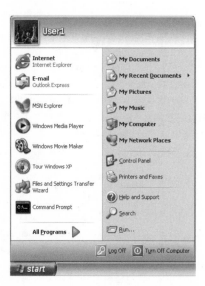

Toolbar Settings

Toolbars are located in every Windows application and are initially found at the top of the screen. Toolbars are specific to an application and can generally be customized within each application for the user. An application might have many toolbars, each with different settings and locations on the screen. We will discuss configuring and troubleshooting applications in greater detail in later chapters, but you should know that toolbar settings can affect what users can see and therefore what they think they can do. Figure 4.3 is an example of a toolbar in Microsoft Word for Office System 2003.

FIGURE 4.3   A toolbar in Microsoft Word for Office 2003

Control Panel Options

Control Panel contains all of the programs used to configure system settings. There are two ways to view Control Panel, and which one is used depends largely upon the preferences of the user. There are two views, Category view and Classic view, and you can be toggle between each view on the left-hand side of Control Panel.

Classic view is the way most people have used Control Panel, and it has remained essentially unchanged, with minor exceptions, since Windows 95. It is organized by functional program, so a user has to know which program will make the changes they desire.

Category view, on the other hand, is new to Windows XP and requires a bit less knowledge about the individual programs involved. It is more intuitive in that the different functions and configuration settings are logically grouped together so a user doesn't necessarily need to know what icon they need to select to perform a task. They simply look at the category they need.

It's important to note that the icons that appear in Classic and Category view are different. So, if you are taking a call from a user who is trying to adjust their desktop resolution, for example, and they tell you that Appearance and Themes does not appear as an option in Control Panel, it's because they are using a different view than you are. In those cases, it may be best for either you or the user to temporarily switch views so you are both looking at the same thing. You can see both views in Figures 4.4 and 4.5.

Accessibility Options and Features

Windows XP has built-in features and settings to enable a person with physical disabilities to use a computer. These are divided into two groups: *accessibility options* and *accessibility features*. You should know how to configure and troubleshoot these settings. In the following sections, we will discuss the location of accessibility options and accessibility features and show how to configure and troubleshoot each of them.

FIGURE 4.4   The Classic-style Control Panel

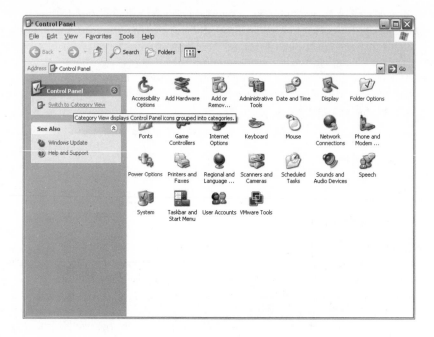

FIGURE 4.5   The Category-style Control Panel

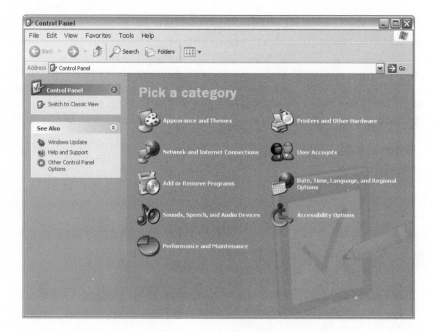

Accessibility Options

Accessibility options are methods of modifying an existing tool to enhance its capabilities for a person who has a physical disability. You can select and apply these options by opening Control Panel and then clicking Accessibility Options. Figure 4.6 shows the Keyboard tab of the Accessibility Options dialog box. The following is a list of tools and the options that you can apply to each tool:

- Keyboard
  - StickyKeys: Automatically locks keys to allow users to press single keystrokes to accomplish multiple-keystroke combinations such as, for example, Ctrl+Alt+Delete.
  - FilterKeys: Sets Windows to ignore brief or repeated keystrokes.
  - ToggleKeys: Plays tones when the Num Lock and ScrLk keys are pressed.

FIGURE 4.6   Accessibility Options dialog box

- Sound
  - SoundSentry: Gives a visual warning to indicate that Windows is playing a sound (e.g., flashes the window).
  - ShowSounds: Works with programs to display captions of sounds that are being played.

- Display
  - High Contrast: Enables very high-contrast colors for individuals with a visual impairment.
  - Cursor Options: Alters the width and blink rate of a cursor.
- Mouse
  - MouseKeys: Enables the control of the mouse pointer from the arrow keys on the numeric keypad of the keyboard.
- General
  - Automatic Reset: Shuts off the accessibility options after a set idle time.
  - Notification: Alerts the user that the options are being turned on or off.
  - SerialKey Devices: Allows the connection and configuration of special input devices.
  - Administrative Options: Determines whether settings apply to just the current user or to all users who log on to the computer.

Accessibility Features

Accessibility features are additional tools or programs that enhance the usability of a computer for a person who is physically disabled. These features can be started and controlled from the All Programs ➤ Accessories ➤ Accessibility menu. The following list shows the accessibility features included in Windows XP and the function of each:

- Accessibility Wizard: Adjusts Windows display settings and configures accessibility options.
- Magnifier: Enlarges part of the screen, as configured by the user, to make it much easier to see and read.
- Narrator: Converts on-screen elements to speech and reads the content and text on the screen for a person who is blind or has a severe vision impairment.
- On-Screen Keyboard: Creates a virtual keyboard on the computer screen on which users can point and click with the mouse to enter text and commands into the computer.
- Utility Manager: Indicates which of the accessibility programs are currently running and allows configuration for automatic startup of accessibility programs when a user logs on or locks the Desktop.

Pointing Device Settings

Most users utilize a keyboard and a pointing device, usually a mouse, to communicate with a computer. Some users utilize other pointing devices, such as a roller ball or touch pad. Since all users are unique, pointing device settings must be flexible enough to adjust to each user. You can configure and troubleshoot the type and behavior of the pointer in the Mouse settings in Control Panel, as shown in Figure 4.7.

FIGURE 4.7   Mouse settings in Control Panel

Fast User Switching

Users who share computers in a workgroup can use *Fast User Switching* to save time logging on and off. Fast User Switching allows a user to let another user log on without the first user logging off or even closing any programs. For example, if Bob is in the middle of a project and Sue just wants to check her e-mail, Bob can let Sue log on and check her e-mail without having to log off or close the project. When Sue is finished, she can log off and Bob will be returned to the program just as he left it. Sounds great, doesn't it?

Well, don't get too attached to it, because Fast User Switching is not available when a computer is a member of a domain. Since most organizations use domains, you probably won't get the opportunity to configure or troubleshoot Fast User Switching very often, at least not at work. You should be aware that Fast User Switching is available for computers that are members of a workgroup and that it can be configured in the User Accounts settings of Control Panel. You should also know that Fast User Switching is not an option if a computer is configured for Offline Files and Folders, which we discussed in Chapter 2, "Managing and Troubleshooting Access to Resources."

You should know that using Fast User Switching may slow down the performance of the computer for each of the users who are logged on. This performance reduction may or may not be noticeable depending on the applications in use.

Multiple Languages or Multiple Locations

Large organizations might contain users from many countries and regions. Windows XP and Windows 2000 Professional software can be configured to accommodate users from all over the world. Microsoft offers special options on the English version of the Windows XP software as well as special variations of the software itself.

The three distinct variations of Windows XP are as follows:

- English version: Standard U.S. version
- Localized versions: 24 varieties of Windows XP
- Windows XP Multilanguage User Interface (MUI)

These variations provide two levels of multilingual support for Windows XP and Windows 2000 Professional: *Localization* and *Regional and Language Options*. In the following sections, we will discuss the difference between these offerings and how to configure and troubleshoot each of them.

Localization

Localization refers to the language that is displayed by the operating system itself on the Start menu, Taskbar, and help screens. There are 24 localized languages for Windows XP. This means that you can buy the software in any of 24 different languages. You can also buy a *Multilanguage User Interface (MUI)* version that contains all 24 Localizations. You cannot change the Localization of Windows XP unless you are using the MUI version of the software. You should also make sure that you have the latest service pack installed before attempting to change the Localization of the MUI version of the Windows XP operating system.

You should know how to change the Localization of the MUI version of Windows XP. Exercise 4.2 walks you through the steps to change the language setting.

EXERCISE 4.2

Changing the Localization of Windows XP MUI Version

1. On the Desktop of Windows XP MUI version, click Start, and then choose Control Panel.

2. Select Date, Time, Language, and Regional Settings, and then choose Regional and Language Options.

3. On the Languages tab, select the language that you want to use under Language Used in Menus and Dialogs.

4. Click the Advanced tab, select the Apply All Settings to the Current User Account and to the Default User Profile check box, and then click OK.

The steps in this exercise are appropriate for a Windows XP computer with the Control Panel display option set to the default setting of Display as a Link.

Regional and Language Options

Regional and Language Options provides the ability to view, edit, and print documents that are *Unicode enabled* in any localized version of Windows. In addition, it provides the ability to change the standards and formats that the operating system uses to specify local currency units, number formatting, time and date, and so on. Collectively, these format and style settings are known as *regional settings*.

You should know how to configure regional settings and choose input languages in Windows XP localized versions. Exercise 4.3 walks you through the steps to configure these settings in Regional and Language Options.

EXERCISE 4.3

Configuring Regional Settings and Input Languages

1. On the Windows XP Desktop, click Start, and then choose Control Panel.

2. Select Date, Time, Language, and Regional Options, then choose Regional and Language Options.

3. On the Regional Options tab, set the regional settings by selecting your language and location.

4. On the Languages tab, click Details to select the default input languages and install additional input languages, and then click OK.

The use of additional input languages may require a special keyboard or a special overlay for the user's keyboard.

Security Settings and Local Security Policy

A security policy is a combination of security settings that affect the security of a computer. When a computer is a member of a workgroup and not a domain, it is subject only to the local security policy for which it is configured. In other words, computers that are members of a workgroup control their own security policies. On the other hand, when a computer is a member of a domain, then the local security policies may be overridden by network security policies. You should know how to configure and troubleshoot local security policies and when to escalate a network security issue to the network administrator.

Configuring and Troubleshooting Local Security Policy Settings

Security policies can be used to configure the following:

- Who accesses the computer
- Which resources users are authorized to use on their computer
- What actions a user may perform on their computer
- Whether a user's or a group's actions are recorded in an event log

There are many individual settings in a computer's Local Security Settings dialog. You can configure each of these settings individually for a computer that is a member of a workgroup:

- Account Policies: These are policies defining password restrictions and account lockout for incorrect logons.
- Local Policies: These settings that define audit policies, user rights assignments, and security options related to the local computer.
- Public Key Policies: These policies define the certificates and data recovery agents used by the Encrypting File System (EFS).
- Software Restriction Policies: These policies define whether a user is prevented from installing specified software on the computer.
- IP Security Policies on Local Computer: These policies define how and when your computer will communicate with other computers on the network (e.g., the encryption and authentication protocols that will be used).

You should know how to configure the settings for local security policies on a computer. Exercise 4.4 walks you through the steps to configure security policy settings.

When a local security policy is changed on a computer in a workgroup, only the computer on which the policy is changed is affected.

EXERCISE 4.4

Configuring Local Security Policy for a Computer

1. On the Windows XP Desktop, click Start, and then choose Control Panel.

2. In Control Panel, select Administrative Tools, and then select Local Security Policy. (If Administrative Tools is not listed, right-click Control Panel in the Start menu and choose Explore.)

3. Click the plus sign (+) of each category in the console pane (on the left) to expand each category and view the options.

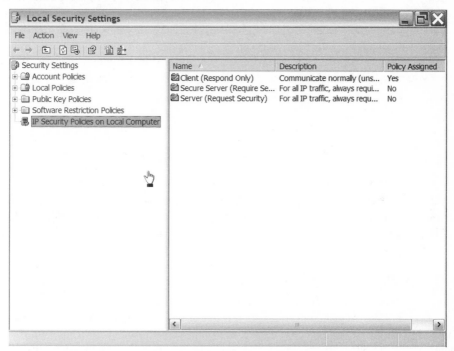

4. Right-click each option in the details pane (on the right), and choose Properties to configure the option or choose Help to find more information about the option.

5. When you have finished configuring options, close the Local Security Policy console. Note that some changes may require that you restart the computer.

WARNING   Be careful when adjusting the settings in your local security policies because incorrect settings or settings that are incompatible with other computers on the network may cause connectivity or resource access issues.

Recognizing Network Security Policy Settings

Windows security in a domain environment is often managed using Group Policy. Group policies are groups of configuration settings and security policies that are used to manage users and computers in sites, domains, and organizational units. They can be used to control what users can view and access and what actions they can perform. Since group policies can be applied to all levels of a hierarchy, more than one may apply to an object in the hierarchy. For example, if a user account is in an organizational unit that is in a domain that is in a site, and if each of these containers has its own group policies applied, then the user account will be subject to all of the group policies in all of the containers—but it's not quite that simple.

Actually, all of the policies will be run for the user account, but if any of the settings on the policies that are run last conflict with the settings of the policies that were run previously, then the last settings applied take precedence and will be the effective settings. The settings that do not conflict will all apply to the user, like a snowball effect.

Now you might be asking, "Well, which ones run first and which ones run last?" We're glad that you asked. The order in which the policies are always run is as follows:

1. Local computer policy

2. Site policy

3. Domain policy

4. Organizational unit policy

5. Child organizational unit policy

If you think about it, it makes sense that the policies that are closest to where the object actually resides (in this case, the child organizational unit) will be the ones that take precedence. The group of settings that ends up taking precedence is called the *Resultant Set of Policy (RSoP)*. The challenge for you is to determine which policies apply to the user or computer.

Using the Gpresult Tool in Windows XP

One way to determine whether group policies apply to a user or computer is to use a tool that is built into Windows XP called *gpresult*. This tool examines the policies that apply to the computer and the currently logged-on user. You should know how to use the gpresult tool to determine if group policies are being applied to a computer or user. Exercise 4.5 walks you through the steps to use the gpresult tool.

Local User and Group Accounts

User accounts are created by an administrator to uniquely identify individuals and define the actions that they can perform in the Windows operating system environment. Each user account is assigned a security identifier (SID) by the operating system. The SID is always unique and is never reused, even if an account is deleted and a new account is created with the same name. Windows uses the SID to control a user's access to resources based on permissions that are assigned to the user or to a group of which the user is a member.

EXERCISE 4.5

Using the Gpresult Tool

1. On the Windows XP Desktop, click Start and then choose Run.

2. On the Run line, type **cmd** and then press OK.

3. At the Windows XP command prompt, type **gpresult**.

4. Examine the output to determine which group policies are applied to the computer and the currently logged-on user.

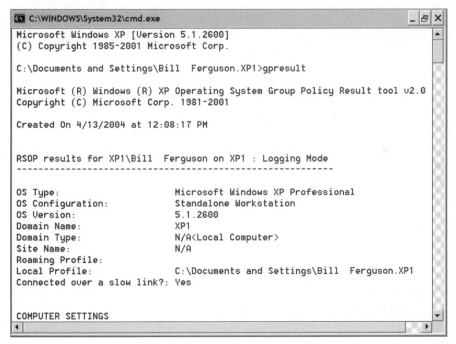

```
C:\WINDOWS\System32\cmd.exe                                          _ ☐ ✕

Microsoft Windows XP [Version 5.1.2600]
(C) Copyright 1985-2001 Microsoft Corp.

C:\Documents and Settings\Bill  Ferguson.XP1>gpresult

Microsoft (R) Windows (R) XP Operating System Group Policy Result tool v2.0
Copyright (C) Microsoft Corp. 1981-2001

Created On 4/13/2004 at 12:08:17 PM


RSOP results for XP1\Bill  Ferguson on XP1 : Logging Mode
---------------------------------------------------------

OS Type:                 Microsoft Windows XP Professional
OS Configuration:        Standalone Workstation
OS Version:              5.1.2600
Domain Name:             XP1
Domain Type:             N/A<Local Computer>
Site Name:               N/A
Roaming Profile:
Local Profile:           C:\Documents and Settings\Bill  Ferguson.XP1
Connected over a slow link?: Yes


COMPUTER SETTINGS
```

WARNING   If a user account is deleted and one is then created with same name, all privileges, rights, and permissions to resources, as well as memberships in groups, must be re-created as well. Windows sees these user accounts as different accounts with different SIDs.

Users can also inherit rights to perform actions within the operating system based on their group membership. You should understand the different types of user accounts and group accounts that you can use within the Windows operating system. In this section, we will discuss the different types of user accounts and group accounts and how to configure and troubleshoot each of them.

Local User Accounts

Local user accounts are specific to the individual computer they are created on and control access to resources and allow privileges on that computer alone. Windows includes several types of built-in local user accounts. You should understand the differences between these accounts and know how to create new local accounts on a Windows XP client computer. Windows XP uses the following types of accounts:

Administrator account   This account type allows users to log on to a computer with full administrative access rights to the computer. An administrative account named Administrator is installed in every computer running Windows XP and Windows 2000 Professional. The administrator can create new administrative accounts.

System account   This account is used by the operating system itself to allow access to resources to run hardware, software, and applications within the computer. This account also has full administrative rights to the local computer and is not used to log on interactively to the computer by users.

Guest account   This account allows users to log on temporarily without the need to create a new account. It should be used only for temporary logons and should be given very few rights and permissions.

Local accounts   This is a broader term that includes all of the accounts mentioned previously in addition to any accounts that an administrator creates for the purpose of giving access to local resources or rights to perform actions locally.

Domain accounts   This type of account is not local. Domain accounts give access to resources that are in the domain, not just the local computer. These accounts are generally created and controlled by network administrators. They reside in the Windows Active Directory, a shared database, not just on one computer.

Viewing and Creating User Accounts

There are two main tools that you can use to view user accounts and create new user accounts on a computer, *User Accounts* and *Local User Accounts and Groups*. Although these tools are located in different places and have some different options, both can be used to manage local user and group accounts, to include creating and deleting accounts, resetting passwords, and granting membership to groups. For example, you can add and manage groups using the Local

Users and Groups tool but not in the User Accounts tool in Control Panel. Fast User Switching, on the other hand, can be enabled and disabled using the User Accounts tool but not with the Local Users and Groups applet. You should know how to use each of these to configure and troubleshoot local user accounts. Exercises 4.6 and 4.7 walk you through the steps to view and configure user accounts with these Windows XP tools.

EXERCISE 4.6

Viewing and Creating Accounts with the User Accounts Tool

1. On the Windows XP Desktop, click Start and choose Control Panel.

2. In Control Panel, select User Accounts.

3. Each account is represented with its name and a unique picture. You can replace the "automatic picture" with an image of your choice.

4. Choose from the options in Pick a Task or select an account to change its specific prop-erties. You can change the name, the account type, or the picture or even delete the account with this tool.

EXERCISE 4.6 *(continued)*

5. To create a new account, select Create a New Account from the Pick a Task list, name the account, specify the account type, and then click Create Account. You can then select the account from the list to modify its properties.

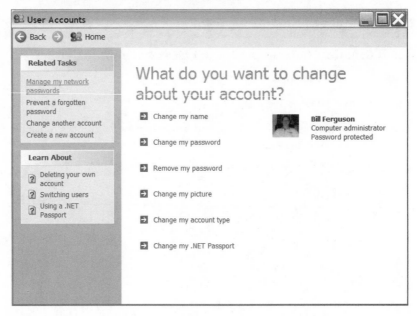

Troubleshooting User Accounts

Most problems associated with a user account stem from the type of account that is being used to access a resource. You should use the User Accounts and Local Users and Groups tools to determine whether an account has limited rights that are keeping it from using a resource. You should also understand that local accounts give access only to a resource that is on the local computer. If the resource is on another computer in the domain, then a domain account will be required.

EXERCISE 4.7

Viewing and Configuring User Accounts with the Local User Accounts Tool

1. On the Windows XP Desktop, right-click My Computer and choose Manage.

2. In the Computer Management console, expand System Tools and select Local Users and Groups.

3. Expand Local Users and Groups in the console pane (on the left) and choose Users.

EXERCISE 4.7

4. View the list of users in the details pane (on the right). Note that the system and support accounts are also listed.

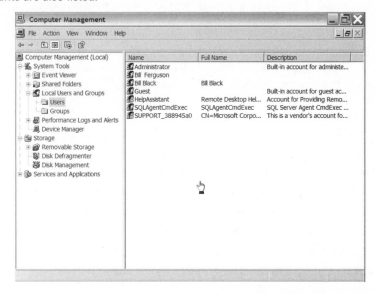

5. To create a new account, right-click Users in the console pane and choose New User.

6. Type the name and password of the user. You can also type a description and indicate whether the user must change their password when they log in.

Groups

Microsoft recommends that you give a user permissions to use resources and rights to perform actions based on being a member of a group rather than directly assigning the permissions and rights to the user account. This makes management of resources much more efficient. By granting permissions to a resource to a group, you do not have to grant permissions to each individual user that accesses that resource. You only have to add the user to the group membership and they will automatically gain permissions to resources that are already assigned to the group. For this purpose, Windows XP includes many default user groups with each computer installation. You can give a user rights to perform actions by making the user a member of one of these groups. You can also create your own groups to assign permissions to resources. Windows XP has the following built-in groups:

Administrators   This group has full, unrestricted access to the operating system configuration and use. By default, the local Administrator account is automatically a member of this group. Other users can be added into this group to give them full administrative access to the computer, but this should be done sparingly.

Backup Operators   This group has the right to back up and restore files and folders.

Guests   This group initially has the same rights as users, but it should be restricted and used only for temporary access.

Network Configuration Operators   This group has some administrative rights to manage networking features.

Power Users   This group has most of the administrative rights on a computer with some restrictions. It is primarily used to allow users to run legacy applications and certified applications.

Remote Desktop Users   This group allows members to log on remotely.

Replicator   This group contains system accounts that support file replication in a domain. User accounts should not normally be added to this group.

Users   This group contains the users that are created by the administrator. By default, all users created are automatic members of this group. It has limited rights as assigned by the administrator.

Help Services Group   This group contains system accounts that are used for the Help and Support Center.

Viewing and Creating User Groups

You should know how to use the Local Users and Groups MMC to view and create user groups. The Local Users and Groups MMC is part of the Computer Management console. Exercise 4.8 walks you through the steps to view and create user accounts.

EXERCISE 4.8

Viewing and Creating User Accounts with the Local Users and Groups MMC

1. On the Windows XP Desktop, right-click My Computer and choose Manage.

2. In the Computer Management console, expand System Tools and select Local Users and Groups.

3. Expand Local Users and Groups in the console pane (on the left), and then choose Groups.

4. View the groups that are listed in the details pane (on the right). Note that a brief description is listed with each group.

5. To add a new group, right-click Groups in the console pane and choose New Group.

6. Type the name of the group and a brief description of the purpose of the group.

7. To add members to the group, click Add, and then type or click Advanced to search for the names of the users or groups that you wish to add.

8. When you have finished configuring the group, click Create.

Troubleshooting User Groups

Most issues with user groups concern a user's membership in more than one group. As we discussed in Chapter 2, if a user is a member of a group that is explicitly denied access to a resource, they will be denied access to the resource even if they are also a member of other groups that are allowed access. This applies to local groups as well as domain groups. You should examine a user's group membership using the Local Users and Groups tool. Exercise 4.9 walks you through the steps to troubleshoot group membership for a user.

EXERCISE 4.9

Troubleshooting Group Membership for a User

1. On the Window XP Desktop, right-click My Computer and choose Manage.

2. On the Computer Management Console, expand System Tools and select Local Users and Groups.

3. Choose Users, right-click the user that you want to troubleshoot in the details pane, and then choose Properties.

4. Select the Member Of tab in the user's Properties dialog box to view the groups of which the user is a member.

5. You can also choose Groups and then right-click the group and choose Properties to view the membership of each group.

System Startup and User Logon

No matter how many resources a computer or network may have, users will not be able to access any of them until they can successfully start a computer and log on to the computer or log on to the domain. For this reason, you should know what is supposed to happen and what can go wrong when a user attempts to start a computer and log on. Problems can occur in three areas: system startup, user logon to a computer, and user logon to a domain. In the following sections, we will discuss troubleshooting each of these areas.

System Startup

We refer to the act of starting up a computer as "booting" it. Did you ever wonder why? After all, we are not kicking it! Booting a computer comes from "bringing it up by the bootstraps," or starting at the very beginning. Every time a computer is started, it goes through a series of phases that verify the presence of and test the components that the computer needs in order to function properly. These phases are collectively referred to as a *boot sequence*. Since errors can potentially occur in each of these phases, you should know what is supposed to happen so you can troubleshoot any errors that occur. In this section, we will discuss the major phases of system startup.

The five major phases of the boot sequence are as follows:

Preboot   The pre-boot phase begins when the computer is first started, before the operating system is loaded. The computer runs a power-on self-test (POST) that identifies the hard drives and other hardware necessary for operation. Also, any Plug and Play devices are located and installed in this phase. Then, the basic input/output system (BIOS) locates the master boot record (MBR), which it uses to locate and start the operating system.

Boot   In the boot phase of the boot sequence, the startup files that we discussed in Chapter 3, "Configuring and Troubleshooting Hardware Devices and Drivers," are used to begin the process of starting the operating system. First, the NTLDR file is used to initialize the system and change the microprocessor from real mode to 32-bit flat memory mode, which is used by Windows XP, Windows 2000 Professional, and Windows NT. Next, NTLDR, ntdetect.com, and the boot.ini files are used to locate and load the operating system. If any of these files are missing or corrupt, the operating system cannot start. You can use the Recovery Console, as illustrated in Chapter 3, to troubleshoot this phase.

Kernel load   During the kernel load phase of the boot sequence, the NTLDR file loads the Ntoskrnl.exe file (NT Kernel) but does not initialize it. NTLDR also loads the Hardware Abstraction Layer (HAL), which provides a filter that allows a wide variety of hardware devices to be used by the system. NTLDR then loads the HKEY_LOCAL_MACHINE Registry key. This Registry key is used to load the device drivers and services for some of the computer's low-level components. (The information that is created at this phase is called the *control set*.) After this is done, NTLDR initializes and passes control over to the NT Kernel.

Kernel initialization   Up to now, the screen has been in text mode. At this point, the Microsoft logo with the multicolored window is displayed in the middle of the screen. During the kernel initialization phase, four tasks are accomplished. First, the hardware key is created using the data found by `ntdetect.com`. Second, the clone control set is created. The clone control set is a copy of the control set that was created in the kernel load phase. Third, the kernel initializes the low-level device drivers that were loaded in the kernel load phase and loads and initializes the higher-level device drivers that are dependent upon the low-level device drivers. Finally, the Session Manager loads all of the highest-level services, including the Win32 Subsystem. The Win32 Subsystem controls the graphical user interface, the video display, and all I/O devices. The Session Manager also starts the WinLogon process.

Logon   In the logon phase, `Winlogon.exe` starts the *Local Security Authority (LSA)*, which provides the logon screen, which is also called the Graphical Identification and Authentication (GINA). At this point you may log on to the system, even though some services may be still starting in the background. After a successful logon, the system copies the clone control set to the *Last Known Good Configuration (LKG)* control set. The LKG control set will not be changed again until the next successful logon.

Check the Simple Solutions First

One day a user called us in a panic. She said that she absolutely had to get her computer running again and that we had to help her. We asked her to calm down and describe the problem. She took a couple of deep breaths and then began to tell us about it.

"I just finished installing some new software that I thought would help me do my job better, but it messed up my computer really badly!" she said. She continued, "As soon as I finished installing the software, the computer said that it had to reboot to finish the installation, and that's when the problem started. When I rebooted the computer, it would not come back up!"

We asked her if there was an error message, and she said, "Yes, it said that it couldn't find the `ntoskrnl.exe` file. Is that bad?" At first we were envisioning trying to walk her through the Recovery Console or possibly a reinstallation of the software. This would have been an interesting challenge over the phone. Then, we decided to check one more thing.

We asked her if there was a floppy disk in the floppy disk drive. She said, "Yes, that's what the software was on. Should I take it out now?" We told her to remove the floppy disk and restart the computer. She did, and of course, everything was fine.

As you might have guessed, the floppy disk was higher in the boot order and was therefore being read instead of the hard drive. Of course the system couldn't find the `ntoskrl.exe` file on the floppy disk! This would have been obvious to us if we had been there with her, but because of her panic and the fact that we couldn't "see" the whole situation, we nearly missed the obvious solution to the problem.

The main point here is that a user might be very upset and think that they have a huge problem. If you get caught up in the emotion of the situation, you might miss an obvious and simple solution to the problem. You should, therefore, always think it through and check the simplest of solutions first.

User Logon to a Computer

Logging on to a computer is a process of authentication and validation. Authentication occurs when a user provides a set of credentials to prove their identity. These credentials can be in the form of a username and password, a smart card, or some type of biometric identification, such as a fingerprint or retinal scan. After the user provides the credentials, the computer checks the Security Accounts Manager (SAM) database to locate the account and validate the logon. If the account is validated, the user receives an access token and is permitted to log on to the computer. A successful logon to a computer provides a user with access to the resources for which they have permissions and on that computer only. If the account cannot be validated in the SAM database, the user will receive an "Access is denied" message. Note that only local logons are authenticated through the SAM; logons using a domain account are authenticated to a domain controller running Active Directory.

User Logon to a Domain

Logging on to a domain is similar to logging on to a computer except that the user is authenticated by a domain controller instead of just the local computer. In Windows 2000 and Windows Server 2003 networks, the domain controller has a copy of Active Directory, which lists all of the accounts and their credentials. When users enter their credentials, they are compared with the account database in Active Directory. If the credentials match those of an account in the Active Directory database, then the domain controller provides the user rights and group membership information to the LSA of the computer, which then creates the access token. If the domain controller cannot be located, the user may be allowed to log on with *cached credentials*. In other words, if the user has logged on before, they can log on again with the same rights and permissions that they had on their last logon. By default, a Windows XP computer caches the last 10 successful logons unless this is disabled in either the local security policy or Group Policy. A successful logon to a domain gives the user access to resources in that domain and any trusted domains provided they have the permissions to use the resources.

WARNING One of the most common errors in logging on occurs when a user enters their domain logon credentials and then accidentally selects to log on to the local computer rather than the domain or vice versa.

System Performance

Just as a chain is only as strong as its weakest link, a computer is only as strong as its weakest essential resource. There are four resources that are essential to the performance of a computer: processor, memory, disk subsystem, and network subsystem. If any of the components are not adequate or are malfunctioning, the computer's performance could be affected in all areas. A weakness that is in one resource and affects all of the other resources is referred to as a *bottleneck*. You should monitor the computer resources to create a standard of configuration that allows the best system performance for the available resources. This standard is referred to as a *baseline*. As a desktop support technician, you must know how to identify and troubleshoot bottlenecks and create a baseline of performance.

There are several tools included with Windows XP that can assist you in monitoring resources, identifying bottlenecks, and creating a baseline. These include system configuration tools in Help and Support, Task Manager, and the Windows Performance tool. You should know how to use each of these tools to identify and troubleshoot problems associated with system performance. In the following sections, we will describe the four resources that affect a computer's performance and discuss how to use the system performance tools built into Windows XP.

Computer Resources

In order for a computer to perform properly, it must have the proper amounts of four essential resources. A lack of any of the essential resources can cause a bottleneck, which can affect the performance of the entire computer. You should be familiar with each of the four essential resources for a computer and know how they might affect system performance. In this section, we will describe each resource and its role in system performance.

Processor   The processor, or central processing unit (CPU), is the main chip that makes the computer, well, a computer. The faster the processor is, the more work the processor can do in any given period of time. At the time this book is being written, the fastest processors are about 3GHz, or 3 billion cycles per second. Most client computers have only one processor. Some client computers and most servers have multiple processors. Normally, processor utilization is the key factor in determining whether or not the processor is a bottleneck and needs to be replaced. Processor utilization may occasionally spike if there is a heavy workload on the machine in a given moment, but it normally should not exceed 80 percent for long periods of time.

Memory   The memory that the computer uses consists of physical memory, referred to as RAM, and virtual memory that is actually stored on the hard drive and then moved into RAM just before being used. The process of moving the memory between the hard drive and the RAM chips is called *paging*. The area of the hard drive that temporarily stores the virtual memory is called the *page file*. It takes longer to use memory that is on the page file than it does to use memory in physical RAM. For this reason, you should avoid excessive paging to improve system performance. Excessive paging can be reduced by adding RAM to the system.

Adding RAM is often a good answer on a test as well as a good solution to many real-world problems.

Disk subsystem   The disk subsystem consists of the hard disks and hard disk controllers. Disks come in all sizes and speeds. The hard disk in a client should be large enough to store the data and software that users need and still have extra space for paging and other functions, such as a printer spooling. If a disk becomes too full, performance can be affected because the computer will have to use more processor time to write to the disk. You can also use high-speed Small Computer System Interface (SCSI, pronounced "scuzzy") disks to speed up disk performance if needed. SCSI disks are often used in servers.

Network subsystem   The network subsystem consists of the network interface cards and other communications components within a computer and within the network to which it is connected. Most of today's network interface cards are dual-speed 10Mbps/100Mbps depending on the network devices to which they are attached. You can speed up the network subsystem by using bus-mastering cards that have their own processor and can "think" for themselves instead of having to rely on the CPU. Since the CPU is responsible for all of the processing that occurs in a computer, a card that can bypass the CPU can in effect "take a shortcut" and therefore speed up the network performance of a computer.

Performance Monitoring Tools

Windows XP comes with a set of tools that you can use to monitor system performance and create a baseline of performance. Each computer and each network is unique, so the use of these tools is as much of an art as it is a science. In the following sections, we will discuss the tools that you will use most often. These include a set of tools that can be found in *Help and Support* as well as *Task Manager* and the *Windows Performance tool*.

Help and Support Tools for Performance

Windows XP contains a set of tools that specifically enable you to maintain the performance of a computer. You should know how to access these tools so that you can use them yourself and teach others to use them. These tools are located in the Performance and Maintenance section of the Help and Support Center, as shown in Figure 4.8. The Help and Support Center will guide you or the user to the appropriate tools or features in the operating system based on the description of the tasks that you want to perform. To access these tools, choose Help and Support from the Start menu (or press F1 from the Desktop).

Task Manager

Windows Task Manager is an easily accessible tool that provides information about performance and displays details about programs and processes that are currently running on the computer. You should know how to use Task Manager to troubleshoot problems related to applications and networking. To access Task Manager, right-click the Taskbar and choose Task Manager. As illustrated in Figure 4.9, Task Manager contains the following tabs:

- Applications: Displays a list of the programs that are running on the computer and the status of each one.

- Processes: Displays information about the processes running on the computer. You can use the View menu's settings to add more details to this tab. This tab can tell you which processes are using the most CPU time.

FIGURE 4.8   The Performance and Maintenance section within Help and Support

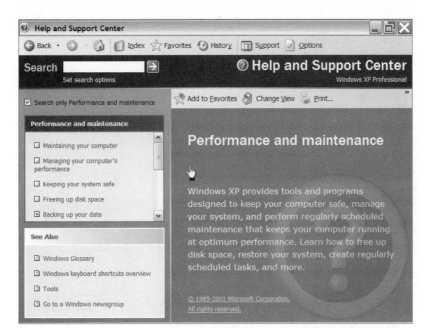

- Performance: Displays a dynamic overview of the computer's performance, including graphs for CPU and memory usage.

- Networking: Displays a graph of network performance. This enables you to determine the status of the network to which the computer is connected. This tab is displayed only if a network interface card is installed in the computer.

- Users: Displays a list of users who can access the computer and the status of each user. This tab is available only for computers that are members of a workgroup and that are enabled for Fast User Switching.

Windows Performance Tool

The Windows Performance tool is actually two tools in one. You should be familiar with both tools and understand the difference between them and when each tool should be used. You can access Windows Performance through Administrative Tools. As shown in Figure 4.10, the two tools contained in Windows Performance are the following:

- System Monitor: This tool can be used to collect real-time information about processor, memory, disk subsystem, and network subsystem components. You can display this information in digital form or on a graph.

- Performance Logs and Alerts: This tool can be used to record performance data over a specified period of time. You can use the recorded data to establish a baseline of performance.

As a desktop support technician, you should know how to use the Windows Performance tool to capture and record performance data. It is a good practice to collect data over a few days or even weeks to establish a baseline of performance. Exercise 4.10 walks you through the steps to create counters that capture and record the data that you specify.

FIGURE 4.9   The Task Manager dialog box

FIGURE 4.10   The Performance tool

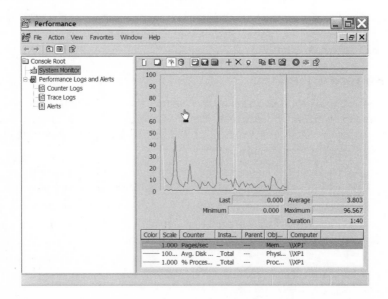

EXERCISE 4.10

Capturing and Recording Data

1. On the Windows XP Desktop, click Start, and then choose Control Panel.

2. In Control Panel, select Administrative Tools and then choose Performance.

3. On the console pane (on the left) of the Performance console, double-click Performance Logs and Alerts.

4. Right-click Counter Logs and choose New Log Settings.

5. In the New Log Settings dialog box, type the name for your new log (any name will suffice).

6. On the General tab in the dialog box for your new log, click Add Objects to record all possible counters for the selected object or Add Counters to specify counters for each object.

7. Continue to select the objects and counters. You should select at least one counter for each of the main resources of processor, memory, disk subsystem, and network subsystem. You can then set the interval at which to collect each counter. Setting the interval to a lower value will increase the load on your processor.

8. Click the Schedule tab to start the log immediately or set the date and time to start the log. You can also schedule the time to stop the log.

9. After all options are set, click OK to save the log. To view the logs that you have set, select Counter Logs in the console pane and view the list of logs in the details pane.

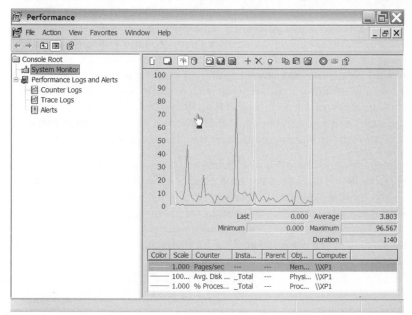

Case Study: XYZ Corp Desktop Configuration

XYZ Corporation is a multinational conglomerate with a diverse IT infrastructure. It has an Active Directory domain that most client computers belong to, but due to some security and political constraints, it has some offices that must be in a workgroup configuration as well. This diverse environment introduces a wide variety of challenges to the IT department, not the least of which is desktop management.

The director of IT has mandated that all client computer desktop configurations be centrally managed whether or not they are part of a domain or a workgroup. This includes security configuration settings, user environment settings, and account management. She has tasked you to come up with a strategy. What should your desktop management strategy be?

In this scenario, there is no one single solution for this problem. Since the environment is so diverse, you will need to approach each piece separately and develop solutions that are right for each part of the network while adhering to the IT director's mandate for centralized management.

First, the client computers that are part of the Active Directory domain can be centrally managed and secured using Group Policy. Standardized desktop settings such as having the company logo as the desktop background, Control Panel views, and so forth can be managed through a group policy that applies to the domain level. Security settings and account management are also controlled through Group Policy and the domain account policy. Any approved exceptions to the standardized settings could be applied in a lower-level policy and applied at the organizational unit to those clients that require the exceptions.

Centralized management of computers that are stand-alone or part of a workgroup will be more of a challenge because they cannot be controlled through Group Policy. However, standardized settings can still be applied manually through security templates applied to each workstation, and mandatory profiles can be set up on each machine that enforce any settings the administrator desires. Unfortunately, account management in the workgroups is also problematic in that accounts cannot be managed from Active Directory. These computers have their own accounts and account policies, so each machine will have to be visited by an administrator in order to set up standardized accounts and passwords.

Desktop management can be hectic in this kind of network, especially one that contains workgroups. A best practice would be to keep the workgroup configurations to a minimum and always look for a way to reduce them while keeping in line with the requirements of the organization. If a group of computers has account or security requirements that differ from those of the domain, a child domain or even another domain tree can be created to fill these needs and is preferable solution over a workgroup because it allows the centralized management that makes a support technician's job much easier.

Summary

Users will be much more productive if they are comfortable with their computer and if their computer is performing well. As a desktop support technician, you are responsible for setting up and maintaining computers and user environments that offer comfort and performance to the users. There are six main factors associated with user comfort and computer performance: user environment, multiple languages and multiple locations, security settings and local security policies, local user and group accounts, system startup and user logon, and system performance.

Windows XP provides a user environment that includes configurable Taskbar, Start menu, toolbar, and pointer device settings to enable users to customize the operation of their computer. In addition, Windows XP provides accessibility options and accessibility features for users who have special needs because of a physical handicap. Correct configuration of these settings can improve a user's productivity.

Windows XP is available in 24 different languages, or localized versions. In addition, you can configure regional settings and input languages on any of the localized versions. You can also install and configure multiple languages of the Windows XP operating system on the same computer using the Multilanguage User Interface (MUI) version of Windows XP software.

Local security policies can be used to control computers that are part of a workgroup. These policies control who accesses the computer, which resources they are allowed to use, and whether their actions are recorded in an event log. When computers are members of a domain, group policies on the network can override the local security policies on the computer. You can determine whether group policies are affecting the user or computer by using the gpresult tool included with Windows XP software.

User accounts uniquely identify a user and can provide access rights and permissions to use resources. A local user account gives a user only the right to log on to a local computer and access the resources on that computer. Domain user accounts give a user the right to log on to a domain as authenticated by a domain controller, which provides access to any resources on the domain for which they have permissions. You generally place users into group accounts to assign the access rights and permissions rather than directly applying them to the user. You can view and configure user accounts using User Accounts in Control Panel or Local Users and Groups in the Computer Management console. You can also use Local Users and Groups to view and configure local groups.

Users cannot access any resources until they are logged on to a computer that has successfully started. Problems can occur in any of five phases: pre-boot, boot, kernel load, kernel initialization, and logon. In each phase, specific tasks that are required for the next phase are performed. Understanding what happens in each phase can assist you in troubleshooting failed startups and failed logons.

Users can be productive only if their computer is working properly. Proper performance of a computer is dependent upon adequate amounts and the correct balance of four primary resources: processor, memory, disk subsystem, and network subsystem. You can use Help and Support, Task Manager, and the Windows Performance tool in Windows XP to monitor and troubleshoot these resources. You should create a baseline of acceptable performance for a computer. This baseline can be used as a comparison to troubleshoot the computer later on.

Exam Essentials

Know how to configure the Taskbar, Start menu, and toolbar settings.   You should know how to configure the Taskbar, Start menu, and toolbar settings in Windows XP and applications that use Windows XP. These include settings for the clock, the notification area, and the Quick Launch area. In addition, you should know how to autohide the Taskbar and how to troubleshoot this option for a user.

Know the difference between accessibility options and accessibility features and where to configure each of them.   You should know that the accessibility options include settings such as StickyKeys and SoundSentry and that these are located in Control Panel. In addition, you should know that the accessibility features include tools such as Magnifier and Narrator and that these are located in the Accessories menu of the All Programs menu. Finally, you should know how each of these options and/or tools operates and how they might be related to a troubleshooting issue.

Know the difference between Localization and Regional and Language Options.   You should know that Localization refers to the language that is in the Windows XP software itself (e.g., on the Start menu and in the help screens). In addition, you should know that Regional and Language Options are available on all localized versions of Windows XP software and on the Multilanguage User Interface (MUI) version as well. Finally, you should know how to configure each of these settings.

Understand local security policy and Group Policy.   You should understand that local security policy can fully control a computer only if the computer is a member of a workgroup and not a domain. In addition, you should know that if a computer is a member of a domain, the network's group policies might override the local security policy of the computer. Finally, you should know how to troubleshoot network group policies and determine which policies are affecting the computer by using the gpresult tool.

Understand the difference between local accounts and domain accounts.   You should know that local user accounts reside in the Security Accounts Manager (SAM) database on each computer and can be used to log on locally to the computer and gain access to resources that are on that computer provided the user has permissions for the resource. In addition, you should know that domain user accounts reside in Active Directory and can be used to log on to a domain and gain access to resources anywhere in the domain provided the user has permissions for the resources. Finally, you should know that one of the most common logon mistakes is accidentally attempting to log on locally to a computer with a domain user account because of an incorrect logon setting.

Know and understand the Windows XP boot sequence.   You should know the five phases of the Windows XP boot sequence and what actions are performed at each step. You should understand the process of logging on to a computer and how it differs from logging on to a domain.

Know and understand the resources involved with system performance.   You should know the four main resources that a computer uses and understand how a lack of or a malfunction in any of these resources can cause a bottleneck. In addition, you should know how to use the Help and Support and Task Manager tools to maintain and troubleshoot system performance. Finally, you should know how to create a baseline of performance using the Windows Performance tool in Windows XP.

Review Questions

1. You are the desktop support technician for your company. A user complains that his Windows XP desktop does not have a clock in the Taskbar at the bottom of the screen. What should you tell him?

   A. The clock option is an advanced option that is available only on special versions of Windows XP software.

   B. He can add the clock by using Regional Options in Control Panel.

   C. He can add the clock by accessing the Taskbar properties and removing the check mark from Hide the Clock.

   D. He can add the clock by accessing Taskbar properties and placing a check mark on Show the Clock.

2. You are the desktop support technician for your company. Two users share the same computer. One of the users needs the Start menu and help screens to be displayed in English, while the other would like to have them displayed in French. The computer currently has the English version of Windows XP installed. Which of the following should you do?

   A. Add the French language to Regional and Language Options on the English version.

   B. Install the French version of Windows XP over the English version.

   C. Add the French language to the Localization options in the English version.

   D. Install the MUI version of Windows XP and then add the required Localization options.

3. You are the desktop support technician for a large company with many users. A user complains that he does not have rights to perform volume maintenance tasks, such as running Disk Defragmenter on his Windows XP computer in your domain. You change the local security policy to allow the user to run the tool, but less than one hour later he is disallowed again. What is the likely cause of this problem?

   A. Users are never allowed to run the Disk Defragmenter tool. It just took the computer some time to take away the rights again.

   B. The group policy of the domain is overriding the local security policy on the computer.

   C. You did not save your change to Active Directory.

   D. You were not allowed to make the change in the local security policy of the computer, so the change was reversed.

4. You are the desktop support technician for a large company. A user complains that she cannot install software on her computer. She says that she is receiving an error that states that she doesn't have the rights to install the software. You suspect that group policies are affecting her computer or her user account. Which of the following tools should you use to troubleshoot this issue?

    A. Active Directory Users and Computers

    B. Computer Management

    C. Task Manager

    D. Gpresult

    E. Nslookup

5. You are the desktop support technician for a large company. A user is attempting to log on to a computer but access is denied. You have administrative rights for the computer. You wish to view all of the accounts on the computer, including the system accounts. Which tool should you use to view accounts on the computer and create a new user account if necessary?

    A. Local Users and Groups

    B. User Accounts

    C. Active Directory Users and Computers

    D. Task Manager

    E. My Computer

6. You are the desktop support technician for a large organization. A user complains that he cannot access a file server on the domain. You examine his permissions for the file server and find that his account has been given Full Control access to the file server. The file server is available on the domain, and other users can gain access to it. Which of the following could be causing this issue? (Choose two answers.)

    A. The user should not have been given Full Control. Only the administrator should have Full Control, so the system is denying access to the user.

    B. The user is a member of a group that is denied access to the file server.

    C. The file server is not operating properly.

    D. The user is logged on to his own computer instead of the domain.

7. You are the desktop support technician for a large organization with many users. A user named Tom has recently been promoted to executive. With this promotion, he is supposed to have access to the executive files. Tom complains that although he can log on to the domain, he still does not have access to the executive files. You verify with the network administrator that Tom's account has been added to the executive group, which has permissions to the files. Other executives are currently able to access and use the files. Which of the following could be causing this problem? (Choose all that apply.)

    A. Tom is a member of group that is explicitly denied permissions to the executive files.

    B. The domain controller is logging Tom on with cached credentials.

    C. Tom has not restarted his computer.

    D. The server with the executive files is not available.

8. You are the desktop support technician for your company. A user complains that he logged onto a computer with his local account but he cannot view or access any of the domain resources. What should you do first?

A. Ask the network administrator to re-create the corrupted local account to give the user access to the domain.

B. Change the user permissions for the domain resources so that he has access to them with his local logon.

C. Tell the user that he must log on to the domain with a domain user account to gain access to the resources of the domain.

D. Run gpresult to make sure that the local user account is not affected by the group policies of the domain.

9. You are the desktop support technician for your company. You want to create a log that represents a baseline of performance for a computer. Which of the following tools should you use? (Choose all that apply.)

A. Task Manager

B. System Monitor

C. Performance Logs and Alerts

D. Disk Management

10. You are the desktop support technician for a large organization. To begin to troubleshoot a user's computer, you want to see a list of all of the applications that are currently being used and the status of each application. You also want to be able to close multiple applications at the same time and open some applications if needed. Which tool should you use?

A. Task Manager

B. Computer Management

C. The Taskbar

D. My Computer

11. You are a desktop support technician with XYZ Corporation. Sarah, one of your users in the graphic arts department, calls you and tells you that the icons and bitmaps on her computer screen are too large. Where do you tell Sarah to go to fix this issue?

A. Accessibility Options

B. Computer Management, Screen Options

C. Display Properties, Settings

D. Control Panel, Fonts

12. A user named Chuck wants to have an icon that launches a program he frequently uses on the Start menu for quick access. How would you add a shortcut to the user's Start menu to launch his program?

    A. Add a shortcut icon for the user's program to the pinned items list on the Start menu.

    B. Add a shortcut icon for the user's program to the most frequently used programs list on the Start menu.

    C. Add a shortcut icon for the user's program to the Start menu using the Desktop Properties applet in Control Panel.

    D. Add a shortcut icon for the user's program to the Start menu by right-clicking the Start menu and choosing Add.

13. A user has asked you to help her adjust her display settings over the phone. When you tell her to click the Appearance and Themes icon in Control Panel, she says it is not there. How will you enable her to see that particular icon?

    A. Ask to user to go to Control Panel, click Add and Remove Programs, and add the Appearance and Themes program to Control Panel.

    B. Ask the user to switch to Category view in Control Panel.

    C. Ask the user to switch to Classic view in Control Panel.

    D. Have the user right click on the Desktop area and select Appearance and Themes.

14. A user complains that he cannot access offline files on his Windows XP Professional computer. After asking him questions about how he logs on, you suspect that Fast User Switching is enabled, preventing him from enabling offline files. How do you tell the user to resolve the problem?

    A. Instruct the user to go into the Local Users and Groups tool in Computer Management and disable Fast User Switching.

    B. Instruct the user to log off the local computer account and log on using a domain account.

    C. Instruct the user to disable Fast User Switching using the Account Logon applet in Control Panel.

    D. Instruct the user to disable Fast User Switching using the User Accounts applet in Control Panel.

15. You are conducting maintenance on a Windows XP Professional computer that has been performing poorly lately. You determine that the computer is using excessive paging when under a heavy workload. What should you do to correct this issue?

    A. Add an additional processor.

    B. Add a larger hard disk drive.

    C. Increase the amount of physical RAM in the system.

    D. Increase the size of the paging file.

16. Which option presents the correct boot sequence of a Windows XP computer?

A. Pre-boot, boot, kernel load, kernel initialization, and logon

B. Pre-boot, boot, GINA load, kernel load, and logon

C. Boot, kernel initialization, kernel load, GINA load, and logon

D. Boot, pre-fetch sequence, kernel initialization, kernel load, and logon

17. What are the primary characteristics of authentication using a local account and authentication using a domain account? (Choose two answers)

A. Local accounts are authenticated through a domain controller running Active Directory and are used to access resources on the local network.

B. Local accounts are authenticated through the local Security Accounts Manager (SAM) database and are used to access resources on the local computer only.

C. Domain accounts are authenticated through the local Security Accounts Manager (SAM) database and are used to access resources across the domain.

D. Domain accounts are authenticated through a domain controller running Active Directory and are used to access resources across the domain.

18. Bobby is a user in the accounting department and calls you with a problem. Since your company does business with several different countries, he needs to be able to change the way currencies and times are displayed and used in Windows. How will you change these options for Bobby?

A. Use the International Options applet in Control Panel to configure these options.

B. You must install the Windows XP Multilanguage User Interface version.

C. Use Date, Time, Language, and Regional Options in Control Panel, and then choose Regional and Language Options.

D. Install the Windows update packs for each of the countries you require different settings for in Windows.

19. You have a user in your network who has a physical disability affecting the use of his hands. As a result, he requires that the keyboard settings be adjusted to ignore repeated keystrokes. Which option do you need to configure in Accessibility Options to accommodate this user?

A. StickyKeys

B. FilterKeys

C. ToggleKeys

D. MouseKeys

20. You administer a small workgroup of 10 computers for your company. You have received a new policy from the IT director that requires users to have passwords consisting of a minimum of 8 characters. How would you configure these computers to enforce this policy?

    A. Use a group policy applied to the company's domain.

    B. Configure an account policy in Local Security Policy for each individual computer.

    C. Configure a group policy and apply it to the entire workgroup.

    D. Configure an account policy in Local Security Policy for one computer in the workgroup and force it to replicate to each computer that is a member of the workgroup.

Answers to Review Questions

1. D. The clock option in the Taskbar is available and selected by default on all versions of Windows XP. If the user does not see the clock in the Taskbar, then someone has removed the check mark from Show the Clock in the Taskbar properties. He should put the check mark back in to show the clock.

2. D. Since the Start menu and help screens in the operating system need to be available in both English and French, you will need to install the Multilanguage User Interface (MUI) version of Windows XP. Regional and Language options can be used to change the input language but not the language displayed in the operating system itself, referred to as Localization.

3. B. Group polices in a domain can override the local security policy set on a computer. You were able to make the change in the local security policy, but the change was only temporary until the group policy refreshed itself

4. D. You should use the gpresult tool from a command prompt. The gpresult tool shows the group policies that are applied to the current computer and to the currently logged-on user. Active Directory Users and Computers, Computer Management, and Task Manager will not give you this information. Nslookup is a tool that is used to troubleshoot hostname resolution on Domain Name System (DNS) servers.

5. A. Since you wish to view all of the local accounts on the computer, including the system accounts, you will have to use the Local Users and Groups tool in the Computer Management console. You can view the local user accounts and add a user account with the User Accounts tool in Control Panel, but you cannot view the system accounts in User Accounts. You would not use Active Directory Users and Computers to view or create local user accounts. Task Manager and My Computer are not used to view and create accounts.

6. B, D. If the user is a member of a group that is explicitly denied access to the file server, then he will be denied access as well, even if he has Full Control permissions assigned to his account. If the user is logged on to his own computer (locally) instead of the domain, then the user will not have access to the file server on the domain. Administrators can give Full Control permissions to users if they choose to, although it is generally not recommended. The file server must be operating properly because other users are gaining access to it.

7. A, B. If Tom is a member of a group that is explicitly denied access to the executive files, then he will be denied access as well, even if he is a member of the executive group. If the Active Directory has a problem and the domain controller is logging Tom on with cached credentials, then he will have the same permissions as he did before he was an executive, so he will be denied access to the executive files. Tom should not need to restart his computer. The server with the executive files must be available because other executives are currently using it.

8. C. Local user accounts give access only to resources that are located on the local computer, not to those on the domain. The user will need a domain user account to gain access to domain resources. His local account is probably not corrupt, and it would not be affected by group policies on the domain.

9. C. The only tool that you need to use to create the log is Performance Logs and Alerts in the Windows Performance tool. Task Manager is a readily accessible tool that lists applications that are currently running and some basic performance information, but it cannot be used to create a log. System Monitor is a tool in the Windows Performance tool that enables you to view real-time data in digital form or on a graph, but it cannot create a log. Disk Management would not be used to create a log.

10. A. Task Manager is the only tool listed in this scenario that enables you to list the applications that are running and view the status of each application. You can also open new applications with Task Manager if needed. Computer Management does not enable you to view a list of applications running on a computer. The Taskbar does enable you to view the applications that are running, but they are not in list form and you cannot see the status of the applications. My Computer does not enable you to view a list of applications that are running on the computer.

11. C. The Settings tab in Display Properties gives you the ability to change your screen resolution, which is what will fix Sarah's problem. There is no Screen Options in Control Panel. Accessibility Options won't change the screen resolution, nor will the Fonts applet in Control Panel.

12. A. The pinned items list contains items that should be permanently visible on the Start menu, so the shortcut icon for the user's program should be added here. Option B is not the correct answer because Windows automatically adds shortcut icons to programs that are frequently used, so no action would be necessary, but if the program is not used after a while, the shortcut created in the most frequently used programs list may be deleted. C and D are incorrect because there are no such options.

13. B. The user should switch to Category view in Control Panel because functions are organized by category in that view and the Appearance and Themes icon will be present. C is incorrect because the user must already be in Classic view if she does not see the Appearance and Themes icon. Both A and D are invalid choices because these options do not exist.

14. D. Fast User Switching is incompatible with offline files caching and must be disabled in order to use offline files. Option D is the correct answer because the User Accounts applet in Control Panel is used to disable and enable Fast User Switching. Option A is incorrect because Fast User Switching cannot be configured using the Local Users and Groups tool in Computer Management. Option B is incorrect because Fast User Switching is automatically turned off when a Windows XP Professional computer is added to the domain, so you know that it would already be disabled if this were the case. Option C is invalid because there is no Account Logon applet in Control Panel.

15. C. Increasing the amount of physical RAM in a system can help alleviate excessive paging to the page file on the hard disk. Adding an additional processor will not prevent information from being paged to the hard drive when the RAM on the system becomes full. A larger hard disk would be ineffective for the same reason. Increasing the size of the paging file would allow more data to be paged to the hard disk but would not prevent paging from happening as frequently as it does. Only more RAM on the system will help in this case.

16. A. The correct sequence is the pre-boot phase, then the boot phase, followed by the kernel load and kernel initialization, and finally the logon sequence. All other options are either out of order or contain invalid phases.

17. B, D. Local accounts can only be used to access resources on the local computer and are authenticated through the local Security Accounts Manager database on the local computer. Domain accounts, on the other hand, are used to access resources throughout the domain and are authenticated through a domain controller running Active Directory.

18. C. You must use Date, Time, Language, and Regional Options in Control Panel and choose Regional and Language Options in order to change the currency and time display settings. There is no International Options applet in Control Panel, and there are no Windows update packs for different counties. You do not need the Multilanguage User Interface edition of Windows XP simply to change these settings.

19. B. FilterKeys is used in Accessibility Options to instruct Windows to ignore repeated keystrokes. StickyKeys is used to automatically lock keys to allow users to press single keystrokes to accomplish multiple-keystroke combinations, such as the Ctrl+Alt+Delete key combination. Toggle-Keys plays tones when the Num Lock and Scroll Lock keys are pressed. MouseKeys allows the control of the mouse pointer from the arrow keys on the numeric keypad of the keyboard.

20. B. The setting to force a user's password to be a certain number of characters long is located in the Account Policy section of the computer's Local Security Policy. Additionally, since Local Security Policy is unique to each computer, it must be configured separately on every single computer that belongs to the workgroup. Group Policy does not apply in this scenario because Group Policy applies only in an Active Directory domain environment and cannot be applied in a workgroup configuration. Workgroups cannot replicate data between their members.

Chapter
5

Recovering Windows XP from Failure

MICROSOFT EXAM OBJECTIVES COVERED IN THIS CHAPTER:

✓ **Perform and troubleshoot an attended installation of a Windows XP operating system.**

  ▪ Troubleshoot and complete installations in which an installation does not start. Tasks include configuring the device boot order and ascertaining probable cause of the failure to start.

  ▪ Troubleshoot and complete installations in which an installation fails to complete. Tasks include reviewing setup log files and providing needed files.

  ▪ Perform postinstallation configuration. Tasks include customizing installations for individual users and applying service packs.

✓ **Configure and troubleshoot storage devices.**

  ▪ Answer end-user questions related to configuring hard disks and partitions or volumes.

  ▪ Manage and troubleshoot disk partitioning.

✓ **Configure and troubleshoot display devices.**

  ▪ Configure display devices and display settings.

  ▪ Troubleshoot display device settings.

✓ **Configure and troubleshoot I/O devices.**

  ▪ Configure and troubleshoot device settings.

  ▪ Configure and troubleshoot device drivers for I/O devices.

There will be times when Windows XP will fail to a point where it is not recoverable using standard tools. Corrupt device drivers, failing hard drives, and viruses are just few problems that could damage the operating system beyond booting capabilities. Operating systems and their associated hardware are very picky in how they must be configured. It won't take much to render an entire partition unusable. You should be familiar with the tools that a desktop support technician must use in order to recover a failed operating system. There are many tools available to a technician that can assist in repairing and recovering Windows XP. Understanding what processes Windows XP goes through when booting up and what can go wrong can prove very useful in the field.

In this chapter, we will cover the boot process and the tools that are used to recover Windows XP.

The boot process   Understanding the boot process is critical to properly troubleshoot hardware and operating system failures. The boot process is a fairly lengthy and complicated process, but simply being able to follow the screens and understand what is happening can enable you to determine a good starting point for troubleshooting.

Last Known Good   During the boot process and even on into the login process, your system monitors changes to the system configuration and key files. Windows XP enables you to revert to the last successful boot in which a login occurred. You should be familiar with the components that are recoverable using the Last Known Good Configuration feature. Reverting to the Last Known Good Configurationn is a great early troubleshooting step that will save you lots of time and energy when used properly.

Safe Mode   There are many different flavors of safe mode available in Windows XP. It is important to know which version of safe mode to use when recovering Windows XP from failure. Each version offers specific functionality under certain circumstances and can be extremely useful when the operating system isn't cooperating with you.

Recovery Console   The Recovery Console is a command-line interface that will allow you to perform advanced configuration on a system that won't even allow you to boot into safe mode. The Recovery Console can be installed or used as a component of the bootable Windows XP CD. You should be familiar with the basic commands and features of this tool.

Automated System Recovery   Automated System Recovery is a last-resort recovery method used to recover the operating system. There are limited options to choose from and it will not recover any user data, only the operating system and it configuration. You should use this only if no other recovery method works.

The Boot Process

The boot process has been around since the introduction of DOS back in the early days of Microsoft. Obviously, a lot has changed with both computer hardware and operating systems since then. Actually, the most drastic change came with Windows NT. Microsoft totally redesigned the boot process to allow for more reliable and functional features in the operating system. Windows XP is built on Kernel 5.1 where Windows NT is built on Kernel 4.0. There are a few differences between the NT boot process and the XP boot process, but those are mostly because of advances in hardware technology. There are 3 phases of the boot process: the boot phase, the kernel load phase, and the logon phase. In the following sections, we will cover each phase in the boot process in detail.

Boot Phase

The boot phase starts just after the successful initialization of the computer's hardware. Once the BIOS has gathered all of the required information and prepared the hardware, it checks the CMOS for a reference to the correct physical drive and the master boot record (MBR).

Boot Initialization

The MBR will call the boot loader into RAM so that it can locate the files that are required to boot the system. Once the boot loader is sure of the location of the boot files, it will start loading them into RAM. One of the first files loaded to RAM is the NTLDR file. The NTLDR file will assist throughout the boot process. The NTLDR will begin its duties by starting the file system drivers that will allow the operating system to interact more closely with the items on the file system. FAT32 and NTFS will load at about the same speed, unless the partition is very large. NTFS is better at dealing with large partitions. The NTLDR file will reference the file system's allocation tables; these are basically maps of the files on disk. This allows it to easily find files and directories when necessary. Before you get too far into the boot process, you need to make a decision. What operating system will you boot from?

Operating System Selection

Assuming you have multiple operating systems or at least the ability to choose different partitions to boot from, you will be prompted to choose during the Operating System Selection portion of the boot process. The NTLDR will actually verify the existence of the `boot.ini` file, the file that contains the list of operating systems and their associated locations. Once the `boot.ini` file has been parsed and loaded to RAM, it will display a text list of the available boot options. Usually this list will be available only if there are multiple operating systems installed on the system. If the `boot.ini` file does not exist, the NTLDR will attempt to boot from the system partition of the first disk available. The list of available boot options will be displayed until you choose an option or the preset timer counts down. As you can see in Figure 5.1, you can use the system configuration utility to make changes to how Windows XP boots. Table 5.1 lists the available options for the `boot.ini` file, and Exercise 5.1 shows you how to configure it.

TABLE 5.1 Boot Options in Msconfig

Boot Option	Description
/Safeboot	Allows you to force safe mode without having to choose it during boot.
/Noguiboot	Forces windows to wait until later in the boot process to initialize any VGA drivers.
/Bootlog	Causes Windows to write a log of the boot to the file %SystemRoot%\Ntbtlog.txt.
/Basevideo	Forces the default VGA driver load during boot.
/SOS	Verbose boot mode; allows you to see what is loading and its specifications.

In addition to the boot options shown in Table 5.1, there are advanced options available, as seen in Figure 5.1, for more granular control, although they are rarely needed.

FIGURE 5.1 Custom boot options in msconfig

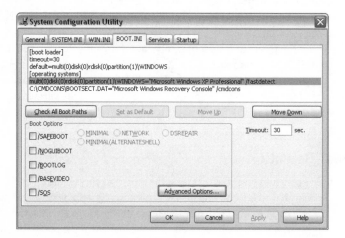

If you perform an upgrade incorrectly, you might have an additional entry in boot.ini. You can remove this entry using the system configuration utility.

Configuring the Boot.ini **File**

1. Click the Start button and choose Run.

2. Type msconfig in the Run box and click OK.

3. Click the BOOT.INI tab of the system configuration utility's dialog box.

4. Choose the appropriate options and click OK.

5. You will be prompted to reboot to test the changes. Click Reboot Now.

Hardware Detection

Once you have determined the correct operating system to boot from, you need to detect and configure the hardware in the system. This is the next phase in the boot process. The hardware detection portion is very straightforward. You can usually tell if incompatible or misconfigured hardware is causing your system problems if you fail at this stage. A good trick to use here is to configure your system to dual-boot, even if you don't have multiple operating systems. This will allow you to determine exactly where the boot process is failing. If it fails after the operating system selection stage but before the configuration selection, your hardware is most likely the problem. This will usually happen after a device that is not on the Hardware Compatibility List (HCL) has been installed or a device has been installed with faulty drivers. Because of this behavior, it often easy to determine the problem device.

Configuration Selection

The configuration selection phase of the boot process will allow you to choose between existing hardware profiles. Hardware profiles are simple templates that enable or disable hardware components. If you have created a hardware profile other than the default, you will be prompted here to choose the appropriate one.

Kernel Load Phase

Once you have selected the appropriate configuration selection, it's time to load the Windows XP kernel. The kernel is a collection of core system files that make up the heart of the operating system. Loading the kernel takes quite a few steps.

Kernel Initialization

While the NTLDR, shown in Figure 5.2, is still in control of the system, it will start loading the system kernel by loading ntoskrnl.exe into RAM. Another important file that is loaded at this time, hal.dll, is key in separating the hardware from the software. You can see hal.dll and ntoskrnl.exe in the system32 directory in Figure 5.3. The hal.dll file will allow the operating system to accurately send signals between the kernel and the hardware components.

FIGURE 5.2   The NTLDR file

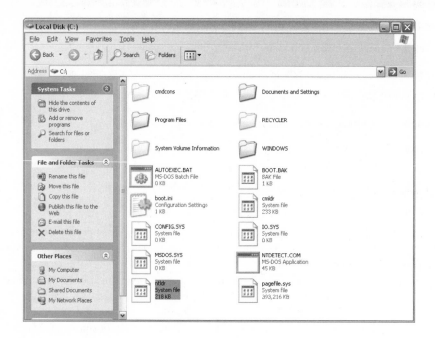

FIGURE 5.3   The ntoskrnl.exe and hal.dll files

Hardware Key

NTLDR now loads device drivers that are marked as boot devices. While loading these drivers, NTLDR releases control of the computer. NTLDR reads control set information from the HKEY_LOCAL_MACHINE\SYSTEM Registry key, which is created from the \System32\Config\System file, so that NTLDR can determine which device drivers need to be loaded during startup. Typically, several control sets exist, with the actual number depending on how often system configuration settings change. If the /SOS switch is used, each filename is printed, as seen in Figure 5.4.

FIGURE 5.4   Output when booting with the /SOS switch

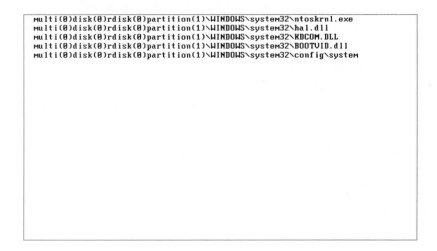

```
multi(0)disk(0)rdisk(0)partition(1)\WINDOWS\system32\ntoskrnl.exe
multi(0)disk(0)rdisk(0)partition(1)\WINDOWS\system32\hal.dll
multi(0)disk(0)rdisk(0)partition(1)\WINDOWS\system32\KDCOM.DLL
multi(0)disk(0)rdisk(0)partition(1)\WINDOWS\system32\BOOTVID.dll
multi(0)disk(0)rdisk(0)partition(1)\WINDOWS\system32\config\system
```

Each driver that is listed under HKEY_LOCAL_MACHINE\SYSTEM\ControlSet001\SERVICES has a start code associated with it. As you can see in Figure 5.5, the CD-ROM, for example, will always start with the system. Table 5.2 shows you the available options for configuring start options.

TABLE 5.2   Start Options in Services

Key Value	Meaning
0	Specifies a driver that is loaded (but not started) by firmware. If no errors occur, the kernel starts the driver.
1	Specifies a driver that loads at kernel initialization by using Windows XP Professional drivers.
2	Specifies a driver or service that is initialized at system startup by Session Manager.

TABLE 5.2 Start Options in Services *(continued)*

Key Value	Meaning
3	Specifies a driver or service that is manually started by a user, a process, or another service.
4	Specifies a disabled driver.

FIGURE 5.5 The values for CD-ROM

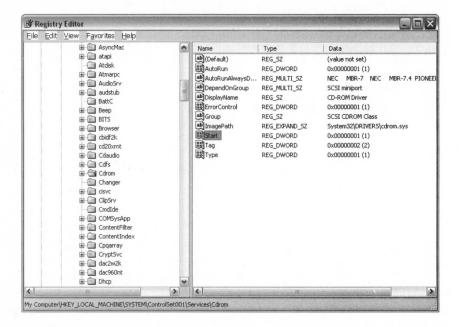

Service Configuration

Now that you have successfully initialized the devices in your system, you will attempt to load the operating system services. A component called the Session Manager Subsystem (SMSS) begins to load services one by one. System services are key for a graphical system that a user can interface with. If at any time a key driver or service fails to load, you either will be prompted with an error onscreen or the system will reboot. If the system reboots, it may automatically attempt to use the Last Known Good Configuration.

Logon Phase

The logon phase will finally allow you to log in to the system. The SMSS will continue to load drivers and devices while the logon phase is starting up.

The XP boot process is not considered complete until a user has successfully logged onto the system. The process is begun by the `winlogon.exe` file, which is loaded as a service by the kernel and continued by the Local Security Authority (`lsass.exe`), which displays the logon dialog box shown in Figure 5.6.

FIGURE 5.6   Graphical logon box displayed by lsass.exe

Last Known Good

The Last Known Good Configuration is a backup set in the Registry that allows you to revert back to a previous, functional configuration. You will generally use the Last Known Good Configuration to recover after a driver or service has been loaded to the system and will not allow it to complete the boot process. The Last Known Good Configuration is only useful if you have not logged onto the system since the last reboot.

Current Control Set

The current control set is a key component of the Last Known Good Configuration. It is a complete set of the configuration data required to start devices and system services. The system always maintains at least two control sets in the Registry. It identifies one as the current control set and the other as the Last Known Good control set. The current control set is the one that was most recently used to start the system. The system stores its control set designations in the System subkey, as seen in Figure 5.7.

FIGURE 5.7 Entries in the System key

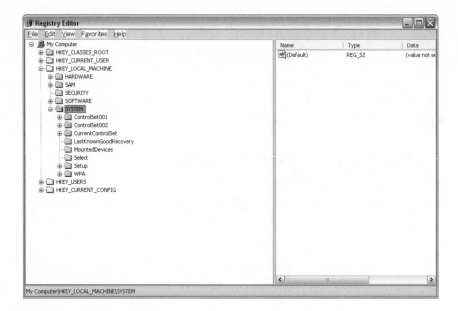

Creation of the Control Sets

The various control sets are created at different times during the startup and shutdown processes. There are three different control sets used in Windows XP: the default control set, the current control set, and the Last Known Good control set.

Default Control Set

The default control set is used much like a control that would be used in an experiment. It is saved during the shutdown process after a successful Windows session. When you boot your system up, it will use the default control set.

Current Control Set

The current control set is initially a copy of the default control set. During the boot process, it is modified to match the configuration of the system as it stands during the boot process. After all of the modifications have been made and the user logs onto the system successfully, the copy is renamed and moved to the current control set.

Last Known Good Control Set

The Last Known Good control set is created when a user successfully logs onto a system. The system assumes that, because you were able to log on, the newly modified control set is going to be successful in the future. During a session, the current control set and the Last Known Good control set are usually the same. This may not be true if you make system configuration modifications during the session. If you make any modifications to the system configuration, it will be saved to only the current control set, not the Last Known Good. Once you shut the system down, the current control set is copied over the default control set and is used during the next startup process.

Using Last Known Good

Using the Last Known Good Configuration is actually very straightforward. You will generally use the Last Known Good if you have changed the system configuration and, following that change, the computer will not successfully complete the boot process. These changes can include modifications to the Registry, driver changes, and other boot configuration changes. This does not included modifications or deletions of core system files. Exercise 5.2 explains how to boot into Last Known Good.

EXERCISE 5.2

Booting to Last Known Good

1. Power on your system.

2. After the BIOS graphical display goes away, start pressing the F8 button.

3. A text display of several options will be on the screen.

```
Windows Advanced Options Menu
Please select an option:

    Safe Mode
    Safe Mode with Networking
    Safe Mode with Command Prompt

    Enable Boot Logging
    Enable VGA Mode
    Last Known Good Configuration (your most recent settings that worked)
    Directory Services Restore Mode (Windows domain controllers only)
    Debugging Mode

    Start Windows Normally
    Reboot
    Return to OS Choices Menu

Use the up and down arrow keys to move the highlight to your choice.
```

4. Choose Last Known Good Configuration from the options.

5. Your computer should boot up successfully and display a logon prompt after a few moments.

Safe Mode

Safe mode has been the staple for recovering Windows since its earliest days. There have been many developments and variations of safe mode over the years. Microsoft Windows XP has several flavors of safe mode, each with its own functionality. The basic idea of safe mode is to have the ability to load Windows without all of the additional, noncritical components. This should allow you to disable services, drivers, and other problem components.

In the following sections, we will discuss each of the different versions of safe mode.

Safe Mode

The original safe mode has several features that are important to remember. Safe mode will disable quite a few features, mainly network and high-quality graphics. Most of the luxury functionality is disabled. This is important because it will help reduce the factors that can cause problems when troubleshooting. Enabled components include the following:

- Drivers for serial or PS/2 mouse devices
- Standard keyboards
- Hard disks
- CD-ROM drives
- Standard VGA devices
- USB mouse
- USB keyboard
- System services
- Event log
- Plug and Play
- Remote procedure calls
- Logical Disk Manager

You can view the components of safe mode by viewing the HKEY_LOCAL_MACHINE\SYSTEM\CurrentControlSet\Control\SafeBoot\Minimal Registry key, as seen in Figure 5.8. Exercise 5.3 steps you through one recovery method in safe mode.

FIGURE 5.8   Safe Mode registry settings

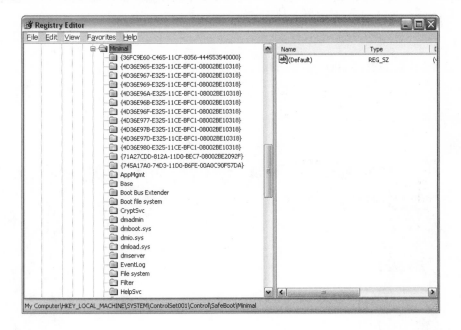

It Just Won't Die!

Spyware and malware seem to be popping up all over the place. Even in a locked-down, protected network you will find spyware and other variations of malicious code on users' systems. I got a call from a good friend who was working on a client PC in the field. He was extremely distressed; it seems that he had tried every trick he knew, but some seriously rough spyware was hanging on to the system he was working on. He was desperate to find a way to remove it. I'll never forget what he said: "This spyware just won't die." Apparently, the spyware was so integrated into various running components, no spyware removal tool could remove it. My solution was very simple: if the spyware is causing problems because it integrates into running processes, just boot into safe mode. Because safe mode disables all but the most necessary system components, anything the spyware uses will most likely be disabled in safe mode. After booting into safe mode and running the spyware removal tool, he was able to get the system working again. Imagine that!

EXERCISE 5.3

Recovering from Failure Using Safe Mode

1. Boot up the system.

2. Press F8 after the BIOS text mode has been displayed.

3. Choose Safe Mode from the text options.

4. Log onto the system using administrative privileges.

5. Use msconfig to remove problem startup components.

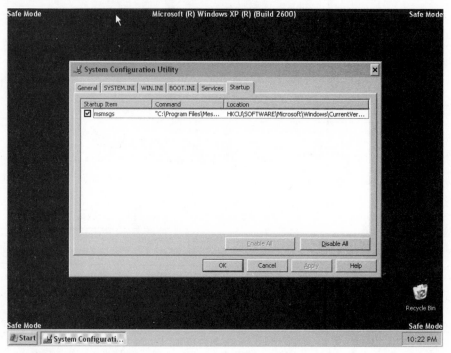

6. Use Device Manager to disable problem devices and drivers.

7. Use the Add/Remove Programs applet to remove problem applications.

Safe Mode with Networking

Safe mode with networking is exactly what it sounds like: safe mode, but with networking components enabled. This simply allows you to have network or Internet access when attempting to resolve issues on your system. This is most often used for problem video drivers. You would choose safe mode with networking because you can use the network or Internet to download and install the correct video driver. This might also allow you to correct system misconfigurations while looking at the proper configuration online.

In Exercise 5.4, you can step through recovering a bad video driver using safe mode with networking.

EXERCISE 5.4

Recovering from a Video Driver Failure

1. Boot up the system.

2. Press F8 after the BIOS text mode has been displayed.

3. Choose Safe Mode with Networking from the text options.

4. Log onto the system using administrative privileges.

5. Depending on the scenario, choose from the following:

    a. If you have recently upgraded or changed your video driver, you can choose to roll the driver back.

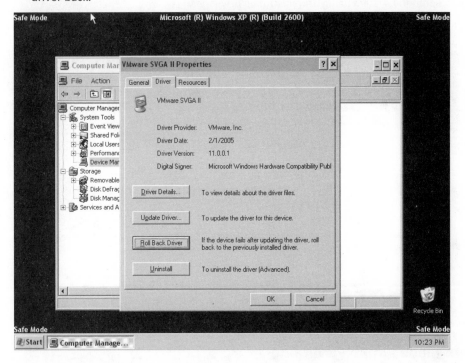

    b. If your driver has never worked properly, you can download a new driver from the manufacturer's website.

Safe Mode with Command Prompt

In some very extreme circumstances, you will not even be able to use the default VGA video driver. It might have been corrupted or accidentally deleted or disabled. Your only resort is to boot the system without a graphical interface. Obviously this will disable nearly everything that is not a critical component of the operating system. In Exercise 5.5, you can step through using safe mode with a command prompt.

EXERCISE 5.5

Recovering from a Video Driver Failure in Safe Mode with Command Prompt

1. Boot up the system.

2. Press F8 after the BIOS text mode has been displayed.

3. Choose Safe Mode with Command Prompt from the text options.

4. Log onto the system using administrative privileges.

5. At the command prompt, type **compmgmt.msc**.

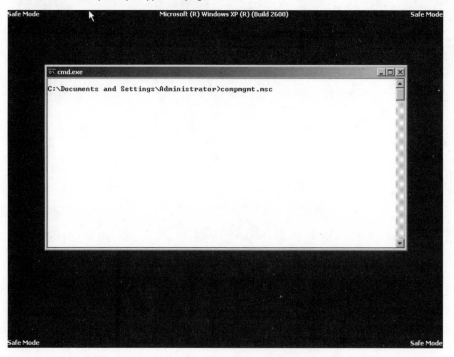

6. Use the computer management console to work with existing drivers.

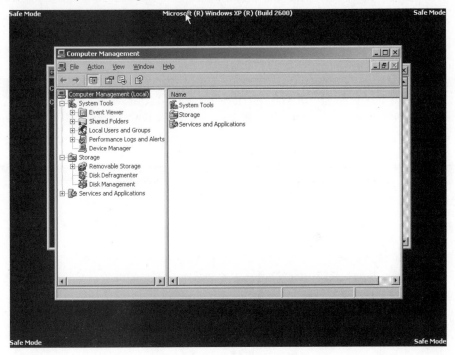

 Don't use safe mode with networking if you are attempting to remove spyware and viruses. Many variations of malicious code will utilize any type of
Internet connection to update itself or report to the code writer. This could
spell bad news if you are trying to remove it!

Recovery Console

The Recovery Console is like a set of jumper cables for your car. If your battery dies, you
can easily jump your car. The only problem is that owning the jumper cables won't help you
if they aren't in your car! This is also true for the recovery console; it is extremely valuable
when attempting to recover your computer from failure, but it won't do you any good if you
don't install it beforehand. Although you can actually use the Windows installation CD to

crank up the Recovery Console after failure, it is not as valuable unless you have previously installed it on your system. The Recovery Console is basically a command-line utility that allows you to perform administrative tasks on your system and, particularly, to use tools to recover your system.

Installing the Recovery Console

Installing the Recovery Console takes only a few moments, but it can become extremely valuable when your system fails. This installation will require that you have an Install CD for Windows XP or have the installation files on your local system. You can also install it from a server if the installation files have been copied to a network share. Exercise 5.6 will walk you through installing the recovery console.

EXERCISE 5.6

Installing the Recovery Console

1. Insert the Windows XP Professional CD-ROM into your CD drive.

2. Click the Start menu and choose Run.

3. Type *CD drive letter*:\i386\winnt32.exe /cmdcons and press Enter.

4. The confirmation screen will pop up. Click Yes to confirm that you want to install the recovery console.

EXERCISE 5.6

5. The process will initialize and attempt to contact the Microsoft website for updated files.

6. If you have an active connection to the Internet, you can choose try again; otherwise, choose to skip this step.

7. The install will run for a few moments and show a confirmation dialog telling you that the Recovery Console was installed successfully. Click OK.

You have installed the recovery console.

Using the Recovery Console

There are many options available to you when using the Recovery Console for repairing the Windows XP operating system. You should be very familiar with each of the commands in Table 5.3.

TABLE 5.3   Available Commands in the Recovery Console

Command	Function
attrib	Changes the attributes of a file or a folder.
del	Deletes a file.
fixboot	Writes a new Windows boot sector on the system partition.
more	Displays a text file to the screen.
set	Displays or modifies environment options.
batch	Runs commands that are specified in a text file.
delete	Deletes a file.
fixmbr	Repairs the MBR of the boot partition.
mkdir	Creates a directory.
systemroot	Sets the current working folder to the %SystemRoot% folder.
bootcfg	Handles boot configuration and recovery.
dir	List files and folders in the current or specified directory.
format	Creates a file system on a specified partition.
type	Displays a text file.
cd	Changes directory.
disable	Disables a Windows system service or driver.
help	Displays available commands and switches.

TABLE 5.3   Available Commands in the Recovery Console *(continued)*

Command	Function
net	Not usable from the Recovery Console, but is available. (There isn't a good explanation for this.)
chdir	Changes directory.
diskpart	Partitions a hard disk.
listsvc	Displays all services or drivers that are eligible to be disabled.
rd	Deletes a folder.
chkdsk	Repairs or recovers a specified drive.
enable	Enables a Windows system service or driver.
logon	Lets you choose what installation of Windows to log into.
ren	Renames a file.
cls	Clears the screen of commands and output.
exit	Quits the Recovery Console.
map	Lists drive letters, file system types, partition sizes, and mappings to physical devices.
rename	Renames a file.
copy	Copies files.
expand	Extracts files from CABs and other collections.
md	Makes a directory.
rmdir	Deletes a folder.

As you can see, there are many commands available in the Recovery Console. You will most likely use only a few of them for each problem computer. In addition to each command, there are switches and syntax that must be used to perform certain functions. Exercise 5.7 will walk you through using the Recovery Console to repair the boot sector.

EXERCISE 5.7

Repairing the Boot Sector using the Recovery Console in Windows XP

1. Reboot your computer.

2. When the option to choose between installations becomes available, choose Microsoft Windows Recovery Console.

```
Please select the operating system to start:

    Microsoft Windows XP Professional
    Microsoft Windows Recovery Console

Use the up and down arrow keys to move the highlight to your choice.
Press ENTER to choose.







For troubleshooting and advanced startup options for Windows, press F8.
```

3. The Recovery Console will load and show you all installations of Microsoft Windows. Choose the appropriate installation and press Enter.

```
Microsoft Windows XP(TM) Recovery Console.

The Recovery Console provides system repair and recovery functionality.

Type EXIT to quit the Recovery Console and restart the computer.

1: C:\WINDOWS

Which Windows installation would you like to log onto
<To cancel, press ENTER>? ▪
```

4.   Type the administrator password and press Enter.

```
Microsoft Windows XP(TM) Recovery Console.
The Recovery Console provides system repair and recovery functionality.
Type EXIT to quit the Recovery Console and restart the computer.

1: C:\WINDOWS

Which Windows installation would you like to log onto
<To cancel, press ENTER>? 1
Type the Administrator password: ▪
```

5.   You will now be at a `C:\Windows` prompt; you can begin using the Recovery Console commands.

```
Microsoft Windows XP(TM) Recovery Console.
The Recovery Console provides system repair and recovery functionality.
Type EXIT to quit the Recovery Console and restart the computer.

1: C:\WINDOWS

Which Windows installation would you like to log onto
<To cancel, press ENTER>? 1
Type the Administrator password: ********
C:\WINDOWS>▪
```

EXERCISE 5.7 *(continued)*

6. To recover the boot sector, you should type either **fixmbr** or **fixboot**.

```
Microsoft Windows XP(TM) Recovery Console.

The Recovery Console provides system repair and recovery functionality.

Type EXIT to quit the Recovery Console and restart the computer.

1: C:\WINDOWS

Which Windows installation would you like to log onto
<To cancel, press ENTER>? 1
Type the Administrator password: ********
C:\WINDOWS>fixmbr

** CAUTION **

This computer appears to have a non-standard or invalid master
boot record.

FIXMBR may damage your partition tables if you
proceed.

This could cause all the partitions on the current hard disk
to become inaccessible.

If you are not having problems accessing your drive,
do not continue.

Are you sure you want to write a new MBR? ▪
```

7. You will be warned about the problems that could be associated with rebuilding the MBR. Type **Y** to confirm the command.

```
Type EXIT to quit the Recovery Console and restart the computer.

1: C:\WINDOWS

Which Windows installation would you like to log onto
<To cancel, press ENTER>? 1
Type the Administrator password: ********
C:\WINDOWS>fixmbr

** CAUTION **

This computer appears to have a non-standard or invalid master
boot record.

FIXMBR may damage your partition tables if you
proceed.

This could cause all the partitions on the current hard disk
to become inaccessible.

If you are not having problems accessing your drive,
do not continue.

Are you sure you want to write a new MBR? y
Writing new master boot record on physical drive
\Device\Harddisk0\Partition0.

The new master boot record has been successfully written.

C:\WINDOWS>▪
```

Automated System Recovery

There will come a time when all recovery options fail and you are faced with either calling it quits or reinstalling the operating system. Luckily for us, Microsoft has a last-ditch tool that will allow you recover the operating system without totally reinstalling and reconfiguring it. The biggest problem with simply reinstalling the operating system is that any system configurations or settings will be lost. This might not seem like a huge deal, but most large organizations have dozens if not hundreds of custom settings that are performed on systems in the network. Windows XP is no exception. Automated System Recovery (ASR) will allow you to recover the system and all system settings with relative ease. The major drawback of ASR is that it will recover only operating system files and settings; no user data or applications will be included in the recovery of a system when using ASR. ASR is generally a last resort, just shy of reinstalling and restoring from backup.

Preparing for ASR

When preparing ASR, there are many things to take into consideration. Using ASR requires that you have already made a full backup of your system, especially if you plan on recovering user-created data. You will also have to create the disks for ASR to use when rebuilding the operating system, commonly called the ASR set. Finally, you will need the operating system installation media, such as a bootable Windows XP CD. Exercise 5.8 walks you through preparing for Automated System Recovery.

EXERCISE 5.8

Preparing for Automated System Recovery

1. Format a floppy disk with the FAT file system and insert into the floppy drive.

2. Click the Start button and click Run, type **ntbackup**, and press Enter. (There are many ways to start the Windows Backup program. We just chose the easy way.)

EXERCISE 5.8 *(continued)*

The backup program will start in wizard mode.

3. Click the Advanced Mode link.

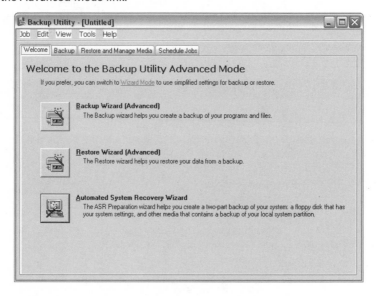

4. Click on the Automated System Recovery Wizard button.

5. Click on the Next button to proceed. You be prompted to find a location for the system backup.

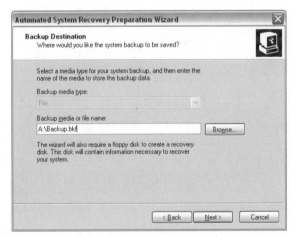

EXERCISE 5.8 *(continued)*

6. Once you have selected the location, click Next to start the backup process.

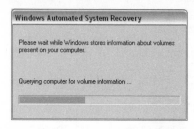

7. When the system backup is finished, you will be prompted to insert a formatted floppy disk. It should already be in the drive, so just click Next.

8. After the system copies recovery information, you will be prompted to remove the disk and label it.

9.   You can also print a report of the backup. It is always a good idea to print the backup report when possible; this way you have documentation in the case of an audit.

```
backup02 - Notepad                                                    _ □ X
File  Edit  Format  View  Help
Backup Status
Operation: Backup
Active backup destination: File
Media name: "Backup.bkf created 11/20/2005 at 3:32 PM"

Backup (via shadow copy) of "C: "
Backup set #1 on media #1
Backup description: ""
Media name: "Backup.bkf created 11/20/2005 at 3:32 PM"

Backup Type: Copy

Backup started on 11/20/2005 at 3:32 PM.
Backup completed on 11/20/2005 at 3:37 PM.
Directories: 589
Files: 7320
Bytes: 761,061,775
Time:   5 minutes and  4 seconds
Backup (via shadow copy) of "System State"
Backup set #2 on media #1
Backup description: ""
Media name: "Backup.bkf created 11/20/2005 at 3:32 PM"

Backup Type: Copy

Backup started on 11/20/2005 at 3:37 PM.
Backup completed on 11/20/2005 at 3:40 PM.
Directories: 134
Files: 1993
Bytes: 332,171,108
Time:   2 minutes and  22 seconds
Backup (via shadow copy) of "C: "
Backup set #3 on media #1
Backup description: ""
Media name: "Backup.bkf created 11/20/2005 at 3:32 PM"

Backup Type: Copy

Backup started on 11/20/2005 at 3:40 PM.
Backup completed on 11/20/2005 at 3:40 PM.
Directories: 3
```

Using ASR

Once a system fails, you should immediately go through the procedure discussed so far in this chapter. Microsoft has set an ordered process for recovering systems:

1.   Use Last Known Good Configuration.

2.   Boot into safe mode.

3.   Use the recovery console.

4.   Use the Automated System Recovery.

Following this guideline, we have covered each process in detail. Assuming you tried the first three options and are not able to recover the system, its time for ASR. Exercise 5.9 walks you through recovering Windows XP from failure using ASR.

EXERCISE 5.9

Performing an Automated System Recovery

1. Reboot the system, and boot to the Windows XP installation media or CD-ROM.

2. When the system is loading files from the installation media, you have a brief moment to press the F2 key to start ASR.

3. When prompted, insert the ASR set or floppy disk you created in Exercise 5.8.

4. You will be notified that the system will destroy all existing data. Press C to confirm this.

5. After the system is scanned and configured, you will be prompted for the backup media. Point the ASR process to your backup location.

6. Reboot the system to confirm it has been "Automatically Recovered."

Case Study: Total Failure

Shelly calls the help desk: "I was walking through some of my exercises for my MCDST course and I think I have broken my computer."

It appears as though her screen is locked up. Your attempt to connect to her computer with a third-party utility fails, so you walk over to her department to see what problems might have arisen. Upon arrival, you notice the problem that she's talking about.

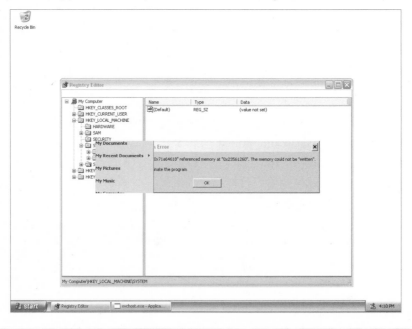

It appears a though her screen has frozen with the Registry Editor open and with the svchost service throwing an error. You can probably assume that the Registry was improperly edited. After performing a hard reboot, you receive another disturbing error.

```
Windows could not start because the following file is missing
or corrupt:
\WINDOWS\system32\config\SYSTEM

You can attempt to repair this file by starting Windows Setup
using the original Setup CD-ROM.
Select 'r' at the first screen to start repair.
```

After pondering a little, you decide use standard procedures to troubleshoot boot errors. You try safe mode first.

```
multi(0)disk(0)rdisk(0)partition(1)\WINDOWS\system32\ntoskrnl.exe
multi(0)disk(0)rdisk(0)partition(1)\WINDOWS\system32\hal.dll
multi(0)disk(0)rdisk(0)partition(1)\WINDOWS\system32\KDCOM.DLL
multi(0)disk(0)rdisk(0)partition(1)\WINDOWS\system32\BOOTVID.dll
multi(0)disk(0)rdisk(0)partition(1)\WINDOWS\system32\config\system

Windows could not start because the following file is missing
or corrupt:
\WINDOWS\system32\config\SYSTEM

You can attempt to repair this file by starting Windows Setup
using the original Setup CD-ROM.
Select 'r' at the first screen to start repair.
```

Apparently safe mode is not the answer this time. On to the next option, Last Known Good Configuration. This time you actually get a graphical "loading windows" screen, but after watching a blank, black screen for over 10 minutes, you decide that Last Known Good didn't work either. Next on your list is the Recovery Console. You try a little trick you were saving from a Knowledge Base article you stumbled across a few weeks ago (`http://support.microsoft.com/?kbid=307545`).

```
The target partition is C:.
Are you sure you want to write a new bootsector to the partition C: ?
Are you sure you want to write a new bootsector to the partition C: ? t
Are you sure you want to write a new bootsector to the partition C: ? y
The file system on the startup partition is NTFS.

FIXBOOT is writing a new boot sector.

The new bootsector was successfully written.

C:\WINDOWS>copy c:\windows\repair\system c:\windows\system32\config\system
Overwrite system? (Yes/No/All): y
        1 file(s) copied.

C:\WINDOWS>copy c:\windows\repair\software c:\windows\system32\config\software
Overwrite software? (Yes/No/All): y
        1 file(s) copied.

C:\WINDOWS>copy c:\windows\repair\sam c:\windows\system32\config\sam
Overwrite sam? (Yes/No/All): y
        1 file(s) copied.

C:\WINDOWS>copy c:\windows\repair\security c:\windows\system32\config\security
Overwrite security? (Yes/No/All): y
        1 file(s) copied.

C:\WINDOWS>copy c:\windows\repair\default c:\windows\system32\config\default
Overwrite default? (Yes/No/All): y
        1 file(s) copied.

C:\WINDOWS>_
```

After rebooting, you breathe a sigh of relief. The Recovery Console is actually good for something!

We wrote this case study to prove that with the right tools, any system can be recovered. In this scenario, the entire operating system was almost lost because the user accidentally deleted a few Registry keys. With a little patience and the right Knowledge Base article, this system was quickly brought back online.

Summary

Systems will crash, and when they do, you will have the knowledge and tools to recover them. Having the ability to quickly and effectively recover failed operating systems can make the difference when it comes down to you versus Windows XP.

Understanding the boot process is essential when troubleshooting problems with Windows XP. Always remember the different phases of the boot process when troubleshooting boot issues.

The Last Known Good Configuration consists of many different components, especially the various control sets that are contained in the Registry. Use Last Known Good after trying safe mode and standard troubleshooting. When Last Known Good is used, any system changes from the previous sessions will be lost.

The various safe mode options will allow you to isolate troubled software and hardware in a manner that is conducive to recovering the system. Remember the flavors of safe mode and what each one will do for you.

The Recovery Console should be installed after a successful installation of Windows XP. This will allow you to use many of the great recovery features that are built into Windows. The Recovery Console provides a secondary operating system to recover your primary system. Although using the Recovery Console can be challenging, there is little doubt that it is one of the most powerful Windows recovery tools available.

Although Automated System Recovery is a quick and easy method to recover a lost operating system, it should be reserved as a last-resort tool. Any user data or applications will be lost when using the Automated System Recovery utility.

Exam Essentials

Understand the boot process.   You should understand how the Windows XP system performs a boot under all scenarios. This includes Registry keys and boot options that are used when troubleshooting problem systems. Be comfortable using the various boot options and configuring special boot options.

Understand troubleshooting problem software and devices.   You should understand how to identify and troubleshoot hardware and software problems related to booting the operating system. This will include problematic configurations of the Registry, system components, and required devices such as the video and hard drive.

Know how to recover Windows XP from failure.   You should understand how each of the recovery options work. This includes the various options available to you for each recovery option, such as the Recovery Console and safe mode.

Know when to use recovery options.   You should understand when and under what circumstances to use each of the available recovery tools for Windows XP. Also be familiar with the requirements for using each tool.

Review Questions

1. You are the senior help desk support technician at your company. Your organization uses Microsoft Windows XP as its mainstream operating system. A user calls the help desk and reports that he receives an error when his system is booting up and is no longer able to access his computer files. The user states that he has already tried the Last Known Good boot option. You need to instruct the user on what to do in order to recover his operating system. What should you tell him?

    A. Use Automated System Recovery to recover the operating system.

    B. Use safe mode to disable any problem drivers or software installed.

    C. Use Last Known Good to enable the system to boot.

    D. Use the Recovery Console and instruct the user to replace all critical system files.

2. You are the senior help desk support technician at your company. Your organization uses Microsoft Windows XP as its mainstream operating system. Your organization installs the Recovery Console on all Windows XP workstations for recoverability. A user calls the help desk and states that he has just installed an application on his system. After the installation he received a stop error and now his system will not boot up properly. What should you do?

    A. Boot using the Last Known Good option.

    B. Boot up using the Windows XP CD and use ASR to recover the system.

    C. Boot into safe mode and uninstall the application.

    D. Reinstall the operating system.

3. You are the senior help desk support technician at your company. Your organization uses Microsoft Windows XP as its mainstream operating system. Your organization installs the Recovery Console on all Windows XP workstations for recoverability. A user calls the help desk and states that she has accidentally deleted most of the files from her C: drive. You need to recover her system as quickly as possible. What should you do?

    A. Boot using the Last Known Good option.

    B. Boot up using the Windows XP CD and use ASR to recover the system.

    C. Boot into safe mode and uninstall the application.

    D. Reinstall the operating system.

4. You are the senior help desk support technician at your company. Your organization uses Microsoft Windows XP as its mainstream operating system. Your organization installs the Recovery Console on all Windows XP workstations for recoverability. A user calls the help desk and states that his system's video is acting very strange after making some driver changes and configuration modifications. The user has also installed a new application that is unrelated to the problem. You need to be sure that the user can perform tasks without problems with his video display. After booting into safe mode, what tools might you use? Choose two answers.

    A. Msinfo32

    B. Msconfig

    C. Device Manager

    D. Last Known Good Configuration

5. You are the senior help desk support technician at your company. Your organization uses Microsoft Windows XP as its mainstream operating system. Your organization installs the Recovery Console on all Windows XP workstations for recoverability. A user calls the help desk and states that each time he logs onto his computer, a service hangs and causes the operating system to fail and restart. You need to enable the user to boot up properly, without rebooting automatically. What should you do? (Choose two options.)

    A. Use Last Known Good to recover the system.

    B. Use ASR to recover the system.

    C. Use safe mode and disable the service.

    D. Use the Recovery Console and disable the service.

6. You are the senior help desk support technician at your company. Your organization uses Microsoft Windows XP as its mainstream operating system. A user calls the help desk and states that he need to modify the safe mode startup devices to include a few additional devices. After the user is pointed to the appropriate Registry key, what number(s) can he configure for each device he wants to start up? (Choose all that apply.)

    A. 1

    B. 2

    C. 4

    D. 5

7. You are the senior help desk support technician at your company. Your organization uses Microsoft Windows XP as its mainstream operating system. Your organization installs the Recovery Console on all Windows XP workstations for recoverability. A user calls the help desk and states that his system shows an error during startup. The error says that his NTLDR file is missing. What should you do?

    A. Boot into safe mode and copy the NTLDR file to the appropriate location.

    B. Boot up using Last Known Good to restore the system file.

    C. Boot into the Recovery Console and copy the NTLDR file to the appropriate location.

    D. Use ASR to replace the NTLDR file.

8. You are the senior help desk support technician at your company. Your organization uses Microsoft Windows XP as its mainstream operating system. Your organization installs the Recovery Console on all Windows XP workstations for recoverability. A user calls the help desk and states that he received a "Stop 0x0000007B" error message when booting his system. You need to ensure that this user can resume normal operation. What should you do?

    A. Restart and use Last Known Good.

    B. Restart into safe mode.

    C. Use the Recovery Console.

    D. Use ASR.

9. You are the senior help desk support technician at your company. Your organization uses Microsoft Windows XP as its mainstream operating system. Your organization installs the Recovery Console on all Windows XP workstations for recoverability. A user calls the help desk and states that after downloading a file from the Internet, he receives an error during startup and cannot successfully boot his system. The error says, "Invalid entry in MBR." You need to resolve this as quickly as possible. What should you do?

    A. Restart and use Last Known Good.

    B. Restart into safe mode.

    C. Use the Recovery Console.

    D. Use ASR.

10. You are the senior help desk support technician at your company. Your organization uses Microsoft Windows XP as its mainstream operating system. Your organization installs the Recovery Console on all Windows XP workstations for recoverability. A user calls the help desk and states that after downloading a file from the Internet, he receives an error during startup and cannot successfully boot his system. The error says, "Could not read from selected boot disk." You need to resolve this as quickly as possible. What should you do?

    A. Edit the `config.sys` file inside the recovery console.

    B. Edit the `boot.ini` file inside the recovery console.

    C. Edit the NTLDR file inside the recovery console.

    D. Delete the `config.sys` file inside the recovery console.

11. You are the senior help desk support technician at your company. Your organization uses Microsoft Windows XP as its mainstream operating system. Your organization installs the Recovery Console on all Windows XP workstations for recoverability. A user calls the help desk and says that his workstation fails to boot properly. He has just recently installed a service-based application, and afterward, his system rebooted. After the reboot, during the service and driver initialization phase, his system froze. You have booted the system to the Recovery Console and you want to disable the service so that it won't hang his system when he boots up. What two commands should be used here? (Choose two answers. Each answer represents a part of the solution.)

    A. `disable`

    B. `expand`

    C. `stop`

    D. `listsvc`

12. You are the senior help desk support technician at your company. Your organization uses Microsoft Windows XP as its mainstream operating system. Your organization installs the Recovery Console on all Windows XP workstations for recoverability. A user calls the help desk and wishes to know in detail what drivers are loaded during startup and what is happening. What should you use?

    A. `/safeboot`

    B. `/SOS`

    C. `/bootlog`

    D. `/syslog`

13. You are the senior help desk support technician at your company. Your organization uses Microsoft Windows XP as its mainstream operating system. Your organization installs the Recovery Console on all Windows XP workstations for recoverability. A user calls the help desk and states that his hard drive has completely failed. You need to get the user back into his operating system, including his data, as quickly as possible. What should you do? (Choose two answers. Each answer is only part of the total solution.)

A. Reinstall the operating system.

B. Run ASR.

C. Restore the user's data from backup.

D. Use Last Known Good

14. You are the senior help desk support technician at your company. Your organization uses Microsoft Windows XP as its mainstream operating system. Your organization installs the Recovery Console on all Windows XP workstations for recoverability. A user calls the help desk and says that during the installation of a known application, his computer blue-screened and rebooted. Now his system boots to a black screen after the operating system choices go away. You are familiar with the application and want to determine what happened during the installation. After booting into the recovery console, what command can be of use here?

A. `more`

B. `del`

C. `fixboot`

D. `less`

15. You are the senior help desk support technician at your company. Your organization uses Microsoft Windows XP as its mainstream operating system. Your organization installs the Recovery Console on all Windows XP workstations for recoverability. After making a modification to the resolution, your user states that when he logs onto his system, his screen is distorted. What recovery method should you use?

A. Safe mode

B. Recovery Console

C. ASR

D. Reinstalling the OS

16. You are the senior help desk support technician at your company. Your organization uses Microsoft Windows XP as its mainstream operating system. Your organization installs the Recovery Console on all Windows XP workstations for recoverability. After installing an unsigned device driver, the system stops responding. The user reboots the system, and it will not come back up. What recovery method should you use?

A. ASR

B. Recovery Console

C. Last Known Good

D. Safe mode

17. You are the senior help desk support technician at your company. Your organization uses Microsoft Windows XP as its mainstream operating system. A user calls the help desk and requests to know when exactly the system records the Last Known Good Configuration in the Registry. What should you tell the user?

   A. During the system shutdown

   B. During the system bootup process

   C. When a user logs off

   D. When a user logs on

18. You are the senior help desk support technician at your company. Your organization uses Microsoft Windows XP as its mainstream operating system. Your organization installs the Recovery Console on all Windows XP workstations for recoverability. You discover that a computer was installed many months ago by a desktop support technician who is no longer with the company. The computer was never joined to the domain, and local accounts were not configured to the company standard. As a result, you are unable to log onto the system or gain access to it in any way. You want to use the computer for a new department manager whose first day is tomorrow. You need to configure the workstation to specifications for your company and join it to the domain. What should you do?

   A. Use ASR.

   B. Use the Recovery Console.

   C. Reinstall Windows XP.

   D. Use Last Known Good.

19. You are the senior help desk support technician at your company. Your organization uses Microsoft Windows XP as its mainstream operating system. Your organization installs the Recovery Console on all Windows XP workstations for recoverability. You have recently hired a new help desk support technician. The new technician is attempting to install a new computer for a new hire in another department. The technician calls you and asks where the installation source is located for the Recovery Console. What should your response be?

   A. The `i386` folder

   B. The `Valueadd` folder

   C. The `support` folder

   D. The `tools` folder

20. You are the senior help desk support technician at your company. Your organization uses Microsoft Windows XP as its mainstream operating system. Your organization installs the Recovery Console on all Windows XP workstations for recoverability. After making changes to a system, one of your trainee support technicians receives a "`User32.dll` is missing" message and the system will not boot to a GUI. What recovery process will most likely provide results?

   A. Last Known Good

   B. Recovery Console

   C. Safe mode

   D. ASR

Answers to Review Questions

1. B. Have the user uninstall any new software or roll back any new drivers that were installed by booting into safe mode and making the appropriate changes.

2. A. When freshly installed device drivers and applications cause stop errors, you should try to boot your computer using the Last Known Good option because it will roll back any system changes since the last successful logon. (`http://support.microsoft.com/default.aspx?scid=kb;en-us;Q314063`)

3. B. Because the core operating system files have been removed, you cannot use Last Known Good or safe mode. This particular case will require either reinstalling the operating system or using ASR. ASR is the preferred method because it will also recover the system configuration.

4. A, C. Msconfig will usually be used for startup issues, whereas Last Known Good Configuration is available only during startup, not in safe mode. Using Msinfo32 will allow you see what drivers and hardware are installed; Device Manager will allow you to roll back or remove problem devices and drivers.

5. C, D. Because the user is logging onto the system, you cannot use Last Known Good. Using ASR is always a last resort. You can use either safe mode or the Recovery Console to disable the problem service.

6. A, B. By setting the string value to 1 or 2, you can be sure the device will attempt to start up when the operating system is initialized.

7. C. Because the system will not start in any mode, you will be forced to boot to an alternate installation. The Recovery Console allows for this and also allows for the replacement of key system files, such as the NTLDR file.

8. A. Because you haven't tried anything yet, following Microsoft's guidelines, you should use Last Known Good.

9. C. The `fixmbr` or `fixboot` options should fix this problem. These commands are only available in the Recovery Console.

10. B. The `boot.ini` file contains the references to each boot location. This error can occur if the `boot.ini` file contains incorrect references to drives or volumes.

11. A, D. You can use `listsvc` to determine which service was installed by the application and use the `disable` command to disable the service.

12. C. Using the startup switch, `/bootlog`, will enable you to see exactly what is happening during the startup process, including what is happening with drivers.

13. B, C. By using Automated System Recovery, you can restore the operating system to its previous functionality. After running ASR, you can restore the user's data from backup.

14. A. The more command allows you to view text files, such as log files from a failed installation. To find out what happened during the installation, you should view the log files generated by the application.

15. A. Using safe mode, you can uninstall the driver and reboot the system. This will force the operating system to reinstall the driver and restore it back to the default resolution, usually 800×600 or 1024×768.

16. C. The Last Known Good option allows you to revert the system configuration back to the last time you successfully logged into the system. This revert included device drivers.

17. D. The Last Known Good is a copy of the current configuration that is in place when a user successfully logs onto a Windows XP or Windows 2000 machine.

18. C. ASR, the Recovery Console, and Last Known Good are system recovery features; they offer no way to recover lost passwords or accounts. The fastest way to solve this problem is to reinstall the operating system to the specifications of the company.

19. A. The installation CD will contain the source files. The i386 subdirectory will have the Winnt32.exe file.

20. D. Because the system did not boot, you can assume that the User32.dll file is a critical system file. Automated System Recovery specializes in recovering the system itself. Recovery Console might work here if you have a replacement User32.dll to extract.

Chapter 6

Troubleshooting Network Protocols and Services

MICROSOFT EXAM OBJECTIVES COVERED IN THIS CHAPTER:

✓ **Troubleshoot TCP/IP. Tools include ARP; the Repair utility; connection properties; and the** `ping`, `ipconfig`, `pathping`, **and** `nslookup` **commands.**

- Answer end-user questions related to configuring TCP/IP settings.
- Configure and troubleshoot manual TCP/IP configuration.
- Configure and troubleshoot automated TCP/IP address configuration.
- Configure and troubleshoot Internet Connection Firewall (ICF) settings such as enable and disable. Considerations include indications of issues related to enabling and disabling ICF.

✓ **Troubleshoot name resolution issues.**

- Configure and troubleshoot hostname resolution issues on a client computer. Considerations include Hosts files and DNS.
- Configure and troubleshoot NetBIOS name resolution issues on a client computer. Considerations include LMHOSTS files and WINS.

✓ **Configure and troubleshoot remote connections.**

- Configure and troubleshoot a remote dial-up connection. Tasks include client-side configuration.
- Configure and troubleshoot a remote connection across the Internet. Tasks include client-side configuration.

✓ **Configure and troubleshoot Internet Explorer.**

  ▪ Configure and troubleshoot Internet Explorer connection properties.

  ▪ Configure and troubleshoot Internet Explorer security properties.

  ▪ Configure and troubleshoot Internet Explorer general properties.

✓ **Configure and troubleshoot end-user systems by using remote connectivity tools.**

  ▪ Use Remote Desktop to configure and troubleshoot an end user's desktop.

  ▪ Use Remote Assistance to configure and troubleshoot an end user's desktop.

Successful communication of networked computers requires three components: a method of connectivity, a common client, and a common communication protocol. You can establish connectivity by using cables to connect the computers or by using wireless connections. The common client for computers running Microsoft operating systems is the Microsoft software that is built into all Microsoft operating systems, referred to as *Client for Microsoft Networks*. A protocol is a set of rules by which communication must take place. There are many different communication protocols, but the protocol that is the most popular today is *Transmission Control Protocol/Internet Protocol (TCP/IP)*. TCP/IP is actually a collection of protocols that provide a variety of services, such as logical addressing, name resolution, application connections, encryption, error correction, and many others. The main reason for the popularity of TCP/IP is that it has become the standard protocol for use on the Internet.

Computers recognize each other by a physical address that is burned into the network interface card installed on each computer. This physical address is referred to as a *Media Access Control (MAC) address*. To facilitate communication between computers in your own network and in other networks, you generally use a logical address configured by the TCP/IP protocol. This address is referred to as an *IP address*. A protocol that is built into TCP/IP called *Address Resolution Protocol (ARP)* is used to convert the IP addresses to MAC addresses so that packets can be sent to the correct computers.

Since IP addresses are not easy to remember, special files and servers are used to convert the cumbersome IP address into a name that can be more easily remembered. Computers then convert these user-friendly names back into IP addresses and eventually into MAC addresses. This process is referred to as *name resolution*. Using TCP/IP and name resolution, the Internet connects computers across the world. You can use your Internet Explorer browser software to connect to servers even though you have no idea where the servers are located. You can also use these same protocols and services to connect to and remotely manage computers in your own organization.

In this chapter, we will discuss configuring and troubleshooting network protocols and services. We will focus our attention on five main areas of configuration and troubleshooting:

TCP/IP   Transmission Control Protocol/Internet Protocol (TCP/IP) is the most common protocol in use today. TCP/IP is used within most networks and is also used to connect all of the networks of the world together through the Internet. As a desktop support technician, you should be able to configure clients to use TCP/IP. In addition, you should know how IP addresses are assigned and how to use tools inherent to TCP/IP to troubleshoot connectivity between computers. You should also be able to configure advanced connection settings, such as the Internet Connection Firewall (ICF).

Name resolution   The logical addresses that TCP/IP uses to identify a computer or a network are called IP addresses. These addresses are long and cumbersome to remember, so people like to use user-friendly names that are easier to remember. Network experts have created files and services that computers use to convert these user-friendly names back into IP addresses. You should know how *Hosts files*, *LMHOSTSLMHOSTS files*, *WINS servers*, and *DNS servers* are used to convert user-friendly names to IP addresses. You should also know when it is appropriate to use each type of file or service. In addition, you should be able to configure and troubleshoot clients to use these name resolution files and services.

Remote connections   In today's business world, many users work from home or from a hotel. It's essential that they be able to connect to your organization's network and use resources just as if they were at a desk in your building, although the connection will probably be quite a bit slower. There are two main types of remote connections that you can use: dial-up and VPN through the Internet. You should know how to configure and troubleshoot both types of remote connections.

Internet Explorer   Most users have no idea how TCP/IP or the Internet actually works. In addition, they don't know where the servers to which they connect are physically located. The reason that they don't know is that they don't have to know; it doesn't matter! Browser software, such as Microsoft's Internet Explorer, enables users to locate resources across the Internet by entering their user-friendly web address or *Uniform Resource Locator (URL) address*. Provided that Internet Explorer is properly configured, a user can browse network resources with very little training or knowledge. You should know how to configure and troubleshoot the properties of Internet Explorer.

Remote connectivity tools   Network administrators and desktop support technicians no longer have to physically visit a user's computer to assist a user and troubleshoot the computer. Remote connectivity tools such as Remote Desktop and Remote Assistance enable them to connect to the user's computer and make configuration changes through the network or even through the Internet. You should understand the difference between Remote Desktop and Remote Assistance. You should also know how to use these tools to configure and troubleshoot common user issues.

TCP/IP

When you want to send data from one physical location to another, you use a network. A network is basically a collection of hardware and software that uses rules called protocols. The primary protocol on networks today is called TCP/IP. TCP/IP stands for Transmission Control Protocol/Internet Protocol. It is a network protocol; actually, it is a collection of different protocols that serve various purposes and provide various functionalities. TCP/IP uses something called a packet to hold and transport data over a network. There are two basic types of packets available when using IP: UDP and TCP. User Datagram Protocol (UDP) is a connectionless, best effort delivery protocol. That basically means that when you send data using UDP, your computer will send the information to the destination, but it will not ensure that it arrives. Transmission Control Protocol (TCP), on the other hand, will follow the data and be absolutely sure that it arrives in the proper location.

Imagine that you are the receptionist at a law firm. One of the lawyers asks you to mail an important document to a client in another state. You take the package to the post office. You get a standard envelope and place the document inside. You purchase a single stamp and drop the envelope in the slot. You have sent the document in the right direction, but you have no idea where it will go from the post office. For all you know, the letter could never make it there! You have created a User Datagram Protocol packet.

Now imagine that you are the same receptionist and the lawyer has asked you to mail the same document. You go to a UPS or FedEx store and request an overnight envelope with delivery tracking and a signed receipt. You hand the package to the person on the other side of the cash register and they immediately walk your package to a truck and send it off to the airport. You then use the tracking number to follow the package to the destination and receive a confirmation of delivery from the recipient and from the delivery company. You have just created a Transmission Control Protocol packet.

There are advantages to using UDP packets. There will be situations in which the connection isn't reliable and you can't ensure data delivery. Because UDP doesn't care when or how a packet reaches a destination, you can actually have huge delays and detours but still reach the remote end point. UDP is often used when you aren't sure if you can reach a destination. The major disadvantage is probably obvious: you can never be sure you'll get to where you are trying to go.

TCP/IP currently uses a 32-bit binary address to provide for unique IP addresses on computers and networks. You usually don't see the binary involved with IP addresses. Most likely you will see an IP address, such as 192.168.1.2 or 172.12.24.6. IP addresses are divided into four octets, basically four sets of numbers separated by decimals.

An octet is a set of digits separated by a placeholder. 1.2.3.4 contains four octets, with the number 1 in the first octet, and 2 in the second octet. Numbers 3 and 4 are in their respective octets.

Those numbers may look intimidating at first, but once you get used to it, they are pretty easy to decipher. An IP address actually consists of two components: a network ID and a node ID. The network ID serves to identify the group of computers that you belong to, called a subnet. Think of a subnet as a street name: it identifies a general area that has many houses. You couldn't find someone's house if you have only their street name. The node ID is like your address number: it uniquely identifies your home, or in this case, your PC, from others in the same group.

The node ID is known by many different names, such as computer ID, host ID, end point ID, and others. You should be able to easily determine the difference between terms used for network IDs and node IDs with a little understanding of the concept.

In order to determine what part of the IP address is the network ID and what part is the node ID, you must have something called a subnet mask. The subnet mask is also a 32-bit binary number, but we will look at its decimal version. The structure of subnet masks is very similar to the structure of IP addresses: four octets separated by decimals. One very common subnet mask is 255.255.255.0. If you combine the IP address with the subnet mask, you are able to determine which numbers are the network ID and node ID. Let's take 192.168.1.77 and 255.255.255.0 for example. The first three numbers in the subnet mask are 255. Any octet that has 255 will match up with the IP address to create the network ID. Because the first three octets are 255 in the subnet mask, you simply use the first three octets of the IP address for the network ID. The network ID is 192.168.1 and whatever is left over will be the node ID—in this case, 77. Another easy way to remember this is to simply place the IP address above the subnet mask and draw a line where the 255s stop; everything on the left of your line will be the network ID and everything to the right of your line will be node ID.

TCP/IP addressing schemes can become very complex and confusing. Fortunately, as a desktop support technician, it is not necessary that you be an expert in regard to TCP/IP or IP addressing. You should, however, know how to configure a client IP address and know how to configure a client to obtain an IP address automatically. In addition, you should be able to configure the Internet Connection Firewall in the advanced settings of a connection's properties. Finally, you should know how to use tools inherent in Windows XP to troubleshoot connectivity for a client.

TCP/IP configuration and troubleshooting can be divided into four main areas:

- Manual IP address configuration
- Automatic IP address configuration
- Windows Firewall, also known as Internet Connection Firewall configuration
- TCP/IP troubleshooting

Let's examine each area in detail.

Manual IP Address Configuration

All Microsoft clients can be configured with an IP address manually. The interface on which this is done varies slightly on different Microsoft operating systems. We will focus on the interface used with Windows XP. Since each computer on the network requires a unique IP address, you should be careful not to use an address that is already in use on the network because this can cause communication errors on your computer as well as on the computer that originally had the address. Exercise 6.1 walks you through the steps to manually configure an IP address on a Windows XP client.

Automatic IP Address Configuration

All Microsoft clients later than Windows 98 are set by default to obtain an IP address automatically. If a client's configuration has been changed to a manually set address and you need the client to obtain an IP address automatically, then you can change the client setting back to automatic configuration. Exercise 6.2 walks you through the steps to configure a client to obtain an IP address automatically.

EXERCISE 6.1

Configuring an IP Address Manually in Windows XP

1. On the Windows XP Desktop, click Start and then select Control Panel. Ensure that Control Panel is in Classic view.

2. In Control Panel, select Network Connections and then choose the connection that you want to configure. Connections represent network interface cards in the computer. Some computers may have multiple connections.

3. Right-click the selected connection and then choose Properties.

4. In the field marked This Connection Uses the Following Items, double-click Internet Protocol (TCP/IP).

5. Select Use the Following IP Address, and then enter an address that is unique for your subnet. If you are not sure of the address to enter, consult your network administrator. It is very important not to use an address that is already in use on the network. You should also consult with the network administrator to determine the correct DNS address to enter.

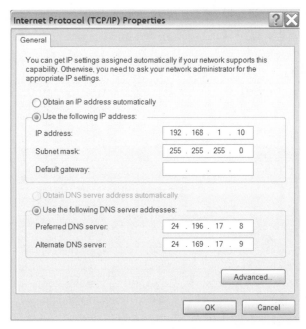

6. When you have finished entering the addresses, click OK, and then click OK again to save the changes.

EXERCISE 6.2

Configuring Windows XP to Obtain an IP Address Automatically

1. On the Windows XP Desktop, click Start and then select Control Panel.

2. In Control Panel, select Network Connections and then choose the connection that you want to configure. Connections represent network interface cards in the computer. Some computers may have multiple connections.

3. Right-click the selected connection and then choose Properties.

4. In the field marked This Connection Uses the Following Items, double-click Internet Protocol (TCP/IP).

5. Select Obtain an IP Address Automatically. Note that it is not necessary to delete the current manually set IP address.

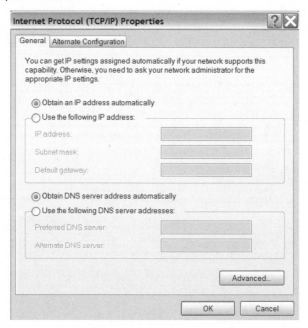

6. You can also set the client to obtain its DNS server address automatically. You should consult with your network administrator to determine this setting.

7. When you have finished making your selections, click OK, and then click OK again to save your settings.

Windows Firewall Configuration

You should know that if you are directly connected to the Internet, the Internet is also directly connected to you! This means that you might unknowingly give other users access to resources and information in your computer. To prevent this from happening, you can use hardware or software to filter traffic to and from your computer or your entire network. This type of hardware and software is referred to as a *firewall*. While most organizations employ a corporate firewall, it's still good practice to use an additional firewall at each client. Windows XP has a built-in firewall called Windows Firewall. If you are using a computer that does not have Service Pack 2 installed on it, then it is referred to as the *Internet Connection Firewall (ICF)*. You should know how to configure both the Windows Firewall and the ICF for a Windows XP client. Exercise 6.3 walks you through the steps to configure the ICF, and Exercise 6.4 shows you how to configure the newer Windows Firewall that comes as part of Service Pack 2.

EXERCISE 6.3

Configuring the Internet Connection Firewall in Windows XP

1. On the Windows XP Desktop, click Start and then select Control Panel.

2. In Control Panel, select Network Connections and then choose the connection that you want to configure. Since connections represent network interface cards in the computer, some computers may have multiple connections.

3. Right-click the selected connection and then choose Properties.

4. In the Properties dialog box, select the Advanced tab.

5. Click the check box marked Protect My Computer and Network by Limiting or Preventing Access to This Computer from the Internet. This will prevent all access to your computer from outside your computer.

6. Click the Settings button to configure access to specific services on your computer. You can also configure logging of packets that flow through the firewall on the Security Logging tab and configure filtering of error and status information on the ICMP tab.

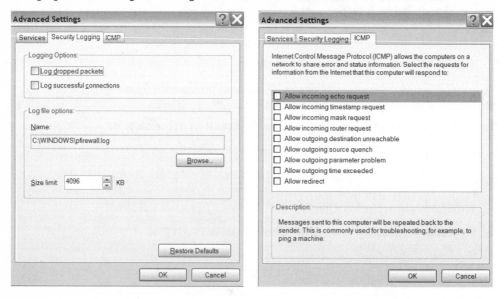

TCP/IP Troubleshooting

As we mentioned before, it's not necessary that you become an expert at the inner workings of TCP/IP to be an effective desktop support technician. You should, however, know how to perform some basic troubleshooting involving IP addresses, connectivity, and name resolution. In the following sections, we will discuss IP address and connectivity troubleshooting. In the next section, we will discuss name resolution troubleshooting.

IP Address Troubleshooting

Network administrators often use servers called *Dynamic Host Configuration Protocol (DHCP) servers* to assign unique IP addresses to client computers when they are connected to the network. Using these centrally managed servers allows IP addressing information to be assigned to a host without requiring an administrator to visit each and every computer on the network and manually assign this information. DHCP servers can assign not only IP addresses, but also subnet masks, default gateways, and DNS and WINS server addresses as well. This process makes managing your client computers much easier and efficient. Additionally, Windows XP and Windows 2000 clients have yet another way of automatically getting IP addressing information configured. Windows XP and 2000 computers can automatically assign the computer an IP address in a special network when no DHCP server is available. This address is referred to as an *Automatic Private IP Address (APIPA)*. You can recognize an APIPA address because it will start with 169.254. Typically an APIPA address on a client indicates that the client was set up to receive IP addressing information automatically from a DHCP server but the DHCP server was not available and the client does not have a valid network address. Windows XP also allows you to set an alternate configuration that will be used instead of the 169.254.*x.y* address in the event that a DHCP server is not available. This can be useful on a laptop that is used in two different networks, especially if one network has a DHCP server and the other does not. You should know how to determine whether a client is configured with an address from a DHCP server, an APIPA address, or just a manual address (either statically assigned or through the Alternate Configuration tab). Exercise 6.5 walks you through the steps to use the ipconfig tool built into Windows XP to determine how a client's IP address is configured. You can see the Alternate Configuration tab in Figure 6.1.

FIGURE 6.1   The Alternate Configuration tab

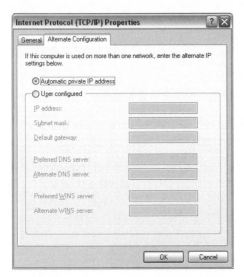

EXERCISE 6.4

Configuring Windows Firewall

1. Open Control Panel (Ensure that the Control Panel view is set to Classic).

2. Click the Windows Firewall icon.

3. Notice that there are two main options listed on the General tab: On and Off. Under the On option is also a check box for you to select whether or not you want exceptions. If this is selected, Windows will not allow any exceptions that are listed on the Exceptions tab.

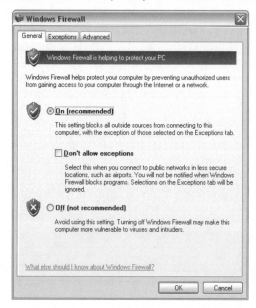

4. There are two other tabs that you can use to configure Windows Firewall Settings: Exceptions and Advanced. Click the Exceptions tab.

5. On this tab, you can configure Windows Firewall to allow certain programs, called exceptions, to enter your network. Windows Firewall will block all other programs. There is already a standard list of programs you can to select, or you can click the Add button and follow the prompts to select one that is not listed.

EXERCISE 6.4 *(continued)*

6. You can also add ports for other programs to use, or edit existing program entries and change their listening ports.

7. If you click the Advanced tab, you will see other options useful for configuring your security settings in Windows Firewall.

8. You can change connections that these Windows Firewall settings apply to by clicking the Settings button in the Network Connection Settings area.

9. You can configure Security Logging options by clicking the Settings button in the Security Logging area.

EXERCISE 6.4 *(continued)*

10. You can also configure how your computer handles ICMP responses (such as pings) in the ICMP area of this tab.

11. Finally, you can reset Windows Firewall settings back to their default on this tab, in case you need to return to the default settings and start over again.

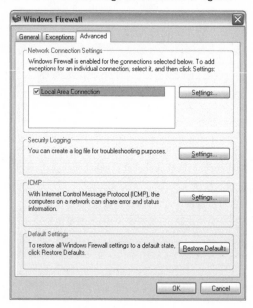

An IP address that starts with 169.254 may indicate that a DHCP server was not available when the client computer was first started. It's possible that the DHCP server could have become available after the client was started. You can force the client computer to ask the DHCP server for an address using the `ipconfig /renew` command. Exercise 6.6 walks you through the steps to force the computer to ask for an address.

Connectivity Troubleshooting

As mentioned earlier, connectivity of computers in a network requires more than just the wires or wireless connections that establish the physical network. To have connectivity, computers must also share a common protocol and configuration information, such as information showing that IP addressing is properly configured. This is referred to as logical connectivity.

EXERCISE 6.5

Using the Ipconfig Tool to Determine How an IP Address Was Configured on a Client

1. On the Windows XP Desktop, click Start and then choose Run.

2. On the Run line, type **cmd** to obtain a command prompt.

3. At the command prompt, type `ipconfig /all`.

4. Read the IP address of the client connection to determine whether it starts with 169.254. If it does, then it is an APIPA address.

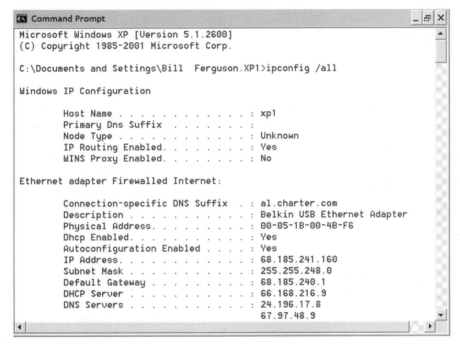

```
Command Prompt                                                    _ 日 X

Microsoft Windows XP [Version 5.1.2600]
(C) Copyright 1985-2001 Microsoft Corp.

C:\Documents and Settings\Bill  Ferguson.XP1>ipconfig /all

Windows IP Configuration

        Host Name . . . . . . . . . . . . : xp1
        Primary Dns Suffix  . . . . . . . :
        Node Type . . . . . . . . . . . . : Unknown
        IP Routing Enabled. . . . . . . . : Yes
        WINS Proxy Enabled. . . . . . . . : No

Ethernet adapter Firewalled Internet:

        Connection-specific DNS Suffix  . : al.charter.com
        Description . . . . . . . . . . . : Belkin USB Ethernet Adapter
        Physical Address. . . . . . . . . : 00-05-1B-00-4B-F6
        Dhcp Enabled. . . . . . . . . . . : Yes
        Autoconfiguration Enabled . . . . : Yes
        IP Address. . . . . . . . . . . . : 68.185.241.160
        Subnet Mask . . . . . . . . . . . : 255.255.248.0
        Default Gateway . . . . . . . . . : 68.185.240.1
        DHCP Server . . . . . . . . . . . : 66.168.216.9
        DNS Servers . . . . . . . . . . . : 24.196.17.8
                                            67.97.48.9
```

5. If the address does not start with 169.254, then read the ipconfig output to determine whether the address was obtained manually or assigned by a DHCP server. If the DHCP Enabled line includes the word *Yes*, then the computer is configured to obtain an address from a DHCP server. You can read the DHCP Server line at the bottom of the output to determine the IP address of the DHCP server that leased the IP address to the client.

EXERCISE 6.6

Using the ipconfig /renew Command

1. On the Windows XP Desktop, click Start and then choose Run.

2. On the Run line, type **cmd** to obtain a command prompt.

3. At the command prompt, type **ipconfig /renew** and then wait a few seconds to deter-
    mine whether the client can obtain an address.

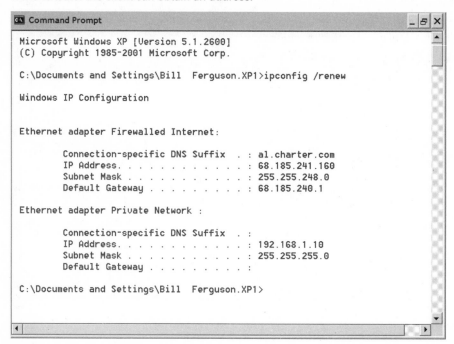

```
Command Prompt                                                    _ 🗗 ×

Microsoft Windows XP [Version 5.1.2600]
(C) Copyright 1985-2001 Microsoft Corp.

C:\Documents and Settings\Bill  Ferguson.XP1>ipconfig /renew

Windows IP Configuration


Ethernet adapter Firewalled Internet:

        Connection-specific DNS Suffix  . : a1.charter.com
        IP Address. . . . . . . . . . . . : 68.185.241.160
        Subnet Mask . . . . . . . . . . . : 255.255.248.0
        Default Gateway . . . . . . . . . : 68.185.240.1

Ethernet adapter Private Network :

        Connection-specific DNS Suffix  . :
        IP Address. . . . . . . . . . . . : 192.168.1.10
        Subnet Mask . . . . . . . . . . . : 255.255.255.0
        Default Gateway . . . . . . . . . :

C:\Documents and Settings\Bill  Ferguson.XP1>
```

4. If the client obtains a valid address from the DHCP server, then the computer should be
    able to communicate on the network. If the client is still unable to obtain a valid IP
    address, then you should escalate the issue to the network administrator.

You can use tools built into Windows XP to test the physical connectivity and logical connectivity of computers in a network. There are two main tools that you can use to test connectivity:
ping and pathping. In the following sections, we will discuss each of these tools and illustrate
how you can use them to troubleshoot connectivity between computers.

Using the Ping Tool

The ping tool is a command-line tool that creates special packets called *Internet Control Message Protocol (ICMP)* packets. When you use the ping tool, you send packets to a specific

address, which then sends them back. You might be wondering why you are sending these packets back and forth in the first place. The main reason you use the ping tool is to see if the packets come back. If the packets can be received by a computer and then be sent back to you, then you know that you have physical and logical connectivity with the computer. If they can't, then you may need to start checking your connections and the link lights on your network interface cards, hubs, and routers. By the same token, you might also need to make sure that you have assigned an address that is valid within the subnet. Exercise 6.7 walks you through the steps to test connectivity using the ping tool.

EXERCISE 6.7

Testing Connectivity between Computers Using the Ping Tool

1. On the Windows XP Desktop, click Start and then select Run.

2. On the Run line, type **cmd** to open a command prompt.

3. At the command prompt, type **ping**, then type a space, and then type the IP address of the computer that you want to ping. For example, if you want to ping a computer at the IP address 192.168.1.105, you would type **ping 192.168.1.105**.

4. View the output to determine whether the packets were received by the destination computer and whether you received the reply.

```
 Command Prompt                                            _ ☐ ☒

Microsoft Windows XP [Version 5.1.2600]
(C) Copyright 1985-2001 Microsoft Corp.

C:\Documents and Settings\Bill  Ferguson.XP1>ping 192.168.1.105

Pinging 192.168.1.105 with 32 bytes of data:

Reply from 192.168.1.105: bytes=32 time=1ms TTL=128
Reply from 192.168.1.105: bytes=32 time<1ms TTL=128
Reply from 192.168.1.105: bytes=32 time=1ms TTL=128
Reply from 192.168.1.105: bytes=32 time=1ms TTL=128

Ping statistics for 192.168.1.105:
    Packets: Sent = 4, Received = 4, Lost = 0 (0% loss),
Approximate round trip times in milli-seconds:
    Minimum = 0ms, Maximum = 1ms, Average = 0ms

C:\Documents and Settings\Bill  Ferguson.XP1>_
```

5. If you received a reply, then your computer has physical and logical connectivity with the other computer. If you did not receive a reply, then you may be lacking physical connectivity, logical connectivity, or both.

If you receive a reply from a loopback test, you can also ping the IP address of the local computer to determine whether the network interface card is functional.

The ping tool can also be used to perform a special test that verifies that TCP/IP is installed and functioning in a computer. This test is referred to as a loopback test. The computer's own network adapter is, by default, assigned a special IP address when TCP/IP is installed, in addition to any IP address you may assign to it manually or that it may get from a DHCP server. This address is called the loopback address, and it is from the 127 address range. Pinging this address tells you whether or not the TCP/IP software (or stack, as it is sometimes called) is installed properly on your machine. Exercise 6.8 walks you through the steps to perform a loopback test.

EXERCISE 6.8

Performing a Loopback Test with Ping

1. On the Windows XP Desktop, click Start and then choose Run.

2. On the Run line, type **cmd** to access a command prompt.

3. On the command prompt, type **ping 127.0.0.1** or type **ping loopback**.

4. View the output to determine whether the packets were sent from and received back to the interface of your computer. If you receive a reply, then TCP/IP is installed and operating. If you do not receive a reply, then the TCP/IP protocol should be reinstalled in the computer.

```
C:\WINDOWS\system32\cmd.exe                                    _ □ x

C:\>ping 127.0.0.1

Pinging 127.0.0.1 with 32 bytes of data:

Reply from 127.0.0.1: bytes=32 time=4ms TTL=128
Reply from 127.0.0.1: bytes=32 time<1ms TTL=128
Reply from 127.0.0.1: bytes=32 time<1ms TTL=128
Reply from 127.0.0.1: bytes=32 time<1ms TTL=128

Ping statistics for 127.0.0.1:
    Packets: Sent = 4, Received = 4, Lost = 0 (0% loss),
Approximate round trip times in milli-seconds:
    Minimum = 0ms, Maximum = 4ms, Average = 1ms

C:\>
```

Real World Scenario

How to Keep from Standing on Your Head!

I've read in many books that tell you the best way to test any new TCP/IP connection is to first ping the loopback, then ping the local address, then ping a computer in your intranet, and finally ping something outside your intranet. Personally, I don't agree with using that method at all—if you set up the connection to connect to the Internet. If that's the case, then why don't you just go to a browser and type an address that you know will be there, such as, for instance, Sybex.com? If you get the Sybex home page, then I can guarantee you that you will be able to ping your loopback address!

However, there is one very good method that you can use to troubleshoot a new connection. In fact, if you do this right, it will literally keep you from standing on your head. Are you interested? Good, then listen closely.

Let's say that you don't get Sybex.com and instead you get the dreaded "Page cannot be displayed" error message. What do you do next? Well, what a lot of people do is begin making sure that their network interface card link lights are lit to eliminate the network interface card as part of the problem. This usually entails pulling the computer away from a wall or desk or leaning way over the computer (standing on your head) to see if the link light on the network interface card is properly lit, indicating that the cable is plugged in and the card is working.

Well, here's an easier way. First ping the local loopback (127.0.0.1) and see if you get a reply. If there is no reply, then reinstall TCP/IP. If there is a reply, then ping the IP address assigned to the computer. (If the IP address is normally assigned by a DHCP server, then assign a temporary address that is not in use, just so you can ping it. The address 1.1.1.1 should do just fine on most networks.) If you get a reply, then the card works! If you don't get a reply, then the card doesn't work. If the card doesn't work, it's either a physical problem or drivers.

Now, reach your hand around the back of the computer and make sure that the RJ-45 plug is securely plugged in. Don't worry about the link light on that end. Next, check the hub or switch for a link light. This is often easier than standing on your head. Remember that both sides would have to be properly connected to get a link light at the hub or switch. If the link light on the hub or switch is lit, then the only thing left is the drivers. You should uninstall the network interface card drivers and restart the computer, look for any connection errors when the computer comes back up, and then reinstall the drivers. Oh, and if the light is not lit, then you may be forced to replace a cable or a network interface card, but at least you didn't have to stand on your head!

Using the Pathping Tool

The pathping tool is a command-line tool that is very similar to the ping tool. You can use the pathping tool to test connectivity between computers. The main difference between the pathping tool and the ping tool is that the pathping tool sends back information about each of the hops that the packets take toward their destination address. If you are in a network that uses a series of routers to connect computers and servers, you can use the pathping tool to determine which of your routers might be down or improperly configured. You can also use pathping across the Internet (from firewall to firewall), but the output may be of limited use to your organization because you don't control all of the routers. Pathping also calculates statistics of packets sent and lost over a 25-second time period and determines the percentage of packet loss. This allows you to identify a connection that is working intermittently, referred to as "flapping." Exercise 6.9 illustrates the use of the pathping tool in Windows XP.

EXERCISE 6.9

Testing Connectivity between Computers Using the Pathping Tool

1. On the Windows XP Desktop, click Start and then select Run.

2. On the Run line, type **cmd** to open a command prompt.

3. At the command prompt, type **pathping**, then type a space, and then type the IP address of the computer that you want to ping. For example, if you want to pathping a computer at the IP address 192.168.1.105, you would type **pathping 192.168.1.105**.

4. View the output to determine the path that the packets are taking as they travel toward their destination and how far they actually get. You can use this information to determine which router may be down or incorrectly configured.

```
Command Prompt                                              _ ⊟ ×

Microsoft Windows XP [Version 5.1.2600]
(C) Copyright 1985-2001 Microsoft Corp.

C:\Documents and Settings\Bill  Ferguson.XP1>pathping 192.168.1.105

Tracing route to 192.168.1.105 over a maximum of 30 hops

  0  xp1.mshome.net [192.168.1.10]
  1  192.168.1.105

Computing statistics for 25 seconds...
            Source to Here   This Node/Link
Hop  RTT    Lost/Sent = Pct  Lost/Sent = Pct  Address
  0                                            xp1.mshome.net [192.168.1.10]
                                0/ 100 =  0%   |
  1    0ms     0/ 100 =  0%    0/ 100 =  0%   192.168.1.105

Trace complete.

C:\Documents and Settings\Bill  Ferguson.XP1>
```

5. The system will calculate lost/sent packets and determine a percentage loss of packets sent. You can use this information to identify a connection that is flapping.

Name Resolution Troubleshooting

As we mentioned earlier, network administrators use user-friendly names rather than cumbersome IP addresses to refer to computers on a network. This makes it easier to manage and troubleshoot a network that contains many computers. They then use files and services to convert the user-friendly names back to IP addresses. Since the client uses these files and services to locate computers and resources in the network, you should know how to configure the client computers to use them. There are two main types of user-friendly names that can be used in a network: NetBIOS names and hostnames. In the following sections, we will define each of these types of user-friendly names and illustrate how you can configure and troubleshoot a client computer for name resolution in a network.

NetBIOS Names

NetBIOS is the name of the standard built-in name resolution method that Microsoft operating systems have used since Windows 3.*x*. It was originally intended for use in very small networks. A *NetBIOS name* is the most basic name that a computer can have, sometimes referred to as a computer name. As you may remember, you enter this name (or accept the default name from the system) every time you install Microsoft operating system software on a computer and indicate that it will be used in a network. This name can be up to 15 characters in length. Computers in the same network can recognize one another by their NetBIOS names, but it's not that simple. Actually, each computer is given several similar NetBIOS names based on services that it can offer the network, so one computer can actually have many NetBIOS names. The only thing that is really different about the names is the end of the name that is assigned by the system, referred to as the 16th character.

As you may remember, computers recognize one another by the MAC addresses burned into their network interface cards. Since you can use ARP only to convert an IP address to a MAC address, you have to use other services to first convert the user-friendly NetBIOS names to IP addresses. There are two main methods of converting NetBIOS names to IP addresses: LMHOSTS files and WINS servers. In the following sections, we will discuss how each of these name resolution methods operates and illustrate how you can configure a Windows XP client to use them.

LMHOSTS Files

An LMHOSTS (stands for LAN Manager Hosts) file is a text file that can be used by a computer to convert a known NetBIOS name to an IP address. Figure 6.2 is a very simple example of a portion of an LMHOSTS file. If LMHOSTS files are used, the network administrators must manually keep them up-to-date. Each computer can have a LMHOSTS file, so anytime there is a change in a computer's NetBIOS name, or if a computer is added to or taken away from the network, this file has to be manually updated on each and every computer using it to reflect the changes. For this reason, only smaller networks using older Microsoft operating system software make use of LMHOSTS files, and they have largely been replaced by more sophisticated and more automatic name resolution methods. You do not need to be an expert at the creation or use of LMHOSTS files, but you do need to know whether your network uses them and how to configure your clients properly based on that knowledge. Exercise 6.10 walks you through the steps to configure a client to use the LMHOSTS files if they are present.

FIGURE 6.2   An example LMHOSTS file

102.54.94.97	SQLsrv
102.54.94.102	app server
102.54.94.123	mailsrv
102.54.94.117	localsrv

WARNING

You should consult with the network administrator before making any change regarding the name resolution configuration of computers. If the LMHOSTS file is incorrect, the computers may not be able to obtain proper NetBIOS name resolution, even if other services, such as WINS, are working properly.

WINS

Windows Internet Name Service (WINS) servers are used by network administrators to automate the process of name resolution. A WINS server works like a hotel registration desk. When a client computer is started on a network, it registers its NetBIOS name (computer name) and its IP address with the WINS server. When another computer wants to convert a NetBIOS name to an IP address, it can consult the WINS server for the address. When users correctly shut down a computer, the NetBIOS name is automatically removed from the WINS database. Network administrators often use DHCP servers to automatically configure the correct WINS address in clients on their networks. It actually gets "a bit" more complicated than that from an administrator's viewpoint, but fortunately for you, you don't have to be a WINS expert. You do, however, have to know how to verify and configure a client's WINS server setting. Exercise 6.11 walks you through the steps to verify a current WINS setting and configure a new setting.

EXERCISE 6.10

Configuring Clients to Use LMHOSTS Files

1.   On the Windows XP Desktop, click Start and then choose Network Connections.

2.   On the Network Connections window, click the connection that you want to configure. On a computer with multiple connections, you can actually choose any connection because the LMHOSTS configuration change will apply to all connections.

3. In the selected connection's Properties dialog box, double-click Internet Protocol (TCP/IP), and then click the Advanced button.

4. In the Advanced TCP/IP Settings dialog, choose the WINS tab.

5. Examine the Enable LMHOSTS Lookup check box in the center of the Advanced TCP/IP Settings dialog box. With a default installation of Windows XP, the check box should be checked, indicating that the computer will use the LMHOSTS files.

6. If the Enable LMHOSTS Lookup check box is not checked, click in the box to place the check mark. You can also click the Import LMHOSTS button to specify the locations of other LMHOSTS files that the computer should also check. You should consult with the network administrator before taking this step.

7. If you have made any configuration changes, click OK three times to exit and save the changes.

EXERCISE 6.11

Verifying and Configuring a Client Computer's WINS Setting

1. On the Windows XP Desktop, click Start and then choose Network Connections.

2. In the Network Connections window, click the connection that you want to configure.

3. In the selected connection's Properties dialog box, double-click Internet Protocol (TCP/IP), and then click the Advanced button.

4. In the Advanced TCP/IP Settings dialog box, choose the WINS tab.

5. At the top of the WINS tab, view the WINS Addresses, in Order of Use field. Clients can be configured with as many as 12 WINS server addresses but typically will have only 1 or 2. Verify with the network administrator that the addresses configured are valid addresses for WINS servers on your network.

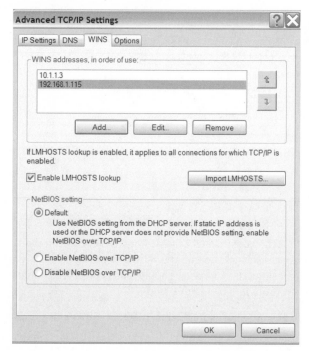

6. Use the Add, Edit, and Remove buttons to make any necessary changes. You can also use the arrows to the right of the field to reorder the use of the WINS servers.

7. Click OK three times to exit and save the changes.

Hostnames

Whereas NetBIOS names can be used effectively within each local area network, they cannot be used between networks, nor can they be used on the Internet. For this reason, network administrators assign yet another type of name to each computer on most networks. This name is referred to as a *hostname*. Since hostnames can be used between networks as well as within the same network, most of the newest client operating systems and applications make use of hostnames instead of NetBIOS names. Windows XP and Windows 2000 Professional clients use hostnames by default to identify computers.

Network administrators use special servers called Domain Name System (DNS) servers to convert hostnames to IP addresses. DNS servers contain databases that pair up a hostname with an IP address. Network administrators once maintained these databases manually, but now much of the process of maintaining the DNS servers has been automated. DNS servers can communicate with other DNS servers to share their information and redirect clients and servers to other IP addresses.

Client computers and applications use the DNS server to convert a known hostname to an IP address so that a client or router can eventually use ARP to convert the IP address to a MAC address. Client computers rely on these servers for communication within their own network as well as on the Internet. For this reason, it's very important that clients be configured with the proper IP addresses for the DNS servers that they need to use. Network administrators often use DHCP servers to automate the configuration of the correct IP address on each client. Again, from a network administrator's point of view, it gets a bit more complex, but you do not need to be a DNS expert. You should, however, know how to verify the DNS hostname of a client and the DNS server addresses that are configured for the client. You should also know how to configure DNS addresses for a client if needed. Exercise 6.12 walks you through the steps to verify and configure a hostname.

EXERCISE 6.12

Verifying and Configuring a Client's Hostname

1. On the Windows XP Desktop, right-click My Computer and then choose Properties.

2. In the System Properties dialog box, choose the Computer Name tab.

3. Read the computer name listed after Full Computer Name field. On Windows XP computers, this is the hostname. The first part of the name is also usually the NetBIOS name of the computer. In this case, the hostname is xpclient and the full computer name is xpclient.bfe.com. The computer is a member of the domain bfe.com.

4. If you need to rename the computer, click the Change button, and then type the new computer name in the Computer Name box. You should consult with the network administrator before renaming a computer since it's very important that all computer names be unique within a network.

5. To save any changes, click OK twice to exit. You will also need to restart the computer to make the changes effective.

Exercise 6.13 walks you through the steps to verify and configure DNS server addresses.

EXERCISE 6.13

Verifying and Configuring DNS Server Addresses for Clients

1. On the Windows XP Desktop, click Start and then choose Network Connections.

2. In the Network Connections window, choose the connection that you want to configure.

3. In the selected connection's Properties dialog box, double-click Internet Protocol (TCP/IP), and then click the Advanced button.

4. In the Advanced TCP/IP Settings dialog box, choose the DNS tab.

5. Examine the DNS Server Addresses, in the Order of Use field at the top of the DNS tab. Verify with the network administrator that the addresses listed are valid DNS server addresses.

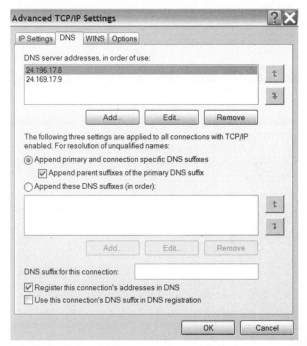

6. Use the Add, Edit, and Remove buttons to make changes to the configuration of the addresses. You can also use the arrows to the right of the field to reorder the use of the DNS servers.

7. Click OK three times to exit and save the changes.

Name Resolution Troubleshooting Tools

Windows XP and Windows 2000 Professional clients have many tools that you can use to troubleshoot name resolution. Many of these tools can be used to troubleshoot other issues as well. In fact, we discussed some of these tools in relation to troubleshooting connectivity and IP addresses. In the following sections, we will focus on the main tools that you can use to troubleshoot name resolution for a client.

Ipconfig

Ipconfig is a very flexible command-line tool that can be used to display, release, and renew IP addresses and name resolution configurations if they are not manually set. You can use the forward slash switch (/) to indicate the option of ipconfig that you want to use. Table 6.1 illustrates the `ipconfig` command options available and the function of each. You can also view these options by typing **ipconfig /?** on a command line and pressing the Enter key.

TABLE 6.1 Command Options for Ipconfig

Command Option	function
/all	Displays all configuration information, including addresses of WINS, DNS, and DHCP servers
/release	Instructs the DHCP server to release the IP address for a specified connection
/renew	Instructs the DHCP server to renew the IP address for a specified connection
/registerdns	Refreshes all DHCP server leases and registers or reregisters the client's DNS name with the DNS server

Ping

Earlier you learned about ping as a connectivity tool, but you can also use ping as a name resolution tool. As you may recall, you can ping the IP address of another computer to establish connectivity with that computer. Well, what if you didn't ping the IP address but instead you pinged the computer name of the computer? Then you would test not just connectivity but also name resolution. In fact, if you pinged the IP address and got a reply and then pinged the computer name and did not get a reply, you could be sure that name resolution was at fault.

Now, you might be thinking, "Yes, but would I be pinging the NetBIOS name or the hostname?" Actually, it depends on which type of client you happen to be using. On Windows XP and Windows 2000 Professional clients, when you ping from a command line, you are pinging the hostname of the client first. On older clients, you are pinging the NetBIOS name first. You can further specify a hostname on a computer that is in a domain by typing the entire hostname and domain name in succession using decimal points between each part. This is referred to as a fully qualified domain name (FQDN). For example, the FQDN of a computer with the name XP1 located in DomainA.com would be XP1.DomainA.com. The name listed as the full computer name for a Windows XP client in a domain will be its FQDN. Only the first part of the name is the NetBIOS name. You can ping the FQDN of another computer from any client to make sure that you are testing hostname resolution and not NetBIOS name resolution.

If you don't get a reply when you ping an IP address or a computer name, then you will receive an error message. Windows clients use three primary error messages to give you hints as to what to fix. You should be familiar with the following three error messages and each of their meanings:

- Destination host unreachable. This error message indicates that there is a problem at the IP routing level between your computer and the remote host. You should escalate this issue to the network administrator.

- Unknown host *hostname*. This error message indicates that none of the name resolution mechanisms recognize the name that you typed. You should check to make sure that you typed the right name and try again. If you are still unsuccessful, then you should escalate this issue to the network administrator.

- Request timed out. This message indicates that at least one name resolution mechanism did recognize the name but the target either did not receive the request or did not respond to it. In this case, you should focus on connectivity between the name resolution mechanism and the remote host.

Nslookup

The *nslookup* tool is a command-line tool that uses DNS to translate a computer name to an IP address. You can use the nslookup tool to test hostname resolution and to verify that the remote computer is registered in the DNS server(s). You can test hostname resolution by typing **nslookup** followed by the FQDN of the computer. The result should be the IP address assigned to the computer.

You can also use several different nslookup options by typing **nslookup** and then typing the appropriate option. You can run the nslookup tool in interactive mode by typing **nslookup** on a command line with no options and pressing the Enter key. In interactive mode, you can view the options available by typing a question mark (**?**) and pressing the Enter key. You see an example of the **nslookup** command in Figure 6.3.

FIGURE 6.3   The nslookup command

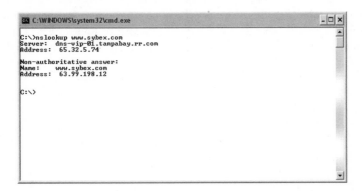

Net

The *net* commands are primarily used to view the network settings assigned to a computer. The net commands also have many options. The main name resolution testing option in the net command tool is the `net config workstation` command, which reports the NetBIOS name and domain name for the computer. You can get more information about the net commands by typing **net help** on a command line.

Nbtstat

You can use the *nbtstat* command to manage NetBIOS name information and display statistics and details regarding current TCP/IP connections. The nbtstat tool has many options as well. You can view all of the options of the nbtstat tool by typing **nbtstat /?** on a command prompt. You should be familiar with the three most common options of the nbtstat tool and the function of each option, as shown in Table 6.2.

TABLE 6.2 Command Options for Nbtstat

Command	Function
nbtstat -n	Lists all of the NetBIOS names registered by a client
nbtstat -c	Displays the NetBIOS name cache showing NetBIOS names recently resolved to IP addresses
nbtstat -R	Manually reloads the NetBIOS name cache with special entries from the LMHOSTS file

Remote Connections

Unfortunately, your work doesn't have to stop just because you leave the office. You and the users you serve can connect to your organization's network from home or from a hotel using *remote connections*. The Network Connections tool in Windows XP enables you to configure two main types of connections: *dial-up* and *Virtual Private Network (VPN)*. You should know how to use the Network Connections tool to configure both types of connections. You should also know the main differences between these types of connections and how to troubleshoot each of them.

VPN stands for Virtual Private Network, but is sometimes used to denote an action, such as Virtual Private Networking

Dial-up Connections

The term *dial-up connections* is most often used to refer to connections that are made using analog modems and ordinary telephone lines. Dial-up connections are generally inexpensive to use and are readily available, but they have very limited bandwidth. These connections are usually temporary in nature and are disconnected when the communication is finished. Other types of dial-up connections include Integrated Services Digital Network (ISDN) connections, which use special lines, provided by the phone company, that offer greater bandwidth. Both types of dial-up connections are sometimes used to provide a backup line of communication for a more costly dedicated line. Dial-up connections are used to connect to an Internet service provider (ISP) or, in the case of remote connections, to a special server located inside your company's network (called a remote access server) to access your company's network resources remotely.

You can use the Network Connections tool to configure dial-up connections for a client computer and a user. This tool provides a wizard to help you configure many types of connections, which can include connections to ISPs as well as other telephone connections to a configured modem. You should know how to configure and troubleshoot dial-up connections in Windows XP. Exercise 6.14 walks you through the steps to configure connections using the Network Connections tool and the New Connection Wizard.

Troubleshooting Dial-up Connections

Troubleshooting dial-up connections, like all troubleshooting, is a process of isolating the problem. You should understand that the main components involved in the communication are your modem, the connection between your modem and the remote modem, and the remote modem. A bad configuration or a problem on either end of the communication can cause the communication to fail. You should first make sure that the username and password are correctly configured on the connection. Then, since modems sometimes malfunction, you should test your modem to make sure that the problem is not hardware related. While you cannot always test the remote modem, you can perform a test on your own modem to determine whether it is working properly. Exercise 6.15 walks you through the steps to test your modem.

EXERCISE 6.14

Configuring Dial-up Connections Using the Network Connections Tool

1. On the Windows XP Desktop, click Start, choose Connect To, and then choose Show All Connections.

2. In the Network Connections tool, view the connections that are set up, and then select Create a New Connection under Network Tasks on the upper-left corner or choose Network Connections. This will open the New Connection Wizard.

3. On the opening screen of the New Connection Wizard, click Next.

4. Select Connect to the Network at My Workplace, click Next, choose the type of dial-up connection, and click Next again.

5. Type a name for your connection (any name will suffice) and then click Next.

6. Type the phone number that you want to dial and then click Next.

7. Click Finish to create the connection and exit the wizard.

EXERCISE 6.15

Performing a Test on a Modem

1. On the Windows XP Desktop, click Start and then choose Control Panel.

2. In Control Panel, choose Phone and Modem Options and then choose the Modems tab.

3. In the Modem Properties dialog box, choose the modem that you want to test and then click Properties.

4. In the Properties dialog box for the modem that you want to test, choose the Diagnostics tab and then click Query Modem.

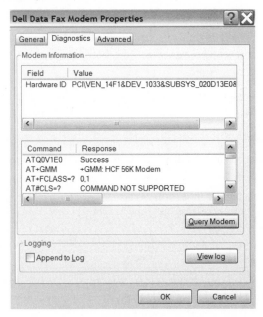

5. View the output in the Response section. A modem that is properly configured and connected to a telephone line should indicate Success. If the output does not read Success, then examine the output for clues as to why the modem did not test successfully (e.g., No Dial Tone Detected).

To perform a very simple test of a remote modem, you can just dial the modem with any telephone and see if it answers. Sometimes the simplest solutions are best!

VPN Connections

In the late 1990s, as remote computing became increasingly popular, dial-up connections presented two problems. First, they required a modem or modem-type of connection for every communication with the server. Second, and most important, the calls from users who were out of town incurred long-distance charges. Businesses needed a way to have secure communications with less cost.

Since the use of the Internet was also growing during this time, businesses began to use the Internet to their advantage for remote connections. VPN emerged as a new technology. Essentially, VPN operates in the following manner:

1. The user dials their Internet service provider (ISP) with a local call.

2. The ISP provides a VPN server that negotiates which tunneling and encryption protocols it will use to provide a secure connection through an unsecured medium, the Internet.

3. The VPN server connects the client to the organization's corporate servers.

4. The client logs on to the corporate servers for secure access to resources.

There are two main types of VPNs:

- Network-to-network (sometimes called site-to-site). This type of connection is used from one office of an organization to another office, such as from a branch office to a main office. These are generally used to save costs compared to leasing expensive dedicated lines. VPN connections are made from one server, at the branch office site, for instance, to a VPN server at the main site. Clients do not have to make any special connections and are virtually unaware of the VPN.

- Host-network. This type of connection is used by a remote office worker in an organization, such as a person who works from home or from a hotel room. The main reasons that this type of VPN is preferred over standard dial-up are that it reduces the cost of maintaining modem pools and it eliminates long-distance charges provided a local ISP telephone number is available.

You can use the Network Connections tool in Windows XP to configure a VPN on a client. All you need to know is the IP address or FQDN of the server to which you want to connect. Of course, the user will have to authenticate to the server after the connection is established. Exercise 6.16 walks you through the steps to configure a VPN connection on a Windows XP client.

Troubleshooting VPN Connections

Since VPN connections are relatively simple to create, they are also relatively simple to troubleshoot. If there is a problem connecting with a VPN, it will most likely involve the IP address or hostname used for the connection. You should recheck the connection and make sure the computer to which you are connecting has not been changed. If you are using the hostname, then try using the IP address instead, just in case the problem has to do with name resolution.

EXERCISE 6.16

Configuring a VPN Connection

1. On the Windows XP Desktop, click Start, choose Connect To, and then choose Show All Connections.

2. In the Network Connections tool, view the connections that are set up, and then select Create a New Connection under Network Tasks in the upper-left corner or choose Network Connections. This will open up the New Connection Wizard.

3. On the opening screen of the New Connection Wizard, click Next.

4. Choose Connect to the Network at My Workplace, and then click Next.

5. Choose Virtual Private Network Connection, and then click Next.

6. Type a name for your connection (any name will suffice), and then click Next. (If you have ISP software installed in your computer, the wizard may also give you the option to let the connection dial the ISP automatically.)

7. Type the hostname (FQDN) or IP address of the computer to which you want to connect, and then click Next.

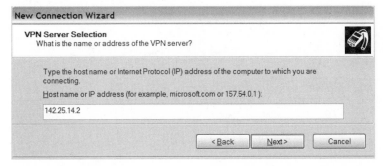

8. Click Finish to create the connection and exit the wizard.

A common problem with VPNs is that a user's Internet services may stop working after they connect to the VPN. This can occur because the VPN is attempting to use the *default gateway* of the remote computer for Internet service rather than its own default gateway. If this occurs on a corporate network, you may be required for security reasons to leave the setting as it is and provide a proxy connection on the remote network for the connection to use. In this case, you should consult with the network administrator to get the proxy address set up. On the other hand, if this occurs on a single computer or even in a small workgroup, you can change the default gateway setting to the local default gateway to provide Internet access for the client while still using the VPN. Exercise 6.17 walks you through the steps to change the default gateway setting for the computer.

EXERCISE 6.17

Changing the Default Gateway of a VPN Connection to the Local Default Gateway

1. On the Windows XP Desktop, click Start, choose Connect To, and then choose Show All Connections.

2. On the Network Connections window, right-click the VPN connection that you want to change and then choose Properties.

3. In the connection's Properties dialog box, click the Networking tab, select Internet Protocol (TCP/IP), and then choose Properties.

4. On the Internet Protocol (TCP/IP) Properties dialog box, click Advanced.

5. On the General tab of the Advanced TCP/IP Settings dialog box, clear the Use Default Gateway on Remote Network check box.

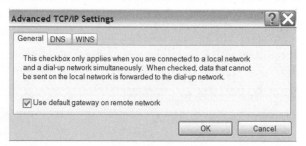

6. Click OK three times to save your settings and exit.

Internet Explorer

Microsoft's Internet Explorer has become the preferred browser of Internet users around the world. What we refer to as the Internet is actually an internetwork of routers, switches, and servers that spans the globe. Most people have no idea how it all works any more than they know how electricity or phone connections come into their home. The main reason that they don't know is that they don't need to know. Browsers such as Internet Explorer make the process of finding websites as easy as dialing a telephone, sometimes even easier!

Actually, browsing with Internet Explorer is easy for a user only if their software is configured properly, so that's where you come in! You should know how to configure and troubleshoot Microsoft Internet Explorer for a user. Most of the configuration of Internet Explorer can be performed via the Tools menu under Internet Options. Your troubleshooting ability relies on your knowledge of what can be configured and how it should be configured. There are seven tabs included in Internet Options: General, Security, Privacy, Content, Connections, Programs, and Advanced. In the following sections, we will discuss all seven tabs with special emphasis on the General, Security, and Connections tabs.

General Tab

The General tab of Internet Options contains three main tools to assist the user in browsing the Internet. As shown in Figure 6.4, the General tab has three main areas of configuration:

Home Page   The home page is the default page that Internet Explorer opens to when you simply click the Internet Explorer icon or the Home icon (which resembles a house) on the toolbar. You can set the default page to any address you choose. You can also browse to a page first and then click Use Current to set that page as the default page. In addition, you can click Use Default to return to the default home page at `msn.com`. Finally, you can click Use Blank to use a blank page for your home page. Whichever you select, you can very easily change it at any time.

Temporary Internet Files   When a user views pages on the Internet, the software automatically stores the addresses of those pages so that they can be accessed when they want to view the same page again. Some pages download special programs to make it easier to access the site when a user returns. These special programs are referred to as *cookies*. You can set the behavior of Internet Explorer in regard to temporary Internet files and cookies. You can click Delete Cookies to remove all of the old cookies from a computer. You can click Delete Files to remove offline and online temporary Internet files. Finally, you can click Settings to view the individual cookies and files and configure the amount of space that will be used on your computer for these types of files and the location of the folder where they will be stored. You can also indicate how often the computer should check for new versions of pages that are in these files.

History   When a user views a page on the Internet, the software keeps a history of the pages that were viewed. This history can be used to quickly access the pages at a later date using the

History icon on the toolbar. You can set how many days of history are stored. This setting can range from 0 (no history) to 999 days! The History tool will sort the pages by the day, week, month, and year that they were last accessed.

FIGURE 6.4 The General tab of Internet Options

Security Tab

Let's face it; the Internet is not always a kind place. There are many sites on the Internet that contain files that might harm your computer. There are also many sites that you probably use every day and that you therefore trust. Internet Explorer has the capability of automatically downloading files and running scripts that can make your browsing experience more enjoyable. Unfortunately, some people can take advantage of these settings to install and run programs on your computer that could damage it and the data it contains.

To get the best of both worlds, you can use the settings on the Security tab of Internet Explorer Security Options to divide all of the sites on the Web into web content zones for the purpose of security; then you can allow specific functions based on zone type. As shown in Figure 6.5, there are four main web content zones:

Internet This is default zone that contains all of the websites that you haven't placed in any other zone. This zone should be configured to give sites limited ability to run scripts or download files that might be harmful to your computer.

Local Intranet   This zone contains the websites that are located on your organization's intranet. This zone should be configured based on how much you trust your own organization's content.

Trusted Sites   This zone contains sites that you trust not to damage your computer or data. Trusted sites are typically given the ability to run scripts and download files that other sites cannot run or download. You can also specify that only secure (`https://`) connections are allowed in this zone.

Restricted Sites   You should add to this list any site on which you discovered harmful content. You should then configure the site to disallow scripts and downloads. The user will still be able to access the site, but their content options will be limited and therefore their computer will be more secure.

You have the ability to configure security settings for each zone. When selecting the zone, simply click the Custom Level button in the area on the Security tab marked Security Level for This Zone. You can then set the different security options for the zone, such as whether to run scripts, allow active content, and so forth.

FIGURE 6.5   Security options and web content zones

Privacy Tab

Have you ever been required to enter your username and create a password in order to access the site? Have you ever accessed that site again from the same computer and found that it was no longer necessary to enter your username and password? If so, then you have used a cookie. Cookies are special files that can contain user information and can give that user information to another party. While cookies can be helpful when used properly, they can be very dangerous to your privacy if they are used improperly. Some cookies can even track all of your browsing activity! The Privacy tab of Internet Options contains settings that allow you to control how cookies can be used on your computer. The Privacy tab settings apply only to the Internet zone and not the other zones.

The privacy settings you can apply to the Internet zone range from very restrictive (Block All Cookies) to very relaxed (Accept All Cookies), with several options in between. Of course, blocking all cookies will prevent a lot of functionality when you are using the Internet, and the opposite extreme, Accept All Cookies, is a very unsecure setting. Usually, one of the in-between settings is right for the Internet zone. These settings include High, Medium High, Medium, and Low. As you select each one, you will get a brief description of what it allows and blocks. By default, the settings are configured for the Medium-High level.

Content Tab

The Content tab is divided into three sections: Content Advisor, Certificates, and Personal Information. Content Advisor contains settings that allow you to use a rating system to determine sites that can be viewed on the computer provided the sites you add to it or visit use this system. Inside the Content Advisor, there are four tabs: Ratings, Approved Sites, General, and Advanced. The Ratings tab lists the categories as defined by the Internet Content Rating Association (formerly the Recreational Software Advisory Council, hence the acronym RSACi above the categories). These categories can be adjusted to specific levels to dictate what content computer users are allowed to view. The Approved Sites tab gives you the opportunity to specifically state which sites are allowed or disallowed regardless of rating or lack thereof. The General tab allows you as the administrator to set a password that you would have to type in to allow a user to view restricted content. The General tab also allows you to find other ratings systems published by other organizations that have differing categories. The final tab, Advanced, allows you to connect with Internet ratings bureaus and get ratings as well as automatically add approved/disapproved sites to your lists. You can see the Content Advisor settings in Figure 6.6.

The Certificates section is used to manage digital certificates that will be used for Secure Sockets Layer (SSL) communication to a website. These certificates, and their publishers, can be added to your machine's store of trusted certificates and publishers. You can also clear your SSL state in this section, which may help clear up connection problems to secure sites when expired, invalid, or corrupt certificates stored on your machine may be an issue. The Personal Information section contains settings for AutoComplete, which stores previous browser entries and suggests matches, and My Profile, which allows you to choose your personal profile from your email address book or create a new profile for use on the Internet. It is not necessary that you create a profile, but it can sometimes be used as a convenience instead of entering information into a form on a web page. In this section, you can also clear out any passwords (as well as prevent their storage in the first place) saved by Internet Explorer for use in frequently visited websites.

FIGURE 6.6   The Content Advisor

Connections Tab

The Connections tab in Internet Options contains two main sections, as shown in Figure 6.7. You should know how to configure all settings in both sections. In the paragraphs that follow, we will discuss each section in detail.

The first section of the Connections tab contains a list of the dial-up and VPN connections configured on the computer. You can configure a default connection to be dialed automatically any time Internet Explorer is used or to dial only if a network connection is not present. You can also configure Internet Explorer to never use a default connection. You can add or remove connections using the Add and Remove buttons. In addition, you can use the Settings button to configure a connection to use a proxy server. In this case, you should obtain the correct settings for the proxy server from your network administrator.

You should be aware that removing a connection on the Connections tab of Internet Options in Internet Explorer will delete the connection from the computer, not just from Internet Explorer.

FIGURE 6.7   The Connections tab of Internet Options

The second section is for local area network (LAN) settings. Click the LAN Settings button to configure manual or automatic settings for network connections and proxy servers. You should consult with your network administrator to obtain the information for these settings. It may also be necessary to choose the LAN settings options and place a check mark in the Bypass Proxy Server for Local Addresses box to give users access to sites that are within your intranet. Incorrect proxy server settings can result in an inability to connect to websites, so this is a key section to check if you are experiencing issues connecting to the Web, after you have already ruled out network connectivity and name resolution as potential problems.

Programs Tab

The Programs tab of Internet Options contains the settings for default applications that Windows will use for specific tasks. Examples include email, Internet calls, contact lists, and so on. You can choose from among the applications that are installed in your computer and have the appropriate functionality. You can use the drop-down box in each category to view the options for that category and make your choice.

Advanced Tab

The Advanced tab contains the settings for fine-tuning all aspects of Internet Explorer. Examples include browsing options, multimedia, and additional security options. You can choose the options that you want by clicking each check box to indicate that you want to configure that option.

Remote Connectivity Tools

The days of having to go to a user's computer to troubleshoot it are long gone. Windows XP provides two tools that enable a network administrator, desktop support technician, or even another user to assist a user in troubleshooting and repairing their computer: *Remote Desktop* and *Remote Assistance*. These two tools are very similar in that they both use the Remote Desktop Protocol (RDP) to provide the remote connection to the computer. There are, however, significant differences in regard to the manner in which they are used and the tasks that can be performed with each tool.

You should know where each of these tools can be found in Windows XP. You should also understand how to use Remote Desktop and Remote Assistance to troubleshoot a user's computer. In addition, you should know what situations call for the use of one tool over the other. In the following sections, we will discuss the use each of these tools in detail.

Remote Desktop

The Remote Desktop tool enables a computer to control another computer remotely over the local intranet or even over the Internet. Once you have established a Remote Desktop connection, you can control the remote computer as if you were sitting in front of it. The computer that is establishing the connection is referred to as the client computer. The computer that it is connecting to is referred to as the remote computer. You should know the requirements for each of these computers to use Remote Desktop. You should also know how to set permissions for users of Remote Desktop. Finally, you should know how to configure, connect to, and troubleshoot Remote Desktop for intranet- as well as Internet-based connections. We will discuss each of these concepts in detail.

Remote Desktop Requirements

The requirements for Remote Desktop are as follows:

- The remote computer must be running Windows XP Professional.
- The remote computer must have Remote Desktop connections enabled.
- The client computer must be running Windows 95 or later and must have Remote Desktop connection client software installed.
- Only one connection (local or remote) is possible.

Remote Desktop Permissions

By default, the following users can connect to the remote computer with Full Control permissions:

- The account currently logged on to the computer
- All members of the local Administrators group
- All members of the local Remote Desktop Users group

You can add users and groups to the default permissions using the Remote tab in System Properties in Control Panel. Just as with local files, permissions can be used to define the type of access that a user or group is granted in Remote Desktop. For example, you can allow some users to read information in files without giving them the ability to change the information, while other users can read the information and change it.

Configuring the Remote Computer

To connect to the remote computer running Windows XP Professional by using the Remote Desktop utility, you must enable Remote Desktop on the remote computer. Exercise 6.18 walks you through the steps to enable Remote Desktop on Windows XP.

EXERCISE 6.18

Configuring Remote Desktop on Windows XP

1. On the Windows XP Desktop, click Start and then select Control Panel.

2. In Control Panel, choose System.

3. On the Remote tab of the System Properties dialog box, select the Allow Users to Connect Remotely to This Computer check box.

4. Click OK to exit and save the changes.

Using Remote Desktop over an Intranet

Within a local network, any computer running the Remote Desktop client can easily connect to any Windows XP Professional computer that has Remote Desktop enabled. Exercise 6.19 walks you through the steps to connect to the remote computer using another Windows XP client.

EXERCISE 6.19

Connecting to a Remote Computer over an Intranet

1. On the Windows XP Desktop, click Start ➢ All Programs ➢ Accessories ➢ Communications ➢ Remote Desktop Connection.

2. On the Remote Desktop Connection window, type the NetBIOS name or the IP address of the remote computer in the Computer field and then click OK. The client computer will connect to the remote computer, and then you can log on to the remote computer.

Using Remote Desktop over the Internet

You can connect to a remote computer over the Internet with the same tools as those used to connect to a remote computer on an intranet, but there are some differences of which you must be aware. The following items should be considered:

- If the remote computer uses a modem, the modem must be installed and functional.
- If the remote computer is behind a firewall, then TCP port 3389 must be open.
- You will have to use the IP address of the remote computer, which may be more difficult to obtain, especially if it is assigned by a DHCP server. You should ask a user at the location of the remote computer to run the `ipconfig` command to determine the IP address.

Remote Assistance

Remote Assistance is a tool that is specifically designed to enable an administrator, desktop support technician, or even another user to help a user solve a computer-related problem. In order for Remote Assistance to work effectively, both users must be present at their computers and must agree to the establishment of a Remote Assistance connection. Remote Assistance requires either a Windows XP Professional or Windows XP Home Edition computer. You should know how Remote Assistance operates and the issues related to the configuration of Remote Assistance. In the following sections, we will discuss both of these concepts in detail.

Using Remote Assistance

The two parties involved in the Remote Assistance session are referred to as the expert and the novice. The Remote Assistance session is initialized in the following way:

1. The novice sends a Remote Assistance request, using either Windows Messenger or email. The user can also initiate this process by clicking Start, choosing All Programs, and then choosing Remote Assistance. This opens the Remote Assistance tool in Help and Support Center, shown in Figure 6.8. The request creates an invitation that is valid for a limited time as defined by the novice, with a default of one day.

FIGURE 6.8 The novice's Remote Assistance console

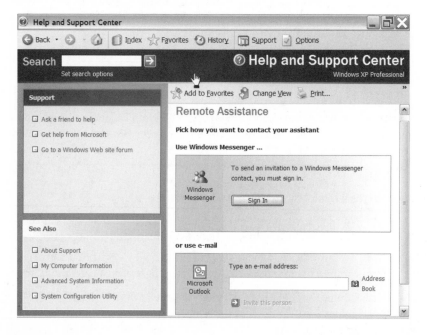

2. The expert accepts the invitation, which opens a terminal window displaying the desktop of the novice's computer along with the Control Panel for the expert, as shown in Figure 6.9. The expert can view the novice's computer in read-only mode and chat with the user. If the users have a headset or a microphone and speakers, they can even talk to each other through the network connection.

3. The expert can then request to take control of the novice's computer by clicking the Take Control button in the console on the expert's computer. This sends a message to the novice that the expert wants to take control.

FIGURE 6.9   The expert's Remote Assistance console before the expert takes control

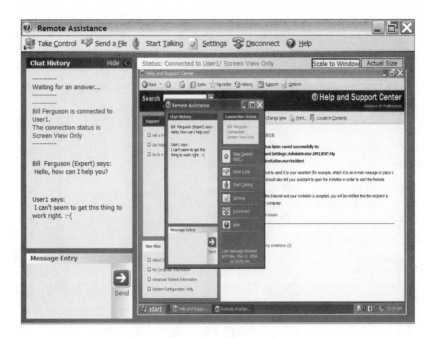

4. The novice must allow the expert to take control of the computer.

5. After the novice has allowed the expert to take control, the expert can transfer files to and from the novice's computer and change the computer's configuration to troubleshoot the problem.

6. After the problem has been repaired, the expert can click the Release Control button, shown in Figure 6.10, to give control back to the novice. The exert will not be able to start another Remote Assistance session without another invitation from the novice.

Configuring Remote Assistance

Remote Assistance is mostly configured by default, but you should be aware of the following:

- The computer must be a least a Windows XP Home Edition or Windows XP Professional computer.

- If the default settings have been changed, then you can use the Remote tab of the System Properties dialog box to configure the settings that control the issuance of invitations and the ability to take control of the computer. These are enabled by default.

- Using Remote Assistance through a firewall requires that TCP port 3389 be open.

- Using Remote Assistance through Network Address Translation (NAT) may require some additional configuration. In that case, you should consult with your network administrator.

FIGURE 6.10 The expert's Remote Assistance console after the expert takes control and begins to work

Case Study: Troubleshooting Network Connectivity

Troubleshooting is as much an art as a science. Not only do you need a well-rounded, solid foundation in the technologies you are using, you also need lots of experience to eventually be a good troubleshooter. There's an old saying that states, "Good judgment comes from experience. Experience comes from bad judgment." This is true even in the world of network connectivity troubleshooting. Take this case of a young desktop support technician for the Global Widgets Manufacturing Corporation, for example.

Bob was a desktop support technician newly assigned to the help desk for the Global Widgets Manufacturing Corporation. He was an experienced technician and had been working with small networks and Windows XP clients for a couple of years already before taking this new job. To learn the ins and outs of his new job quickly, he spent a considerable amount of time learning how the network was laid out, including the names and IP addresses of the DNS and WINS servers, the different client subnets, the proxy server settings, and anything else about the infrastructure he could get his hands on. By the end of his first week on the job, he felt confident that he could tackle any network connectivity issue unassisted. At least, until he got a phone call from a power user named Gerald.

Gerald reported that he could not connect to his email, shared network drives, or the Internet. To Bob, this seemed like a simple case to resolve, so he began to ask Gerald a few questions over the phone, the first of which was to find out if Gerald had changed any network settings himself. Of course, Gerald stated that he had not. So Bob began with the basics, as he'd been taught, and was sure he'd find the problem quickly. First, he asked Gerald to make sure the network cable was connected securely to the network card on the back of the computer, and Gerald confirmed that it was.

He then asked Gerald to ping his loopback address, and after he had explained to Gerald how to get to a command prompt and use the `ping` command, Gerald reported that he could ping his loopback. So far, so good. That meant that at least TCP/IP was working correctly. He next asked Gerald to run the `ipconfig` command on the machine. When asked about the results, Gerald reported that the he received a "Media disconnected" message. This meant to Bob, of course, that the cable wasn't properly connected to the network card. So he once again asked Gerald to check the cable connection. Once again, Gerald reported that the cable was securely connected. At this point, Bob was fairly certain that the network cable connection must be bad and decided he would go down the five floors that separated his office from Gerald's and fix the broken connector. As he headed out the door, he grabbed a RJ-45 crimp kit and a cable tester.

When he arrived at Gerald's desk, he got down on the floor, and although the area under Gerald's desk where his computer was located was dark and had cables and electrical cords running everywhere, Bob felt around and managed to find the network cable and unplugged it. He attached it to a cable tester first, and surprisingly, the cable tester reported it as a good connection. Shrugging his shoulders, he decided to reterminate the cable anyway.

Afterward, he tested the cable again, and once again, the cable tested as good. But when he plugged it back into the PC after fumbling around under the desk, the network connection still showed as "Media disconnected." Now Bob was irritated and baffled. What should have been a simple 20-minute troubleshooting job had now turned into an hour and a half with no results. After thinking about it for a minute, he decided that there must be a problem with the switch Gerald's computer was plugged into.

After about 20 more minutes of tracing poorly marked cables through the ceiling down to the switch closet, he located Gerald's cable and plugged it into another port. He then went back to Gerald's computer and got exactly the same results as before, "Media disconnected."

By now, Bob was quite mystified. He called an experienced network administrator and explained the entire problem to her, including all of his troubleshooting steps and results, from start to finish. She confirmed that Bob had taken all the necessary steps and agreed to check the switch for problems. After a few more minutes, she called back and confirmed that the switch tested as good on all ports. She suggested Bob go back and start over again from the beginning and retest the computer's connection and the cable.

By now, Bob was about three hours into this job and was quite frustrated. In addition, his customer, who had several production deadlines to meet, was also frustrated and demanding results. Bob decided to try to start all over again by trying to calm Gerald down and asked him once again if he had changed any settings or deleted anything from the computer. Once again Gerald, in a very angry voice, said that he had not. Bob then, in desperation, asked him had anything at *all* unusual happened to the computer. Gerald thought for a second and then said, "Well, now that you mention it, Sally from the cubical next to me plugged her new paper shredder into one of my power outlets under my desk. Afterward, I noticed the network connection had problems, so I reached under the desk and discovered that she had accidentally unplugged the network cable. But I plugged it back in, so that can't be an issue."

A little bit more frustrated at the late revelation of this new and likely important piece of information, Bob decided to get a flashlight and pull Gerald's computer out from under the desk. It was difficult due to the limited space and all of the many tangled cables in the way, but Bob finally got it out from under the desk. He followed the network cable he had recently plugged in and traced it to the network card in Gerald's PC, where, sure enough, it had a solid connection. Sighing and thinking he was going to have to just replace the network card itself, it was only then that he looked up and saw an additional network card installed in Gerald's computer! He thought to himself, "Oh, no, it can't be that, can it?" and plugged the network cable into the other network card. Immediately the link light on the network card came on, and Gerald asked from above the desk what he'd done, since his network icon in his task bar had just changed to say "100 Mbps connected." Apparently, Gerald's computer had two network cards installed, one of which was disabled, and when he had plugged the cable back in, as Bob had done subsequently, he had plugged the cable into the disabled network card instead of the live one.

From this case study, you can see that there are several important lessons to be learned. First, a technician should never get overconfident in their abilities because even the simplest of problems can be overlooked and cost wasted time and resources. Second, a technician should always ask their probing questions of a customer in more than one way. Technicians must also always be customer and service oriented. Never let your inability to solve a problem allow you to get frustrated with the customer, even if they help cause the problem. And definitely don't let your pride make you afraid to ask for help when you've hit the troubleshooting "wall."

On the technical side, a good technician should also be prepared to visually inspect any and all connections and termination points to ensure that not only is a cable plugged in correctly, but into the correct place! Additionally, relying on a checklist in this case may have forced Bob to look at the computer itself, and having a hardware/configuration record for Gerald's PC may have helped Bob look at the issue of the two network cards sooner.

In any case, this experience will teach Bob—and you—a lesson in troubleshooting and give you a better perspective.

Summary

To be an effective desktop support technician, you must understand how to configure network protocols and services at the client level. You must also understand which problems you can troubleshoot and which problems you will have to escalate to the network administrator. You are not required to be a networking expert, but you are required to understand the principles of client configuration in regard to TCP/IP, name resolution methods, remote connections, and Internet Explorer. You should also be able to configure the settings of the Internet Connection Firewall and the newer Windows Firewall. In addition, you should be able to configure remote connectivity tools such as Remote Desktop and Remote Assistance and use them to troubleshoot client computers remotely.

TCP/IP is a communications protocol that is used by most networks today. It provides for logical addressing of computers and facilitates communication within an intranet as well as throughout the Internet. You can manually assign IP addresses to a computer or use a network service, referred to as a DHCP server. It is extremely important that each computer have its own unique IP address within a network. TCP/IP comes with its own set of tools. The ipconfig tool enables you to determine a computer's current configuration and to release and renew addresses from DHCP servers. There are many other tools included with TCP/IP that can assist you with troubleshooting IP addresses, connectivity, and name resolution.

Name resolution on a network is necessary because people can't remember long IP addresses such as 192.168.1.105. Computers and routers communicate using IP addresses and eventually MAC addresses; any other addresses are strictly for the benefit of people. There are two main types of user-friendly names used on a network: NetBIOS names and hostnames. NetBIOS names are the older type of name, used by clients earlier than Windows 2000 Professional and applications written at or before that time period. Computers use LMHOSTS files and WINS servers to convert these names to IP addresses. NetBIOS names are valid only in a local intranet. Hostnames can be used within an intranet and on the Internet as well. Windows 2000 Professional and later clients use hostnames, as do most applications written today. Computers use Hosts files and, more often, DNS servers to convert hostnames to IP addresses. TCP/IP has tools such as nslookup and nbtstat that assist you in troubleshooting name resolution issues.

The most important assets in a company are not its buildings but rather its people. Whether users are in the building, at home, or "on the road," they need to have access to the resources of the network in order to remain productive to the organization. Users can connect to a network remotely and use the resources as long as the network and the client computers are configured properly. The network is the responsibility of the network administrator, but the clients are the responsibility of the desktop support technician—you. There are two main types of connections that you can configure on a client computer using the New Connections Wizard: dial-up and VPN. The type of connection that you configure will depend completely on the type of configuration and the equipment that is provided by your organization. Companies can save money in the long run by enabling users to use VPN connections to connect through the Internet with a local call to their ISP. VPNs won't necessarily provide more bandwidth if you are still using an analog modem on the client side, but they can save on long-distance charges and they can provide enhanced security over that of dial-up connections. Troubleshooting remote connections is a process of isolating the problem between the client side, the server side, and the connection between. You can use tools built into Windows XP to test the modem on the client and eliminate it as the source of the problem. All other issues will probably require escalation to the network administrator.

Most users know how to use a browser to get to their favorite web page, even though they have no idea how it all works. Many users know "enough to be dangerous" about the settings that can affect their browsing experience. Since users are, by default, allowed to make changes to their Internet Explorer settings, you should know what changes are possible so that you can repair what they "fixed!" Most of the configuration options are located in the Internet Options section of the Tools menu in Internet Explorer. Tabs on this tool include General, Security, Connections, and many others. If you know what is included with each tab, you will be able to recognize what the user might have changed.

With the use of new tools, administrators and desktop support technicians no longer have to physically go to a user's computer to assist the user and troubleshoot the computer. Tools such as Remote Desktop and Remote Assistance make troubleshooting possible over an intranet and even over the Internet. Remote Desktop is primarily a troubleshooting tool that is used by administrators and desktop support technicians. It can be used to remotely control any Windows XP Professional computer that has the service enabled. Remote Assistance is a tool that can be used by administrators, desktop support technicians, or any two users. Typically, the person who is asking for help is referred to as the novice, and the person who provides the help is referred to as the expert. The expert can assist the novice while continuing a chat conversation. The novice must first issue an invitation to the expert and then must give the expert permission to take control of the computer. Once a novice has given the expert permission to take control, the expert can upload files, download files, and make configuration changes necessary to repair the computer. If you are the expert, then your knowledge of all of the topics discussed previously will be a key to assisting the user.

Exam Essentials

Know IP address configuration and how to troubleshoot it.   You should know how to determine the IP address of a client and whether it was manually assigned or automatically configured by DHCP or APIPA. You should also know how to manually configure an IP address on a client and how to force DHCP to release an address and configure a new one. Finally, you should be able to use the ping and pathping tools to troubleshoot connectivity between computers.

Understand the various methods of name resolution.   You should understand that computers recognize one another by their MAC addresses and that ARP is used to convert an IP address to a MAC address. You should also understand that NetBIOS names and hostnames are user-friendly names created because people would rather remember them than IP addresses. In addition, you should know the names of the files and services that are used for name resolution, both NetBIOS and hostname. Finally, you should know the appropriate tools to use to troubleshoot each type of name resolution.

Know the types of remote connections.   You should know that there are two types of remote connections, dial-up and VPN, and that you can configure both using the New Connections Wizard. You should also know that VPN connections use the Internet and an ISP to make a connection to an organization's server. In addition, you should know that VPNs are being used more often now because they eliminate long-distance charges and provide greater security than do dial-up connections. Finally, you should know how to troubleshoot the client side by checking the configuration and testing the modem.

Be able to configure Internet Explorer for users.   You should know that Internet Explorer has become the most popular browser partly because of its tremendous flexibility. You should also know that most of the client configuration settings for Internet Explorer are located in the Internet Options section of the Tools menu. In addition, you should know that users, by default, have the permissions to make changes to these settings. Finally, you should know where each setting is located and what it does so that you can fix errant configurations for users.

Know how to use the remote connectivity tools.   You should know that there are two main remote connectivity tools: Remote Desktop and Remote Assistance. You should also know that Remote Desktop is available only on Windows XP Professional. In addition, you should know that Remote Assistance is available on Windows XP Professional and Windows XP Home Edition. Finally, you should understand how to install and configure both of these remote connectivity tools and how to use them to troubleshoot a user's computer.

Review Questions

1. You are the desktop support technician for your organization. A client complains that she cannot connect to the network servers. You direct her to a command line and ask her to type the `ipconfig` command. She says that the IP address reads 169.254.11.15. Which of the following should you do next?

    A. Immediately escalate the issue to the network administrator.

    B. Tell her to type `ipconfig /renew`.

    C. Tell her to restart her computer immediately.

    D. Stop and restart the DNS server.

2. You are the desktop support technician for a large company. A user complains that when he uses his laptop at home to connect to the company's server over his VPN connection, he can no longer browse the Internet. As soon as he closes the VPN connection, he can browse the Internet again. Which of the following should you do next?

    A. Reconfigure the VPN connection to use the default gateway of the server.

    B. Change the IP address on the server to an IP address that has Internet connectivity.

    C. Reconfigure the VPN connection to use the local default gateway instead of the remote default gateway.

    D. Tell the user to use a dial-up connection for Internet connectivity while he is using the VPN connection at the server.

3. You are the desktop support technician for a large organization. A user complains that some of his applications are not working properly through the network. You suspect that name resolution is at fault. You ping the application's server by its FQDN, APP1.sybex.com, and receive a reply that the host cannot be found. You now want to confirm that you have connectivity to the server. Which of the following should you do next?

    A. Disconnect and reconnect the client computer's network cable.

    B. Ping the server by its NetBIOS name, APP1.

    C. Type `nslookup app1.sybex.com`.

    D. Ping the IP address of the server.

4. You are the desktop support technician for a large company. Some users are having problems with a legacy application. The errors that the application reports seem to indicate that NetBIOS name resolution is at fault. You suspect that an old file may be the problem. Which of the following should you do?

    A. Ask the administrator to examine the Hosts files on the servers for errors.

    B. Ask the administrator to restart all of the DNS servers.

    C. Ask the administrator to restart all of the WINS servers.

    D. Ask the administrator to examine the LMHOSTS files in the network for errors.

5. You are the desktop support technician for a large company. A user in your building tells you that he can get access to the Internet through the proxy server just fine but he cannot access the sites on your intranet. Which of the following should you do?

A. On the client computer, create a new connection that is specifically for internet access.

B. Change the LAN settings in Internet Explorer to allow bypassing the proxy for local addresses.

C. Change the default gateway on the client computer.

D. Change the client's IP address to the address of the servers in the intranet.

6. You are the desktop support technician for a company with many mobile users. You currently use modems on the users' laptops to connect to a stack of modems in the server closet. Users are dialing in from all over the country, so long-distance costs are very high. Management has asked you for suggestions for lowering costs without sacrificing security. What should you tell management? (Choose two.)

A. You could use VPNs instead of the dial-up connections. This would decrease costs and increase security.

B. You could lower costs by changing from dial-up to VPN, but the trade-off would be an increased security risk.

C. If most of the cost comes from long-distance charges, there is no way to avoid those besides negotiating a better contract with the communications carrier.

D. Using VPNs could eliminate the use of the modems in the network closet.

7. You are the desktop support technician for a company with many Internet users. One of your users calls you complaining that the page that automatically comes up when he starts Internet Explorer has been changed. You want to help the user fix the problem, but you are not in front of a computer. Which tab in Internet Options contains the Home Page setting?

A. Content

B. Programs

C. Advanced

D. General

8. You are the desktop support technician for a company with many Internet users. A user calls you complaining that she cannot download files or run special applications on a web page. You want to walk her through adding the page as a trusted site, but you are not in front of a computer. Which tab in Internet Options contains the appropriate setting?

A. General

B. Advanced

C. Security

D. Privacy

9. You are the desktop support technician for a company that has many users in many different locations. All users are using Windows XP Professional client software. You want to set up a program whereby you will train certain users who will then be able to assist other users over the network. You want the novice users to have to invite the expert users before the expert users can help. Which remote connectivity tool should you use?

    A. Remote Desktop

    B. Dynamic Host Configuration Protocol

    C. Remote Assistance

    D. WINS

10. You are the desktop support technician for a large company with many users. You are considering using Remote Desktop to remotely manage clients in your network. Which of the following are true? (Choose two.)

    A. You can manage any client from a Windows XP Professional computer with Remote Desktop enabled.

    B. You can manage a Windows XP Professional client computer, with Remote Desktop enabled, from any client computer with the Remote Desktop client installed and enabled.

    C. You can manage a Windows XP Home Edition client from a Windows XP Professional client as long as Remote Desktop is enabled.

    D. You can only have one active session, local or remote.

11. You are a desktop support technician for the XYZ Company. You are helping one of your users troubleshoot a network connectivity issue. Which one of the following is a valid troubleshooting step when resolving network connectivity issues?

    A. Reset the computer's account in Active Directory.

    B. Ping the computer's default gateway.

    C. Run the `gpupdate` command to reapply Group Policy.

    D. Have the user run the `ipconfig /connect` command from the command prompt.

12. You are helping one of your users resolve an issue they are having with accessing Internet sites. You have established that the network connectivity is functioning properly by pinging the DNS server. You have also ruled out name resolution as an issue. What other configuration settings should you check?

    A. Open Internet Explorer, click Tools and then Internet Options, and then click the Connections tab. Click LAN Settings, and ensure you have the correct proxy server information configured.

    B. Click Control Panel, switch to Category view, and then click Security Center. Ensure that Windows Firewall is turned off.

    C. Open Control Panel, switch to Classic view, and then click the Windows Firewall icon. On the General tab, ensure that the box Allow Outbound Connections is checked.

    D. Open Network Connections, right-click your network connection icon, select Properties, and check the Allow Outbound Connections check box.

13. What troubleshooting step might you take if you are trying to resolve a user's problems with connecting to a particular secure (`https`) site?

A. Enable IP Security (IPSec) in tunnel mode on the client.

B. Enable the Encrypting File System (EFS) on the client.

C. Remove all of the server certificates from the Trusted Root Certification Authorities store.

D. Click the Clear SSL State button under the Certificates section of the Content tab under Internet Options in Internet Explorer.

14. How would you disable the function of Internet Explorer that allows you to store usernames and passwords for frequently visited sites?

A. Disable Windows Protected Storage in the Registry.

B. Open User Accounts in Control Panel and ensure that the Save User Passwords check box is unchecked.

C. In Internet Options, click the Content tab; then click the AutoComplete button and clear the check boxes for the Use AutoComplete for User Names and Passwords on Forms and the Prompt Me to Save Passwords options.

D. In Internet Options, click the Security tab; then click the Passwords button and clear the Save User Names and Passwords on Forms check box.

15. Under which of the following sections on the Content tab in Internet Options can you configure which sites users are allowed to access based upon their content ratings?

A. Content Restrictions

B. Content Advisor

C. Site Restrictions

D. Site Advisor

16. Which option best describes a computer's loopback address?

A. An IP address in the 127 range that is assigned to the computer when TCP/IP is installed

B. The address assigned by the Automatic Private IP Address function when a DHCP server cannot be located

C. An alternate configuration IP address assigned by an administrator in the event the computer cannot locate a DHCP server

D. A locally assigned Media Access Control (MAC) address

17. Which option is used with the `ipconfig` command to refresh all DHCP server leases and registers or reregisters the client's DNS name with the DNS server?

A. `/renew`

B. `/release`

C. `/refresh`

D. `/registerdns`

18. Which of the following statements about the TCP and UDP protocols best describes these two protocols?

    A. TCP and UDP are both connectionless protocols.

    B. TCP is a connection-oriented protocol and UDP is a connectionless protocol.

    C. TCP and UDP are both connection-oriented protocols.

    D. TCP is a connectionless protocol and UDP is a connection-oriented protocol.

19. Which of the following ICMP error messages might you receive as a response to the `ping` command when there is a problem at the IP routing level between your computer and the remote host?

    A. Destination host unreachable

    B. Unknown host *hostname*

    C. Request timed out

    D. Path not found

20. How would you enable Windows Firewall to allow incoming traffic that it otherwise would not permit?

    A. Turn Windows Firewall off when you require inbound traffic that is not normally allowed.

    B. Add exceptions for this traffic to the Allowed Applications list in the network adapter properties.

    C. Click the Exceptions tab in Windows Firewall and add programs to the Programs and Services list.

    D. You cannot do this.

Answer to Review Questions

1. B. You should tell her to type `ipconfig /renew`. Apparently the DHCP server was not available when the computer was last started, but it might be available now. If her computer still does not obtain an IP address, then she should restart it just to give it one more chance. If it still does not obtain an IP address, the problem should be escalated to the network administrator. The DNS server should not be stopped and restarted; it will not fix this problem.

2. C. You should reconfigure the advanced network settings of the connection. You should remove the check mark from the Use Default Gateway on Remote Network check box. Changing the IP address of the server would not solve this problem. The user would need to have two modems in his laptop and two available telephone lines to use a dial-up connection at the same time he is using the VPN connection; therefore, this is not a viable solution.

3. D. To confirm that you have connectivity, you should ping the IP address of the server. If you get a reply, then you know that you have connectivity and that name resolution is the issue. You should not disconnect and reconnect the client computer's network cable. Pinging the computer by the NetBIOS name will not eliminate all of the name resolution issues. Using nslookup might assist you in determining whether the DNS servers are working properly, but it won't help you establish connectivity between the client computer and the server.

4. D. You should ask the administrator to examine the LMHOSTS files for errors. Since the issue relates to NetBIOS name resolution, the Hosts file and the DNS servers are not part of the problem. The WINS database is dynamic and self-checking, so it is unlikely that the old record is still in the WINS database. If there is an error in the LMHOSTS file, it will cause this problem because the LMHOSTS file is read before WINS.

5. B. You should change the LAN settings in Internet Explorer. You should check the Bypass the Proxy Servers for Local Addresses check box under Proxy Settings. It is not necessary to create a new connection on or change the default gateway of the client computer. Each address in a network should be unique, so you certainly wouldn't want to change the client's IP address to that of the servers.

6. A, D. You should recommend using virtual private networks (VPNs) instead of dial-up connections. VPNs will eliminate the long-distance costs and the need for modems on the server side. VPNs will also increase, not decrease, security versus that of dial-up connections.

7. D. You should direct the user to the General tab in the Internet Options dialog box, accessible from the Tools menu. The Home Page setting is the first option on the General tab. The other options do not contain the Home Page setting.

8. C. You should direct the user to the Security tab of the Internet Options dialog box, accessible from the Tools menu. You should then walk her through configuring the site as trusted. (This is assuming that the user has the permissions to make the configuration change.)

9. C. You should use the Remote Assistance tool built into every Windows XP client. Novice users can invite expert users to help them. Remote Desktop is primarily used by administrators and support personnel and does not have the invitation capability. Dynamic Host Configuration Protocol (DHCP) is a service used to automatically assign IP addresses to hosts, not a remote connectivity tool. WINS is a service that converts NetBIOS names to IP addresses and not a remote connectivity tool.

10. B, D. Only Windows XP Professional supports remote control from Remote Desktop, not Windows XP Home Edition or any other client prior to Windows XP Professional. You can manage a Windows XP Professional client computer from any client computer with the Remote Desktop client installed and enabled. You can only have one active session, local or remote.

11. B. Option B is the only valid troubleshooting step when resolving network connectivity issues. Resetting the computer's account in Active Directory will not help the computer connect to the network. The `gpupdate` command only reapplies Group Policy settings to the local computer, which require network settings to be configured in the first place, and does not resolve connection problems. Option D is incorrect because there is no `/connect` option with the `ipconfig` command.

12. A. If you have established that network connectivity and name resolution are not the problems, a next step could be to check the proxy settings in Internet Explorer and ensure that they are configured correctly. Option B is incorrect because turning the firewall off would be ineffective; you can already connect to the network and resolve Internet hostnames. Options C and D are invalid options.

13. D. Clearing the SSL state is one troubleshooting step you can take when a user has difficulty connecting to a site that uses SSL and server certificates (usually a site that has `https` in the URL). This causes Internet Explorer to reacquire a certificate from the site and reestablish a secure session. Neither IPSec nor EFS is used to connect to sites that use SSL, so both A and B are incorrect. C is incorrect because if you removed all the certificates from the Trusted Root Certification Authorities store, you would have even more difficulty connecting to any site that uses server certificates because your computer would no longer trust any certificate.

14. C. The AutoComplete option under the Content tab in Internet Options is where you can configure Internet Explorer to not save usernames and passwords. Disabling Windows Protected Storage would render many functions, including the ability to store digital certificates, inoperable and may damage your operating system. B and D are incorrect because those options do not exist.

15. B. The Content Advisor section of the Content tab under Internet Options is where you can restrict which sites users are allowed and not allowed to view based upon their content ratings. All of the other options are invalid because these sections do not exist.

16. A. A loopback address is an address that is assigned to the computer when the TCP/IP stack is installed. It is an address in the 127 IP address range, usually 127.0.0.1, and is used for diagnostic purposes. A computer that has had its address assigned under the Automatic Private IP Address (APIPA) function has an IP address in the range of 169.254.*x*.*x*. An alternate configuration address is an IP address assigned by an administrator and is used by a Windows XP computer in the event it cannot locate a DHCP server. Option D is an invalid option because MAC addresses are not locally assigned but are physically burned into the network card when it is manufactured.

17. D. The command `ipconfig /registerdns` refreshes all DHCP server leases and registers or reregisters the client's DNS name with the DNS server. The `/renew` option renews an address lease with the server but does not reregister the client's DNS name with a DNS server. The `/release` option simply releases a client's leased IP address back to the DHCP server for return to the address pool. The option in C does not exist.

18. B. TCP is a connection-oriented protocol and UDP is a connectionless protocol. TCP concerns itself with reliable delivery and has extra overhead built in to it with sequence and acknowledgement numbers as error-correction capabilities. UDP does not concern itself with reliable delivery and leaves it up to higher-level protocols or the applications themselves to ensure delivery.

19. A. You will receive a "Destination host unreachable" error message when there is a problem at the IP routing level between your computer and the remote host. An "Unknown host *hostname*" error message indicates that none of the name resolution mechanisms recognize the name that you typed. A "Request timed out" message indicates that at least one name resolution mechanism did recognize the name but the target either did not receive the request or did not respond to it. A "Path not found" error message is not a response to the `ping` command.

20. C. Programs and services that would not otherwise be permitted to enter the computer through Windows Firewall can be added to the list of allowed programs on the Exceptions tab. Turning off Windows Firewall is not advisable because then any and all traffic would be allowed into the computer, including undesirable traffic. Option B is invalid because there is no Allowed Applications list in the network adapter properties, and D is incorrect because this action can be done as stated in option C.

Supporting Users and Troubleshooting Desktop Applications on a Microsoft Windows XP Operating System

Chapter

7

Configuring and Troubleshooting Applications

MICROSOFT EXAM OBJECTIVES COVERED IN THIS CHAPTER:

✓ **Configure and troubleshoot Office applications.**

- ▪ Answer end-user questions related to configuring Office applications.
- ▪ Set application compatibility settings.
- ▪ Troubleshoot application installation problems.
- ▪ Configure and troubleshoot email account settings.

✓ **Configure and troubleshoot Internet Explorer.**

✓ **Configure and troubleshoot Outlook Express.**

- ▪ Answer end-user questions related to configuring Outlook Express.
- ▪ Configure and troubleshoot newsreader account settings.
- ▪ Configure and troubleshoot email account settings.

✓ **Configure the operating system to support applications.**

- ▪ Answer end-user questions related to configuring the operating system to support an application.
- ▪ Configure and troubleshoot file system access and file permission problems on multiboot computers.
- ▪ Configure access to applications on multiuser computers.
- ▪ Configure and troubleshoot application access on a multiple user client computer.

Although any of the information in this book could be very useful on both the MS 70-271 and MS 70-272 exams, most of what we have covered so far has focused on the MS 70-271 exam. We are now moving into information that is more likely to be useful for the MS 70-272 exam. The information in the remaining chapters of this book is more specific to applications and the relationship of applications to the Windows XP operating system.

As user friendly as Windows XP is, most people still don't start up a computer and log on to it just to gaze at the operating system. Most of the time, they want to use an application that is installed on the operating system. There are many different types of applications from which a user can choose. Some of these are produced by Microsoft and others are produced by third-party companies. In this chapter, we will focus first on some of the applications that are produced by Microsoft to run on the Windows operating system. As a desktop support technician, you should be able to install, configure, and troubleshoot the most common Microsoft Windows applications. After we have discussed Microsoft applications, we will turn our attention to applications in general, discussing how to configure old and new applications on single-user computers as well as multiuser computers. First we will discuss Microsoft Office, Internet Explorer, and Outlook Express, and then we'll take a look at configuring the operating system to support different versions of applications.

Microsoft Office   Microsoft Office is a family of products that are designed to assist users in completing common business tasks. These products are available individually and in suites, which are groups of programs bundled together to address related business requirements. You should know the members of the Office family and have an understanding of how to install, activate, configure, and troubleshoot these products for the various Windows operating systems in your user environment.

Internet Explorer   As we discussed in Chapter 6, "Troubleshooting Network Protocols and Services," Internet Explorer is the browser of choice for most Internet users. It comes standard with all Microsoft client operating systems later than Windows 95. You should know how to configure and troubleshoot all of the client settings for Internet Explorer.

Outlook Express   Outlook Express is a messaging tool that is built into Windows operating systems later than Windows 95. Many people use Outlook Express for email transactions and newsgroup communications. Using the tools in Outlook Express, more than one person can use the same computer for email and each person can have their own identity in the computer. You should know how to configure and troubleshoot email settings and newsgroup settings for users of Outlook Express.

Application support   Applications and operating systems have evolved over time. Some applications that were designed to run on older operating systems can now run on Windows XP provided that it is configured properly. Computers that have multiple users or multiple operating systems present a special challenge. You should know how to configure and troubleshoot applications on the most common Windows operating systems in various computer and user configurations.

Microsoft Office

Since *Microsoft Office* is the best-selling suite of applications in the world today, many of the calls that you receive from customers may relate to one or more of the Microsoft Office products. As a desktop support technician, you should be able to provide support for users of Microsoft Office applications. In the following sections, we will discuss installing Microsoft Office and the individual applications within it. In addition, we will examine how you should configure, manage, and troubleshoot existing Microsoft Office applications. Finally, we will discuss how to configure email account settings for Microsoft Outlook users.

Installing Microsoft Office

Microsoft Office has evolved since its first release in 1995. It contains many applications, such as Word, Excel, PowerPoint, and so on. There are many versions and editions of Office that you might encounter in your network. It's essential that you have knowledge of these applications and their different versions. We will discuss the older versions of the software later in this chapter. In this section, we will focus on the latest Microsoft Office suite of applications, Office 2003. You should know how to acquire the software, determine the disk space requirements, select an installation methodology, perform the installation, and activate the new software. We will discuss each of these concepts in detail.

Acquiring Microsoft Office 2003

There are many editions of Microsoft Office 2003. Depending on the nature of your organization and the edition that you require, you will find the software available from many different sources. Table 7.1 illustrates the editions that are available for Office 2003. Stand-alone applications are also available through retail outlets, *original equipment manufacturers (OEMs)*, and volume licenses.

TABLE 7.1 Editions of Microsoft Office 2003 and Their Availability

Microsoft Office Edition	Availability
Office Professional Enterprise Edition	Volume license and academic volume license
Office Professional Edition	Retail, OEM, and academic volume license
Office Standard Edition	Retail and all volume licenses
Office Small Business Edition	OEM only
Office Student and Teacher Edition	Retail and academic volume license

Determining Disk Space Requirements

How much hard disk space Office requires is largely dependent on the options that you select. You can choose to install all of the applications, just the most commonly used applications, or just the applications that you want. Table 7.2 illustrates the approximate space required on the hard disk for each of the installation options.

TABLE 7.2   Disk Space Requirements for Office 2003

Type of Installation	Disk Space Needed	Description of Installation
Typical	331MB	Installs the most commonly used components of Microsoft Office
Complete	577MB	Installs all of Microsoft Office on your computer, including all optional components and tools
Minimal	251MB	Installs Microsoft Office with only the minimum required components
Custom	Based on selected features	Enables you to select the applications and features that will be installed on your computer

Selecting an Installation Methodology

A methodology is simply a way of doing something. There are three ways to install Microsoft Office onto Windows 2000 and Windows XP clients:

- Manual installation: This type of installation can be accomplished by using the CD or a network share with the required files. You begin the installation and continue to follow all of the onscreen prompts until the installation is complete. You can specify files that are installed and advanced settings.

- Automated installation: This type of installation proceeds according to an installation script. The script installs the application based on preselected choices. Scripts and other types of automated software installations can be run using Group Policy in Windows 2000 and Windows Server 2003 networks. You can also use Microsoft Systems Management Server (SMS) to perform installations on multiple computers in any type of Microsoft network with any Microsoft client later than Windows 95.

- Upgrade installation: This type of installation is performed on a computer with a previous version of Office installed. The purpose of this type of installation is either to update the Office version or to install additional components on the current version. This type of installation can be performed manually or can be automated using Group Policy or SMS software.

Performing the Installation

The actual steps involved in the installation will vary depending on your installation methodology. In the following sections, we will focus on the manual installation and upgrade installation methodologies using the Microsoft Office 2003 CD. Automated installations and network share installations are beyond the scope of this text because they are not generally performed by a desktop support technician.

 You should make sure that you have closed all other programs and deactivated antivirus software before performing any new installation or upgrade.

Performing a New Installation of Office 2003 from a CD

The number of decisions that you make during the installation will vary depending on whether you select to perform a Typical installation or a Custom installation. Exercise 7.1 walks you through the steps to perform a Typical installation of Office 2003.

EXERCISE 7.1

Performing a Typical Installation of Office 2003 from a CD

1. Insert the Office CD in the CD-ROM drive to launch the Office Setup program. If Setup does not run automatically, you can manually run the setup.exe program located in the root folder of the CD.

2. Enter the product key displayed on the label on the Office CD container in the Product Key dialog box, and then click Next.

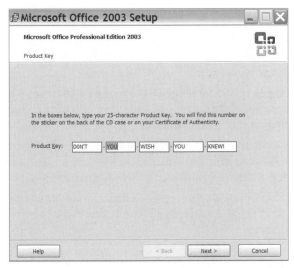

EXERCISE 7.1 *(continued)*

3. Enter the appropriate information in the User Name, Initials, and Organization fields, and then click Next.

4. Accept the terms in the license agreement, and then click Next.

5. Select Typical Install for the installation type, and click Next.

6. Setup will display a list of applications that will be installed. Click Install to complete the installation.

If you select Custom Install for the installation type, you will have the option to choose which programs will be installed and how they will be run on your computer. You should understand the following options in the Custom Setup box:

- Run from My Computer: The component will be installed so that it can be run directly from the hard drive without the use of the CD. Other underlying components and options may not be installed, to save hard disk space.

- Run All from My Computer: The component and all of the underlying components and options will be installed on the hard drive so that they can all be run from the hard drive without the use of the CD. This option consumes the most hard disk space.

- Installed on First Use: Office will prompt the user to install the component the first time they attempt to use it. The user will have to have access to a CD or to a network share to perform the installation.

- Not Available: The system will not install the component or any of the underlying components or options.

> If you have a previous version of a component on your computer, then you can select whether to uninstall the previous version or leave it in place.

Performing an Upgrade Installation of Office 2003 with a CD

The term *upgrading* refers to the process of installing a more recent version of a software component that currently exists on your computer. Upgrading Office 2003 is very similar to installing it for the first time. Exercise 7.2 walks you through the steps to perform an Upgrade installation of Office 2003.

EXERCISE 7.2

Upgrading to Office 2003 from a CD

1. Insert the Office CD in the CD-ROM drive to launch the Office Setup program. If Setup does not run automatically, you can manually run the setup.exe program in the root folder of the Office CD.

2. Complete the first three Setup dialog boxes and in the Product Key dialog box, enter the product key displayed on the label of the Office CD container.

3. Select Upgrade as the installation type.

4. Setup will examine your computer for currently installed Office 2003 components and then display a list of applications that will be installed. Click Install to complete the installation.

Activating Office 2003

Activation is the newest form of protection from piracy of software. It is designed as a countermeasure to the most prevalent form of copyright infringement, casual copying. It works by associating hardware components of a computer with a specific installation of software. After the software has been associated with a specific set of components, it cannot be activated on another computer that does not have the same specific set of components. Exceptions are made for volume license versions of software that is purchased by large organizations.

After you install or upgrade Office 2003, you are required to activate it. This can be accomplished using the Activation Wizard and an Internet connection. The Activation Wizard will appear the first time that you run an Office Application. You can activate the software easily through the Internet. If you do not have an Internet connection, then the wizard can give you the correct telephone number to dial to activate the software. You will either speak with a Microsoft representative or use an automated system, depending on your region. After you have given the product key information to Microsoft, they will give you an activation code to activate the software.

Software activation can cause major problems in a corporate environment, mostly because of the automated method of installation. Most large companies utilize some sort of remote software deployment. Programs like SMS and Group Policy make deploying new and updated software much easier, unless those new software packages require activation. You might also find a problem if your company uses PC imaging as an operating system deployment method. Both of these mechanisms can offer great flexibility when deploying software to a large user base. Microsoft offers volume licensing for companies with solutions such as these. Volume License versions of office and Windows do not require activation and therefore are more suitable for automated delivery.

Configuring, Managing, and Troubleshooting Microsoft Office Applications

Simply knowing how to install Office 2003 will not get you very far as a desktop support technician. To be effective, you must also know how to troubleshoot the installation and maintain the installation for the user. In addition you should know how to apply updates, add and remove components, reinstall and repair components, and assist the user to recover data whenever possible. In the following sections, we will discuss each of these concepts in detail.

Troubleshooting an Installation of Office 2003

Because of the evolution of the Office software itself and the manner in which it operates with other applications on your computer, there a number of problems that can occur when installing or upgrading Office 2003. If you are performing an upgrade installation with an upgrade CD, then you should make sure you have a previous version of the software that you are trying to upgrade currently installed on the computer; otherwise, you will receive a "No Qualifying Product" error.

The other errors that could occur during an installation depend on the hardware and software installed on a computer and are too numerous to mention here. Often, the best method is to simply uninstall the software, restart the computer, and then reinstall the software. If this still does not eliminate the problem, you should examine the following files created during the installation:

- `Office Professional Edition 2003 Setup(000x).txt`
- `Office Professional Edition 2003 Setup (000x)_Task(000x).txt`
- `MSI*.log`
- `Offcln11.log` (If you have uninstalled Microsoft Office 2003 previously)

Applying Updates to Office 2003

The Microsoft Office website is the online extension of Office that assists you in keeping your applications up-to-date. Microsoft adds new content to the site on a regular basis, so you can always get the most recent updates and fixes to protect a user's computer and keep it running efficiently. You can access the Office Update website at `http://office.microsoft.com/officeupdate/default.aspx`. Office Update scans your computer and then provides a list of critical updates and optional updates. Critical updates are considered essential for the operation and/or security of your computer. Optional updates could be new features and/or functionality. As a desktop support technician, you should scan for updates regularly or advise your clients to scan for them on a regular basis. Exercise 7.3 walks you through the steps to scan for updates on the Microsoft Update website.

EXERCISE 7.3

Scanning for Updates

1. In the location bar in your browser, type `http://office.microsoft.com/officeupdate/default.aspx`.

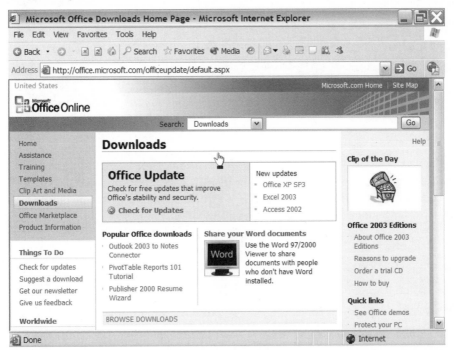

EXERCISE 7.3 *(continued)*

2. Click Check for Updates. The system will scan your computer and generate a list of recommended updates. The updates that are considered critical will already be selected. You can read information about each of the updates on the links provided and make your own decisions regarding which updates you want to install.

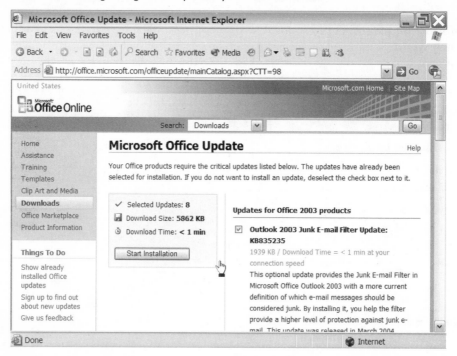

3. When you have selected all of the updates that you want, click Start Installation and accept any user license agreements provided. Some updates may require that you restart your computer to complete the installation.

 You can also access Windows Update from the Help menu of most Office 2003 applications.

Adding and Removing Office Components

Over time, users' needs are bound to change. They might need Office components they didn't need before. By the same token, they might have components installed on their computers they never use that are just taking up hard drive space that could be used for something else. You should know how to assist users in making these adjustments to their Office software without affecting any other components in the system. Exercise 7.4 walks you through the steps to add or remove Office components.

EXERCISE 7.4

Adding or Removing Office Components

1. On the Windows XP Desktop, click Start, choose Control Panel, and then choose Add or Remove Programs.

2. Select the Microsoft Office program from the program list, and then click Change.

3. In the Maintenance Mode Options dialog box, click Add or Remove Features, and then choose Next. Setup will display the same installation options displayed at the original Setup Screen.

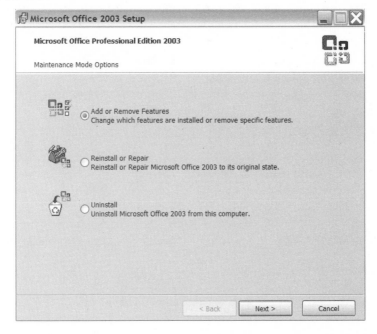

4. Change only the features that you want to change; the rest of the installation will not be affected.

5. When you have finished making your choices, click Install. The system will make the changes to create the installation that you chose. You may have to restart the computer to complete the installation.

EXERCISE 7.5

Reinstalling and Repairing Office

1. On the Windows XP Desktop, click Start, choose Control Panel, and then choose Add or Remove Programs.

2. Select the Microsoft Office program from the program list, and then click Change.

3. In the Maintenance Mode Options dialog box, click Reinstall or Repair, and then click Next. In the Reinstall or Repair Office Installation dialog box, select one of the following options:

   a. Reinstall Office: This option instructs Setup to reinstall all Office files and reset all Registry settings whether or not they appear to be defective.

   b. Detect and Repair Errors in My Office Installation: This option instructs Setup to detect defective files or settings and make just the repairs that are necessary. You should check the Restore My Start Menu Shortcuts check box if you have changed or deleted any of the default shortcuts and you want them restored.

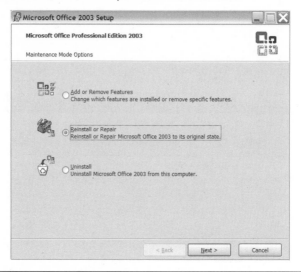

Repairing Office Components

Microsoft Office 2003 uses the *Microsoft Windows Installer* to enable self-repairing features. The Microsoft Windows Installer is a special tool that is designed to streamline the process of installing and configuring products and applications. If a resource that is required to start a program is missing or corrupt, such as a Registry key, then Windows Installer will detect that the resource is missing and repair the program. You can read more information about Windows Installer on the Microsoft Developer Network (MSDN) library at http://msdn.microsoft.com.

If you or your customers are having problems with an Office component, you can attempt to reinstall and repair it yourself or let the system detect and repair the problem. Exercise 7.5 walks you through the steps to attempt to reinstall and repair a problem in Office.

In Office 2003, you can also choose the Detect and Repair option from the Help menu in any Office 2003 application.

Recovering Office Application Files

Microsoft Office 2003 has built-in features to prevent users from losing data. There are new tools that you can use manually as well as new services that run in the background automatically. In the following sections, we will discuss the three main tools and services that you and your users can use to recover Office application files: Microsoft Office Application Recovery, AutoRecover, and Shadow Copy.

Microsoft Office Application Recovery Tool

The Microsoft Office Application Recovery tool provides a way to keep from losing data when an application crashes or hangs. Instead of using the old familiar End Task button in Task Manager, users now have another option that may allow them to restart the application and recover the documents. Exercise 7.6 walks you through the steps to use the Microsoft Office Application Recovery tool.

EXERCISE 7.6

Using the Microsoft Office Application Recovery Tool

1. On the Windows XP Desktop, click Start and then choose All Programs ➢ Microsoft Office ➢ Microsoft Office Tools ➢ Microsoft Office Application Recovery.

2. Select the name of the application that you want to recover, and then click Recover Application. This will terminate the application and cause it to attempt to save any unsaved changes before terminating.

Be warned: Selecting the End Application option in the Microsoft Office Application Recovery tool will cause the specified application to terminate without attempting to save your data.

AutoRecover

AutoRecover is a feature included in Office 2003 and Office XP that recovers data in Office applications if it's lost. It is especially useful in the event of a power outage on a desktop or laptop. The service works by automatically saving files at a specified interval. If you suddenly lose power, the only data that you will lose will be anything that has changed since the last AutoRecover save. Exercise 7.7 walks you through the steps to recover files using AutoRecover.

EXERCISE 7.7

Recovering Files Using AutoRecover

1. Open the Office application that you were using when the power outage occurred.

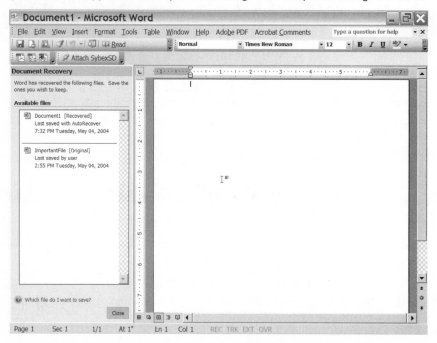

2. Scan the files listed in the Document Recovery task pane and decide which file you want to keep. Files that have the word *Recovered* in the title are usually the newest files.

3. Select the file in the Document Recovery task pane, click the arrow next to the file's name, and then do one of the following:

    a. To work with the file, click Open.

    b. To save the file, click Save As and name the file. The newly named file will be saved in the same folder as the original file. If you type the same name as the original file, then the original file will be overwritten with the recovered file.

Shadow Copy

Shadow Copy is a new technology included with Windows Server 2003 that tracks the history of all documents stored in a particular volume on a server. Shadow Copy allows users to roll back changes made to documents or restore them on the file server if they were accidentally deleted. Client computers must be Windows XP or Windows 2000 Professional and must have the Shadow Copy client software, ShadowCopyClient.msi, installed on them to use this feature. You can obtain this software from Microsoft's downloads site at http://microsoft.com/downloads. The client software will create a new tab in the file and folder properties called Previous Versions. You can use this tool to recover accidentally deleted files and folders or to recover a file that was accidentally overwritten.

Exercise 7.8 walks you through the steps to recover a deleted file.

EXERCISE 7.8

Recovering a Deleted File with Shadow Copy

1. Navigate to the folder in which the deleted file had been stored.

2. Position your cursor over a blank space in the folder.

3. Right-click, select Properties, and then choose the Previous Versions tab.

4. On the Previous Versions tab of the folder's Properties dialog, select the version of the folder that contained the file before it was deleted, and then click View.

5. View the folder and select the file that will be recovered.

6. Drag and drop or cut and paste a copy of the file to the user's local computer.

Exercise 7.9 walks you through the steps to recover a deleted folder:

EXERCISE 7.9

Recovering a Deleted Folder with Shadow Copy

1. Position the cursor in a blank space in the folder that contained the folder that will be recovered.

2. Right-click and select Properties, and then choose the Previous Versions tab.

3. Select Restore to recover everything that was in the folder or Copy to copy the older version to another location.

Exercise 7.10 walks you through the steps to use Shadow Copy to recover an overwritten or corrupt file.

EXERCISE 7.10

Using Shadow Copy to Recover an Overwritten or Corrupt File

1. Right-click the overwritten or corrupt file and then click Properties.

2. Select the Previous Versions tab.

3. To view an older version of the file, choose the version and then click View. To replace the current version with the older version, click Restore. To copy the older version to another location, click Copy.

The Real Value of Shadow Copy

Suppose that you are normal user working on a PowerPoint presentation that contains over 300 slides. You are preparing the presentation for a meeting that will take place this afternoon. You've been working hard on it for about two months and you are just putting on the finishing touches. There is only one copy of the presentation, which is located on the file server. You feel safe with this because the file server is backed up on a nightly basis.

There is only one thing about the presentation that bothers you—the style of the slides. You're not sure whether you have chosen a look that is professional enough. You decide to get a second opinion, so you call a colleague to ask her to review a shorter version of the presentation for style only. She agrees and asks you to send her just 10 or 12 slides.

This is where the problem starts. You decide to select the slides that you don't want to send her and cut them out of the current presentation. You decide to cut all but the ten slides you want to send to her You select about 290 slides and delete them from the current presentation. You then intend to save the presentation with a different filename, but you become distracted and you make a rather large error. You save the file with the same name that it had before and overwrite the 300-slide presentation with the 10-slide presentation. You have effectively lost 290 slides!

The fact that you should have just created a new file and then copied the slides into it is no longer relevant at this point. What is relevant is that the only copy that is left of that presentation is the one that is on the backup tape of the file server. How well do you know the network administrator? Will he understand the significance of this emergency and restore your file before the meeting? What else does the network administrator have to do today besides fix your mistake? The network administrator might be able to bail you out this time, but suppose it happens again; would you even have the courage to ask for another favor? Maybe you should talk to the desktop support technician instead!

Now suppose you are the same user and you are working on the same file but you know about Shadow Copy. You accidentally click Save instead of Save As and realize that you have just copied over your original presentation. You simply right-click on the file that you still have and select a previous version of it. Depending on how often the shadow copies are made (as defined by the network administrator), you may have to redo the finishing touches that you added today. That's it!

The real value of Shadow Copy is that it lets people be people. We all make mistakes at times and do things that we can't believe we actually did. This example, or something like it, probably has happened to you or someone you know. If your organization uses Shadow Copy, you should educate your people about its use so that their mistakes don't have to become your emergencies.

Configuring and Troubleshooting Outlook Email Accounts for Clients

Microsoft Office includes a program called Outlook. This program provides an integrated solution for managing and organizing email messages, schedules, notes, contacts, tasks, and other information. You should know how to configure Outlook for your user environment. You should also know how to troubleshoot Outlook for clients.

Outlook can be configured for general Internet access or for a specialized server that stores an organization's messages, called Exchange Server. In the following sections, we will discuss how to configure Outlook for each of these options and how to troubleshoot common user problems for each of them. A detailed discussion of Exchange Server is beyond the scope of this book.

Configuring Outlook for Internet Email and Exchange

Configuring Outlook is a two-step process. First, you create a *profile* that identifies the user and stores their messages. Then, you configure a mailbox in which to receive the messages. We will discuss both of these steps in detail.

Creating an Outlook Profile

A profile is a group of email accounts, address books, and personal folders. A user can create any number of profiles for different uses. In addition, multiple profiles can be very useful when more than one person uses the same computer. Exercise 7.11 walks you through the steps to create a new Outlook profile.

Configuring Mailboxes

Before users can receive email in Outlook, they need to have a mailbox that is properly configured. There are many different types of mailboxes that you can configure for a user. Which type will depend upon how you are using Outlook in your organization. In the following sections, we will discuss the configuration of Outlook mailboxes for Internet email (POP3), Internet Message Access Protocol (IMAP), Hypertext Transfer Protocol (HTTP), and Exchange.

EXERCISE 7.11

Creating an Outlook Profile

1. On the Windows XP Desktop, click Start and then choose Control Panel.

2. In Control Panel, choose Switch to Classic View, and then double-click Mail.

3. In the Mail Setup dialog box, click the Show Profiles button.

4. On the General tab, select the Prompt for a Profile to Be Used check box, and then click Add.

5. In the Profile Name field, type a name for the new profile. The name should describe the user or the type of accounts that will be contained in the profile.

6. In the Email Accounts dialog box, click the Add a New Email Account button, and then click Next.

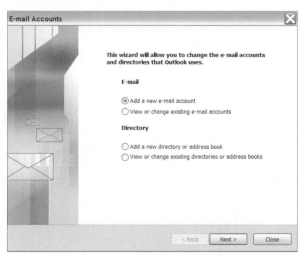

EXERCISE 7.11 *(continued)*

7. Select the appropriate server type for your new email account, and click Next.

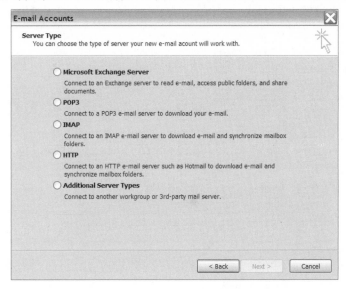

8. Fill in the information as prompted, and then click Next and Finish as needed.

9. Click OK.

CONFIGURING MAILBOXES FOR INTERNET EMAIL (POP3)

Before a user can receive email through the Internet, they must have a mailbox that is correctly configured with their *Post Office Protocol, version 3 (POP3)* account, provided by the ISP. Exercise 7.12 walks you through the steps to configure a POP3 mailbox for a user.

EXERCISE 7.12

Configuring a Mailbox for POP3 Delivery

1. In Microsoft Outlook, choose the Tools menu and then choose Email Accounts from the Tools menu.

2. In the Email Accounts dialog box, choose Add a New Email Account, and then click Next.

3. In the Server Type dialog box, choose POP3, and then click Next.

EXERCISE 7.12 *(continued)*

4. In the Email Accounts dialog box, enter the username, email address, and logon information, and then fill in the POP3 and SMTP server addresses as provided by the ISP. The POP3 address is for incoming mail, while the SMTP address is for outgoing mail.

5. If the outgoing server requires authentication, click the More Settings button, and then choose the Outgoing Server tab. Select the My Outgoing Server (SMTP) Requires Authentication box.

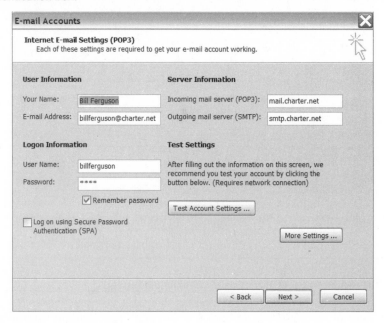

6. Configure the username and password for your outgoing server. If the outgoing server will use the same credentials as the incoming server, you can simply select the Use Same Settings as My Incoming Mail Server option.

7. Click Test Account Settings to test the POP3 and SMTP addresses that you entered. The system will send out and receive a message that proves that the accounts are working properly.

8. Click Next, and then click Finish.

This is the only configuration necessary if a user is using only one computer to check their email. If the user is using more than one computer, you may want to configure the mailbox to leave a copy of the messages on the server; otherwise, once messages have been downloaded onto one computer, they will not be accessible from the server to download to another computer. Exercise 7.13 walks you through the steps to configure the user's mailbox to leave a copy of messages on the server.

EXERCISE 7.13

Configuring a Mailbox to Leave Messages on the Server

1. In Microsoft Outlook, click the Tools menu, and then choose Email Accounts.

2. In the Email Accounts dialog box, click View or Change Existing Email Accounts, and then click Next.

3. Select your POP3 email account and click Change.

4. Click More Settings.

5. On the Advanced tab, select Leave a Copy of Messages on the Server, and then click OK.

6. Click Next, and then click Finish.

CONFIGURING MAILBOXES FOR IMAP

IMAP is a method for email programs to access email and bulletin board messages that are stored on a mail server. IMAP allow the user to view the headings and the senders of email and then decide whether to download the entire message. Unlike POP3, a user can search for a specific message without downloading all of their email. Because all email messages are maintained on the server, the user can access the messages from more than one computer. Exercise 7.14 walks you through the steps to configure a mailbox for IMAP email service.

EXERCISE 7.14

Configuring a Mailbox for IMAP

1.   In Microsoft Outlook, click the Tools menu, and then choose Email Accounts.

2.   In the Email Accounts dialog box, choose Add a New Email Account, and then click Next.

3.   In the Server Type dialog box, choose IMAP, and then click Next.

4.   On the Internet Email Settings (IMAP) screen, enter the required user and logon information.

5.   Enter the name of the IMAP server for incoming mail and the name of the SMTP server (provided by the ISP) for outgoing mail.

6.   Click Next, and then click Finish.

CONFIGURING MAILBOXES FOR HTTP MAIL ACCOUNTS

Some email accounts are based on the Web, such as Hotmail accounts. You can configure a user's Outlook software to create a mailbox for messages received in web-based accounts. Exercise 7.15 walks you through the steps to configure mailboxes for web-based accounts.

EXERCISE 7.15

Configuring a Mailbox for an HTTP Mail Account

1.   In Microsoft Outlook, click the Tools menu, and then choose Email Accounts.

2.   In the Email Accounts dialog box, choose Add a New Email Account, and then click Next.

3.   In the Server Type dialog box, choose HTTP, and then click Next.

EXERCISE 7.15 *(continued)*

4.   On the Internet Email Settings (HTTP) screen, enter the required user and logon information.

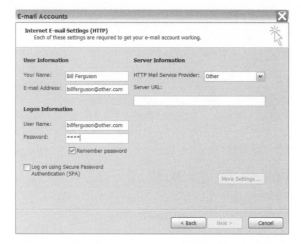

5.   Enter the server information. If your server is not available, choose Other from the drop-down list and enter the URL of the server.

6.   Click Next, and then click Finish.

CONFIGURING MAILBOXES FOR EXCHANGE

Configuring Outlook mailboxes for Exchange is relatively simple. When Outlook is first started after installation, a wizard guides the user through the entire process. You can also add an Exchange mailbox to a user's account. Exercise 7.16 walks you through the steps to add an Exchange mailbox to an existing profile.

EXERCISE 7.16

Adding an Exchange Mailbox to an Existing Account

1.   Ensure that Microsoft Outlook is closed. In Windows XP, click Start and then choose Control Panel.

2.   In Control Panel, choose Switch to Classic View, and then double-click Mail.

EXERCISE 7.16 *(continued)*

3. In the Mail Setup dialog box, choose Show Profiles.

4. On the General tab, choose the profile that you want to use, and then click Properties.

5. In the Mail Setup dialog box, choose Email Accounts.

6. In the Email Accounts dialog box, select Add a New Email Account, and then click Next.

7. In the box labeled Server Type, select Microsoft Exchange Server.

8. In the box labeled Exchange Server Settings, enter the required information, including the name of the Exchange server and the username.

9. Select Check Name to make sure that the server recognizes the name.

10. Click Next and then click Finish.

11. In the Mail Setup dialog box, click Close and then click OK.

CONFIGURING MICROSOFT OUTLOOK FOR DIGITAL CERTIFICATES

Email has become an integral part of business today, and as a result, email is often used to send confidential and highly sensitive information. There are many ways to ensure that your data is both digitally signed and encrypted. It is often difficult to accurately determine the true identity of an email author. It is very easy to obtain a free email account using someone else's name. You can use digital certificates to digitally sign emails, therefore ensuring their origin. You can also use digital certificates to encrypt data so that it can only be read by its intended recipient. There a few requirements that must be met before you can use the security features of Microsoft Outlook. First, you have to obtain a digital certificate. Then you must configure Outlook to use them. Finally, to use encryption, you must have a copy of the recipient's digital certificate. Exercise 7.17 will show you how to configure Outlook to use email security.

EXERCISE 7.17

Configuring Microsoft Outlook for Secure Email

1. Open Microsoft Outlook and choose Tools ➢ Options from the menu bar.

2. Click the Security tab in the Options dialog box. At the bottom you will see the Digital IDs (Certificates) section.

3. If you already have a digital certificate, you can click Import/Export; otherwise, you should click Get a Digital ID.

4. If you are importing a digital certificate, you can simply browse to it.

5. Once you have imported the digital certificate, you are ready to send signed messages. Open a new message and choose Options on the toolbar.

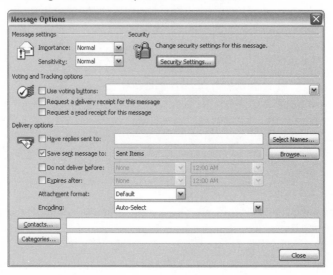

6. Click the Security Settings button.

7. Check the Add Digital Signature to This Message box to digitally sign your email.

8. Fill out your email information and send it off. It is now digitally signed.

WARNING Be sure to purchase your certificate from a trusted vendor. If the recipient cannot verify your certificate, they might not be able to open your message, or they might receive a message that the certificate can't be verified.

TROUBLESHOOTING MAILBOX CONFIGURATION

As you can see, there are many settings involved in mailbox configuration. Since users by default have the permissions to create their own mailboxes, you may be asked to troubleshoot what a user has attempted to configure. Table 7.3 lists the most common configuration errors and their solutions.

TABLE 7.3   Common Mailbox Configuration Errors and Their Solutions

Error	Solution
The username or password is incorrect.	Remember that the password and username may be case sensitive depending on the ISP. Check your settings in the Email Accounts dialog box.
Server times out.	Increase the setting in the Email Accounts dialog box.

TABLE 7.3 Common Mailbox Configuration Errors and Their Solutions *(continued)*

Error	Solution
Order of account processing is incorrect.	For users with multiple accounts, you can change the order in which the accounts are processed. The account that is used most often should be processed first.
Deleted messages remain on the server.	If you do not want this to occur, you can change the settings in the Email Accounts dialog box by selecting More Settings.
Copies of messages are not stored on the server.	Make sure that the settings on the computer with which you are accessing the server are configured to leave the messages on the server. Make sure that you have not set the messages to be deleted after a set number of days and that the ISP does not have a policy of deleting messages after a period of time.
ISP requires secure password authentication.	Configure this setting in the Email Accounts dialog box by selecting the check box.
Outgoing email server requires authentication.	Configure the required authentication in the Email Accounts dialog box under the More Settings option on the Outgoing Server tab.

REPAIRING CORRUPT PST FILES

PST files are very similar to databases. They store data in an organized manner that allows for fast access. Unfortunately, that means that they are plagued with the same problems as databases, namely, corruption. File corruption occurs because the data file isn't cleanly closed or has been fragmented beyond recovery. Scanpst.exe is a tool that is built into the Office installation that can allow you recover and repair the corrupted data files created and used by Microsoft Outlook. You can find the scanpst.exe file in the C:\Program Files\Common Files\System\MSMAPI*xxxx*\ directory, where *xxxx* is your local installation number, as seen in Figure 7.1. You can see the steps related to recovering corrupt PST files in Exercise 7.18.

There is an alternate repair tool that works for OST (offline data files) named scanost.exe.

For some reason, each time you run the repair tool, it will find errors in your data file even if it is not corrupt. You should only use the repair tool if Outlook gives an indication of a corrupt data file. If you repair a data file that is not corrupt, you could end up corrupting it!

FIGURE 7.1   Scanpst.exe

EXERCISE 7.18

Recovering Corrupt PST Files

1. Open Windows Explorer and navigate to `C:\Program Files\Common Files\System\MSMAPI\`*xxxx*`\` where *xxxx* is your local installation number.

2. Double-click on the `scanpst.exe` file to open the Inbox Repair Tool dialog box.

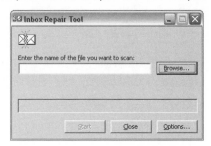

3. Select your PST file using the browse button and start the scan.

Note that your PST file is usually located inside your user profile (for example, `C:\Documents and Settings\brad\Local Settings\Application Data\Microsoft\Outlook\outlook.pst`).

4. If the repair tool finds any errors, you should keep the default option to make a backup of the PST file to ensure that you don't destroy it during the repair process.

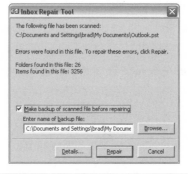

Internet Explorer

As we discussed in Chapter 6, "Troubleshooting Network Protocols and Services," Internet Explorer has become the browser of choice for most people who use the Internet. Users can easily connect to resources across the street or across the world without even knowing the actual location of the server that contains the information. In Chapter 6, we focused on the

Connections, General, and Security tabs as they related to using Internet Explorer as a connectivity tool. In this chapter, we will focus on the Programs, Content, Privacy, and Advanced tabs and discuss the settings that you can apply to Internet Explorer to enhance its functionality as an application.

Programs

You can configure the default program that Internet Explorer will use for each of six Internet-related tasks, such as writing an email message or editing an HTML document. Figure 7.2 shows the Programs tab of the Internet Options dialog box. You can click the drop-down arrows to the right of each of the six tasks to choose the application that the computer will use. The list of available programs that displays in the drop-down list will depend on which applications are installed on the computer. If Internet Explorer does not find an applicable program, the list will be blank. If you want the computer to recognize an older application that it cannot locate, you can manually edit the Registry.

FIGURE 7.2   The Programs tab of Internet Options

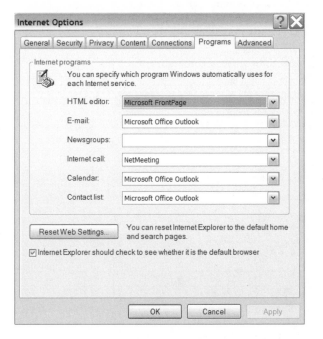

For information about manually adding program choices to the Windows XP Registry, go to the Microsoft Library at the following address: msdn.microsoft.com/library.

Content

The Internet is an extremely diverse environment that provides access to a wide variety of information. Some information may not be suitable for all viewers, to put it mildly! You can use the Content Advisor within the Content tab to help control the types of content that a user can access on the Internet. The Content tab also contains tools to control the behavior of digital certificates on the computer. Certificates can be used to protect a user as well as the computer itself. Finally, the Content tab contains the Personal information section, which includes tools that will complete web addresses for a user if the address has been typed before and other tools that allow a user to create a profile that can be used to automatically supply information for a website. In the following sections, we will discuss each of these concepts in greater detail.

Content Advisor

The purpose of the *Content Advisor* is to keep users from accessing websites that contain material that could be considered offensive. The Content Advisor works by a system of ratings that judge content based on four areas: Language, Nudity, Sex, and Violence, as shown in Figure 7.3. You must be logged in with an account that has administrative rights to activate the Content Advisor. You can enable the Content Advisor by setting a password that only you know. You will then need this password to change the settings in the future. Any settings that you apply in the Content Advisor will apply to all users of the computer.

FIGURE 7.3   Content Advisor in Internet Options

When you first enable the Content Advisor, the settings that are least likely to allow a user to access offensive content are in effect by default. You can adjust these settings to meet your own preferences. You can also use ratings bureaus to identify and block objectionable content. Unfortunately, not all Internet content is rated, and the content on the Internet changes on a daily basis, so maintaining an effective ratings system is a full-time job. You can also set exceptions for sites that can always be viewed or sites that can never be viewed regardless of any rating.

One of the problems with the content advisor is that it goes from one extreme to another. You can configure it to either block unrated sites or allow unrated sites. An approved ranking system is used to accurately identify the level of content on a particular site. There is supposed to be a mandate that forces all sites to build the ratings into their code; unfortunately, that has not been properly enforced. This lack of enforcement has led many sites to be "unrated." Because of the sheer number of unrated sites, setting the Content Advisor to block all unrated sites would result in the inability to view some safe sites. Setting the Content Advisor to allow all unrated sites will result in most unsafe sites being allowed.

Most enterprise and corporate environments use a third-party content filter that is more suitable and accurate.

Certificates

Digital certificates can be used to verify the identity of a person or the security of a website. Certificates are "electronic keys" that identify a user or a computer and are signed by a certificate authority (CA). A certificate authority is generally a highly trusted third party that is relied upon to verify the identity of an individual or a company. It's not necessary that you be an expert in regard to public key infrastructures, but you should be able to recognize and locate the various kinds of certificates to assist the network administrator in troubleshooting an Internet Explorer issue regarding certificates.

There are four kinds of digital certificates that are used on the Internet:

Personal certificates   Personal certificates identify individuals. They are used with email and other specialized applications, such as banking software, to prove the identity of the user. Once personal certificates are installed, they work transparently for the user. On the Content tab of the Internet Options dialog box, choose Certificates and then choose the Personal tab to view the list of personal certificates installed on a computer.

Server certificates   Server certificates identify servers that participate in secure communications with other computers using communication protocols such as Secure Sockets Layer (SSL). Servers use these certificates to prove their identity to their clients. Server certificates follow the X.509 certificate format that is defined by the Public-Key Cryptography Standards (PKCS).

Software publisher certificates   Software publisher certificates inform the user whether or not the software publisher is participating in the infrastructure of trusted publishers and CAs. Using only software from a certified publisher decreases the risk of downloading and installing software that might damage your computer or your data. To view a list of the trusted software publishers, choose Publishers on the Content tab of the Internet Options dialog box.

Certificate Authority certificates   Certificate authority certificates are divided into two categories: Root CAs and Intermediate CAs. Root CAs are self-signed; in other words, a company is in essence verifying itself. Root CAs can assign certificates to Intermediate CAs, which then issue personal, server, and publisher certificates or even certificates for other Intermediate CAs. This is referred to as a certificate hierarchy. You can view all of the trusted Root CAs and Intermediate CAs that are recognized by your computer by choosing Certificates on the Content tab.

Personal Information

The Personal information section of the Content tab contains two main tools: AutoComplete and Profile Assistant. Both of these tools can be used to increase the speed and ease of use of Internet Explorer. In the section, we will discuss the configuration of each of these timesaving options.

AutoComplete

You can configure AutoComplete to remember what a user has done in the past and then make suggestions as the user types. If the suggestions are correct, the user can simply press the Enter key to accept the suggestion. You can specify whether you want AutoComplete to remember web addresses, form information, usernames and passwords on forms, or all of the above. Figure 7.4 shows the AutoComplete Settings dialog box within the Content tab.

FIGURE 7.4   The AutoComplete Settings dialog box

Profile Assistant

The Profile Assistant stores a user's personal information, such as name, address, telephone number, email address, and so on. When the user accesses a website that requests this information, the Profile Assistant can enter the information for the user. You or the user should click the My Profile button on the Content tab and then complete all of the information that you want the Profile Assistant to automatically enter in future transactions. After the information is entered, the Profile Assistant will automatically complete the matching required information on website forms. This can be a great time-saver for the user.

You can remove an item from the list of items suggested when you're typing passwords and information in web by clicking the item and then pressing the Delete key.

Privacy

When you access a website on the Internet, the website also accesses you! As you browse the content on the website, it can download files, called cookies, into your computer and read the cookies that are already there. This can work to your advantage if it helps you to browse the websites more quickly in future. It also helps the vendor on the website make suggestions about what you might be interested in based on what you've done before. Some people consider cookies to be harmless and maybe even a little helpful at times. Other people consider cookies to be a blatant invasion of privacy!

How you feel about cookies will probably be determined by how your organization regulates their use. You can adjust the settings that affect a computer's use of cookies on the Privacy tab of Internet Options, shown in Figure 7.5. You can adjust the slider control on a continuum between block all cookies and accept all cookies. You can also override the default settings on a per-site basis.

FIGURE 7.5   Privacy settings in Internet Explorer

For more information about the Privacy settings in Internet Explorer, see Microsoft Knowledge Base article 283185.

Advanced

You can use the Advanced tab to customize many aspects of Internet Explorer. The settings on the Advanced tab fall into eight categories:

- Accessibility: Settings for configuring accessibility options for users with physical disabilities
- Browsing: Settings for configuring how web pages are viewed
- HTTP 1.1: Settings that specify how the Hypertext Transfer Protocol (HTTP) is used by the browser
- Microsoft VM: Settings for configuring Java operations on Internet Explorer (if Java is installed)
- Multimedia: Settings for configuring support for sound, a joystick, and so on
- Printing: Settings that control background print operations
- Search: Settings that control the default search options
- Security: Settings for configuring the use of certificates, Secure Sockets Layer (SSL), and other security options

You can choose Restore Defaults on the Advanced tab to reset all settings to their original installation state.

Outlook Express

Outlook Express is a simple messaging tool that comes bundled with the Windows operating system. It does not come bundled with Microsoft Office software. Most organizations prefer to use Outlook because of the additional functionality and security that it provides. Some organizations may use Outlook Express to avoid purchasing additional messaging software. In addition, users may use Outlook Express on their home computers to receive work-related email or newsgroups. For these reasons, you should know how to configure Outlook Express for your users. In the following sections, we will discuss configuring and troubleshooting Outlook Express for email accounts and for newsgroups.

Configuring and Troubleshooting Outlook Express for Email Accounts

You can configure POP3, IMAP, and HTTP accounts in Outlook Express using the same tool. Since users also have access to this tool, they might ask you to help them fix a setting that they have attempted to configure. You should be able to recognize the most common configuration errors and provide the appropriate solutions. In the following sections, we will discuss both of these concepts in detail.

Configuring Outlook Express Email Accounts

Accounts in Outlook Express can be POP3, HTTP, or IMAP based. You can use the same tool to create all three types of accounts. Exercise 7.19 walks you through the steps to create a POP3 account. The other types of accounts are very similar to create, and the wizard guides you through the steps.

EXERCISE 7.19

Creating a POP3 Account in Outlook Express

1. In Microsoft Outlook Express, choose Tools and then choose Accounts.

2. In the Internet Accounts dialog box, click Add.

3. Choose Mail to open the Internet Connection Wizard.

4. Enter the username and then click Next.

5. Enter the email address of the user and then click Next.

6. Select POP3 from the drop-down list.

7. In the Incoming Mail Server field, enter the POP3 address assigned by the ISP.

8. In the Outgoing Mail Server field, enter the SMTP address assigned by the ISP, and then click Next.

9. Enter the user's password for the account, and then click Next.

10. Click Finish.

Troubleshooting Outlook Express Email Accounts

Troubleshooting Outlook Express can be a challenge because there are so many configuration options to consider. You should remember that the key to troubleshooting is isolating the problem. In Outlook Express, there are really only two problems that users can have: either they cannot send email or they cannot receive email.

If a user can receive email but cannot send email, the problem is most likely based in the SMTP settings for their accounts. By the same token, if they can send email but cannot receive email, then the problem is most likely based in the POP3, IMAP, or HTTP settings. If they can do none of the above, they may not be online or may have a general connectivity problem. If you examine all of the settings and cannot pinpoint the problem, you may want to create a new account for the user.

Outlook Express stores its information a little differently from Microsoft Outlook. Instead of using PST files, Outlook Express uses individual data files that are named after their contents. You can find your data files by checking for their location inside of Outlook Express. Usually, your Outlook Express files will be located inside your profile folder, such as `C:\Documents and Settings\User\Local Settings\Application Data\Identities\`*xxxx*`\Microsoft\Outlook Express`, where *xxxx* is a local install number. Exercise 7.20 walks you through backing up Outlook Express.

Configuring and Troubleshooting Outlook Express for Newsgroups

A newsgroup is a forum on the Internet that is used for threaded discussions on a specified topic or range of topics. You can find newsgroups on everything from business ethics to fly-fishing. A newsgroup consists of articles and follow-up postings. Each newsgroup has a name that consists of a series of words separated by periods. The words become more specific as you read from left to right, such as rec.fishing.flyfishing. You can configure Outlook Express to locate newsgroups as long as your ISP offers links to one or more news servers called Network News Transfer Protocol (NNTP) servers. Users can subscribe to their favorite newsgroups to make them easier to access. Some newsgroups are public, while others are private, requiring an account name and password to connect.

In the following sections, we will discuss how to make Outlook Express the default newsgroup reader. We will also discuss how to create a newsgroup account and how to subscribe to a newsgroup. Finally, we will discuss how to troubleshoot common problems associated with newsgroups.

EXERCISE 7.20

Backing up Outlook Express Data Files

1. Open Outlook Express and choose Tools ➤ Options.

2. Choose the Maintenance tab in the Options dialog box.

3. Click the Store Folder button and copy the path displayed in the Address bar.

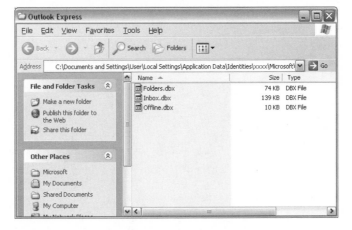

4. Paste the path into the Windows Explorer address bar.

5. Copy the files to an alternate location.

Creating and Subscribing to a Newsgroup Account

In order for a user to be able to read newsgroups messages, a newsgroup account must be properly configured for the user. To create the newsgroup account, you will need to know the following:

- The name of the NNTP server to which you want to connect
- Your account name and password if one is required

Exercise 7.21 walks you through the steps to create a newsgroup account.

EXERCISE 7.21

Creating a Newsgroup Account

1. In Microsoft Outlook Express, choose Tools and then choose Accounts.

2. In the Internet Accounts dialog box, click Add, and then select News to open the Internet Connection Wizard.

3. Provide a display name for the new account (any name will suffice).

4. Provide your email address, and then click Next.

5. Type the name of the NNTP server. If this is a private newsgroup, select My News Server Requires Me to Log On, click Next, and enter your credentials.

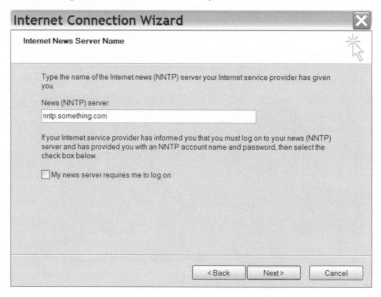

6. Click Finish.

Making Outlook Express the Default Newsgroup Reader

After you have created a newsgroup account, you can configure Outlook Express to be the default newsgroup reader for a user. This simplifies using newsgroups for the user by opening Outlook Express anytime they choose a newsgroup link on a web page or a newsreader command in a browser. Exercise 7.22 walks you through the steps to configure Outlook Express as the default newsgroup reader.

EXERCISE 7.22

Configuring Outlook Express as the Default Newsgroup Reader

1. In Microsoft Outlook Express, choose Tools and then choose Options.

2. On the General tab, in the Default Messaging Programs area, next to This Application Is NOT The Default News Handler, click Make Default.

3. Click OK.

Troubleshooting Newsgroups

Troubleshooting newsgroups is similar to troubleshooting email accounts; it's all based on isolating the issue that is causing the problem. If the user cannot connect to any NNTP servers but can connect to the ISP, then you should review the settings on the newsgroup account. If the user can connect to some NNTP servers but not others, then the problem may be at the news server or may be one involving authentication. In this case, you should review the credential settings for any accounts that require authentication. You can also adjust the search time-out in the Advanced settings for the connection to give the news server more time to respond to the request for a connection.

Application Support

If you are old enough to remember when DOS first hit the market, then you will recall that we only had the DOS prompt with which to work. There were no windows to open and there was no mouse to click. Only one user could be logged on to a computer at a time, and only one application could be running at a time. Software has come a long way over the last 20 years!

As application software and operating system software evolved over time, Microsoft decided to make much of each new operating system backward compatible with the old applications. This meant that you could continue to use the software to which you had become accustomed even if you upgraded to the latest operating system. This backward compatibility came in many different forms over the last 20 years, depending on the operating system and the type of applications that were to be supported. While backward compatibility is a convenience for the user, it can be a troubleshooting issue for a desktop support technician. Another troubleshooting challenge occurs when more than one person uses the same computer. In the following sections, we will discuss each of these concepts in greater detail.

Backward Compatibility

Backward compatibility in regard to operating systems is the capability of an operating system to create an environment that supports an older application. In other words, it's the capability of a computer to simulate the environment that the older application is expecting. For example, programs designed for DOS can be run in the newer operating systems using a special application environment called a *Windows NT Virtual DOS Machine (NTVDM)*. Also, programs that were designed for 16-bit operating systems such as Windows 3.1 and the original Windows 95 can be run in a 32-bit environment using a program called Win16 on Win32 (WOW), which operates in the context of an NTVDM. Windows XP takes backward compatibility to a new level with tools such as Application Compatibility Mode, which can simulate the correct environment for an application, and the Program Compatibility Wizard, which can help troubleshoot application compatibility issues. We will discuss each of these concepts in greater depth.

NTVDM

Many 16-bit applications that were developed during the late 1980s and early 1990s are still in use today. While these applications don't have the intense graphics or extreme power of 32-bit applications, some of them are still perfect for their intended use and have no successor. Since businesses continue to use these applications, you should know how to install them on a computer that runs one of the newer operating systems, such as Windows XP.

In order for a 16-bit application to run on a 32-bit operating system, the 32-bit operating system must simulate a 16-bit operating system like the one for which the application was designed. You can use a computer running Windows XP to simulate one or many "mini operating systems" for 16-bit applications. These mini operating systems are referred to as NTVDMs. They enable you to run DOS applications as well as 16-bit Windows applications in a Win32 environment such as Windows XP.

When you launch a DOS-based application in Windows XP, the operating system automatically creates an NTVDM. Each additional DOS-based application that you launch will be assigned its own NTVDM. This is because DOS can run only one application at a time. When you launch 16-bit applications, all 16-bit applications will be launched into the same NTVDM by default. This simulates a Windows 3.1 environment. You can also decide to launch each 16-bit application in its own NTVDM. You can customize the NTVDMs for 16-bit applications by changing the settings in their program information file (PIF). PIFs are used by the operating system to start the 16-bit application. They specify the simulated environment that will be created. To change the PIF on an installed 16-bit application, you should right-click the application and choose Properties. Each application will vary in regard to what can be configured, but you can generally configure the amount of memory that the application will use and whether the application will run in a window or in full-screen mode.

WARNING   You should be aware that if one 16-bit application crashes inside an NTVDM, it could cause all the other applications inside the same NTVDM to crash as well.

WOW

Win16 on Win32 (WOW) is a program that runs inside an NTVDM, enabling applications that were written for 16-bit Windows to run in a 32-bit Windows environment. WOW translates the 16-bit calls from applications into 32-bit calls. This process is referred to as "thunking." You can determine whether 16-bit applications are currently running on a computer by examining the Processes tab in Task Manager for an executable named `ntvdm.exe`, as shown in Figure 7.6. You will also see the `wowexec.exe` and the executable name of each 16-bit program that is running in the WOW virtual machine.

FIGURE 7.6 Task Manager with 16-bit applications running

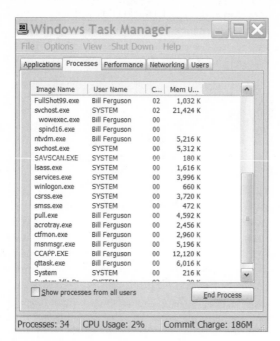

Application Compatibility Mode

Application Compatibility Mode is a special environment within the Windows XP operating system that closely simulates the behavior of the Windows NT and *Windows 9x* operating systems. Application Compatibility Mode resolves most of the issues that have prevented older programs from working correctly on the Windows 2000 Professional client. You can configure a program to run as if it were running in the previous operating system. You can even choose the resolution and color depth that the application will use. Exercise 7.23 walks you through the steps to configure programs to run in Application Compatibility Mode.

Program Compatibility Wizard

Windows XP includes a program called the Program Compatibility Wizard, which allows you to test an application in different modes or with different settings. You can set the application and the computer to run as if they were running on a previous version of the operating system. The main difference between the Program Compatibility Wizard and Application Compatibility Mode is that the Program Compatibility Wizard actually changes the settings and drivers in the computer to accommodate the application, so you should use caution when testing applications with the Program Compatibility Wizard. The Program Compatibility Wizard, shown in Figure 7.7, is located by default in the Accessories menu of Windows XP.

EXERCISE 7.23

Configuring Programs in Application Compatibility Mode

1. In Windows XP, right-click the shortcut of the program that you want to configure, and then choose Properties.

2. On the Compatibility tab, check Run This Program in Compatibility Mode For, and then select the operating system in which you want to run the program.

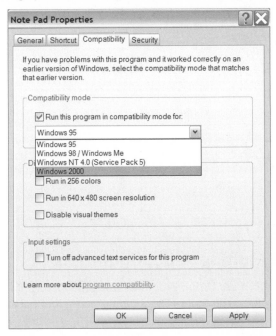

3. In the Display Settings area, select the display mode that the application requires, and click Apply.

4. Click OK to close the dialog and save the settings.

The Compatibility tab used for Application Compatibility Mode is available only after programs are installed on the hard drive. In contrast, you can use the Program Compatibility Wizard to test programs that are on a CD/DVD, but the settings will not remain in effect when you close the program.

FIGURE 7.7   The Program Compatibility Wizard

Multiuser and Multiboot Configuration

Network administrators can use Group Policy and IntelliMirror technology to create a multiuser computer with managed desktops. The computer settings of the multiuser computer allow users to configure some parts of their own desktop but not others. You should be aware of how managed desktops can affect your ability to configure a computer for a user and your need to escalate the issue to network administrator.

A multiuser computer configuration works best when the computer is in a public environment, such as a library, laboratory, or public computing center. Since the multiuser desktop experiences high traffic, it is protected so it's reliable for all users. It is also somewhat flexible so that users can customize it to some degree. You should understand what you have permissions to change on a computer that is a multiuser managed desktop and what you will have to escalate.

With the multiuser desktop configuration, users can do the following:

- Modify Internet Explorer settings
- Run applications that are assigned or published through Group Policy
- Configure some Control Panel options that relate to appearance

With the multiuser desktop configuration, users can be prevented from doing the following:

- Using the Run command in the Start menu or at a command prompt
- Adding, removing, or modifying hardware devices

As we discussed in Chapter 1, you and the users can install multiple operating systems on the same computer. If you choose to perform a multiboot installation, you should install each operating system in its own separate partition. You should be aware that each operating system will have its own Registry, which records the installation of applications and manages their use. For this reason, each operating system will require a separate installation of most application software.

You can share data files across operating systems as long the operating system that is being used to retrieve the files can use the file system that stored them. For example, Windows 98 can use only the FAT and FAT32 file systems; therefore it cannot be used to retrieve files that have been stored in NTFS volumes. For this reason, when you multiboot computers and share data files with multiple installations, you should format the partition that will store the files with a file system that is compatible with all of the operating systems on the computer.

Case Study: ABC Company Application Issues

Jim is working with you to deploy and configure Microsoft Office 2003 to 10,000 users throughout his organization. Jim has a mix of various previous versions of Microsoft Office as well as other desktop productivity suites. Most Windows 2000 PCs have either Open Office 2.0 or Star Office installed. Note that Star Office and Open Office are open source, or free versions of Microsoft Office.

All Windows XP Professional computers are running Microsoft Office 2002. Jim will also need to configure Microsoft Outlook on each PC to use the in-house Exchange server. The company also uses two custom DOS-based programs to export data from a database into a comma-separated (CSV) file. Once the file has been exported, it is imported into Microsoft Excel for use by the analyst department. All analyst computers are configured to dual-boot between Windows XP and Windows 98. In addition to configuring the entire company's computers for use with Microsoft Office 2003, Jim must ensure that the analyst users will always have access to their data.

Problem 1: Migrate users from open-source desktop productivity software to Microsoft Office 2003, ensuring the proper configuration of Microsoft Outlook.

Solution 1a: Use Control Panel to uninstall the third-party productivity software and install and configure Microsoft Office manually.

Solution 1b: Use an automated tool such as SMS or Group Policy to deploy Microsoft Office while uninstalling the third-party software. Use SMS to deploy a preconfigured MSI file that contains Microsoft Outlook configuration settings.

Answer 1: Each of the solutions offers a benefit. Solution 1a will be very expensive and take many man hours, but it also offers a lot of flexibility. If problems arise during the installation, the onsite technician can make adjustments. If there are multiple Exchange servers, this may be the only way to correctly configure each workstation. On the other hand, solution 1b offers a rapid deployment for the entire company. This option will also be the cheapest, not needing any "hands-on" assistance. The largest problem here is that the environment varies from one PC to the next. Each PC will require a certain configuration, whether it is removing software or configuring Office on multiple operating systems. Jim would need more information from upper-level management to make an accurate decision.

Note that the system folder for Windows 2000 is usually named WINNT whereas the system folder for Windows XP is usually named WINDOWS.

Problem 2: Ensure that all analysts are able to continue to use the custom DOS-based applications. Make all database information available to both of the operating systems installed. Ensure access to Microsoft Office for Windows XP.

Solution 2a: Manually configure the analysts' workstations with the Microsoft Office installation on the C: drive so that it can be used with Windows 98. Install the DOS-based applications in Windows XP and place its working directory on the NTFS drive so that both operating systems can have access to the data files generated from the database.

Solution 2b: Use an automated installation method such as SMS or Group Policy to deliver Microsoft Office 2003 to Windows XP. Configure the DOS-based applications to run in Windows XP and use the C: drive as the working directory to allow both operating systems to access the data.

Answer 2: Solution 2a would not meet the objectives. Installing Microsoft Office 2003 on the FAT32 file system would not allow Windows 98 to use the software. In addition, using an NTFS file system would restrict the availability of the data files to Windows XP. Solution 2b would meet the objectives with the minimal effort. Jim can use SMS or Group Policy to deliver the software to Windows XP. Because Windows XP includes WOW and NTVDM, Jim can emulate a DOS environment and use the custom applications to retrieve data from the database. Because Jim is storing the data on the C: drive, which is formatted with FAT32, he can be sure that both operating systems will have access to the required data.

Summary

With a complex scenario such as we have here, you want to take all things you have learned into consideration. You know that multiboot systems will have the older operating system installed first, meaning that the C: drive will be formatted with FAT32 or FAT. Any data files that require access from both of the installed operating systems will need to be stored on the older file system. Because you need to configure Microsoft Outlook accurately, you should be sure that you are prepared for the possibility of multiple Exchange servers. You should also be aware of Windows XP's compatibility option with older DOS-based applications.

Summary

It's not enough that you understand the Windows operating system; you must also understand the most common applications that users are running on the operating system, such as Microsoft Office, Outlook Express, and Internet Explorer. In addition, as a desktop support technician, you must understand how the newer operating systems, such as Windows XP, can simulate the environment that older applications were designed to work within, making it possible for organizations to continue to use older applications on the latest operating systems. Finally, you should understand the additional issues and challenges that you may encounter when you have more than one user or more than one operating system on the same computer.

Microsoft Office has become the leading suite of business applications in the world today. The newest release, Office 2003, comes in many editions, which include program bundles designed for a specific environment, such as a business enterprise or an academic environment. Programs include Word, Excel, PowerPoint, Outlook, and so on, each having its own specific business use. You can purchase these programs over the retail counter or through special channels, depending on your type of business. You can install Office 2003 using the CD, through the network, or by using an automated method such as SMS. Office 2003 includes new features that protect your data, including the Application Recovery Tool and AutoRecover.

Outlook, one of the programs included in Microsoft Office, is an email and scheduling program that is designed to increase worker productivity. Outlook helps users manage email messages, notes, contacts, tasks, and other information. It can be configured for general Internet access or for a specialized server that stores an organization's messages, referred to as Exchange Server. Configuring a user for Outlook email is a two-step process: First you create a profile for the user, and then you configure the mailbox or mailboxes that user will utilize. Troubleshooting Outlook is usually a process of examining the settings that were configured by a user.

Internet Explorer is the browser that most people use to access the Internet. It has many configuration options to accommodate the user and make browsing the Internet as safe and pleasant as possible. You can configure Internet Explorer to automatically call on other programs installed on your computer from within the browser when they are required for specific tasks, such as email or HTML editing. In addition, you can adjust the settings on the Privacy tab to control how the computer allows special personal information files called cookies to be used by websites. You can fine-tune eight categories related to Internet Explorer on the Advanced tab in Internet Options.

Outlook Express is a simple messaging tool that comes bundled with the Windows operating system, but it does not come with Microsoft Office. Organizations may use Outlook Express to avoid purchasing other email software. Users may use Outlook Express at home for email as well as newsgroups. You can configure POP3, HTTP, and IMAP email accounts and NNTP newsgroup accounts using the same set of tools and the Internet Connection Wizard. Troubleshooting these accounts is a process of isolating the problem and checking the appropriate configurations.

Windows XP can, of course, run all of the latest software, but it can also run most of the old software that was designed for earlier operating systems, such as Windows 95, Windows 98, and Windows NT Workstation. This backward compatibility is accomplished using NTVDMs,

WOW, and Application Compatibility Mode. An NTVDM is a virtual machine that is created automatically when a 16-bit application is launched in Windows XP. With Application Compatibility Mode, you can run programs that were designed for older 32-bit operating systems in Windows XP as if you were running them in the operating system for which they were designed. The Program Compatibility Wizard lets you experiment with an application and the computer settings both before you install the application and after, but you should use the program with caution because it changes settings that might affect other programs.

Special challenges can result when you troubleshoot computers that are configured as multiuser computers by the network administrator. Users do not have the ability to change many of the configuration settings of the computer, such as the hardware settings or network connection settings. This may cause a need to escalate the issue to the network administrator, even when you might know the solution to the problem.

Client computers can also be configured with multiple operating systems. This is referred to as a multiboot configuration. Each operating system should be installed in its own partition. Each operating system will have a separate Registry and will require its own installation of applications. You can share data across operating systems provided that the operating system that is retrieving the data supports the file system in which the data is stored. You should know how to assist users with these multiboot application issues.

Exam Essentials

Know how to install and repair Microsoft Office 2003. You should know how to install, configure, and troubleshoot Microsoft Office 2003. You should also know how to activate the software over the Internet and over the telephone. In addition, you should know how to scan for updates on the Office Update website. Finally, you should know how to add and remove components and repair Office installations when needed.

Know how Microsoft Office 2003 AutoRecover works. You should know that AutoRecover automatically saves versions of files so that you can use them in an emergency. In addition, you should know that AutoRecover works best when the emergency is a power interruption on a desktop or even a laptop. Finally, you should know that AutoRecover works automatically when the application is restarted.

Understand when to use Shadow Copy. You should understand that Shadow Copy is a service that the network administrator can run on a file server to protect data for users. In addition, you should know that the Shadow Copy service stores versions of an entire volume of files sorted by time. Finally, you should know that users can utilize this service only if they have the software client installed on their computer.

Be able to configure Microsoft Outlook. You should know how to configure Outlook for Internet email and for Exchange email. Specifically, you should know how to create an Outlook profile and then configure mailboxes for POP3, IMAP, HTTP, and Exchange accounts. You should also know how to troubleshoot common issues with mailbox configurations.

Be able to configure Internet Explorer.   You should know how to configure the Programs, Content, Privacy, and Advanced tabs of Internet Explorer's Internet Options dialog box. You should become familiar with all of the options on each of these tabs and how they can affect the user. You should also know how to troubleshoot errant configurations set by users.

Know how to configure Outlook Express.   You should know how to configure Outlook Express for email accounts and newsgroups. Specifically, you should be able to configure POP3, IMAP, HTTP, and NNTP accounts for Outlook Express. You should also know how to troubleshoot the most common issues regarding Outlook Express.

Know how to support older applications in Windows XP.   You should know that Windows XP can support many different types of applications, even those designed for much older operating systems. Specifically, you should know how NTVDMs are used by the operating system to create a simulated environment for 16-bit applications. In addition, you should know how Windows XP's Application Compatibility Mode can run older 32-bit applications as if they were running in the older operating system. Finally, you should know how to use the Program Compatibility Wizard to test an application on a computer using various settings.

Be able to troubleshoot multiuser issues.   You should know the specific troubleshooting issues regarding application support on computers configured as managed multiuser computers. Specifically, you should know that since users cannot configure the hardware or the network connection settings on these computers, you probably can't configure them either. You should know that users cannot use the Run command in the Start menu or on the Taskbar. Finally, you should be aware that these limitations may cause you to escalate the issue to the network administrator, even though you might know the solution to the problem.

Be able to troubleshoot multiboot computers   You should know that computers that have more than one operating system installed will need to have a separate instance of most applications installed for each operating system. In addition, you should know that each operating system will have a separate record of each application in its Registry. You should also know that each operating system should be installed on its own partition. Finally, you should know that these computers can share data across the operating systems as long as the data is formatted in a file system that all of the operating systems can use.

Review Questions

1. You are the desktop support technician for your organization. You are performing a manual installation of Microsoft Office 2003. You wish to install only the Microsoft Word program, but you do not want to install all underlying optional components. Which of the following should you do?

   A. Choose Typical Install, and then select Word.

   B. Choose Custom Install, and then choose Run All from My Computer for Word and Do Not Install for all other components.

   C. Choose Typical Install, and then choose Run from My Computer for Word and Not Available for all other components.

   D. Choose Custom Install, and then choose Run from My Computer for Word and Not Available for all other components.

2. You are the desktop support technician for your company. You want to upgrade a user's applications from Office 2000 to Office 2003. You insert the CD into the drive and close it, but the program does not automatically run as expected. You want to start the program manually. Which of the following should you do?

   A. Access the Office folder on the CD and double-click the `autorun` file.

   B. Access the root folder of the CD and double-click the `setup.exe` file.

   C. Access the Office folder on the CD and double-click the `setup.exe` file.

   D. Access the Office 2003 folder on the CD and double-click the `setup.exe` file.

3. You are the desktop support technician for a large organization. All users are directed to store their important files on a centrally located file server rather than on their own hard drives. The data is backed up on a nightly basis. You want to recommend a method of further protecting the user data on the file servers. Which of the following should you recommend?

   A. AutoRecover

   B. Application Recovery Tool

   C. Shadow Copy

   D. Microsoft Windows Installer

4. You are the desktop support technician for a large company with many email users. You receive a call from a user who has attempted to set up a mailbox to his ISP, but he is receiving an error indicating that the ISP requires Secure Password Authentication. You do not have immediate access to a computer. Which dialog box contains the setting that the user needs to change?

   A. The Global Security Settings dialog box for Outlook

   B. The Security settings for the mailbox

   C. The Email Accounts dialog box for that specific account

   D. The Global Email Accounts dialog box

5. You are the desktop support technician for a large company with many users. A user asks you if there is any way to automatically fill in the information on websites that ask for name, address, telephone number, email address, and so on. There are no security restrictions in your organization that prevent this action. Which of the following features should you show the user?

   A. AutoComplete

   B. AutoRecover

   C. Public Key Cryptography

   D. Profile Assistant

6. You are the desktop support technician for a large company. Many of your users work from home, using Microsoft Outlook Express to send and receive email. You receive a call from a user who says that he thinks that one of his friends tampered with his email settings and now he can receive email normally but nobody seems to be receiving his email and he keeps getting errors. Which of the following settings should you direct the user to examine?

   A. SMTP address

   B. IMAP address

   C. NNTP address

   D. POP3 address

7. You are the desktop support technician for your company. Users in the research department make extensive use of newsgroups to get the latest information and industry trends. A user calls you complaining that she cannot connect to some newsgroup servers but she can connect to others. What should you do to allow the user to connect to all newsgroup servers? (Choose all that apply.)

   A. Check the network connection settings on the computer.

   B. Check the search time-out setting on the NNTP connection.

   C. Check the authentication settings on the connections for the NNTP servers with which she cannot connect.

   D. Check the SMTP settings for all connections.

8. You are the desktop support technician for a large company with many users. All users have desktop computers running Windows XP Professional. Some users still utilize 16-bit applications that were designed for DOS or the Windows 3.1 operating system. You want to determine whether there are any applications currently running on a user's computer that were designed for DOS or Windows 3.1. Which of the following should you do?

   A. Open Task Manager and search the Applications tab for the presence of the NTVDM application.

   B. Open Task Manager and search the Performance tab for the presence of the `ntvdm.exe` file.

   C. Open Task Manager and search the Performance tab for the presence of the `ntvdm.exe` application.

   D. Open Task Manager and search the Processes tab for the presence of the `ntvdm.exe` executable file.

9. You are the desktop support technician for a large company. All users have computers that run Windows 2000 Professional. Some users need to utilize applications that were designed for Windows 98. Some of these applications do not run well on Windows 2000. Your management team is considering upgrading the client computers to Windows XP Professional. Which feature(s) can you use for the Windows 98 applications after the upgrade is complete? (Choose all that apply.)

   A. NTVDM

   B. WOW

   C. Application Compatibility Mode

   D. Program Compatibility Wizard

10. You are the desktop support technician for a large company. You receive a call from a user who says that his Windows XP computer is not connecting to the network. He says that it's a computer that he shares with other users and they can't connect either. You tell the user to click Start and then choose Run. The user tells you that there is no Run Option in his Start menu. Which of the following could be causing this to happen?

    A. The network administrator has applied group policies to the computer and is managing it as a multiuser managed desktop.

    B. Windows XP is improperly installed.

    C. The user has accidentally deleted the Run Option from the Start menu.

    D. Windows XP does not have a Run Option in the Start menu.

11. You are the lead desktop support technician for your organization. Your company uses Windows XP as its primary desktop operating system. You receive a call from a user who claims to have changed some settings in Internet Explorer. Each time she attempts to access a website, Internet Explorer prompts her to either allow or deny the cookies delivered by the site. You need to ensure that the user can use Internet Explorer without interruption. What should you do?

    A. Verify settings on the Programs tab of the Settings dialog box.

    B. Verify settings on the Content tab of the Settings dialog box.

    C. Verify settings on the Connection tab of the Settings dialog box.

    D. Verify settings on the Privacy tab of the Settings dialog box.

12. You are a desktop support technician for your company. Your company uses Outlook Express as its default email client. You set up your POP email server so that each user account has the same name and password as the regular user account. You ask each user to configure their mail client to use the new POP server. One of the users reports that Outlook Express prompts him for his password each time he checks his email. You verify that other users are not experiencing this problem. You need to ensure that this user can access his email without having to type his password. What should you do?

    A. The user's account is locked out on the email server. You should reset it.

    B. The user's password has expired on the email server. You should request that the user choose a new password.

    C. The user is incorrectly entering his password. Verify that the Caps Lock key is not enabled.

    D. Make sure the option to save the password is not set in Outlook Express.

13. You are the senior help desk technician for your organization. A user calls into the help desk and says that each time she attempts to access an Internet address that starts with `https://`, she receives an error message. She has no problems accessing websites with `ftp://` and `http://` prefixes. You verify that no other users are having this problem. The user is using Internet Explorer to access websites. What should you do?

A. Reinstall Microsoft Windows XP on the user's PC.

B. Reinstall Internet Explorer on the user's PC

C. Configure SSL 2.0 and SSL 3.0 on the Advanced tab of the Internet Settings dialog box.

D. Request that the user type `http://` instead of `https://`

14. You are a help desk support technician for your company. Your company uses Windows XP Professional as its operating system of choice and Microsoft Office 2003 as its desktop productivity suite. One of your users says that some features in Microsoft PowerPoint do not work properly. You verify that this is an issue with all users. After contacting Microsoft support, you determine that these issues were addressed in a service pack released 30 days ago. You need to be sure that these features are available to all users. What should you do?

A. Reinstall Microsoft Office.

B. Use the Microsoft Windows Update tool to obtain the fix.

C. Guide the users to the Office Update website and ask them to scan for new updates.

D. Use the Detect and Repair option of Microsoft Office to resolve the issue.

15. You are a help desk support technician for your company. Your company uses Windows XP Professional as its desktop of choice. A user calls the help desk and reports that a legacy application will not run properly on her new Windows XP computer. The user states that the application is mission critical and must be working as soon as possible. What should you do?

A. Uninstall and reinstall the application.

B. Go online and attempt to find a compatible version of the application that works on Windows XP.

C. Configure the application to run in Application Compatibility Mode.

D. Reboot into safe mode and try to run the application again.

16. You are a help desk support technician for your company. Your company uses Windows XP Professional as its desktop of choice. A user is attempting to open Microsoft Word. Each time the user double-clicks the shortcut, the application fails to start and shows a "There is not enough Memory to perform this operation" error. You open Task Manager and verify that there are only 12MB of RAM available. When you view the list of running processes, you notice that the WOW and NTVDM processes are running, although they show minimal memory usage. You need to get Microsoft Word functional as quickly as possible. What should you do?

A. Reset the computer.

B. Assign the WOW and NTVDM processes the "low" priority.

C. Assign the WOW and NTVDM processes the "high" priority.

D. Select WOW and NTVDM and choose End Task.

17. You are the lead desktop support technician for your organization. Your company uses Windows XP as its primary desktop operating system. Your company has deployed shadow copies on all of your Server 2003 file servers. A user calls the help desk and says that he has accidentally overwritten his copy of an important PowerPoint presentation that is due in one hour. The slide show wasn't edited in over a week before the user overwrote it. You must ensure that the user can obtain the original copy of the PowerPoint presentation. What should you do?

A. Contact the backup administrator and request that the slide show be restored from backup.

B. Instruct the user to select the Previous Versions tab in the file's Properties dialog box and restore an original copy.

C. Tell the user that he is out of luck and to attempt to re-create the presentation.

D. Copy the original from the Shadow Copy cache on the root of the server to the user's desktop.

18. You are the desktop support technician for a large company with many users. All users have desktop computers running Windows XP Professional. One of the members of the application deployment team has been given an older 16-bit application to deploy to all finance users in the company. The member is not sure that the program will run on Windows XP. When he runs the application, it seems to try to run, but the screen resolution get messed up and the application fails after a few seconds. You need to make sure the member can run the older 16-bit application successfully on Windows XP. What should you do?

A. Instruct him to configure each finance machine to dual-boot to Windows 95 and to run the 16-application under the Windows 95 installation.

B. Tell him that because Windows XP is a 32-bit operating system, the 16-bit application will not run properly.

C. Instruct him to use the Program Compatibility Wizard to determine the proper configuration for the 16-bit application.

D. Use Windows Update to get the latest updates to the operating system so that the application will run properly.

19. You are the desktop support technician for a large company with many users. All users have desktop computers running Windows XP Professional. Your company uses Microsoft Outlook 2003 as its default email client. A user calls the help desk and states that when he attempts to click a Mail To link in Internet Explorer, it opens the Outlook Express Configuration Wizard. The user does not know how to configure Outlook Express. You need to ensure that user can utilize Mail To links in Internet Explorer. What should you do?

A. Show the user how to configure Outlook Express.

B. Reinstall Microsoft Outlook so it will reset to the default email client.

C. Instruct the user to configure the default email program on the Programs tab of the Internet Options dialog.

D. Reinstall Internet Explorer to reset the default email client.

20. You are the lead desktop support technician for your organization. Your company uses Windows XP as their primary desktop operating system. Your company uses Microsoft Office 2003 edition for desktop productivity software. A user with a laptop has called the helpdesk and states that her laptop battery ran out of power when she was writing an important report in Microsoft Word. She states that she had been writing the report for over an hour and never saved the document. She needs to turn in the report to her boss today. What should you do?

A. Instruct the user to quickly get back to work on the document to have it retyped by the end of business today.

B. Instruct the user to go the properties of the file and use the shadow copy recovery feature to recover the file.

C. Instruct the user to use the Microsoft Office Application Recovery Tool to recover her document.

D. Use a copy of the report from another user's directory on a shadow copy enabled share on the network.

Answers to Review Questions

1. D. You should choose Custom Install first to make the other options available. Then you should choose Run from My Computer for Word to install the program without installing all of the other underlying optional components. Finally, you should choose Not Available for all other Microsoft Office components to prevent them from being installed.

2. B. You should access the root folder of the CD and then double-click the `setup.exe` file. The `setup.exe` file is not contained in the Office folder or the Office 2003 folder. The `autorun` file is not contained in the Office folder.

3. C. You should recommend that the network administrators use Shadow Copy on the file servers. You should install the Shadow Copy client in each user's computer and train the users to use the Previous Versions tab. AutoRecover and the Application Recovery Tool are components on the client, not on the file server. Microsoft Windows Installer is a service that ensures that an application can start and run, but it does not protect data.

4. C. You should direct the user to use the Tools menu to access the Email Accounts dialog box for that specific account. You should then tell him to place a check mark on the box labeled Log On Using Secure Password Authentication (SPA). The Global Security settings for Outlook do not contain the SPA setting.

5. D. You should show the user the Profile Assistant on the Content tab of the Internet Options dialog box in Internet Explorer. The Profile Assistant can automatically fill in personal information on websites. AutoComplete makes suggestions as you type based on websites that you have visited before. AutoRecover makes version copies of files and stores them on the local computer's hard drive in case of a power failure. Public Key Cryptography is used for security within a network or through the Internet.

6. A. Since the user can receive email but not send it, you should direct him to the Simple Mail Transfer Protocol (SMTP) settings for his account. The IMAP and POP3 address could affect receiving email but not sending it. The NNTP address will affect only newsgroups, not email.

7. B, C. You should check the settings for authentication and search time-out for the NNTP servers' connections that will not connect. It is not necessary to check the network connections for the computer since some of the NNTP servers are connecting. The SMTP settings would affect a user's ability to send email, not to connect to NNTP servers.

8. D. You should open Task Manager and search the Processes tab for the presence of the `ntvdm.exe` executable file. The presence of this file in Processes indicates that at least one 16-bit application is currently running on the computer.

9. C, D. After the upgrade to Windows XP Professional is complete, you can use Application Compatibility Mode and the Program Compatibility Wizard to test and run the applications in an environment that closely simulates the Windows 98 operating system environment. NT virtual DOS machines (NTVDM) are used to run 16-bit applications on a 32-bit operating system. Win16 on Win32 (WOW) is used to convert 16-bit Windows calls to 32-bit Windows calls and vice versa.

10. A. Windows XP does normally have a Run option on the Start menu. The reason that the Run option does not appear for the users is that the network administrator has configured the computer as a managed multiuser desktop. You will have to escalate the issue to the network administrator. The users do not have the permissions to use the Run option or to change the hardware and/or connection settings on the computer. An improper installation will not cause the Run option to be inaccessible. The user cannot accidentally delete the Run option from the Start menu.

11. D. The Privacy tab of the Internet Options dialog box contains settings that allow you dictate how Internet Explorer will react to websites reading, creating, and modifying cookies on your hard drive. Setting the options back to the default here should allow the user to browse the Internet without receiving the prompts.

12. D. User accounts generally do not get "locked out" on email servers. If the user's Active Directory account had been locked out, the user would not have been able to log into the computer. In addition, the email client will usually notify the user that his account has been locked. Outlook and Outlook Express have the option to save the password so that authentication is not required to check your mail.

13. C. `https://`is the URL prefix for sites on which Secure Sockets Layer, or SSL, is used. If the sites are using SSL versions 2 or 3, then the user needs to have the proper options selected in the Advanced tab in the Internet Options dialog box. Reinstalling the operating system or Internet Explorer will not resolve the inability to connect to SSL-enabled sites. Typing `http://`instead of `https://`will cause an error; most HTTPS sites will not reply to non-HTTPS requests.

14. C. Microsoft Office updates are available only from the Office Update website. It is accessible at `http://office.microsoft.com/en-us/officeupdate/default.aspx`. Reinstalling or repairing Office will not resolve the problem because it was fixed in a later release. Windows Update does not check for Office updates.

15. C. Windows XP has the built-in ability to run older 16-bit applications in Compatibility Mode so that they function properly. Reinstalling the application won't fix the problem because the question doesn't say the install failed. Safe mode is going to fail as well; it's not a device driver or setting that is causing the application to fail.

16. D. Even though the Task Manager shows the WOW and NTVDM processes as using minimal memory, the application they are supporting is most likely experiencing a memory leak, meaning it doesn't release memory space when it is finished using it. Over time, this problem can cause the system to run low on physical memory.

17. B. Files that are stored on Shadow Copy-enabled volumes can be restored by using the Previous Versions tab in the Properties dialog box of the affected file. Although restoring the file from backup will solve the problem, it will most likely put the user over his one-hour deadline.

18. C. Windows XP has a built-in compatibility configuration tool called the Program Compatibility Wizard that will automatically determine the proper configuration for older applications that were not meant to run Windows XP. You can also save the configuration so that it can be deployed to other users.

19. C. All external programs used by Internet Explorer can be configured on the Programs tab of the Internet Options dialog box in Internet Explorer. You can also configure these options in Control Panel using the Internet Options applet.

20. C. Microsoft Office has a built in application called the Microsoft Office Application Recovery Tool that can recover lost documents. This program can be found under All Programs ➢ Microsoft Office ➢ Microsoft Office Tools ➢ Microsoft Office Application Recovery.

Chapter

8

Resolving Usability Issues

MICROSOFT EXAM OBJECTIVES COVERED IN THIS CHAPTER:

✓ Resolve issues related to Office application support features. Tasks include configuring Office applications and interpreting error messages.

✓ Resolve issues related to Internet Explorer. Tasks include configuring Internet Explorer and interpreting error messages.

✓ Resolve issues related to Outlook Express features. Tasks include configuring Outlook Express and interpreting error messages.

✓ Resolve issues related to operating system features. Tasks include configuring operating system features and interpreting error messages.

In the real world, applications don't always function without any problems. You should know how to configure the most commonly used software components to ensure continued usability for clients. You should also know how to interpret the error messages that you might encounter with each of these software components. In this chapter, we will discuss configuring and troubleshooting these software components to resolve issues related to usability.

The four components that are most commonly used on Microsoft networks are as follows:

Microsoft Office   You can reduce the risk of having problems related to Microsoft Office by installing only the components that a user requires. We will discuss how to customize an installation for a user's needs. Unfortunately, no matter how well you configure the installation, you may still have problems. These problems will often be revealed in an *error message*. We will discuss the tools that you can use to interpret error messages and troubleshoot problems associated with Microsoft Office.

Internet Explorer   There are many settings in Internet Explorer that can affect a user's experience. We will discuss how to configure the settings to make Internet Explorer more user-friendly. In addition, we will discuss how to use the Help menu built into Internet Explorer. Finally, we will discuss how to interpret error messages and troubleshoot the issues.

Outlook Express   Efficient use of Microsoft Outlook Express requires more than just the ability to set up a mailbox. There are many features that can enhance the usability of the software for each user or even for multiple users on the same computer. We will discuss the tools located within the File, Edit, View, Tools, and Message menus of Outlook Express. In addition, we will discuss using the Help menu and other tools to interpret and troubleshoot the error messages.

Operating system features   You can enhance the usability of the computer and the applications that it contains by understanding the configuration of the operating system itself. There are many features and options you can use to configure the computer for each user. We will focus on the Desktop of the latest operating system, Windows XP Professional, and discuss some of the options that you can configure to enhance the usability of the computer, including Start menu properties, Taskbar properties, and shortcuts. In addition, we will discuss interpreting and troubleshooting error messages related to the operating system.

Microsoft Office

Microsoft Office is one of the most commonly used applications on the network, partly because of all of the components that it contains. Users can utilize the software for word processing, spreadsheets, presentations, and more. In fact, there are so many tools contained in the Typical installation of Microsoft Office that it is unlikely that most users will need to use all of them. You can make your job a little easier by installing only the components that a user needs so there is less chance for programs to interfere with one another. Of course, no matter how well you install the software, there will be some problems. As a desktop support technician, you should know how to interpret error messages associated with Microsoft Office. In the following sections, we will discuss each of these concepts in greater detail.

Microsoft Application Customization

Within Microsoft Word there are many options available to you for customization. You will usually customize individual applications for usability purposes. Most of Microsoft's applications have customizable menus. In Exercise 8.1, we will examine some common customization options.

EXERCISE 8.1

Customizing Microsoft Word

1. Open Microsoft Word and examine the existing menu layout.

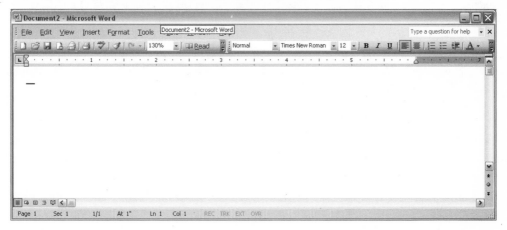

2.   Right-click on the menu bar and choose Customize.

3.   The Toolbars tab in the Customize dialog box allows to you add and remove toolbars on the default display.

4. The Commands tab allows you to customize the displayed commands in Microsoft Word.

5. The Options tab allows you to reset defaults and manipulate menu animations.

6. Once you have configured the customization options, simply click the Close button to commit the changes.

Microsoft Office Customization

The best way to troubleshoot a problem is to do all that you can to keep it from occurring in the first place. The more software a user has on their computer, the greater chance there is for a problem to develop. As a desktop support technician, you should ensure that users have the software required to perform their jobs. You should also ensure that they do not have software that is not required, especially if that software might cause problems. You can accomplish this goal in relation to Microsoft Office by customizing the installation whenever possible. You should ask users about their roles and make a decision about the software that they will need based on what they do. You should not ask them what software they want installed because most users won't know and some users will just tell you to install "everything you've got."

In Chapter 7, "Configuring and Troubleshooting Applications," we illustrated how to perform a Typical installation of Office 2003. While this type of installation generally provides the tools that users require, it also might install applications that they will never use. For example, a user might never need to use Excel because their job does not require the use of spreadsheets. These unnecessary tools not only take up space on the hard drive, they also create a potential source for future problems. To give user only what they require, you should know how to customize an installation of Office 2003. Exercise 8.2 walks you through the steps to perform a customized installation of Office 2003.

EXERCISE 8.2

Performing a Customized Installation of Office 2003

1. Insert the Office CD in the CD-ROM drive to launch the Office Setup program. If Setup does not run automatically, you can manually run the setup.exe program located in the root folder of the CD.

2. Enter the product key displayed on the label of the Office CD container in the Product Key screen, and then click Next.

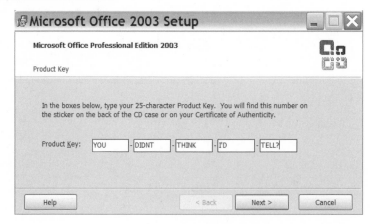

EXERCISE 8.2 *(continued)*

3. Enter your username, initials, and organization, and click Next.

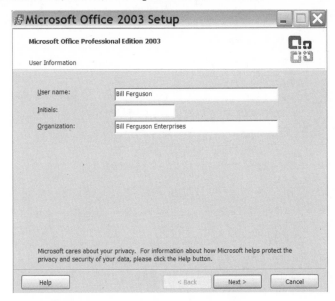

4. Accept the terms in the license agreement, and click Next.

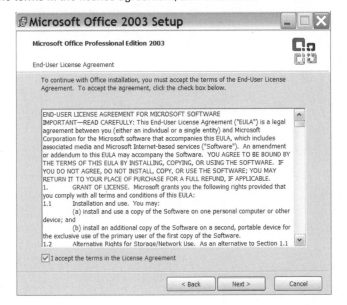

EXERCISE 8.2 *(continued)*

5. Select Custom Install for the installation type, and click Next.

6. Choose the specific applications for the user based on their use of the computer, select Choose Advanced Customization of Applications, and then click Next.

EXERCISE 8.2 *(continued)*

7. Examine the list of applications that will be installed, and ensure that only the appropriate applications are selected.

8. Click on the name of each selected application to fine-tune its installation, and then click Next. (Refer to Chapter 7 for the advanced installation options.)

9. Review the Summary page to ensure that only the applications you selected are listed and that the advanced options you selected are listed. Click Back to make any changes or Install to begin the installation. (You can also click Cancel to cancel the entire installation at this point.)

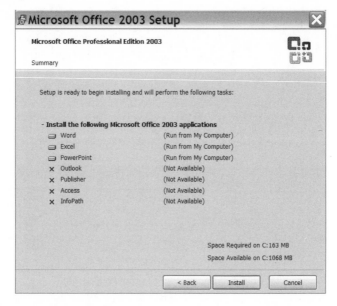

10. The system will begin the installation process and continue through each of the steps until the software is completely installed on the computer. When the installation is finished, the Setup Completed box will appear.

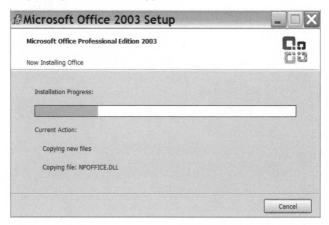

11. Select the Check the Web for Updates and Additional Downloads option to get the latest updates for the software that you have installed. This will automatically connect the computer to the Windows Update website provided that a connection to the Internet is established. You will also need to activate the software over the Web or by telephone. (Refer to Chapter 7 for details on activating software.) Click Finish to complete the installation.

Interpreting Microsoft Office Error Messages

No matter how well you install and maintain a user's computer, problems will still occur within and between applications. The good news is that the problems will often tell you about themselves if you know how to listen to and interpret what they are telling you.

There are two general categories of problems that you can encounter in regard to Microsoft Office: those caused at installation and those that occurred after installation. Depending on when the problem occurred, you can use specific tools to find out more information about it. While the details of each potential problem with each application in Microsoft Office cannot be listed in this chapter, or even in this book for that matter, the tools that you can use to find out more information are the same for many problems. In this section, we will discuss the tools that you can use to interpret error messages in Office 2003.

The two main tools that you can use to troubleshoot Microsoft Office problems are the log files and the Microsoft Knowledge Base. Let's look at each in detail.

Log Files

During installation, Office 2003 automatically creates log files in your /temp folder. These files contain information about the specific tasks that were accomplished during installation and any errors that occurred. Typically, an error will also be reported to you in an error message during installation, but not always. Sometimes the error that occurred prevents the error message from being created. Therefore, you should know how to locate and examine the log files created during installation. Table 8.1 lists the log files that are created. You should examine these log files only for errors that pertain to the issue that you are experiencing.

Many log files contain errors that can be ignored because the issue corrected itself later in the setup. You should examine the log file only for entries that pertain to the issue that concerns you at this time.

TABLE 8.1   Office 2003 Log Files Created at Setup

Log File For	Log Filename
Setup.exe	Microsoft Office 2003 Setup(####).txt
Windows Installer (System Files Update)	Microsoft Office 2003 Setup(####)_Task(0001).txt
Windows Installer (Office Installation)	Microsoft Office 2003 Setup(####)_Task(0002).txt

The #### characters in the log filenames are numbers that start with 0001. They increment by one each time you run Setup. Therefore, the log file that has the highest number is the log file for the most recent time you ran Setup.

The Microsoft Knowledge Base

As you may have realized by now, chances are very good that you will receive error messages or read errors in a log file that you do not understand. This is quite normal. There is no way that anyone can know everything there is to know about troubleshooting all Office applications and their relation to the operating system. To make matters worse, some error messages ask you for permission to proceed or not! For this reason, Microsoft has developed the Knowledge Base.

Actually, the articles about Microsoft Office make up just a small portion of the Microsoft Knowledge Base. You can use the Microsoft Knowledge Base to interpret error messages and gain more information about all Microsoft operating systems and applications. It has been developed over time by administrators and network technicians who have experienced the same issues and found solutions. You can access the Microsoft Knowledge Base through the Microsoft Help and Support page, as illustrated in Figure 8.1.

FIGURE 8.1   The Microsoft Help and Support page

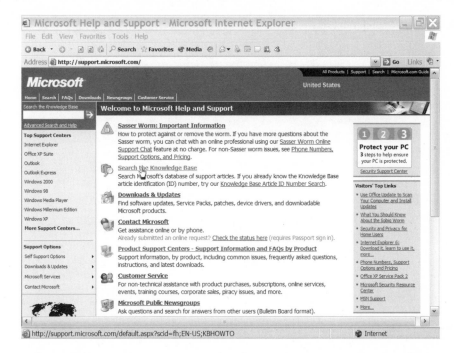

Exercise 8.3 walks you through the steps to troubleshoot an error message using the Microsoft Knowledge Base. In this case, the error message reads as follows:

"You have not entered a valid product key. Please check the number located on the sticker on the back of your CD case or on your Certificate of Authenticity."

You can also use the Microsoft Knowledge Base to find a specific article when you are referred to it from another publication and therefore already know the article number, such as a reference to KB 836178.

EXERCISE 8.3

Using the Microsoft Knowledge Base

1.   On a browser and type **support.microsoft.com** to access Microsoft's Help and Support website, which contains the Microsoft Knowledge Base.

EXERCISE 8.3 *(continued)*

2. Choose Search the Knowledge Base to access the Microsoft Knowledge Base home page.

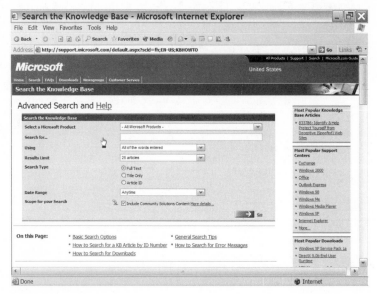

3. Click the drop-down arrow next to Select a Microsoft Product, and choose Office 2003 from the drop-down list.

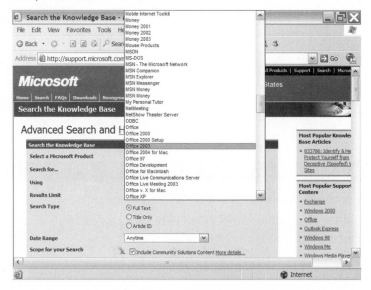

4. Enter as much information as possible about the error message or text in the log file. You can even copy and paste parts of a message or the entire error message. You can also select to use all of the words, any of the words, or only an exact phrase on the drop-down list next to Using. The trick here is to type the key information to narrow the search as much as possible.

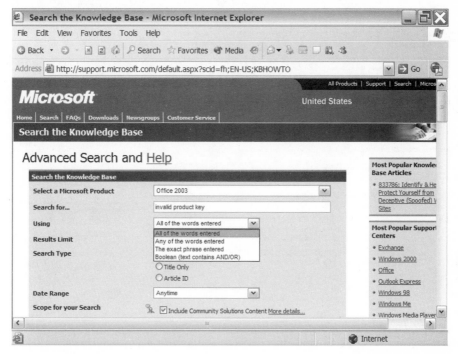

5. If you wish to narrow your search even further, you can select Search Type, Date Range, and Scope options for your search.

6. When you have finished entering information and making selections, click Go.

7. Examine the selections that the search engine finds to determine whether any of them contain the error that you are experiencing.

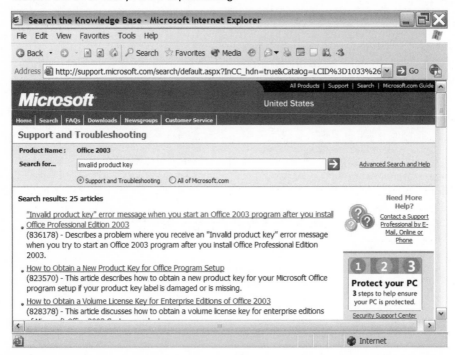

8. If you find an article that matches your problem, read the article and follow its instructions. If you do not find an article that matches your problem, you may want to widen or narrow your search to use the search engine in a different manner.

Internet Explorer

There is more to Internet Explorer than meets the eye and more than just the Internet options in the Tools menu. As a desktop support technician, you should be familiar with all of the tools that can enhance the usability of Internet Explorer. You should also know how to use the Help menu and the Microsoft Knowledge Base and Support Center to interpret error messages related to Internet Explorer. In the following sections, we will discuss each of these concepts in detail.

You Don't Have to Know Everything!

A user called me and said that icons were disappearing from his Desktop and then reappearing! At first, I thought either he was crazy or someone was playing a joke on him. After talking with him for a little while longer, I realized that this was no joke.

The computer that he was using was at his home and it was not subject to any group policies or network administration of any kind. He was also using a firewall to prevent access from intruders. He seemed to know how to protect his computer, yet the icons continued to disappear.

I considered that he might have a virus of some kind. I researched my information on the latest viruses and did not find any that just caused icons to disappear. Now, I was totally perplexed!

As my "one last shot," which should have been my first shot, I decided to check the Microsoft Knowledge Base to see if there was any information about disappearing icons. Was there ever! As it turned out, there were many combinations of features that can make icons disappear for no apparent reason. In some cases, Microsoft doesn't even try to explain why they disappeared; the articles just tell you how to get them back! Check for yourself on KB articles 307077, 321213, 822721, and 324250. You can also just select Windows XP in the Knowledge Base and then type **disappearing icons**; that's what I did.

My point is that I should have checked the Microsoft Knowledge Base first instead of last. What I did was try to solve the problem with only my own intellect. I figured that I must know the answer to this problem. In other words, I let my ego get in the way.

The moral of this story is that you don't have to know everything in order to be an effective desktop support technician; sometimes you just have to know where to find the information. The Microsoft Knowledge Base is compiled by hundreds of experts who have likely experienced the same problems that you are experiencing. Don't use it as a last resort. Use the Knowledge Base as your first resource and you will solve many problems faster than you ever thought possible!

Internet Explorer Settings

It may seem as if we discussed every possible option involving Internet Explorer in Chapter 6. In reality, we only scratched the surface in regard to its usability because we focused our entire discussion on one dialog box, Internet Options. In this section, we will discuss all of the settings contained in the File, Edit, View, Favorites, Tools, and Help menus.

The File Menu

The File menu contains tools to create new windows, messages, and other communications. You can also configure settings for printing and saving web pages. In addition, you can import and export your favorites and cookies files to and from other applications on your computer.

Figure 8.2 shows the options contained in the File menu. In this section, we will discuss each of these options in greater detail.

FIGURE 8.2   The File menu

New   You can choose New from the File menu to create a new window for the currently displayed page. You can also use New to connect to other applications installed on the computer to create a new email message, newsgroup post, contact record, or Internet call.

Open   You can select Open and then type the Uniform Resource Locator (URL) of the resource that you want to open. You can also simply type this information in the address line on the browser.

Edit and Save   These options are generally not available when you are working online, but you can use them when you are working with documents through your browser offline.

Save As   You can choose Save As to save a web page for later viewing. You should use this option when you feel that the information may not continue to be available online.

Page Setup, Print, and Print Preview   You can choose the Page Setup option to configure the manner in which web pages will be printed. You can use the Print Preview option to view an example of the document in its printed form on the screen before you print. You can choose the Print option to select the printer on your computer to which you will send the page.

Send   You can choose Send to send a copy of a web page or a link to the web page through your default e-mail program. You can also create a shortcut to a web page on your Desktop with this tool.

Import and Export   You can choose Import and Export to copy favorites and cookies to and from other applications on your computer or computers connected to your computer in your network.

Properties   You can select Properties to view general information about a page, such as the page type and the URL.

Work Offline/Work Online   You can use the Work Offline/Work Online option to control the use of the browser as a tool to access resources on the Internet or your intranet—or just to access resources on the computer itself.

Close   You can choose this option to close Internet Explorer. You can also close it by clicking on the *X* in the upper-right corner of the program.

The Edit Menu

The Edit menu contains the tools to cut, copy, and paste portions of the page or the entire page. In addition, you can use the Edit menu to search for text on a web page. Figure 8.3 shows the Edit menu, which contains the following options:

Cut, Copy, Paste   These are functions that enable you to move or copy text from a website on your browser to another application. These options are also available by right-clicking the mouse when it is positioned over the web page.

Select All   This option can be used to quickly select the entire web page to prepare for a printing or copying operation.

Find (on This Page)   This option enables you to search for specific words within the web page.

FIGURE 8.3   The Edit menu

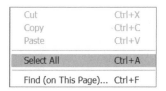

The View Menu

The View menu enables you to decide which tools will be visible during a user's normal utilization of the browser. You can also use the View menu to refresh a page or to go to a specific web page. In addition, the View menu enables you to the view the source information for a website and its encoding type. Finally, the View menu allows you to control the size of the text and use the Full Screen mode of the browser. Figure 8.4 shows the View menu, which contains the following settings:

Toolbars, Status Bar, and Explorer Bar   These settings control the toolbars that will be displayed for the user. The toolbars include Standard Buttons, Address Bar, Links, Favorites, Media, and others, depending on what other software is installed on the computer. You should select only the toolbars that the user will utilize.

Go To, Stop, and Refresh   These settings are used to navigate to websites. Go To enables you to go directly to the home page or to move forward or backward from your current location. Stop causes the current navigation attempt to cease and returns the previous web page to the screen. Refresh retrieves the latest copy of the web page that you are currently viewing.

Text Size   This setting enables you to adjust the text size of most web pages to a larger or smaller size relative to the current size of the font. Some fonts on some web pages do not respond to this setting.

Encoding   This setting enables you to adjust the way the browser will display the information contained on the website. You should usually leave the encoding set to the default.

Source   Choosing the Source option enables you to view the metadata that composes the web page. The metadata for the page will be displayed in Notepad when you select the Source option.

Privacy Report   This setting allows you to view and change settings related to how your computer will handle the cookies from a specific website. The report will indicate the websites that have contributed content to the current page. You can adjust your Privacy settings from this page provided you have Administrative rights to the computer.

Script Debugger   This setting will open the default script debugger installed in your computer. If you do not have a script debugger installed, then this setting will not be visible.

Full Screen   This setting will open the current page in Full Screen mode for the maximum viewing area. Your standard icons will still appear at the top of screen. You can also press the F11 key to toggle between Full Screen and Normal view.

FIGURE 8.4   The View menu

The Favorites Menu

The Favorites menu contains the links to the web pages that a user has marked. You can add as many favorites as you need, organize them in folders, and sort the sites and folders to make them easier to find. Figure 8.5 shows the Favorites menu, which contains the following options:

Add to Favorites   You can choose Add to Favorites to add the website you're currently viewing to the Favorites menu. You can give the website a name of your choice that will help you remember why you saved it. If you have created folders, then you can add the site to a specific folder within Favorites to make it easier to find.

Organize Favorites   You can choose Organize Favorites to create, rename, move, and delete folders that contain websites.

Lists of Favorites   You can click any of the favorites in your list to instantly navigate to the corresponding web page. You can sort the favorites by right-clicking the list and then choosing Sort by Name. You can also store a copy of a user's favorite web page on the computer by right-clicking the favorite of your choice and then choosing Make Available Offline.

FIGURE 8.5   The Favorites menu

The Tools Menu

As you may remember, we discussed the Internet Options dialog box accessible through the Tools menu in great detail in Chapter 7. The Tools menu also contains other options that you can configure for a user. You can use the Tools menu to synchronize a user's offline web pages with the online web page from which they originated. In addition, you can use the Tools menu to connect to the Windows Update site at Microsoft. Finally, you can also use the Tools menu to navigate directly to your default email and newsgroup applications. Figure 8.6 shows the Tools menu, which contains the following options:

Mail and News   You can choose the Mail and News option to automatically open your default email and newsgroups applications.

Synchronize   When a user stores web pages offline, they are very likely to change online. You can use the Synchronize option to configure the computer to automatically synchronize these web pages when the user logs on or logs off or on a set schedule. Simply click the Setup button in the Synchronize dialog box to configure these settings.

Windows Update   This setting opens the Microsoft Windows Update website at its most current location. You can update your operating system and the Microsoft applications that it contains from this site.

Messenger   This setting opens the Microsoft Messenger program. You can add contacts so that you can send instant messages, files, and photos to other users who are online with Messenger.

Show Related Links   This setting shows other websites that appear to the search engines to be related to the current website.

FIGURE 8.6   The Tools menu

The Help Menu
================

The Help Menu

The Help menu contains information about the browser that you are currently using. It also contains links to a tremendous amount of information that may be very useful for configuring and troubleshooting Internet Explorer. Figure 8.7 shows the Help menu, which contains the following settings options:

Contents and Index   The Contents and Index tool provides information related to configuring and troubleshooting Internet Explorer. We will discuss this tool in greater detail later in this chapter.

Tip of the Day   You can choose the Tip of the Day option to display a helpful tip at the bottom of the screen. The tips change on a daily basis.

For Netscape Users   This is specific help designed to show users who are currently using Netscape Navigator how to use the similar features in Internet Explorer.

Online Support   Choose this option to be automatically connected to Microsoft's Help and Support Home page. You can get the latest updates on viruses, downloads, and other information. You can also search the Knowledge Base or contact Product Support Centers from this site.

Send Feedback   Choose this option to be instantly connected to the Microsoft Internet Explorer Contact Us page. You can use this page to reach the Product Support, Product Suggestions, Frequently Asked Questions, and Microsoft Internet Explorer website Feedback pages.

About Internet Explorer   Choose this option to view the version and product number information for the browser that you are using. You may need this information for troubleshooting purposes to determine whether you have the latest version of the browser. Click OK to close the dialog box and remove it from view.

FIGURE 8.7   The Help menu

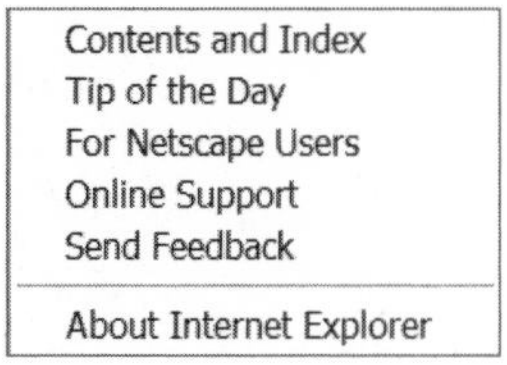

Contents and Index
Tip of the Day
For Netscape Users
Online Support
Send Feedback

About Internet Explorer

Interpreting Error Messages in Internet Explorer

There are two main categories of errors that users might encounter when using Internet Explorer: those that keep them from accessing a specific page and those that keep them from browsing at all. Depending on the type of error and whether Internet access is available from another computer, you have a few tools from which to choose to interpret the error message and troubleshoot the problem. If you do not have an Internet connection, then you should check the configuration settings that we discussed in Chapter 6 and the general connectivity of your computer. The tools that you can use to troubleshoot Internet Explorer errors include the following:

The Help menu   Many errors are caused by improper configuration. Even if you cannot obtain an Internet connection, you can find a tremendous amount of information regarding the proper configuration and use of Internet Explorer in the Help menu within the Contents and Index section. You can browse the contents or search the index for the configuration information that you need.

The Microsoft Knowledge Base   If you have an Internet connection, then you can navigate to the Microsoft Knowledge Base through the Support Tools at `support.microsoft.com`. You can choose the browser that you are using (for example, Internet Explorer 6) from the Select a Microsoft Product drop-down list and then type the key information regarding the error in question to obtain the latest articles and other support information.

The Microsoft Product Support Centers   If you have an Internet connection, you can navigate to the product support centers through `support.microsoft.com`. You can choose Internet Explorer from the products listed and view the latest support information and frequently asked questions about the product. You can also enter key information in the Search line of product support centers to be redirected to a search of the Microsoft Knowledge Base.

This is by no means an exhaustive list because new articles and websites that might assist a user may emerge on the Internet on a daily basis. You can use the normal search engines such as MSN and Google to find more information about error messages.

Outlook Express

Creating a user-friendly email and newsgroup management tool involves much more than just setting up a mailbox. You can enhance the user's experience with Outlook Express if you know all of the features and options that are available. As with other applications, users will sometimes have problems with the software. As a desktop support technician, you should know how to interpret the error messages regarding Outlook Express and troubleshoot the problems. In the following sections, we will discuss each of these concepts in detail.

Outlook Express Settings

There are many menus in Outlook Express that contain settings to enhance the usability of the program for the user. All of the tools are located by default at the upper-left corner of the screen. You should be familiar with these tool menus so that you can enhance the settings for users as well as troubleshoot any settings that they have "adjusted." We will discuss the File, Edit, View, Tools, Message, and Help menus and the settings and options that they contain.

The File Menu

The File menu contains tools that enable a user to organize the mailbox, open new messages, import and export address books and messages, and print messages. A user can also manage multiple identities from the File menu. This is useful when more than one person is using the computer or when one user has more than one account. Figure 8.8 shows the File menu, which contains the following settings:

New   You can use the New option to open a new email message, news message, instant message, folder, or contact. You can also use the icons on the Outlook Express toolbar to perform these actions.

Open   You can choose the Open option to open a selected email or news message. You can also simply double-click the message to open it.

Save As   You can use the Save As option to make a copy of a message and store it in a folder on the computer or on another computer in your network.

Save Attachments   You can use the Save Attachments option to copy attachments from the temporary folder where they are stored by default to a folder of your choice on your computer or another computer in your network. You can also use Save Attachments by right-clicking the attachment itself.

Save as Stationery   When you receive an email on digital stationery that you like, you can add that stationery to your options by choosing Save as Stationery.

Folder   You can use this option to create new folders for messages and to move, rename, manage, compact, and delete folders.

Import/Export   You can use this option to quickly move messages and email address books from one computer to another. This is especially useful when a user changes computers.

Print   You can choose this option to be directed to the printer tools, where you can choose a printer and other advanced options and preferences before printing.

Switch Identity/Identities/Exit and Log Off Identity   When more than one person is using the same computer, this option enables each user to create their own personal message management system. We will discuss this in greater detail in Chapter 9, "Resolving Application Customization Issues."

Properties   This option enables you to view details related to the selected message. These include general properties, such as the time that the message was sent and received, as well as details such as the addresses of all of the other recipients of a message.

Work Offline   This option allows you to compose email messages offline to be sent when you are back online. This is especially useful when you are working with a dial-up connection that you don't want to stay on because it is shared or because the connection has long-distance charges associated with it.

Exit   You can choose this option to close Outlook Express. You can also close it by clicking on the *X* in the upper-right corner of the program.

FIGURE 8.8   The File menu

The Edit Menu

The Edit menu contains options to organize messages and mark them as Read or Unread. In addition, you can use the Edit menu to control the use of the folders that you created with the File menu. You can also use the Edit menu to find a specific message based on information about the message itself. Finally, you can delete messages using the Edit menu. Figure 8.9 shows the Edit menu, which contains the following options:

Copy/Select All   You can use the Copy and Select All tools to select messages in preparation for moving them or printing them. You can also hold down the Ctrl key and select multiple messages or hold down the Shift key and select a range of messages.

Find   You can use the Find option to locate a message based on information about the message. You can enter parameters on which to search, including whom the message was to or from and the subject and date of the message. You can also use the Find option to locate specified text within a message. Finally, you can use the Find option to locate people in your address book or through Internet services.

Move to Folder/Copy to Folder   You can use these options to move or copy selected messages from one folder to another or from the Inbox to a specified folder.

Delete   Choosing the Delete option will place the selected message(s) in the `Deleted Items` folder. You can then control how often the messages in the `Deleted Items` folder are actually deleted. This is a precaution to prevent users from deleting messages by mistake.

Empty 'Deleted Items' Folder   Choosing this option will override the normal schedule to delete items in the `Deleted Items` folder and delete the items immediately. When you choose this option, Outlook Express will ask you if you are sure that you want to permanently delete the items. If you choose Yes, then the items will be deleted. If you choose No, then you will cancel the deletion of the items.

Mark as Read/Mark as Unread/Mark Conversation as Read/Mark All Read   The Mark options enable you to keep track of which messages you have read and which messages you have yet to read. Messages that are unread will appear in bold text by default. You can also configure Outlook to automatically mark a message as read after you have viewed it for a set amount of time, for example, 5 seconds. We will discuss this customization option in Chapter 9.

FIGURE 8.9   The Edit menu

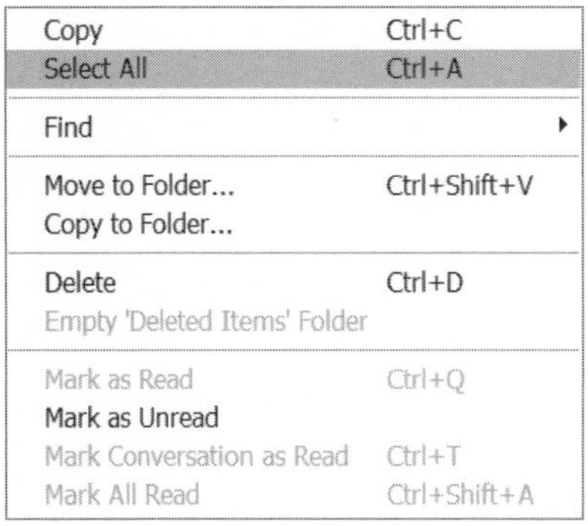

Copy	Ctrl+C
Select All	Ctrl+A
Find	▶
Move to Folder...	Ctrl+Shift+V
Copy to Folder...	
Delete	Ctrl+D
Empty 'Deleted Items' Folder	
Mark as Read	Ctrl+Q
Mark as Unread	
Mark Conversation as Read	Ctrl+T
Mark All Read	Ctrl+Shift+A

The View Menu

The View menu enables users to control the messages that are displayed and how they are sorted. They can also control the text size in the message and the message encoding. In addition, the View menu contains tools that enable users to navigate to and from messages and folders. Figure 8.10 shows the View menu, which contains the following options:

Current View   The Current View option enables you to display all messages or to hide the messages that you have already read or have decided to ignore. You can also create customized views. In addition, you can use the Current View menu to group messages by conversation. This sometimes makes a conversation string easier to follow.

Sort By   You can use the Sort By option to control the order in which the messages will be displayed. For example, messages can be displayed by date, subject, priority, and so on. You can also simply click on the column heading to sort the messages by the parameter of that column.

Columns   You can choose the Columns option to select the column heading that will be shown for the messages. Keep in mind that you are limited by your screen area unless you want to scroll over to see information. You can change the font and the resolution to bring more columns into Normal view.

Layout   The Layout option allows you to further customize the look of Outlook Express and the tools that you have available. We will discuss the Layout option in greater detail in Chapter 9.

Text Size   You can choose this option to increase or decrease the size of the text used in the messages.

Encoding   You can use this option to change the manner in which Outlook Express interprets and displays the message information. In most cases, you should leave this setting at its default.

FIGURE 8.10   The View menu

Previous Message/Next/Go to Folder/Expand/Collapse   You can use these tools to navigate messages and folders. This is especially useful when you have many messages and folders through which to navigate.

Stop   You can use the Stop option to cancel a previous command. For example, if the system is having trouble locating a message but is continuing to try, then you can cancel that command using the Stop option and then try to locate the message by another parameter.

Refresh   This option repaints the screen with the latest information and messages.

The Tools Menu

The Tools menu contains many options that control sending and receiving email and receiving newsgroup messages. You can also create and control user accounts through the Tools menu. Most of the Tools menu relates directly to customizing Outlook Express for a user. For this reason, we will discuss the Tools menu in depth in Chapter 9.

The Message Menu

The Message menu relates directly to creating and replying to messages. Users can also use the Message menu to block messages from specified senders and to flag messages so they stand out. In addition, users can set the options to watch a specific conversation or ignore a conversation of messages that they have previously received. A conversation includes the original email and all of the replies. Figure 8.11 shows the Message menu in Outlook Express, which includes the following options:

New Message/New Message Using   Both of these options create a new message. New Message creates the message with no stationery. New Message Using enables you to select the stationery that you will use to create the message.

Reply to Sender/Reply to All/Reply to Group   All of these options send a reply to a message. Reply to Sender sends the reply only to the person who originated the message. Reply to All sends a copy of the reply to all of the users who were copied on the message when it was sent. Reply to Group enables you to select a recipient out of the entire list of recipients to this message.

Forward/Forward as Attachment   Both of these options send a copy of the message to another recipient as specified by the user. Forward sends the message just as it was received, although the user can add text within the message to introduce the message or make comments. Forward as Attachment converts the message into an attachment and provides a new email message box for the user to introduce the message attachment or make comments about the message.

Create Rule from Message   Users can automatically forward a message, place it in a folder, highlight it, flag it, and even delete it based on the information about the message. This is one of the customization options that we will discuss in detail in Chapter 9.

Block Sender   You can use this option to create a quick rule that will block any further messages from the sender of the currently selected email. The sender will be added to the blocked senders list. The system will also ask you if you want to remove, from the current folder, all messages from the selected sender.

Flag Message/Watch Conversation/Ignore Conversation   These options enable you to customize your use of Outlook Express. You can identify messages and conversations that you want to pay close attention to and those that you want to ignore completely. We will discuss these options in greater detail in Chapter 9.

Combine and Decode   Sometimes a very large message that contains pictures, audio files, or other large attachments must be broken down into multiple messages to be sent. You can use Combine and Decode to put the messages back together into one message. You should first select the messages that you want to combine and then choose Combine and Decode. The tool will enable you to put the messages in the right order regardless of the order in which you received them.

FIGURE 8.11   The Message menu

New Message	Ctrl+N
New Message Using	▶
Reply to Sender	Ctrl+R
Reply to All	Ctrl+Shft+R
Reply to Group	Ctrl+G
Forward	Ctrl+F
Forward As Attachment	
Create Rule From Message...	
Block Sender...	
Flag Message	
Watch Conversation	
Ignore Conversation	
Combine and Decode...	

The Help Menu

The Help menu is a great source of information for troubleshooting. You can use the Contents and Index tool offline or a host of tools online. As a desktop support technician, you should be familiar with the Help menu, and you should make users familiar with it as well. Figure 8.12 shows the Help menu, which includes the following options:

Contents and Index   You can use the Contents and Index option to connect to a tremendous source of configuration and troubleshooting information on your computer. You can use this tool even if you do not have a connection to the Internet.

Read Me   This option doesn't do much except tell you that the Read Me information is in the `Readme.doc` file at the root of the Windows CD.

Microsoft on the Web   This option enables you to quickly connect to many websites, such as the Windows Update, Product News, Frequently Asked Questions, and Online Support sites. You can also send feedback to Microsoft through this option and connect to Hotmail and the MSN home page.

About Microsoft Outlook Express   This option shows the current product information, version information, and specific files used by the program. You may need to view this information for troubleshooting to make sure that you have the latest software available.

FIGURE 8.12   The Help menu

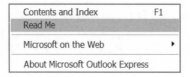

Interpreting Outlook Express Error Messages

Since Outlook Express has many features and settings, it can also generate many types of error messages. As with Internet Explorer, we can group these error messages into two categories: those that are related to general connectivity issues and those that are related to Outlook Express configuration issues. If a user cannot connect to the Internet with any application, they might just have a general connectivity issue, so you should check all of the general connectivity settings first. On the other hand, if they have connectivity to the Internet but are still having a problem sending and/or receiving email, you can be fairly sure that the problem is related to the configuration settings of Outlook Express.

Depending on the type of error encountered and your access to the Internet, you can use a few tools to assist you in interpreting Outlook Express error messages and troubleshooting the problem:

The Help menu   As with Internet Explorer, many errors are caused by improper configuration. The Help menu within the Contents and Index section is a great source of information about proper configuration of Outlook Express. You can browse the contents or search in the index for the configuration information that you need.

The Microsoft Knowledge Base   Assuming that you have an Internet connection, you can navigate to the Microsoft Knowledge Base through Microsoft Help and Support at support.microsoft.com. Choose Outlook Express from the Select a Microsoft Product drop-down list and type the key information regarding the error in question to obtain the latest articles and other support information.

The Microsoft Product Support Centers   Also, if you have an Internet connection, then you can navigate to the Product Support Centers through support.microsoft.com. Choose Outlook Express from the products listed and view the latest support information and frequently asked questions about the product. Enter key information in the Search line of Product Support Centers to be redirected to a search of the Microsoft Knowledge Base. The Product Support Centers will often contain the latest updates and patches to enhance the performance of the program.

Operating System Features

Regardless of the application(s) the user is utilizing, you can enhance the usability of the computer by configuring components of the operating system to meet the user's needs. While there are many components of the operating system that you can configure, the most prominent components are the Start menu, the Taskbar, and shortcuts on the Desktop. Since users will sometimes have problems with the operating system, you should know how to interpret and troubleshoot error messages related to the operating system. In the following sections, we will discuss both of these concepts in detail.

Configuring Operating System Features

Most users use the operating system only as a platform to gain access to applications. For this reason, the Start menu, Taskbar, and Desktop shortcuts are the most important configuration options in the operating system since they are the tools that enable the user to gain access to applications. As a desktop support technician, you should know how to configure and troubleshoot these important tools for the user. We will discuss configuring each of these tools to enhance their usability.

The Start Menu

The Start menu is usually the first navigational tool that the person uses when they log on to a computer to access applications. You can configure the Start menu in Windows XP so that it contains repeatedly used applications, making them readily available for the user. When you or a user adds an application to the operating system, it is automatically added to the All Programs menu in the Start menu. As a desktop support technician, you should know how to configure the Start menu properties for a user.

There is only one main configuration option for the Start menu: Start menu or Classic Start menu. The rest is all customization. In the following sections, we will discuss only the main configuration option for the Start menu. We will discuss customizing the Start menu in Chapter 9.

Start Menu for Windows XP

The default Start menu option for Windows XP is simply called Start menu. You can view this setting by right-clicking the Taskbar, choosing Properties, and then choosing the Start Menu tab. Figure 8.13 shows the Start menu properties settings. The Start menu settings allow easier access to the most commonly used programs and remembers the programs that you use, making them easier to access next time. They also contain the user's name and the picture that the user has chosen for the account. Figure 8.14 shows an example of a Start menu with the default Windows XP settings.

FIGURE 8.13   Start Menu properties

FIGURE 8.14   Windows XP default Start menu

Classic Start Menu

If users are accustomed to the Start menu in Windows 95, Windows 98, and Windows 2000 Professional and prefer to use what is familiar to them, then you can configure their computers with the Classic Start menu. This configuration does not contain the sections for previously used programs and does not remember programs that users have previously used. It also does not contain the user's name or picture. Figure 8.15 shows the Classic Start menu in Windows XP. To switch to the Classic Start menu, simply right-click the Taskbar and choose Properties, click the Start Menu tab, and select Classic Start Menu from the options shown.

FIGURE 8.15   The Classic Start menu

All Classic Start menus contain the name of the operating system written from the bottom and running toward the top of the menu. This started with Windows 95 and continues through Windows XP.

The Taskbar

The Taskbar contains information regarding applications and services that are running. You can also configure the Taskbar with miniature icons called Quick Launch icons. The Taskbar is located at the bottom of the screen by default. There are many options for customizing the Taskbar, which we will discuss in Chapter 9.

In the following sections, we will we focus on Taskbar properties, shown Figure 8.16.

FIGURE 8.16   Taskbar properties

There are two main groups of settings on the Taskbar tab: Taskbar Appearance and Notification Area. We will discuss each of those groups of settings in detail.

Taskbar Appearance

The Taskbar Appearance properties control the general appearance of the Taskbar during normal use of the computer. There are five options that relate to the Taskbar's appearance. You should be familiar with these options so you can adjust them for a user or troubleshoot a problem related to their use.

The five Taskbar appearance settings are as follows:

▪ Lock the Taskbar: You can use this setting to prevent the user from accidentally changing settings on the Taskbar. While the Taskbar is locked, most other changes are disabled. Administrators can use a group policy to prevent the user from unlocking the Taskbar.

- Auto-Hide the Taskbar: This setting causes the Taskbar to disappear from the screen when it is not being used. This frees up space on the screen and reduces clutter. When you return the mouse pointer to the area where the Taskbar is located, the Taskbar will appear again.

- Keep the Taskbar on Top of Other Windows: This setting is checked by default. If you remove the check mark, the Taskbar will disappear when you begin to use another application. You can switch to the Desktop to regain the use of the Taskbar.

- Group Similar Taskbar Buttons: This setting is an enhancement to Windows XP that automatically puts similar programs into groups in the Taskbar. For example, if you have several Microsoft Word documents open at the same time, then Windows will group the documents in the Taskbar and indicate how many are in the group. You can click the group icon to view the items that it contains and manage each item separately. Groups are indicated with a triangle pointing downward. Figure 8.17 shows a Taskbar with groups.

- Show Quick Launch: You can use this setting to create miniature icons for the most commonly used applications in the Taskbar. The initial Quick Launch icons include Internet Explorer, Outlook Express, and the Desktop toggle icon. You can add more icons by dragging icons from the Desktop to the Taskbar.

FIGURE 8.17   A Taskbar with groups

Notification Area

The notification area is located by default on the right side of the Taskbar. This area was referred to as the system tray in previous versions of Windows. It shows the services that are running on your computer to support applications, such as Microsoft Messenger. It can also contain the date and time. When you install new hardware and software in your computer, it can indicate their presence. You can control which icons are displayed and when they are displayed.

The Notification Area section of the Taskbar tab contains the following settings:

- Show the Clock: You can use this setting to display or not display the time and date.

- Hide Inactive Icons: You can use this setting to reduce the clutter in the notification area by not displaying icons that are inactive. You can further customize the display of these icons by choosing Customize and then selecting when to hide or show each icon.

Desktop Shortcuts

The more quickly users can find their applications, the more productive they can be. Many applications ask whether to add a shortcut on the Desktop during their installation. If the application does not ask, or if the user chose no, there are still many ways to add a shortcut to the Desktop for that application. In the following sections, we will discuss two methods of adding shortcuts to a Desktop: from the All Programs menu and from the Desktop using the Create Shortcut Wizard.

From the All Programs Menu

If the application is installed in Windows XP, then it is most likely in the All Programs menu of the Start menu. If it is, you can simply navigate to the application in the Start menu, right-click the application name, choose Send To, and then choose Desktop (Create Shortcut). Figure 8.18 shows the steps to create a Desktop shortcut for Microsoft Office Excel 2003 from the All Programs menu.

FIGURE 8.18   Creating a Desktop shortcut from the All Programs menu in Windows XP

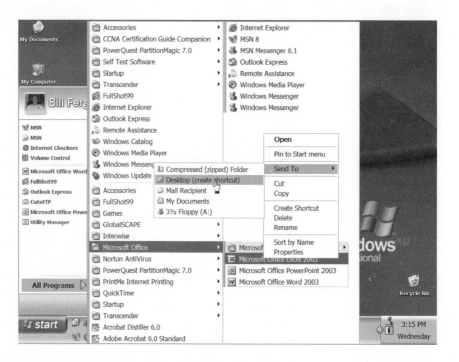

From the Desktop Using the Create Shortcut Wizard

If the application is not listed in the All Programs menu, such as an older application or an application that has been deleted from the All Programs menu, then you can create the shortcut from the Desktop by using the Create Shortcut Wizard. Exercise 8.4 walks you through the steps to create a Desktop shortcut using the Create Shortcut Wizard.

EXERCISE 8.4

Creating an Application Shortcut with the Create Shortcut Wizard

1. On the Windows XP Desktop, right-click in an open area and choose New.

2. On the expanded list from New, choose Shortcut. This will start the Create Shortcut Wizard.

3. Type the location of the executable file for the application for which you creating the shortcut, or click Browse to search for the file. In this example we will use Solitaire (sol.exe).

EXERCISE 8.4 *(continued)*

4. After the wizard enters the location of the executable file, choose Next to continue.

5. Type the name that you want to use for the shortcut.

6. Click Finish to add the shortcut to the Desktop.

Interpreting Error Messages Related to the Operating System

Just as applications will sometimes have "issues," so will the operating system. You should know how to interpret error messages that are related to the operating system and trouble-shoot the problem for the user. As with applications, the main tools that you should use are

Help menus and the Microsoft Knowledge Base on the Internet. With Windows XP, however, the Help menu is greatly enhanced to provide a tremendous amount of information that you can use for configuration and troubleshooting. In the following sections, we will discuss the tools that you can use to troubleshoot the operating system: the Help and Support Center, the Microsoft Knowledge Base, and the Microsoft Product Support Centers.

The Help and Support Center

The Help and Support Center contains tools that can be used online as well as tools that can be used offline. The tools are arranged in categories to make it easier to find the one that you need. Many of the offline tools provide links to online tools. Figure 8.19 shows the Help and Support Center. You can access the Help and Support Center through the Start menu or by pressing the F1 key.

FIGURE 8.19   The Help and Support Center

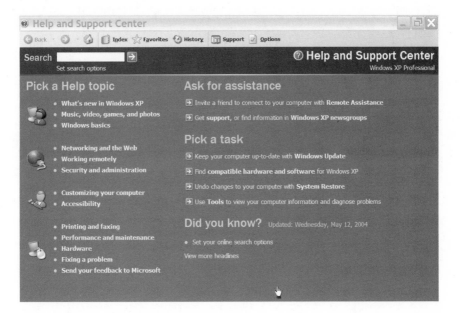

The Microsoft Knowledge Base

If you have an Internet connection, then you can navigate to the Microsoft Knowledge Base through the Support Tools at `support.microsoft.com`. Just choose Windows XP from the Select a Microsoft Product drop-down list and type the key information regarding the error in question to obtain the latest articles and other support information.

The Microsoft Product Support Centers

If you have an Internet connection, then you can navigate to the Product Support Centers through support.microsoft.com. Simply choose Windows XP from the products listed and view the latest support information and frequently asked questions about the product. You can also enter key information in the Search line of the Product and Support Centers to be redirected to a search of the Microsoft Knowledge Base. The Product Support Center will often contain highlights and important issues regarding the operating system. Figure 8.20 shows the Microsoft Product Support Center for Windows XP.

FIGURE 8.20   The Microsoft Product Support Center for Windows XP

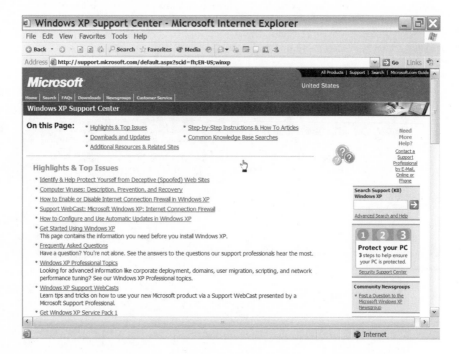

Case Study: Troubleshooting Applications

Troubleshooting applications will probably take up a significant part of your average workday as an MCDST. Knowing the different installation options, locations of log files, and where to turn for help online are some key things that will assist you in doing your job each day.

Every now and then, however, you'll find that no matter what you do, you can't find the answer to the problem or get the application to start/stop doing what it should/should not be doing. There are lots of possible causes for applications to behave unexpectedly.

One thing that may cause applications to hang or behave incorrectly is a problem with another program or application. Sometimes programs are simply incompatible with each other due to a variety of reasons; addressing each other's memory, attempting to use the same devices or resources, and using different versions of the same required DLLs are a few of the reasons. If something like this happens, you may have to contact the manufacturers of the applications to see if there are any known fixes for these issues. If the issue can't be resolved any other way, you may have to uninstall one of the applications and simply use it on a different computer.

Other things that can cause applications to not function may be external to the application itself. Network connectivity (reliance on shared drives, for example), file permissions, administrative rights to the computer, and Group Policy are some examples of external causes of application issues. Normally, these issues can be resolved with a little bit more in-depth troubleshooting, and looking outside the box for the cause.

Ultimately, when no other solution works, you may wind up having to uninstall the application and reinstall it with different options. This is an extreme solution, but it does become necessary.

Troubleshooting applications is like troubleshooting anything else in the computer world. Technical knowledge goes a long way, but the ability to think outside the box and sometimes try unorthodox solutions will definitely help as well.

Summary

As a desktop support technician, you are responsible for configuring a user's operating system and applications to prevent as many problems as possible. It's impossible to prevent all problems, but correct configuration of the operating system and the most common applications is a large step in the right direction. You should know how to configure the most common applications and the operating system to maximize usability for the user. You should also know how to interpret error messages that relate to the operating system and the most common applications, such as Microsoft Office, Internet Explorer, and Outlook Express.

When you install Microsoft Office for a user, you can prevent many issues by installing only the components that the user will use. You should ask the user about their job roles and determine which components they need. You should then perform a Custom installation, which installs only the components they will use. While this will prevent many problems from occurring, it will not prevent them all. You should know how to use the Setup log files and the Microsoft Knowledge Base to troubleshoot a problem with a Microsoft product for a user.

One of the most commonly used applications other than Microsoft Office components is the Microsoft browser, Internet Explorer. There are many configuration options within Internet Explorer that can enhance its usability and make the product more user-friendly. You should know how to configure the options in Internet Explorer to allow for safe, efficient browsing. You should also know how to use the Help menu and the Microsoft Knowledge Base and Product Support Centers to interpret and troubleshoot error messages.

Outlook Express will be the email program of choice for many of your users, especially at home. You need to know the options that are available in Outlook Express so that you can configure them for the user and teach the user to configure them. These options control the manner in which messages are displayed, read, sent, stored, and so on. You should also know how to use the Help menu and the Microsoft Knowledge Base and Product Support Centers to interpret and troubleshoot error messages.

Users will be more productive if their applications are organized so that they can easily find the ones they need. Windows XP has the most user-friendly interface of any Microsoft client. You can configure the Start menu, Taskbar, and Desktop shortcuts so that applications are easy to locate and use. You should also know how to use the Help and Support Center, the Microsoft Knowledge Base, and the Product Support Centers. Knowledge of these tools will assist you in interpreting error messages and troubleshooting the operating system and the Microsoft applications that run on it.

Exam Essentials

Know how to perform a Custom installation of Office 2003.   You should know how to perform a Custom installation of Office 2003. This includes selecting only the components that the user requires and configuring the components to provide maximum usability.

Be able to use the Microsoft Knowledge Base.   You should know how to access the Microsoft Knowledge Base on the Internet and use it to interpret error messages. You should know that the Microsoft Knowledge Base can assist you in troubleshooting Windows operating systems and most Microsoft applications.

Know how to configure Internet Explorer.   You should know how to configure all of the menus of Internet Explorer so that you can assist users with configuration. In addition, you should know how to troubleshoot errant configurations by users. Finally, you should know how to use the Help menu and the various online resources to interpret error messages and troubleshoot Internet Explorer.

Know how to configure Outlook Express.   You should know how to configure all of the menus of Outlook Express to create a usable email and newsgroup tool for the user. You should know the menus so well that you can assist the user over the phone without looking at the software yourself. In addition, you should know how to use the Help menu and the various online resources to interpret error messages and troubleshoot Outlook Express.

Know how to configure the Windows XP Desktop.   You should know how to configure the Start menu, Taskbar, and Desktop shortcuts on the Windows XP Desktop to make applications easily available to users. In addition, you should know how to troubleshoot users' errant configurations.

Be able to troubleshoot Windows XP.   You should know how to use the offline and online tools of Help and Support Center to troubleshoot Windows XP. In addition, you should know how to use the Microsoft Knowledge Base and Product Support Centers to interpret error messages and troubleshoot problems.

Review Questions

1. You are the desktop support technician for your company. A user calls you to request that Microsoft Word be added to her computer so that she can read email attachments. She has never needed any Microsoft Office products in the past. Which should you do?

    A. Perform a Typical installation of Microsoft Office.

    B. Perform a Custom installation, selecting only Word.

    C. Ask the user what other email attachments she has received and what types of tasks she needs to perform, and then install only the software that you think she will require in the near future.

    D. Ask the user what applications she needs to have installed on her computer along with Word.

2. You are the desktop support technician for your company. You have recently installed Microsoft Office on a user's computer, but you are experiencing errors. Which of the following resources can you use to interpret the error messages? (Choose two.)

    A. The Microsoft Knowledge Base

    B. The Computer Management Console

    C. The Setup log files

    D. Device Manager

3. You are the desktop support technician for your company. A user calls you complaining that the font on some web pages is very small and that he can't read it. He does not want to make any changes that will affect the size of any icons or the text of any other applications. You are not in front of a computer at this time. To which Internet Explorer menu should you direct the user?

    A. Tools

    B. View

    C. Edit

    D. Options

4. You are the desktop support technician for a large company. A user calls you from a remote location and tells you that he cannot gain access to the Internet through Internet Explorer. He can send and receive email. Which of the following should you do?

    A. Ask the user for all of his network connection information, IP address, default gateway, and so on.

    B. Ask the user if he is receiving an error message and then use the Microsoft Knowledge Base to interpret the error message.

    C. Tell him to restart his computer.

    D. Walk him through uninstalling and reinstalling Internet Explorer.

5.   You are the desktop support technician for your company. A user calls you to say that she is upgrading to a new computer at home but she is worried because all of her Outlook Express email messages and address books are on the old one. She is afraid that she will have to start over. What should you tell her?

   A.   She should make sure to move the old hard drive over to her new computer to keep all of the email messages and address books intact.

   B.   She will have to start all over, but everything will be better when she gets it all in there again.

   C.   She can simply find the folders where all of the messages and address are contained and then move them over to the My Documents folder on her new computer.

   D.   She can export the email messages and address books from her computer and then import them into the new computer.

6.   You are the desktop support technician for your company. A user is experiencing problems with Outlook Express and is receiving some very odd error messages that you have never seen before. Which resource should you use first to attempt to interpret the error messages?

   A.   Google

   B.   The Microsoft Product Support Center

   C.   The Help menu in Outlook Express

   D.   The Microsoft Knowledge Base

7.   You are the desktop support technician for your company. A user who is working from home calls you with a question. She has received an email on stationery that she really likes and she would like to add that stationery to her stationery options on Outlook Express. You are not in front of a computer with Outlook Express installed. To which menu should you direct her to find Save as Stationery?

   A.   Edit

   B.   View

   C.   Tools

   D.   File

8.   You are the desktop support technician for a large company. A user who is working from home calls you with a question. He has received an email and he would like to see detailed information about it, including all of the email addresses to which it was sent. To which Outlook Express menu should you direct the user?

   A.   File

   B.   Edit

   C.   Tools

   D.   Message

9. You are the desktop support technician for a large company with many Windows XP computers. Some users complain that they liked the old Start menu that was provided by previous Windows operating systems much better than the one they have now. What should you do?

A. Tell them that there are no other options unless you reinstall the operating system.

B. Direct the users to reinstall the operating system and choose the Classic installation this time.

C. Direct the users to right-click on an empty area of the Desktop and then choose Properties ➢ Start Menu ➢ Classic Start Menu.

D. Direct the users to right-click on an empty area of the Taskbar and then choose Properties ➢ Start Menu ➢ Classic Start Menu.

10. You are the desktop support technician for a large company with many Windows XP computers. A user calls you to say that he is experiencing a problem when he uses many of the applications on his Windows XP computer. He does not have Internet access, but you do. Which of the following should you do? (Choose two. Each answer is part of the solution.)

A. Direct the user to the offline Help and Support Center tools on his computer.

B. Direct the user to the Microsoft Knowledge Base.

C. Tell the user to read the error message to you over the phone.

D. Research the Microsoft Knowledge Base through your computer for information about the error on his computer.

11. What kind of Microsoft Office Installation allows you to give users only the applications needed to do their jobs?

A. Typical

B. Custom

C. Minimal

D. Special

12. What three programs are log files created for during an installation of Microsoft Office?

A. Setup, Error, and Details logs

B. Windows Installer, Update, and Error Logs

C. `Setup.exe`, Windows Installer (System Files Update), and Windows Installer (Office Installation) logs

D. `Setup.exe`, Installed Components, System logs

13. What online resource can you use to interpret error messages and gain more information about Microsoft operating systems and applications?

A. Microsoft Knowledge Base

B. Microsoft Answer Center

C. Microsoft Tech Center

D. Corresponding home page on Microsoft website for each application

14. How would you accommodate a user who wants to see the older-style user interface and Start menu used with Windows 2000?

    A. Create a profile under Windows 2000 and copy it to their new profile under Windows XP.

    B. Manually create their Desktop icons and Start menu items as they were under Windows 2000.

    C. Select the Classic Start menu option under the Start Menu tab in the Taskbar and Start Menu Properties dialog box.

    D. Reinstall Windows 2000

15. Which option prevents users from accidentally making changes to the Taskbar?

    A. Lock the Taskbar

    B. Taskbar Permissions

    C. Auto-Hide the Taskbar

    D. Taskbar Settings

16. Which option in Outlook Express enables different users on the computer to use and manage their electronic mail?

    A. Fast User Switching

    B. Change User

    C. Switch Profile

    D. Switch Identity/Identities/Exit and Log Off Identity

17. Which application comes with a Combine and Decode option to reassemble files received regardless of the order in which they are received?

    A. Internet Explorer

    B. Outlook Express

    C. Windows XP

    D. Microsoft Office

18. What does the Import and Export option in Internet Explorer allow you to do?

    A. Import and export web content across the Internet

    B. Import and export email messages from web-based email services to and from Outlook Express

    C. Import and Export favorites and cookies to and from other applications on your computer or computers connected to your computer in your network

    D. Import and Export connection settings to other computers

19. Which of the following applications specifically requires activation from Microsoft, either over the phone or through the Internet?

    A. Internet Explorer

    B. Outlook Express

    C. Notepad

    D. Microsoft Office

20. Which tool can be used offline as well as online to help resolve issues with applications?

    A. Microsoft Knowledge Base

    B. Microsoft Product Support Center

    C. Help and Support Center

    D. Google

Answers to Review Questions

1. C. You should ask the user how she will be using the computer and then make your decision about what software to install. A Typical installation might install many programs that she will not use but that could cause problems in the future. Installing only Word is a short-range solution to the problem. You should not ask the user what she needs because most users will not know what they need.

2. A, C. You should use the Microsoft Knowledge Base and the Setup log files to find more information about error messages that you receive after installing Microsoft Office. The Computer Management Console and Device Manager will not help you interpret error messages related to Microsoft Office.

3. B. You should direct the user to the View menu and then to Text Size to change the size of the text in Internet Explorer only. The Tools and Edit menus do not have the required option. There is no Options menu in Internet Explorer.

4. B. You should ask the user if he is receiving an error message and then use your Internet connection and the Microsoft Knowledge Base to interpret the error message for him. You do not need his network information since he obviously has connectivity. (He can send and receive email.) Stopping and restarting the computer probably won't fix the problem. You should not recommend uninstalling and reinstalling Internet Explorer until you have checked the error messages.

5. D. You should tell her to use the Import/Export tools under the File menu in Outlook Express to export the email messages and address books from her old computer and import them into the new computer. She does not have to move the hard drive from the old computer to the new computer. She does not have to start over. She should not just copy the files.

6. D. You should look first at the Microsoft Knowledge Base to interpret the error messages. The Microsoft Knowledge Base has been compiled by experts who have probably experienced the same problems that your user is experiencing. Google, the Microsoft Product Support Center, and the Help menu in Outlook Express would all be good alternatives for information, but they should not be your first choice.

7. D. You should tell the user to select the email with the stationery that she wants and then choose Save as Stationery from the File menu of Outlook Express. Then she can name the stationery so it will be made available to her when she composes email. The Edit, View, and Tools menus do not contain the Save as Stationery option.

8. A. You should direct the user to the File menu, and then to Properties, and finally to the Details tab to see the details of the message. You could also direct the user to right-click on the email and choose Properties. The Edit, Tools, and Message menus do not contain the required information.

9. D. You should direct the users to change to a Classic Start menu by right-clicking an empty area on the Taskbar and then navigating to the Start menu's properties. You do not have to reinstall the operating system to change the Start menu's properties. You should direct them to right-click an empty area on the Taskbar, not the Desktop.

10. C, D. You should assist the user by asking him to read the error message to you and then researching the error message on the Microsoft Knowledge Base with your Internet connection. You should not direct the user to his own offline Help and Support Center tools. The user will not be able to access the Microsoft Knowledge Base without Internet access.

11. B. A Custom installation allows you to pick and choose which Office components a user will get during an installation. A Typical installation installs commonly used components and does not allow you to select the ones you want. Options C and D do not exist.

12. C. The three logs created during an installation of Microsoft Office are the `Setup.exe`, Windows Installer (System Files Update), and Windows Installer (Office Installation) logs. All other answers are invalid choices.

13. A. The Microsoft Knowledge Base is an online resource can you use to interpret error messages and gain more information about Microsoft operating systems and applications. All other answers are invalid choices because they do not exist.

14. C. Users desiring to see the older-style Start menu from Windows 2000 and older Microsoft operating systems can select the Classic Start menu option under the Start Menu tab in the Taskbar and Start Menu Properties dialog box. B and D are not necessary to achieve this, and option C is an invalid choice because it will not accomplish what you are after.

15. A. Selecting the Lock the Taskbar option prevents users from making changes to the Taskbar. Options B and D are invalid choices, and option C merely causes the Taskbar to disappear when other applications are in use.

16. D. Switch Identity/Identities/Exit and Log Off Identity is the correct answer. Option A applies to switching users in Windows XP, and options B and C are invalid choices.

17. B. Outlook Express allows you to use the Combine and Decode option to reassemble many files that come as attachments regardless of the order in which they are received. The other applications listed do not have a Combine and Decode option.

18. C. The Import and Export option in Internet Explorer allows you to send your favorites and cookies to and from other computers, so that you can log on to another computer and still retain those settings.

19. D. Microsoft Office requires activation after installation by contacting Microsoft either over the phone or through the Internet. The other applications mentioned do not specifically require activation.

20. C. The Help and Support Center can be used offline as well as online to help resolve application issues. All other options require the user to be online and connected to the Internet.

Chapter

9

Resolving Application Customization Issues

MICROSOFT EXAM OBJECTIVES COVERED IN THIS CHAPTER:

✓ **Resolve issues related to customizing an Office application.**

- Answer end-user questions related to customizing Office applications.
- Customize toolbars.
- Configure proofing tools.
- Manage Outlook data, including configuring, importing, and exporting data and repairing corrupted data.
- Personalize Office features.

✓ **Resolve issues related to customizing Internet Explorer.**

✓ **Resolve issues related to customizing Outlook Express.**

✓ **Resolve issues related to customizing the operating system to support applications.**

- Answer end-user questions related to customizing the operating system to support an application.
- Customize the Start menu and Taskbar.
- Customize regional settings.
- Customize fonts.
- Customize folder settings.

As a desktop support technician, your main job is to make sure a user's computer and applications continue to function well so that the user can remain productive for your organization. You should understand that every user utilizes an operating system and applications in a unique manner; therefore, you can increase users' productivity by customizing their settings or teaching them to customize them on their own.

The four main components that you can customize are as follows:

Office applications   After you have installed the applications that a user needs to do their job, you can make them easier to learn and easier to use by customizing them. We will discuss customizing toolbars to make them easier to use. In addition, we will discuss tools that can enhance productivity when users are working with multiple languages, such as proofing tools for multiple languages. We will also discuss how to safely import data to and export data from Microsoft Outlook and how to repair corrupted data. Finally, we will discuss how to use the features of Microsoft Office to create a personalized workspace for a user.

Internet Explorer   Perhaps one of the most customized applications is a user's browser. Internet Explorer provides a variety of customization options that let you create a browsing environment that fits a user's needs. We will discuss using and organizing the Favorites tool to make returning to a website as easy as clicking the mouse. In addition, we will discuss password caching to enable the browser to automatically enter a previously entered password. Finally, we will discuss customizing the toolbars in Internet Explorer to create the most efficient browsing environment for each user.

Outlook Express   When you support users who share a computer, you can personalize the Outlook Express mailbox, contacts, and personal settings for each user by creating an *identity* for each user. We will discuss how to create, modify, and delete identities in Outlook Express. In addition, we will discuss how to import a user's email messages and address books into Outlook Express from another computer and how to export them to another computer. Finally, we will discuss how to customize the toolbar for users based on their needs.

The operating system   Just as you can customize applications for users, you can also customize the operating system so that they can gain access to and use the applications more efficiently. We will discuss how to customize the Start menu and the Taskbar to meet a specific user's needs. In addition, we will discuss how to customize the regional settings for a user based on their location. We will also talk about how to customize fonts within the operating system to create a more comfortable and user-friendly environment for each user. Finally, we will discuss how to customize folder settings based on the types of files that are stored in the folder and their intended use.

Customizing Office Applications

Different users utilize applications in different ways. The way a user utilizes an application may be due to their role in the organization, their location in world, or many other factors. As a desktop support technician, you should be able to assist a user to customize their own applications to make them easier to use. Microsoft Office 2003 contains features that enable you to customize the toolbars and personalize the Office environment. You can also install additional proofing tools and language programs that enable a user to work efficiently with documents in multiple languages. In addition, you can safely manage Microsoft Outlook data using the tools provided by the application in Office 2003. These tools enable you to configure data, import data from other applications, and export data from Outlook to other applications. You can also use tools to fix Outlook data if it becomes corrupt. Finally, you can use the extensive Options menu to personalize the software for each user. In the following sections, we will discuss each of these concepts in detail.

Customizing Toolbars

One of the benefits of using Microsoft applications is that there is some standardization in regard to their control. In other words, the Cut, Copy, Paste, Save, and many other tools are about the same for Word as they are for Excel and PowerPoint. Although the tools themselves are standardized, the way that we use them can be customized.

The method you can use to customize toolbars varies only slightly across the applications in Office 2003. We will use Microsoft Word to illustrate this concept, but you should know that the other applications, such as Excel and PowerPoint, function in very much the same manner. Figure 9.1 shows Microsoft Word with a blank document and a standard set of toolbars.

FIGURE 9.1   Microsoft Word 2003 with standard toolbars

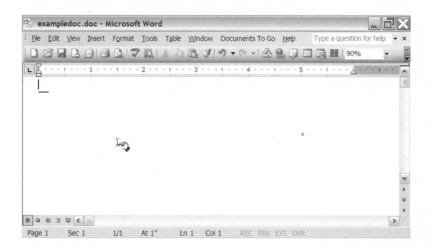

You can add toolbars to Microsoft applications to put the tools that the user needs to do their job in an obvious location on the screen. The types of toolbars that you can add will depend on the software that you are using and on the other software that is installed on the computer. Even some non-Microsoft software can produce toolbars in Office 2003 applications. Exercise 9.1 walks you through the steps to add and organize toolbars in Word 2003.

If the default selection of toolbars is still not sufficient for a user, they can create fully customized toolbars. For example, if a user needs some of the tools from many of the toolbars but does not want the clutter of having all of the toolbars on the screen, they can create their own toolbar that has only the tools that they need. Exercise 9.2 outlines the steps to create a custom toolbar.

EXERCISE 9.1

Adding and Organizing Toolbars in Word 2003

1. In Microsoft Word 2003, choose View from the menus at the top of the screen, and then choose Toolbars. (You can also simply right-click any existing toolbar.)

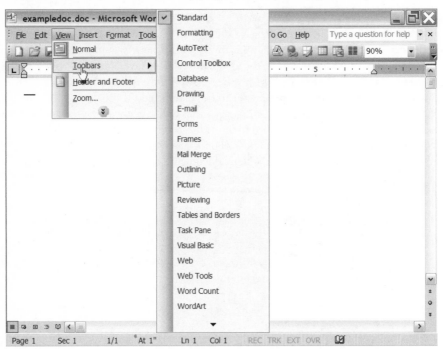

2. Select the toolbar that you want to add by positioning the mouse pointer on it and click-ing. The toolbar will be added to the screen in its default location. In this case we will add the Picture toolbar.

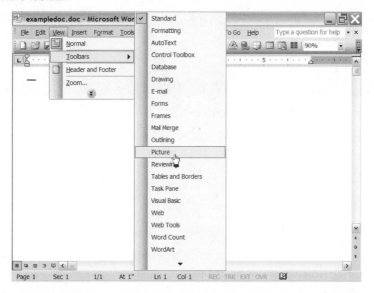

3. If the toolbar is floating in the screen, you can move it to the top, bottom, left side, or right side to anchor it on its own or with other toolbars.

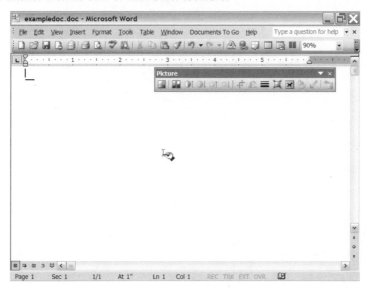

4. If the toolbar is already anchored, you can click and hold the handle on the left side of the toolbar and drag it to any area of the screen. Note that the mouse pointer changes when it is over the handle.

5. You can also resize the toolbar by clicking and holding it on the right side and "pushing" toward the left.

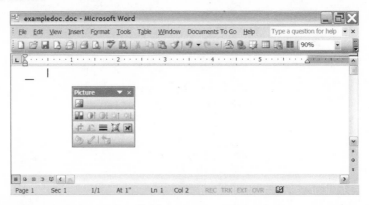

6. You can add as many toolbars as a user needs in this manner. This example shows 10 added toolbars. Note that this is an extreme example and you probably would not use this many toolbars. (You can also add multiple toolbars by choosing Tools ➢ Customize and then selecting the toolbars.)

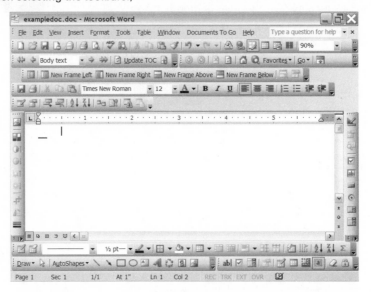

EXERCISE 9.1 *(continued)*

7.   To remove any toolbar, choose View ➢ Toolbars and then click on the toolbar that you want to remove. (You can also right-click on any toolbar to see a selection list of all toolbars.)

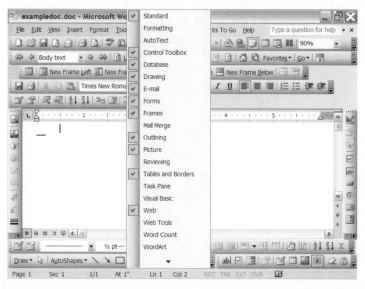

EXERCISE 9.2

Creating a Custom Toolbar

1.   In Microsoft Word 2003, choose Tools from the menus at the top of the screen, and then choose Customize.

2.   In the Customize dialog box, choose New and type a name for your new toolbar; then use the drop-down arrow to choose whether the toolbar will be available only on this document or whether it will be added to the normal.dot template to make it available on all future documents created with this template. Then, click OK to continue. Note that a small toolbar will appear next to the Customize dialog box when you click OK.

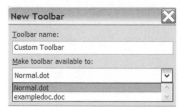

3. In the Customize dialog box, choose the Commands tab and then choose the first category from which you will gather tools for your new toolbar.

4. Click, hold, and drag to your new toolbar each tool that you want from the first category,
and then move on to each additional category and do the same. You can scroll through
the categories on the left and through the tools on the right and choose any of the tools
in any category. When you have finished building your toolbar, click Close to remove the
Customize dialog box. The new toolbar is automatically saved.

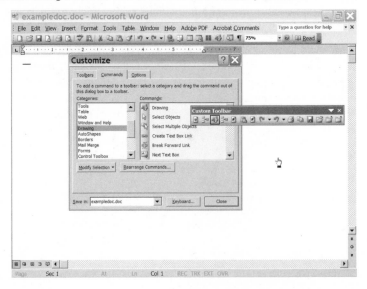

5. You can now anchor the new toolbar and manage it in the same manner as all of the other toolbars.

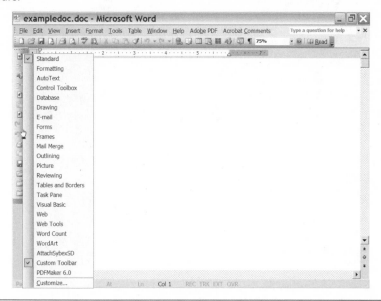

Configuring Proofing Tools

If your organization does business in more than one language, you might want to consider purchasing the *Office 2003 Proofing Tools* software, which can be added to Office 2003. These tools offer a collection of editing technologies that enable a user to proofread and correct documents in multiple languages. They include spelling and grammar checkers, AutoCorrect lists, and options. Administrators can choose from a list of languages when installing Proofing Tools, as shown in Figure 9.2.

If your organization uses only the English language, then all of the proofing tools that you need are included with the English version of Office 2003. In this section, we will focus on configuring the proofing tools for the English version of Office 2003.

Spelling and Grammar Checkers

Let's face it, we are all human and we all make mistakes in spelling and grammar from time to time—that means you, too! For this reason, the more help that we can get from the application in regard to spelling and grammar, the better—at least usually. The reason that we say "usually" is that there are some instances when we know what we want to say or how we want to spell a word (or an acronym), but the application has not yet been trained to accept our input. Because of this, spelling and grammar checkers can irritate users who do not know how to configure them properly. The trick is to configure the tool to be flexible to the way users expresses themselves while at the same time maintaining as much accuracy as possible.

FIGURE 9.2 A custom installation of Microsoft Proofing Tools for Office 2003

FIGURE 9.3 The Spelling & Grammar tab of the Options dialog box

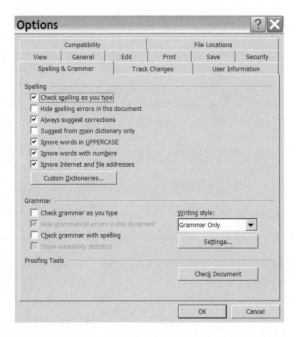

In this section, we will discuss how to configure the spelling and grammar checkers for Microsoft Word 2003. These tools are very similar in the other applications within Office 2003. You can configure spelling and grammar checking from the Tools menu of Word 2003. Click the Tools menu at the top of the screen, choose Options, and finally, choose the Spelling & Grammar tab.

Figure 9.3 shows the Spelling & Grammar tab in the Options dialog box, which includes the following settings:

- Check Spelling As You Type: This setting automatically checks the spelling of each word that you type against the dictionary or dictionaries that you choose and install. It will indicate a word that is not in the dictionary by placing a wavy red line underneath the word.

- Hide Spelling Errors in This Document: You can use this setting in conjunction with the Check Spelling As You Type setting to leave the default setting for documents set so that spelling is checked and the wavy red line is shown while at the same time hiding the wavy red line in only the document in which you apply this setting. If Check Spelling As You Type is not selected, then this setting will be enabled by default.

- Always Suggest Corrections: You can use this setting in conjunction with the Suggest from Main Dictionary Only setting. If this option is checked, then the system will make recommendations from the dictionary or dictionaries to correct your misspelling.

- Suggest from Main Dictionary Only: If you are using multiple dictionaries for reference, you can use this setting to limit the recommendations to only your main dictionary.

- Ignore Words in UPPERCASE: Often, words that are written in all uppercase letters are actually acronyms or company names that may not be found in a dictionary. You should use this setting when the user tends to type many of these kinds of words. This setting is selected by default when Word 2003 is installed.

- Ignore Words with Numbers: Words with numbers are usually being utilized for a special purpose and may not be found in a dictionary. You should use this setting when the user tends to use many words with numbers. This setting is selected by default when Word 2003 is installed.

- Ignore Internet and File Addresses: These types of addresses are often used in business but may not be found in a dictionary. You should select this setting when a user utilizes these types of addresses. This setting is selected by default when Word 2003 is installed.

- Custom Dictionaries: You should click the Custom Dictionaries button to add a new dictionary that you have obtained from the Internet or from a third-party source.

- Check Grammar As You Type: When you enable this setting, the application will examine the words that you type and the context in which you type them against the standard rules for grammar. When the application does not agree that what you have typed is grammatically correct, it will indicate this by placing a wavy green line underneath the area with which it has an issue. You can right-click the entry to get suggestions as to how to fix the grammatical error.

- Hide Grammatical Errors in This Document: You can use this setting in conjunction with the Check Grammar As You Type setting to leave the default setting for documents set so that grammar is checked and the wavy green line is shown while at the same time hiding the wavy green line in only the document in which you apply this setting. If Check Grammar As You Type is not selected, then this setting will be enabled by default.

- Check Grammar with Spelling: You should use this setting when you want the application to also check the grammar whenever you specifically select to check the spelling in a document.

- Show Readability Statistics: When you enable this option, the application will automatically display information about the reading level of the document as soon as it finishes a spelling or grammar check. If you are using multiple languages in a document and multiple dictionaries, then you should select the text on which you want to perform a spelling or grammar check. The application can then recognize the language.

- Writing Style and Settings: You can use these options to further customize what will be considered acceptable grammar by the application. You should balance what a user needs to do their job against the need to maintain the highest level of accuracy in regard to grammar.

- Check Document/Recheck Document: If a user has not previously clicked Ignore on any spelling and grammar suggestions, then this button will read Check Document. If the user has clicked Ignore on even one suggestion, then the button will read Recheck Document. Users can utilize this option to recheck potential errors on which they have previously answered Ignore.

Microsoft Word Dictionary

Microsoft Word has a dictionary file that is used as a reference each time a spell check occurs. This is referenced as a custom dictionary. Custom dictionaries have several characteristics that you should be familiar with. First, the custom dictionary contains only words and phrases that you manually add. The actual Word dictionary is a separate file from the custom dictionary. The custom dictionary file can grow to be a maximum of only 65,593 bytes and can contain a maximum of only 5,000 words. We will explore these options in Exercise 9.3.

AutoCorrect Lists and Options

If you are using *AutoCorrect*, then you may not be as good a typist as you think! The application might just be changing your misspellings before you ever get a chance to see them. AutoCorrect is a feature included in Microsoft Word that automatically corrects the most common types of spelling errors. You can also use AutoCorrect to replace a typed entry with another typed entry. This is especially useful for users who tend to use the same long phrase or terminology repeatedly. They can type a much smaller entry and then let AutoCorrect do the rest of the work. You can add in any text and the text with which you want to replace it. Users can utilize plain text or formatted text to express themselves in their documents. The AutoCorrect settings are located within the Tools menu of Word 2003. Figure 9.4 shows the AutoCorrect dialog box. Most of the settings are self-explanatory. You can choose the Exceptions button to list specific instances when you don't want the application to work for you. For example, most of the time it's handy that the application will automatically capitalize the next letter after you type a period, but not if you just typed a word such as *appt.* within a sentence. Users can use exceptions to "train" and customize AutoCorrect so that it works better for them.

EXERCISE 9.3

Configuring the Microsoft Word Custom Dictionary

1. Open Microsoft Word and type a word that is not in the default dictionary; it should be underlined with a red line.

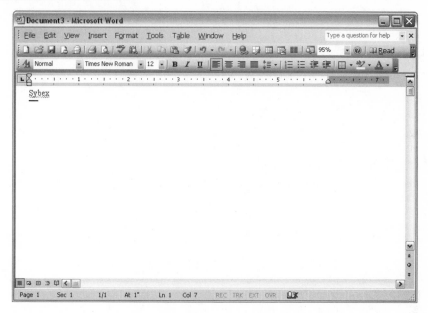

2. To add the word into your custom dictionary, simply right-click on it and choose Add to Dictionary

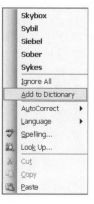

3. Once the word has been added, it should be contained within the custom dictionary. To view words added into the custom dictionary, select Tools from the menu bar and click Options.

4. Select the Spelling & Grammar tab.

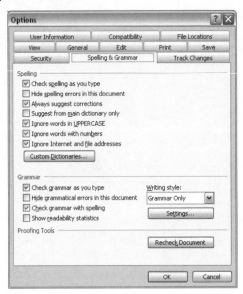

5. Click the Custom Dictionaries button.

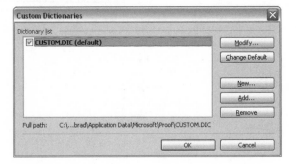

6. Select the appropriate dictionary and click modify.

7. To add a word, simply type it in at the top of the dialog box and click Add.

8. Click Cancel to go back to the Custom Dictionaries dialog box.

9. To add additional dictionaries, click the New button.

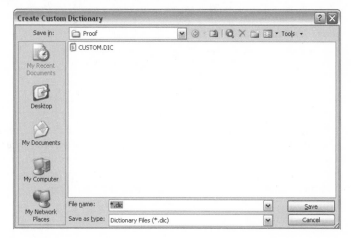

10. Save the new dictionary file and begin use!

Note that you would add additional dictionary files when your initial file becomes too large or has too many words in it.

FIGURE 9.4 The AutoCorrect dialog box

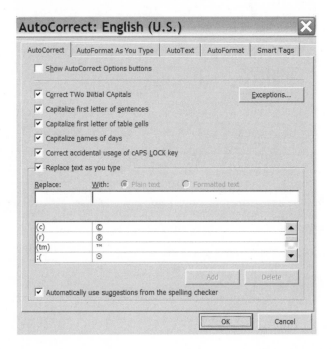

This is by no means a complete list of all of the automatic features of Microsoft Word 2003 or other Microsoft Office 2003 applications; we've included only the features that pertain to proofing the document. To learn more about Word, you should take a good class on the software or read a good book that walks you through all of its features. It will be well worth your time.

Managing Outlook Data

When your users utilize Outlook on a daily basis, they may send and receive email using multiple accounts. This activity will create many contacts, notes, appointments, and so on. This information is vital to the productivity of the users in your organization. Outlook provides many tools that assist you in managing this data for users. You can use personal folders to store user information in a central location. In addition, you can create junk email filters to block a user's receipt of unsolicited email. You can also configure automatic features that manage and organize messages and archive data for users, clearing out the old items in their mailboxes. Finally, you can import data into Outlook from other applications and export data to other applications using the tools built into Outlook. In the following sections, we will discuss each of these concepts in detail.

Personal Folders

A personal folder is a data file with a `.pst` extension that stores information such as messages, appointments, tasks, and journal entries. The storage limit on these files is set to 20GB by default but can be increased to as much as 1 terabyte! Exercise 9.4 shows you how to create a personal folder in Microsoft Outlook 2003.

Junk Email Filters

Unfortunately, many users receive unsolicited advertisements and other unwanted email, called *junk email*. Outlook 2003 includes tools that can automatically move junk email to a user's Deleted Items folder, Junk E-mail folder, or any folder that you specify. Users can also have unwanted email delivered to their Inbox but color coded so it's easy to recognize. Finally, users can specify that all messages from a particular sender be moved to another folder or deleted. We will discuss each of these options in detail.

Setting Junk Email Options in Outlook

Outlook 2003 includes a new feature called the junk email filter. This tool enables you to quickly configure a user's junk email settings and make changes to them whenever necessary. You can access this tool through the Tools ➤ Options menu of Outlook 2003. The Junk E-mail Options dialog box includes the following tabs and settings.

EXERCISE 9.4

Creating a Personal Folder in Outlook 2003

1.   In Microsoft Outlook, choose File ➤ New ➤ Outlook Data File.

2. In the New Outlook Data File dialog box, click OK.

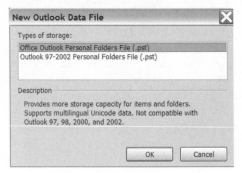

3. In the File Name field, type a name for the file, and then click OK. In this case we used the username Bob Jones.

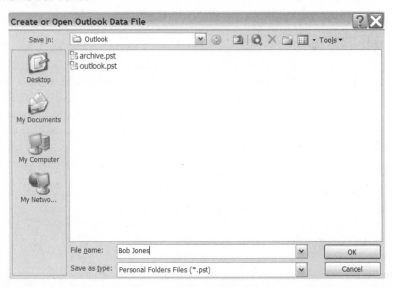

4. In the Create Microsoft Personal Folders dialog box, type the display name for the folder and the password required to access it, and then click OK.

The new folder will be displayed in Outlook 2003 and can be accessed by the user with the password. (You can also specify the type of encryption required by your organization.)

OPTIONS

The Options tab contains the overall settings for filtering junk email. You should configure the settings based on the amount of junk email that a user is receiving. Remember that a setting that is too strict might cause the user to miss an email that they actually need to see. This is because a user will not always remember to check the Junk E-mail folder. Figure 9.5 shows the Options tab of the Junk E-mail Options dialog box, which includes the following settings:

- No Automatic Filtering: Use this tab to have all mail sent to the user's Inbox.

- Low: Use this setting to move only the most obvious junk email to the Junk E-mail folder. All other mail will be filtered and then sent to the user's Inbox.

- High: Use this setting to detect most junk email. Users should understand that some regular email also might be accidentally sent to the Junk E-mail folder. Users should check their Junk E-mail folder regularly when using this setting.

- Safe Lists Only: Use this setting to establish that only email from senders that are listed in the Safe Senders or Safe Recipients lists will be sent to the mailbox. All other mail will be considered junk email. Users should check their Junk E-mail folder regularly after configuring this setting.

- Permanently Delete Suspected Junk E-Mail Instead of Moving It to the Junk E-mail Folder: You should use this setting only after you have established a reliable system to identify and manage junk email.

FIGURE 9.5   The Options tab of the Junk E-mail Options dialog box

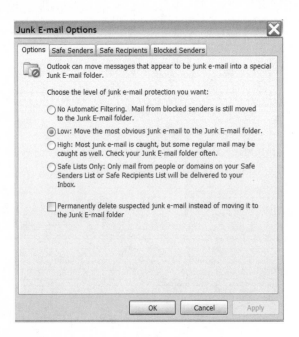

SAFE SENDERS

The Safe Senders tab enables you add users or domains that will never be treated as junk email. You should add the individuals or domains with which you commonly associate to this list. This will prevent these users or domains from being accidentally filtered by the junk email filter. Figure 9.6 shows the Safe Senders tab. You can use the Import from File and Export to File options to copy Safe Senders lists to and from Outlook. The Always Trust E-mail from My Contacts check box allows all recognized email to be sent to the user's Inbox. This option is enabled by default, but you can clear the check box to disable it.

FIGURE 9.6   The Safe Senders tab of the Junk E-mail Options dialog box

SAFE RECIPIENTS

The Safe Recipients tab enables you to add users or domains from which messages will not be considered junk email if users have sent them an email message and they receive a reply to that message. You should add the individuals or domains with which you commonly associate to this list. This will prevent these users or domains from being accidentally filtered by the junk email filter. Figure 9.7 shows the Safe Recipients tab. You can use the Import from File and Export to File options to copy Safe Recipients lists to and from Outlook.

BLOCKED SENDERS

The Blocked Senders tab enables you to add individual names or domains from which messages will always be treated as junk email. You should add names and domains that have been recognized in the past as junk email senders. Figure 9.8 shows the Blocked Senders tab. You can use the Import from File and Export to File options to copy Blocked Senders lists to and from Outlook.

User can quickly add a sender or domain name to these lists by right-clicking the message, pointing to Junk E-mail, and then choosing the appropriate list.

FIGURE 9.7   The Safe Recipients tab of the Junk E-mail Options dialog box

Microsoft Outlook Rules

A Microsoft Outlook rule is a set of conditions, actions, and exceptions to use in processing and organizing messages. Rules help by performing actions automatically based on the conditions of the rule. For example, a rule could be used to automatically move all messages from a specific email address into a folder created for only that address. Rules fall into two categories, as follows:

- Organization rules: This type of rule performs one or more actions on a message. You can create rules that automatically move, forward, and/or highlight messages based on whom the message is from and what it contains.

- Notification rules: This type of rule alerts users when they receive a message with particular characteristics. Users can utilize these rules to have a message sent to their cellular phone or pager when they receive an important email.

Once you create a rule, it will run automatically. In addition, you can run the rule manually to selectively apply it to messages that are already in a user's Inbox or another folder when you create the rule. If you do not want Outlook to apply your rule all of the time, you can create a list of exceptions to the rule.

Exercise 9.5 walks you through the steps to create a rule in Outlook.

FIGURE 9.8   The Blocked Senders tab of the Junk E-mail Options dialog box

Creating Rules in Outlook 2003

1. In Microsoft Outlook, choose Tools ➢ Rules and Alerts.

2. If the user has more than one email account, choose the Inbox that you want; if the user has only one account, proceed to step 3.

3. Click New Rule to open the Rules Wizard.

4. In the Rules Wizard, you can choose to create a rule from a template or start with a blank rule. Either way, the wizard will guide you through the rest of the process to create your new rule by assisting you in selecting a template, editing a rule description, and applying special conditions if necessary.

EXERCISE 9.5 *(continued)*

5. For example, to automatically move messages from a specific sender to a folder, under Stay Organized, choose Move Messages from Someone to a Folder.

6. In the Step 2 area, click the People or Distribution List link, then select the user(s) on which you want the rule to apply, and click OK.

7. Click the Specified link, and then choose the folder to which you wish to send the messages, or select New to create a new folder, and click OK.

8. Apply any specific conditions that are necessary, and then click Next.

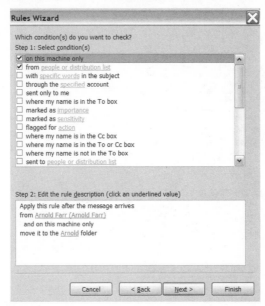

9. Selected any additional actions that you want to perform on the email, such as printing it, for example, and then choose Next.

10. Configure any exceptions to the rule that apply, and then click Next.

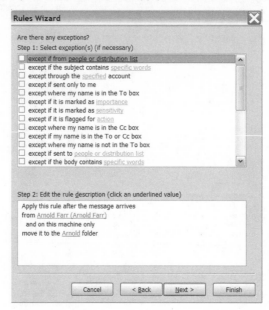

11. Click Finish to complete the configuration of the new rule and turn the rule on. You can also select to run the rule for the messages that are already in the Inbox.

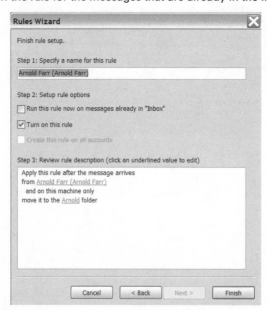

Exercise 9.6 details the steps needed to run an existing rule in Outlook.

EXERCISE 9.6

Running an Existing Rule in Outlook 2003

1. In Microsoft Outlook, choose Tools ➢ Rules and Alerts.

2. Choose Run Rules Now.

3. In the Run Rules Now dialog box, select the rules that you want to run.

4. Click Browse to select the folders that contain the messages on which you want to run the rules. You can also indicate whether you want to include the subfolders within the folders.

5. Click the drop-down arrow to configure the application to run the rule on all messages, unread messages, or read messages.

6. Click Run Now to run the rules that you have selected.

Archiving Data

Microsoft Outlook 2003 includes a tool called AutoArchive that allows users to archive their data at specific intervals. AutoArchive is on by default and runs automatically to clear out old and expired items from folders. You can configure AutoArchive in regard to which folders it clears out and how often it clears them out. You can configure an overall setting for AutoArchive that applies to all folders. To locate these settings, choose Tools ➢ Options ➢ Other ➢ AutoArchive. In addition, you can override the overall setting by applying the AutoArchive settings directly to a folder. Figure 9.9 shows the AutoArchive dialog box, which includes the following settings:

- Run AutoArchive Every __ Days: This setting configures the interval in days for AutoArchive to run automatically.

- Prompt Before AutoArchive Runs: When this setting is enabled, the user is prompted that AutoArchive is about to run.

- During AutoArchive: This is the main configuration menu that controls which items will be deleted and which items will be moved. You can also specify the location to which the old items will be moved.

- Apply These Settings to All Folders Now: Clicking this button automatically applies the new AutoArchive settings to all folders except those that have their own specific settings. You can specify settings for a single folder by right-clicking the folder, choosing Properties, and then choosing the AutoArchive tab.

- Retention Policy: The network administrator can enter a retention policy that will override the settings of a user to be certain that information is retained for the length of time required by the organization.

FIGURE 9.9 The AutoArchive dialog box

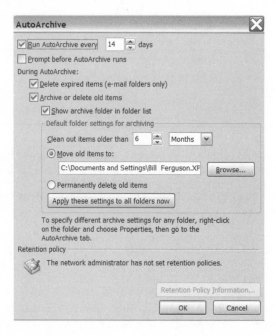

Importing and Exporting Outlook Data

When a user changes computers or software, you can easily move the important data to and from Outlook using the built-in Import and Export Wizard. This wizard enables you to safely import data without damaging or duplicating it in the process.

Exercise 9.7 walks you through the steps to import data using the Outlook Import and Export Wizard.

EXERCISE 9.7

Importing Data Using the Import and Export Wizard

1. In Microsoft Outlook, choose File ➤ Import and Export.

2. In the Import and Export Wizard, choose Import from Another Program or File, and then click Next.

3. Select the type of file that you want to import, and then click Next.

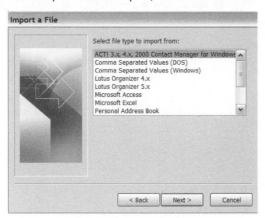

4. Click Browse, select the file that you want to import from, and then choose one of the following:

> Replace Duplicates with Items Imported: This setting will cause existing duplicate data to be overwritten by the data that is being imported.

> Allow Duplicates to Be Created: This setting will allow duplicate data to be added to the Outlook folder.

> Do Not Import Duplicate Items: This setting will prevent duplicate data from being copied into the folder during import. The existing data will be retained.

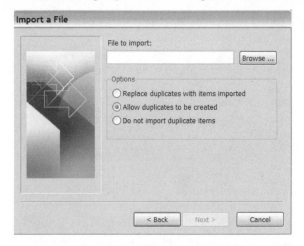

5. Click Next, and then select the folder into which you want to import the data.

6. If necessary, map the fields from the file that you are importing to the Outlook fields, and then click Next.

7. Click OK to import the data.

Exercise 9.8 explains how to export data using the Outlook Import and Export Wizard.

EXERCISE 9.8

Exporting Data Using the Import and Export Wizard

1. In Microsoft Outlook, choose File ➢ Import and Export.

2. In the Import and Export Wizard, choose Export to A File, and then click Next.

3. Select the type of file that you want to export to, and then click Next.

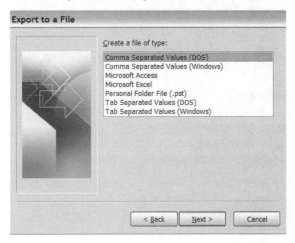

4. Follow the remaining instructions of the wizard; these will vary based on the type of file that you choose.

Repairing Corrupt Data

Office 2003 has a tool called the Inbox Repair Tool that you can use to repair corrupted PST files (files with a `.pst` extension). The Inbox Repair Tool, also called `Scanpst.exe`, is installed automatically during setup. You can typically find the `Scanpst.exe` file at the following location:

`C:\Program Files\Common Files\System\MSMAPI\1033\Scanpst.exe.`

The Inbox Repair Tool scans PST files to verify that the file structure is intact. When it discovers problems, it attempts to repair the corrupt items. Exercise 9.9 shows you how to scan a PST file with the Inbox Repair Tool.

EXERCISE 9.9

Using the Inbox Repair Tool

1. Click Start and then choose Run.

2. On the Run line, type `C:\program files\common files\system\msmapi\1033\scanpst.exe`.

3. In the Inbox Repair Tool dialog box, enter the name of the PST file that you want to scan.

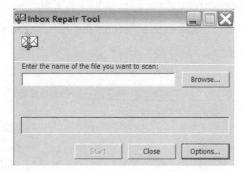

4. Choose Options to specify scan log options, or just click Start.

5. If errors are found during the scan, then you will be prompted to start the repair process. If so, click Repair.

Customizing Internet Explorer

Each user utilizes the Internet Explorer browser in a slightly different manner. You can assist users in customizing their browser so it fits their own needs. This might include using time-saving features such as saving a password for a site so the user doesn't have to remember it or organizing links to their favorite websites so that they are easier to find. You can also customize the toolbar in Internet Explorer to create a user-friendly workspace for the user. In the following sections, we will discuss each of these concepts in detail.

Saving a Password for a Website

When a user attempts to access a website that requires secure access, they have to type their password. You can enable the system to remember the password so they don't have to type it again when they use the same computer. This password caching is on by default and can be controlled in the AutoComplete settings on the Content tab of Internet Options, as shown in Figure 9.10.

FIGURE 9.10   The password caching option in AutoComplete

 Some organizations may have security policies that do not allow password caching. You can disable password caching, but it requires using the Registry Editor or the Internet Explorer Administration Kit (IEAK).

Organizing Favorites

Favorites are simply Internet shortcuts that point to websites that users want to access frequently and quickly. You can assist users in organizing their favorites in order to put the tools that they use on a daily basis at their fingertips. To organize favorites in Internet Explorer, you should choose Favorites ➢ Organize Favorites. Figure 9.11 shows the Organize Favorites dialog box, which includes the following buttons:

- Create Folder: This button creates a new folder. You should give each folder a unique name based on the shortcuts that are in it.

- Move to Folder: Select the shortcuts that you want to move and then click this button. You can then select the folder to which to move the shortcuts. You can also drag and drop the shortcuts.

- Rename: Use this button to rename a shortcut or a folder.

- Delete: Use this button only if you want to permanently delete a folder or a link from Favorites. The system will ask you for confirmation, and if you answer yes, the item will be moved to the Recycle Bin.

> You can also organize favorites within the Internet Explorer Favorites menu. Most operations can be performed by right-clicking the item that you want to manage.

FIGURE 9.11   The Organize Favorites dialog box

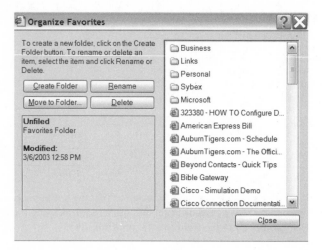

Customizing the Internet Explorer Toolbar

Different users utilize different tools in Internet Explorer. Some users may never use some of the tools that are included in the Standard toolbar. In that case, they are just getting in the user's way. Other users may perform an action for which there is no tool in the Standard toolbar, thereby doing it the hard way. You can assist users in customizing their toolbar to fit their own needs. To customize the toolbar in Internet Explorer, right-click the Standard toolbar and choose Customize. Figure 9.12 shows the Customize Toolbar dialog box, which includes the following settings and options:

- Available Toolbar Buttons: This is a list of all of the buttons that are available for use in Internet Explorer.

- Current Toolbar Buttons: This is a list of all of the tools that are currently installed and the order in which they are displayed, including separators.

- Add/Remove: These buttons enable you to add and remove tools to create a custom toolbar.

- Reset: This button restores the default set of tools that were installed.

- Move Up/Move Down: These buttons enable you to reorganize the order in which the tools will be displayed.

- Text Options: This setting controls the display of text shown with the tool icon.
- Icon Options: This setting controls the size of the icons for the tools. There are only two sizes: large and small.

FIGURE 9.12 The Customize Toolbar dialog box

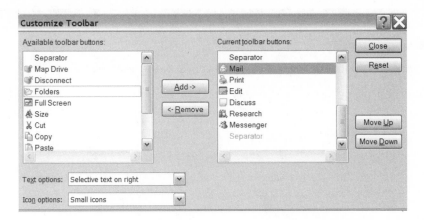

Customizing Outlook Express

When more than one person uses a computer for email messages, you can create an identity for each user so their messages will go into their own Inbox. In addition, when a user changes computers, you can easily and safely import their messages and address books to another computer using the tools built into Outlook Express. You can also assist each user in creating a customized look and feel in Outlook Express by modifying the standard toolbar. In the following sections, we will discuss each of these topics in detail.

Outlook Express Identities

You can create an identity for each user who utilizes Outlook Express email on a computer. Once the identity is created, users can build their own hierarchy of folders that they will be able to see and use each time they log on to the computer. Each identity can also have its own personal settings such as tools, fonts, and so on. You can also manage the identities on the computer for each user and delete identities when they are no longer required. We will discuss each of these subjects in detail.

Creating an Identity

Usually, you will create identities from inside Outlook Express. If a computer has multiple users, you should create an identity for each one. Exercise 9.10 walks you through the steps to create an identity.

Creating an Identity

1. In Microsoft Outlook Express, choose File ➢ Identities ➢ Add New Identity.

2. Type the name of the new user. In this case, **Sam Spade**.

3. If you want to require a password for this identity, select Require a Password and then press enter and confirm the password.

4. Click OK. The system will ask you if you want to switch to the new identity that you created. You can answer yes to switch to the new identity or no to remain on the identity that you used to create the new identity.

Managing and Deleting Identities

Outlook Express provides tools to assist you in managing multiple identities. You can find these tools on the File menu. Choose Identities ➤ Manage Identities. Figure 9.13 shows the Manage Identities dialog box, which contains the following options and settings:

- Identities: This is a list of all of the identities that are currently in the computer.

- New: You can click this button to create new identities from the Manage Identities dialog box.

- Remove: You can click this button to delete an identity that is no longer required. You cannot delete an identity that is currently being used.

- Use This Identity When Starting a Program: You can click the drop-down arrow and then select the default identity that will be used when identity-aware programs are started. If you leave this option unchecked, the user will be prompted to choose the identity.

- Use This Identity When a Program Cannot Ask You to Choose an Identity: You can click the drop-down arrow and then select the default identity that will be used when a program is not identity aware.

FIGURE 9.13   The Manage Identities dialog box

Import and Export Tools

When a user changes computers or changes software, the last thing that they want to have to do is start all over again in regard to messages, address books, and settings in Outlook Express. You can assist a user in safely exporting the data from the old system and importing it to the new system. Table 9.1 lists the types of data and settings that you can import into Outlook Express. You can also export address books and messages from Outlook Express to other email programs. You can use the Import and Export Wizard located on the File menu of Outlook Express. The wizard will guide you through the process of importing and exporting all types of data and settings.

 WARNING
You should know that using a password provides only a minimal level of security. It keeps users from using your identity, but it does not keep them from viewing your files.

TABLE 9.1   Data and Settings That Can Be Imported into Outlook Express

Item	Details
Address books from Microsoft and other products	You can import address book data that uses a comma-separated value (CSV) format.
Messages from other email programs	You can import messages from Microsoft Outlook and older versions of Outlook Express.
Email account settings	You can import most, if not all, of the customization settings such as fonts, mailbox settings, and so on.
Newsgroup account settings	You can import your subscription settings from other Outlook Express programs.

Customizing the Outlook Express Toolbar

As with Internet Explorer, different users will use Outlook Express in very different ways. The Standard toolbar might contain some tools that a user will never utilize. By the same token, the user might be performing tasks the hard way because they are not aware of a tool that would help perform them faster. You can assist the user in creating a customized toolbar that fits their needs. Begin by right-clicking the current toolbar in Outlook Express and choosing Customize. Figure 9.14 shows the Customize Toolbar dialog box for Outlook Express, which contains the following settings and options:

- Available Toolbar Buttons: This is a list of all of the buttons that are available for use in Outlook Express.

- Current Toolbar Buttons: This is a list of all of the buttons that are currently installed and the order in which they are displayed, including separators.

- Add/Remove: These buttons enable you to add and remove tools to create a custom toolbar.

- Reset: This button restores the default set of tools that were installed.

- Move Up/Move Down: These buttons enable you to reorganize the order in which the tools will be displayed.

- Text Options: This setting controls the display of text that appears with the tool icon.

- Icon Options: This setting controls the size of the icons for the tools. There are only two sizes: large and small.

FIGURE 9.14   The Customize Toolbar dialog box in Outlook Express

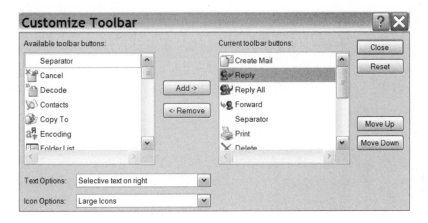

Customizing Windows XP Settings

Windows XP has many features that allow you to customize an environment for users. In Chapter 8, "Resolving Usability Issues," we discussed basic configuration of the Start menu and Taskbar. You can also further customize each of these components for a specific user's needs. In addition, you can configure and customize regional settings to adapt the computer to users from all over the world. You can also customize the font that the operating system uses for each user who logs on to a computer. Finally, you can customize folder settings to make it easier to use the specific types of files that are stored in a folder. In the following sections, we will discuss each of these concepts in greater detail.

Customizing the Start Menu and Taskbar

Both the Start menu and the Taskbar in Windows XP have two levels of settings: general and customized. In Chapter 8 we discussed the general settings for each of these tools. In this chapter, we will discuss how to further customize each of these tools for an individual user.

Customizing the Start Menu

The Start menu in Windows XP is the first tool that most people use to find the programs they need. You can customize the look and feel of the Start menu for an individual user. Begin to customize the Start menu by right-clicking on an empty area of the Taskbar and choosing Properties; then, select the Start Menu tab, shown in Figure 9.15.

FIGURE 9.15   The Taskbar and Start Menu Properties dialog box

To customize the Start menu options, click the Customize button. This will open a new dialog box that contains two additional tabs, General and Advanced, as shown in Figure 9.16. We will discuss each of these tabs in detail.

General

The General tab of the Customize Start Menu dialog box contains settings that control the size of the icons that the user will see and how many shortcuts will be created and remembered in the Start menu. You can also select the Internet and email program that will be shown on the

Start menu when there is more than one program of that type in the computer. The General tab contains the following options:

- Select an Icon Size for Programs: You have two choices, large and small.

- Programs: Use this setting to determine the number of shortcuts that will be remembered on the Start menu. When you choose this number, try to find a balance between making programs available to the user and reducing clutter on the Start menu. You can also clear the memory by clicking the Clear List button.

- Show on Start Menu: Use the drop-down arrow to indicate which Internet and email programs you wish to show on the user's Start menu when the computer has more than one of these types of programs.

FIGURE 9.16   The Customize Start Menu dialog box

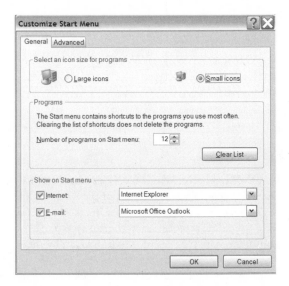

Advanced

The Advanced tab of the Customize Start Menu dialog box contains more detailed settings for many of the components of the Start menu. You can also configure the system to remember the documents that users have recently used so that they can return to them faster. Figure 9.17 shows the Advanced tab, which contains the following options and settings:

- Start Menu Settings: These settings include the options to open submenus when the user pauses on them with the mouse and to highlight newly installed programs for users.

- Start Menu Items: These settings enable you to fine-tune the way items such as Control Panel, My Documents, My Music, and so on are shown in the Start menu.

- Recent Documents: This setting enables users to utilize My Recent Documents from the Start menu to get faster access to documents that they have recently used and then closed.

FIGURE 9.17 The Advanced tab of the Customize Start Menu dialog box

Customizing the Taskbar

When configured properly for a user, the Taskbar in Windows XP can be a control and information center. In Chapter 8, we discussed general configuration of the Taskbar. In this chapter, we will discuss customizing the Taskbar to show or not show items in the notification area. Notification area icons can give users information about hardware and software installed in and running on their computer. The type of information given by the icon varies based on the type of icon.

To begin to customize the notification area of the Taskbar, right-click on an empty area of the Taskbar and choose Properties. Then choose the Taskbar tab and select Hide Inactive Icons (at the bottom of the dialog box). When you select this option, the Customize button will become active, as shown in Figure 9.18. You should then click Customize to open the Customize Notifications dialog box and begin to configure the notification area.

The Customize Notifications dialog box enables you to configure the type of icons that will be shown in the notification area of the Taskbar and under what circumstances they will be shown. As shown in Figure 9.19, each icon can be configured for the following settings:

- Hide When Inactive: Use this setting for hardware or software that is rarely used but might sometimes be needed.

- Always Hide: Use this setting when the presence of the icon in the notification area has no value to the user.

- Always Show: Use this setting for items that show critical information about hardware or software. For example, a notification area icon can show a user that they have a connection with a universal serial bus (USB) device.

FIGURE 9.18   The Taskbar tab of the Start Menu and Taskbar Properties dialog box

FIGURE 9.19   The Custom Notifications dialog box

Customizing Themes

When working inside of Windows XP, you will find that a single set of desktop configuration options simply won't suffice. By utilizing the ability to create and store customized themes, you can have exactly the settings you need, when you need them, and without much hassle. Themes have always been around in the Windows operating system, but in Windows XP, they have become much easier to work with and configure. This may be why people have started using them on a more frequent basis. Because so many programs require specific settings, having a dedicated theme for a particular application or task can save you a significant amount of time. Exercise 9.11 shows you how to customize a theme in Windows XP.

EXERCISE 9.11

Customizing Themes

1. Right-click on an empty space on the Desktop background and choose Properties.

2. Customize your settings as needed. Note that some Desktop settings, such as resolution, are not saved into a theme. Make sure those settings are customized to your liking.

3. Click the Themes tab of the Display Properties dialog.

4. To change themes, simply click the Theme drop-down box and choose the desired theme.

EXERCISE 9.11

5.   Click the Save As button to save your settings to a theme file.

Customizing Regional Settings

In Chapter 4, "Configuring and Troubleshooting the Desktop and User Environments," we discussed regional settings and performed an exercise in which you selected additional input languages. By choosing the region, you chose how the operating system would treat dates, times, numbers, and so on. You may have noticed that there was also a Customize button on the Regional Options tab. In this section, we will discuss how to further customize the regional options in Windows XP.

You should begin to customize the regional options by opening Regional and Language Options through Control Panel. The first tab of the Regional and Language Options dialog box is Regional Options, as shown in Figure 9.20. It enables you to configure the correct settings for most users in most regions.

Click Customize to begin to customize the options for any selected region. This will open the Customize Regional Options dialog box, shown in Figure 9.21. The settings that you can customize on the four tabs are as follows:

- Numbers: This tab allows you to customize how positive and negative integers are displayed and how digits are separated.

- Currency: Here you can customize the currency symbols that are used in a specific region.

- Time: You can customize how times are displayed in the operating system and in applications that get this information from the operating system.

- Date: This tab lets you customize how dates are displayed in the operating system and in applications that get this information from the operating system.

FIGURE 9.20 The Regional Options tab of the Regional and Language Options dialog box

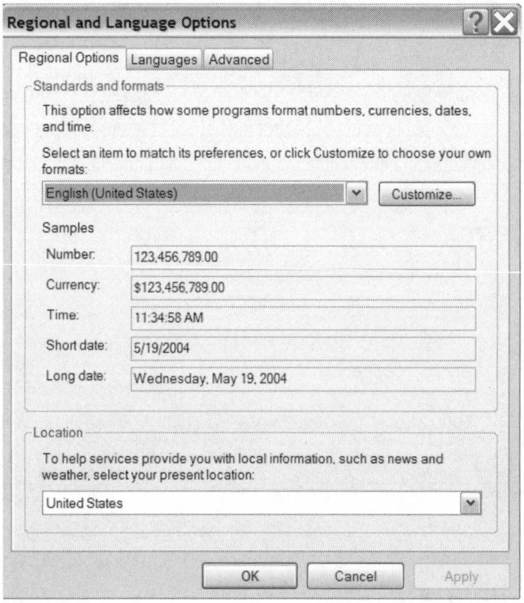

FIGURE 9.21 The Customize Regional Options dialog box

Customizing Operating System Fonts

It stands to reason that users will generally be more productive if they can read what is on their screen! In addition, you can increase user satisfaction and productivity by making the fonts that the operating system uses more pleasing to the user. What is pleasing varies by user, but you can control three main settings that affect the fonts: Appearance, Advanced Appearance, and DPI. In the following sections, we will discuss each of these settings in detail.

Appearance Settings for Fonts

Windows XP makes it simple to change the size of the fonts used by the operating system. Rather than having to choose the size of each font on each type of menu, you can simply configure the system to use larger fonts instead of the normal font size on every menu. You can adjust the size of all fonts by right-clicking the Windows XP Desktop, choosing Properties, and then choosing the Appearance tab, shown in Figure 9.22. Then click the Font Size drop-down arrow to adjust the fonts to normal, large, or extra large.

FIGURE 9.22   The Appearance tab of the Display Properties dialog box

Advanced Appearance Settings for Fonts

If there are specific items or menus on which users would like to have a larger font or a different font style, then you should click the Advanced button on the Appearance tab of the Display Properties dialog box. The Advanced Appearance dialog box enables you to control the size and type of font for many areas of the Desktop and its associated icons, windows, and menus, as shown in Figure 9.23. You will generally use this setting to fine-tune the overall settings.

FIGURE 9.23   The Advanced Appearance dialog box

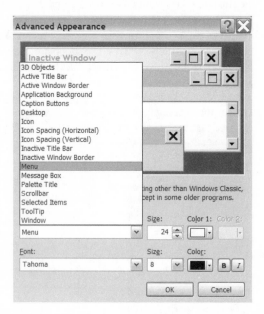

DPI

Dots per inch (DPI) is a standard that is used to indicate how crisp and readable a font will appear. Sometimes a user needs to utilize a very high screen resolution, which makes the fonts very small, in order to view an entire application on the screen. When this is the case, you can increase the readability of the fonts by increasing the DPI setting. This setting will also slightly increase the size of the font. Exercise 9.12 outlines the steps to adjust the DPI setting for all fonts in Windows XP.

EXERCISE 9.12

Configuring the DPI Setting for Fonts

1. On the Windows XP Desktop, right-click and choose Properties.

2. On the Display Properties dialog box, choose the Settings tab and then click Advanced.

3. On the dialog box for your video card, choose the General tab. The name of this box will vary based on the type of video card on your computer.

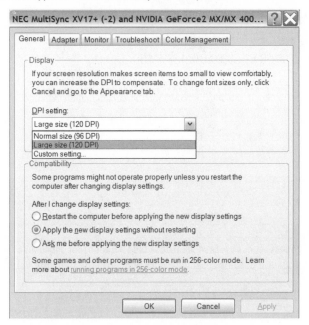

4. Use the drop-down arrow to adjust the DPI setting for all screen items including fonts, and then click OK or Apply. You will be required to restart the computer before all of the settings can take effect.

Customizing Folder Settings

Computer users work with many different types of files in many different ways. Some tools that are very helpful for some types of files do not apply at all to other types of files. For example, if you are working with audio or video files, it might be useful to have an indication of the length of time that the audio or video file runs; however, for any other type of file, this information would not apply. For this reason, Windows XP enables users to customize a folder so that it contains the tools that are useful for the files that it contains. Exercise 9.13 explains how to customize a folder for a user.

EXERCISE 9.13

Creating a Customized Folder

1. In Windows XP, right-click the Start button and then choose Explore.

2. Select the folder that you want to customize.

3. Choose the View menu at the top of the screen and then choose Customize This Folder. (You can also use the View menu in My Documents.)

4. In the folder's Properties dialog box, from the Use This Folder Type as a Template drop-down list, select the type of folder that will work best with the files that your folder contains.

EXERCISE 9.13

5. Click Choose Picture and then choose any picture that you have in the computer to represent the folder.

6. Click Change Icon and then choose any icon to represent the folder and make it stand out within Windows Explorer.

Take the Time to Customize Folders

One of the nicest new features of Windows XP is the ability to customize folders. I doubt that most people take advantage of all that this feature has to offer. Depending on the types of files that are contained in the folder, you can really add some convenient tools.

I tend to work with lots of pictures, so the options to customize the folder for pictures and even for a photo album are of great value to me. They give me the tools to view a slide show and manage the pictures in a much more organized manner. I've also used the customization option for music files to have the ability to quickly play and control the files. Customizing for videos gives me the capability to control the videos in the Windows XP software. I've also found the customized icons for folders to be a handy way to make folders stand out when needed.

Because customizing folders is one of those things that is not urgent, people tend to think it's not that important either, which may be why a lot of people aren't taking advantage of this feature. Do yourself a favor and take the time to experiment with customizing folders. Not only can you introduce the feature to others, you can find new ways to increase your productivity as well as the productivity of the users you serve.

You can also customize folders in the same manner using the My Documents tool.

Case Study: ABC Company, Customizing the End-User Environment

Abby, the lead help desk technician for ABC Company, has been asked to develop a method to deliver customized configurations to two different user groups in the company. She is very familiar with user environment configuration and has a few good ideas on how to deliver these settings. Abby has been given a list of settings that are required for each group, one series of settings for the marketing department and one series of settings for the retail department.

Marketing Configuration Requirements:

- The Desktop resolution must be 1024 × 768.

- Desktop background must be set to the company standard, `Marketingdpt.jpg`.

- Classic Windows settings must be used for appearance, Start menu, and Taskbar.

Because each one of these settings requires different methods of configuration, Abby will have to be creative in her delivery. She knows that Desktop background configuration is part of a theme and that appearance, Start menu and Taskbar configurations are also part of a theme. She can develop a customized theme named Marketing dept and email it each user or use an automated method, such as Systems Management Server (SMS). This will resolve all requirements for marketing users except the resolution. Because the resolution is not included as a configuration option within a theme, she will have to request that users set this manually or force it by use of a group policy.

Once these configurations are made, each Marketing user should have a standard Desktop.

Retail Configuration Requirements:

- Microsoft Word will have a custom toolbar with buttons for custom macros used by the retail group.

- Outlook with have custom Inbox folders and rules to place the appropriate message into the appropriate folder.

Because these changes are within an application, it would prove very difficult for Abby to find a method of automated deployment. Most likely these settings will need to be documented and sent to either the users or a group of field support technicians for implementation. If Abby's company has a method for automated software deployment, they might be able to develop a script or batch program to automatically integrate these settings into the respective application.

Summary

Because Desktop and application customization options exist in a wide variety of places inside the operating system, it proves a difficult task to implement them in an automated fashion. You should avoid creating cosmetic desktop policies if they don't serve a purpose. These settings are often difficult to get into place and will most likely be changed by users; therefore, development and implementation time is pretty much wasted. Most Microsoft Office application customization can be deployed via VBA or VB scripts. This requires very extensive knowledge of the program code, something most desktop support technicians don't have. Select programs, such as Microsoft Word, have built-in macro recording tools so that you can develop and distribute macros to other users. If you decide to use macros to standardize the environment, be aware that most antivirus software and email scanners will block macros because of their use as viruses.

Summary

The productivity of most users can be increased if their tools are customized for the tasks that they are performing. As a desktop support technician, you should know how to assist users in customizing the applications they use most often. In particular, you should know how to customize Office 2003 applications, Internet Explorer, and Outlook Express. In addition, you should know how to assist users in customizing the Windows XP operating system so that they can find and manage applications and data in the most efficient manner.

The most commonly used applications in the world are those in Microsoft Office. Each user utilizes Office for or her own reasons and in a slightly different manner than other users. For this reason, Microsoft Office 2003 has features that allow it to be customized to fit a user's needs. You should know how to customize the standard toolbars in Office 2003 applications and how to create new custom toolbars for the user. You should also know how to assist a user to configure and train proofing tools such as spelling and grammar checkers and AutoCorrect. In addition, you should know how to manage Microsoft Outlook data by creating and managing personal folders. You should also know how to help the user manage Outlook email by configuring a junk email filter and rules that automatically manage messages. Finally, you should know how to attempt to repair corrupted Outlook data using the Inbox Repair Tool in Office 2003.

Each user can utilize Internet Explorer in a unique manner. This is because Internet Explorer has many features that can be customized for each user. You should be able to assist the user in customizing features that will save time. In particular, you should be able to configure password caching for secure sites so that users don't have to remember and enter passwords for sites where they have already been authenticated. You should also be able to assist users in organizing their Favorites menu so they can easily access websites that they use frequently. Finally, you should be able to assist users in customizing the Internet Explorer toolbar so that it contains all of the tools they need and only the tools they need.

Outlook Express can be used as the email program for multiple users on the same computer. Users can have their own Inbox folder and can create their own folder hierarchy. This is accomplished by creating a separate identity for each user. You should know how to create and manage identities for users and how to delete identities when they are no longer required. You should also know how to import messages and address books from other email programs into Outlook Express and how to export them from Outlook Express to other programs or computers. Finally, you should know how to customize the Outlook Express toolbar so that it contains all of the tools that users need and only the tools that they need.

Windows XP is the most customizable Microsoft operating system to date. You should know how to customize the Start menu and Taskbar to put the tools that users need right at their fingertips. You should also know how to customize regional settings for users to configure the operating system and applications for use in many different areas of the world. In addition, you should know how to customize operating system fonts to make the font more legible and pleasing to a user. Finally, you should know how to customize folders based on the types of files that are contained in them.

Exam Essentials

Know how to customize and manage toolbars and create custom toolbars.   You should know how to customize the toolbars in Windows XP, Internet Explorer, and Outlook Express. You should also know how to create custom toolbars in Office 2003 applications, such as Word 2003. Finally, you should know how to manage toolbars on the screen in Office 2003 applications.

Be able to configure proofing tools.   You should know how to configure the spelling and grammar checking tools in Office 2003 applications. You should also know how to install the Microsoft proofing tools for Office 2003 and configure them for multiple languages. Finally, you should know how to configure the AutoCorrect option in Office 2003 applications, such as Word 2003.

Know how to manage Outlook data.   You should know how to create personal folders in Outlook 2003. In addition, you should be able to configure junk email filters to protect a user from unsolicited email but let the regular email get through to their Inbox. You should also know how to use the Rules Wizard to configure rules that manage messages automatically. Finally, you should be able to use the Inbox Repair Tool to attempt to repair a corrupt PST file.

Be able to customize Internet Explorer.   You should know to configure Internet Explorer for password caching to save a user from having to authenticate to a secure website after they have already authenticated once. You should also know how to organize the Favorites feature to save a user time when accessing frequently used websites.

Understand how to create and manage identities in Outlook Express.   You should know how to create an Outlook Express identity for each user of a computer. In addition, you should be able to manage the identities and change properties when necessary. Finally, you should know how to delete the identities when they are no longer necessary.

Know how to import and export messages and mailboxes in Outlook Express and Outlook. You should be able to use the Import and Export Wizard in Outlook Express and Outlook to move messages and mailboxes from one computer to another. You should be able to use the wizard to move many different types of files.

Know how to customize Windows XP. You should know how to customize the Start menu and Taskbar in Windows XP. In addition, you should be able to customize regional settings for users around the world. You should also know how to customize fonts in the Windows XP operating system. Finally, you should understand how to customize folders to work the best with the files that they contain.

Review Questions

1. You are the desktop support technician for your company. A user has asked you how to create a custom toolbar in Microsoft Word with only the tools that he needs. Which of the following items shows the first two steps to create the new toolbar?

    A. Choose Tools ➢ New.

    B. Choose Tools ➢ Toolbars.

    C. Choose Tools ➢ Customize.

    D. Choose Tools ➢ Options.

2. You are the desktop support technician for your company. A user complains that someone has opened so many toolbars in Word that she can hardly see the document anymore. You want to help her remove all of the toolbars except for the Standard toolbar. Which of the following options is the easiest method of accomplishing this task?

    A. Right-click on each toolbar and then choose Close.

    B. Choose Tools ➢ Customize, and then remove all of the toolbars except the Standard toolbar from the list in the Toolbars tab.

    C. Right-click on each toolbar and then deselect it from the list of active toolbars.

    D. Right-click on any toolbar, hold down the Shift key, and deselect all of the toolbars except the Standard toolbar.

3. You are the desktop support technician for your company. A user complains that he doesn't like Word because it thinks it's smarter than him. You ask him to elaborate, and he says that it's always trying to capitalize the next letter after a period and a space, so when he types an abbreviated word such as *etc.* in the middle of a sentence, he has to fight with Word to keep the next letter in lowercase. Which of the following options would fix his problem? (Choose two.)

    A. Create a custom dictionary.

    B. Adjust the spelling and grammar checker options in Word.

    C. Remove the check mark from Capitalize First Letter of Sentences in AutoCorrect.

    D. Create an exception in AutoCorrect for each of the words that are creating the problem.

4. You are the desktop support technician for your company. A user complains that she has to use many acronyms and the spell checker in Word is always bothering her about them. She has added some of them to her dictionary, but there are too many of them and it's an ongoing battle. What should you tell her to do that will fix the problem?

    A. Create an exception for each acronym that she uses.

    B. Replace the Correct Two Initial Capitals check mark that has been removed from the AutoCorrect options.

    C. Turn off grammar checking.

    D. Replace the check mark that has been removed from Ignore Words in UPPERCASE in the Spelling & Grammar options.

5. You are the desktop support technician for your company. A user complains that she is receiving a lot of unsolicited email in Outlook 2003 that just clogs up her mailbox. What should you do to help the user?

A. Ask the administrator to change her username on the network servers.

B. Install a firewall on her computer to block all unsolicited email.

C. Configure the junk email filter to send unsolicited email to the Junk E-mail folder instead of her mailbox.

D. Configure the options on her browser to block all unsolicited communication.

6. You are the desktop support technician for your company. A user would like to receive a phone call automatically if he receives an important email from a specific email address. What feature of Outlook 2003 will enable you to configure this option for the user?

A. Organization rules

B. Personal folders

C. Import and Export Wizard

D. Notification rules

7. You are the desktop support technician for your company. A user complains that after having installed a security update, his Outlook does not work at all. You suspect that the PST file has become corrupt. Which tool should you use to troubleshoot the problem?

A. The Inbox Repair tool

B. The AutoCorrect tool

C. The AutoArchive tool

D. The `scanstate.exe` tool

8. You are the desktop support technician for your company. A user asks you if there is any way that he can avoid remembering all of the passwords that he has to use for secure sites that he accesses frequently from his Desktop. Which feature of Internet Explorer will assist the user?

A. Favorites

B. AutoComplete

C. Customized toolbars

D. Registry Editor

9. You are the desktop support technician for your company. One of your users utilizes Outlook Express to work from home. He has two children who also use Outlook Express on the same computer. He wants to have a completely separate Inbox and folder hierarchy from those of his children. What feature of Outlook Express should you explain to the user?

A. Personal Folders

B. Junk email filtering

C. Identities

D. Customized toolbars

10. You are the desktop support technician for your company. A Windows XP user asks you why he does not have an option to open My Recent Documents from his Start menu. Which tab contains the setting that will fix his problem?

   A. The Start Menu tab in Taskbar and Start Menu Properties

   B. The Taskbar tab in Taskbar and Start Menu Properties

   C. The General tab in Customize Start Menu

   D. The Advanced tab in Customize Start Menu

11. You are the lead desktop support technician for your organization. A user in the marketing department has saved a file in the My Documents folder. The user can not see the file when he opens My Documents but is able to access the file from the Recent Files menu in his application. You need to ensure that the user can find the file in his My Documents folder. What should you do?

   A. Check the path of the file in the Recent Files menu of the application.

   B. Configure the view options of My Documents to show hidden files.

   C. Resave the file into a different location.

   D. Try to save the file on the computer of a user who is not in the marketing department.

12. You are the help desk technician for your company. Your company is using Windows XP as its primary desktop operating system. A user who is using Internet Explorer calls the help desk. Each time the user goes a site that uses cookies, she is prompted to either allow or deny cookies from that site. The user wishes to go to websites and not receive this prompt. What should you do?

   A. Click the Default command button on the Privacy tab.

   B. Click the Default Level command on the Security tab.

   C. Click the Restore Defaults command button on the Advanced tab.

   D. Click the Reset Web Settings command button the Programs tab.

13. You are a help desk support technician at your company. A user calls the help desk and reports that his virus scanner detected a virus in a file he recently received in an email. The file was named `analyst.doc` but was being called an executable by his virus scanner. You need to be sure that the user can determine the true file type of files that are being downloaded as to avoid viruses in the future. What should you do?

   A. Select the Show Hidden Files and Folders option box in the folder options of Windows Explorer.

   B. Select the Display the Full Path in the Title Bar check box in the Windows Explorer

   C. Clear the Hide Extensions for Known File Types option in folder options of Windows Explorer

   D. Clear the Hide Protected Operating System Files (Recommended) check box in folder options of Windows Explorer

14. You are a desktop support technician for your organization. Most users in your company use Windows XP for their operating system and Microsoft Outlook Express as their email client. A user wants to import his contacts from his home computer into his work computer. He has copied his Windows address book file to a floppy disk. How can the user import his addresses?

    A. Use the Import Wizard in Outlook Express.

    B. Use the File and Settings Transfer Wizard.

    C. Use the Synchronization option on the Start menu.

    D. Use the Synchronize Folder option on the Tools menu in Outlook Express.

15. You are the senior help desk technician for your company. Users in your company use Windows XP as their primary operating system. One of these users has requested that his Taskbar be removed from the screen when he is not using it. You need to ensure that the Taskbar will be minimized from view when not in use. What should you do?

    A. Select the Hide Taskbar option in Display Settings.

    B. Clear the Show Taskbar option in Display Settings.

    C. Clear the Auto-Hide the Taskbar option in the Taskbar and Start Menu Properties dialog box.

    D. Select the Auto-Hide the Taskbar option in the Taskbar and Start Menu Properties dialog box.

16. You are a help desk support technician at your organization. Users in your organization use Windows XP as their mainstream desktop operating system. A user calls in to the help desk and says her clock is missing from the system tray. No other users are reporting problems with their system tray. You need to be sure that her clock is visible from the Desktop. What should you do?

    A. Enable the Hide the Clock option on the Taskbar tab in the Taskbar and Start Menu Properties dialog box.

    B. Clear the Hide the Clock option on the Taskbar tab in the Taskbar and Start Menu Properties dialog box.

    C. Enable the Show the Clock option on the Taskbar tab in the Taskbar and Start Menu Properties dialog box.

    D. Clear the Show the Clock option on the Taskbar tab in the Taskbar and Start Menu Properties dialog box.

17. You are the help desk support technician for your company. Users in your company use Windows XP as their desktop operating system. A user calls the help desk to report that Internet Explorer shows all websites in Verdana font. The user needs to be able to view websites in their intended fonts. What should you do?

    A. Click the Restore Defaults button on the Advanced tab in Internet Options.

    B. Click the Reset Web Settings button on the Programs tab in Internet Options.

    C. Clear the Ignore Font Styles Specified on Web Pages check box in Internet Options.

    D. On the View menu in Internet Explorer, point to Encoding and select Unicode.

18. You are the desktop support technician for your company. Your company uses Windows XP as the mainstream desktop operating system. Users rely on Internet Explorer as their web browser. A user reports that his address bar is missing inside of Internet Explorer. The user cannot type in addresses to navigate on the Internet. You need to be sure that this user can use Internet Explorer to browse the Internet. What should you do?

A. Lock the toolbars.

B. Enable the address bar.

C. Enable the links bar.

D. Enable the Standard Buttons toolbar.

19. You are the senior desktop support technician for your company. Your company uses Windows XP as its primary desktop operating system. All Windows XP computers have Microsoft Office 2003 installed. A user reports that when she performs a grammar or spell check, Microsoft Word uses an Arabic dictionary. All documents typed by the user are in English. You need to ensure that documents typed by the user are checked in English. What should you do?

A. In Word, set the spelling and grammar language to English.

B. In Regional Options in Control Panel, choose English as the default language.

C. In Word, clear the Allow Accented Uppercase in French check box in the Edit options.

D. In Regional Options in Control Panel, add United States-International under keyboard options.

20. You are a desktop support technician for your organization. Your company uses Windows XP as its primary operating system. All Windows XP machines have Office 2003 installed. A user reports that he commonly reviews documents that have been modified by other users. He wants to be able to track changes to the document so that they can approved or rejected by other users. What should you do?

A. Select Detect and Repair from the Help menu.

B. Right-click one of the existing toolbars and choose Reviewing from the context menu.

C. Create a `Normal.dot` file in his working directory.

D. Have another user create a document and let him modify it.

Answers to Review Questions

1. C. You should first choose Tools and then choose Customize. The Customize dialog box will enable you to create the new toolbar. None of the other options have the correct tools.

2. B. She should choose Tools and then Customize. On the Toolbars tab of the Customize dialog box, she can deselect all of the toolbars except the Standard toolbar. She could right-click on each toolbar and then deselect it from the list, but this would not be the fastest option. The other options are not valid.

3. C, D. He could remove the check mark from Capitalize First Letter of Sentences within the AutoCorrect options. This would fix his problem, but he would not have the convenient tool that capitalizes the first letter automatically when it's appropriate. He could also create an exception for each of the words with which he is having a problem. The other options will not provide the solution.

4. D. The option Ignore Words in UPPERCASE is selected with a default installation, for the express purpose of ignoring acronyms and company names. Evidently, someone has unchecked this option. She should replace the check mark in the appropriate box on the Spelling & Grammar tab of the Tools ➢ Options dialog box. The other choices will not solve the problem.

5. C. You should configure a junk email filter that automatically sends unsolicited email to her Junk E-mail folder. She can review the mail there to make sure that nothing is filtered that should not be filtered. None of the other options provide a solution to the problem.

6. D. The Outlook 2003 feature that will automatically make a call based on receiving a specific email is notification rules. You can use the Rules Wizard to create this rule provided that a modem is set up to make the call. Organization rules automatically manage messages but cannot be used to make a phone call. Personal folders contain and organize all of the user data. The Import and Export Wizard can be used to transfer data.

7. A. The Inbox Repair tool (`scanpst.exe`) should be used to examine the PST file and, if it's corrupt, attempt to repair it. The AutoCorrect tool corrects errors in typing. The AutoArchive tool cleans up a user's mailbox by removing old items. The `scanstate.exe` tool is used to gather information about the settings on a computer to transfer them to another computer.

8. B. The AutoComplete feature of Internet Explorer can be used to control password caching. This feature can remember passwords for a user. The Favorites tools provide shortcuts to websites but do not remember passwords. Customized toolbars are not a solution to this problem. The Registry Editor can be used to disable the option for password caching but would not be used to enable the feature.

9. C. The user can create identities in Outlook Express for himself and for his children. This will create a completely separate Inbox and folder hierarchy. Personal folders are used in Outlook, not in Outlook Express. Junk email filtering does not address this problem. Customized toolbars do not address this problem.

10. D. The Recent Documents settings are contained in the Advanced tab of Customize Start Menu. This is within the Start Menu and Taskbar Properties dialog box. The other options do not identify the correct tab.

11. B. It is very likely that the file is being saved by the application as a hidden file; Hidden files can only be viewed by configuring the folder's view options to show hidden files. You usually cannot view the path of a recent file inside an application. Resaving the file won't help because it will probably be saved as hidden in an alternate location as well. Saving the file on a non-marketing computer will not make it visible unless the target computer has been configured to show hidden files and the question does not specify that.

12. A. The settings for cookies have most likely been modified inside of Internet Explorer. You should set the cookie settings back to the default configuration to allow most cookies without prompting. Resetting options on other tabs will not affect the configuration of cookies.

13. C. The user was tricked by the virus writer; the real filename was `analyst.doc.exe`. When the file extensions are not shown, it appears to be a Word (`.doc`) file. Once you turn on file extensions, you should be able to spot this common technique for hiding malicious files.

14. A. The Outlook Express program has a built-in component that will import addresses from other emails clients as well as from the Windows Address Book (WAB).

15. D. By right-clicking the Start menu or Taskbar, you can open the Taskbar and Start Menu Properties dialog box. This will allow you select the Auto-Hide the Taskbar option, hiding the Taskbar when it is not in use.

16. C. It appears as though the Taskbar settings have been modified. Simply enabling the Show the Clock option on the Taskbar tab in the Taskbar and Start Menu Properties dialog box will resolve this issue.

17. C. The default options appear to have been modified so that the default website font is displayed in a certain fashion. To restore the ability to view the default fonts, you can remove the ignore font styles restriction in the Internet Explorer settings.

18. B. By simply right-clicking on the menu bar and choosing Address Bar within Internet Explorer, you can restore the address bar so that the user can navigate the Internet.

19. B. Even though you are using Microsoft Word, it will check with the operating system language settings to determine what language to use for options such as spell check. By setting the operating system language to English, you can be sure that all applications will use the English language by default.

20. B. You can customize the available and viewable toolbars by right-clicking on an existing toolbar. This will display a context menu with many toolbar options. Any toolbars already shown will have a check box next to their name in the list.

Chapter

10

Configuring and Troubleshooting Connectivity for Applications

MICROSOFT EXAM OBJECTIVES COVERED IN THIS CHAPTER:

- ✓ **Identify and troubleshoot name resolution problems. Indications of such problems include application errors.**

- ✓ **Identify and troubleshoot network adapter configuration problems. Indications of such problems include application errors.**

- ✓ **Identify and troubleshoot LAN and Routing and Remote Access configuration problems. Indications of such problems include application errors.**

- ✓ **Identify and troubleshoot network connectivity problems caused by the firewall configuration. Indications of such problems include application errors.**

- ✓ **Identify and troubleshoot problems with locally attached devices. Indications of such problems include applications errors.**

Many of the applications that people use in today's modern networks require connectivity to an intranet or to the Internet in order to function properly. For example, applications such as Internet Explorer, Outlook, and Outlook Express are relatively useless if the computer upon which they are installed has no connectivity with other computers. For this reason, connectivity issues can potentially have a very negative affect on the productivity of your users. As a desktop support technician, you should be able to quickly identify and troubleshoot both network and local device connectivity problems with applications. To be able to troubleshoot connectivity problems, you have to know how the connections and configurations are supposed to look. In other words, you should be able to configure them yourself.

In this chapter, we will discuss how to configure the essential elements for connectivity with applications. Once you know how to configure these elements, you will more easily recognize a problem with one of them. We will also discuss the methods of troubleshooting connectivity as they apply to each of these elements. The five elements that are essential to connectivity in regard to applications are as follows:

Name resolution   In order for computers to communicate on a network, they must each have a unique address. Actually, computers can have more than one type of address, based on the way they are used in a network and on the protocol that is used. Name resolution is a process of converting the user-friendly addresses that people use into logical and physical addresses that routers and computers can use. We will discuss the major types of name resolution and how to troubleshoot name resolution.

Network adapter configuration   A network adapter is a device that converts serial communication from the network cable or a wireless device into parallel communication that can be interpreted by the computer. Proper configuration of the network adapters in clients and servers is essential for communication on a network. We will discuss how to configure and troubleshoot network adapters for user computers.

LAN and routing and remote access configuration   There are generally many devices within and between networks that must be configured properly for clients to have connectivity to access resources. While you probably don't have the authority to configure or repair all of these devices, you should be able to identify them as the source of a problem and then give that information to the network administrator. We will discuss the different types of network devices that you might encounter in a network and how to isolate a problem that exists on a network device. In addition, we will discuss configuring the client to connect to these devices for LAN communication as well as remote access configuration.

Firewall configuration   Firewalls are filters that allow you to control what goes into and out of your network. A properly configured firewall is to a network an asset that will keep intruders out and increase productivity in an organization. An improperly configured firewall can become a barrier to legitimate communications and have exactly the opposite effect. While you probably won't be able to modify the configuration of your firewalls, you should know about firewall configuration in general so that you can identify connectivity problems that relate to it. We will discuss the general configuration of network firewalls and the issues that can occur with applications.

Locally attached device configuration   Today's computers are capable of directly connecting to many different types of devices, including printers, faxes, and other locally attached devices. These devices are often configured by Plug and Play, but sometimes problems occur with the connection or the configuration. You should know how to configure and troubleshoot locally attached devices on a user's computer.

Name Resolution

To really comprehend name resolution you have to understand all of the types of names that a computer can have and the services that can be used to resolve them. As we discussed in Chapter 6, "Troubleshooting Network Protocols and Services," computers actually recognize each other by a unique physical address burned into their network interface cards: their Media Access Control, or MAC, address. In order for *packets* to be delivered to the correct location, the MAC addresses must be used. When we build and connect networks, we use logical addresses and names such as protocol addresses, NetBIOS names, and hostnames to facilitate communication to the correct networks and the correct computers within the network. Since the computers cannot use these names and addresses, they must be resolved from logical names and addresses to the physical address, the MAC address, before communication can take place. Many different services and protocols can be involved in this process. In the following sections, we will discuss each of these concepts in greater detail.

Types of Names and Addresses Used by Computers

Depending on how a computer is used in a network, it may be designated by many types of names or addresses. To understand name resolution, you must first understand the nature of each type of name and address assigned to a computer. We will focus on the names and addresses that can be assigned to each computer and the methods that you can use to determine what name or address is assigned to a computer.

MAC Address

A MAC address is a *Data-Link layer* address that is required for every port or device that connects to a LAN and uses the *Ethernet* method of communication. MAC addresses are 6 bytes long and are controlled by the IEEE to make sure they are unique. A MAC address is also known as a hardware address, a MAC-layer address, and a physical address. Computers recognize each other by their MAC address. MAC addresses are expressed in hexadecimal numbers. The first 3 bytes represent the manufacturer of the network adapter and the last 3 bytes should be unique for that manufacturer; for example, 00-05-1B-00-4B-F6 is the MAC address for a Belkin USB Ethernet network adapter. You can view the MAC address of your Windows 2000, Windows NT, or Windows XP computer by typing `ipconfig /all` on the command line. This will generate the output shown in Figure 10.1. The address listed next to Physical Address is the MAC address of the computer.

FIGURE 10.1 An ipconfig /all output showing the MAC address of a computer

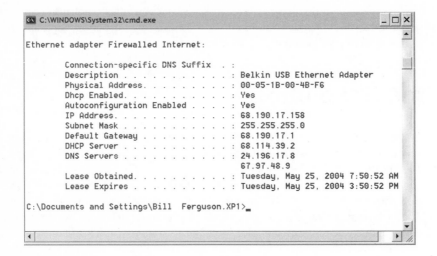

 On Windows 95, 98, and Me clients, enter **winipcfg** on the Run line to view the MAC address of the computer.

Protocol Address

A protocol address is a logical address that is used by networks to move packets to the correct network, often through a series of *routers*. Logical addresses can be assigned to computers on the network in a variety of ways, usually dynamically from a server designed expressly for that purpose or statically (manually) by an administrator. The most common protocol address is an IP address that is used by the TCP/IP protocol suite. (Some networks also use IPX addresses, which are protocol addresses proprietary to Novell NetWare servers and clients.) Each computer in a network must have a unique protocol address. An example of an IP address is 192.168.1.10. The example is given in the decimal form, which is the human-readable form that we usually see and interact with on a daily basis. This type of address is referred to as a 32-bit address and is based on binary. Since computers can work only with ones and zeros, the computer would read the address above as its binary equivalent, 11000000 10100000 00000001 000001010. IP addresses can be likened to telephone numbers in that each network card must have a unique IP address assigned to it to make it identifiable on the network, much as a telephone must be assigned a unique phone number to identify it. IP addresses are broken down into two parts: the network portion and the host portion. The network portion tells us which network (or subnetwork) the computer is assigned to, and the host portion identifies that computer as a particular host. The easiest method of viewing the IP address of a computer is by typing **ipconfig** on the command line, as shown in Figure 10.2. The output will display the IP address of each network adapter card in the computer.

FIGURE 10.2   An ipconfig output showing the IP address of a computer

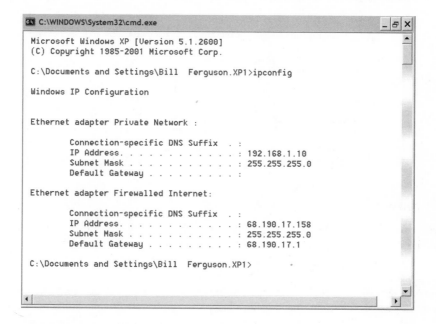

NetBIOS Name

A *NetBIOS name* is a unique computer name assigned to every computer in a Microsoft network. NetBIOS names exist in a *flat name space*, which means that they must be completely unique and are not dependent on the domain in which they reside. They are sometimes referred to as the *computer name*. NetBIOS names can be up to 15 characters in length. A computer can have many NetBIOS names because the operating system adds a 16th character to create multiple NetBIOS names for the same computer. These names designate services that the computer can perform for the network. Some legacy applications rely on these names. You can view the list of NetBIOS names for a computer by typing **nbtstat -n** on a command line. This will generate the output shown in Figure 10.3.

FIGURE 10.3 An nbtstat -n output showing the NetBIOS names of a computer

```
C:\WINDOWS\System32\cmd.exe                                    _ | □ | ×
     Name              Type       Status
    -------------------------------------------
     XP1         <00>  UNIQUE     Registered
     WORKGROUP   <00>  GROUP      Registered
     XP1         <03>  UNIQUE     Registered
     XP1         <20>  UNIQUE     Registered
     WORKGROUP   <1E>  GROUP      Registered
     BILL FERGUSON <03> UNIQUE    Registered

Firewalled Internet:
Node IpAddress: [68.190.17.158] Scope Id: []

              NetBIOS Local Name Table

     Name              Type       Status
    -------------------------------------------
     XP1         <00>  UNIQUE     Registered
     WORKGROUP   <00>  GROUP      Registered
     XP1         <03>  UNIQUE     Registered
     XP1         <20>  UNIQUE     Registered
     WORKGROUP   <1E>  GROUP      Registered
     WORKGROUP   <1D>  UNIQUE     Registered
     .._MSBROWSE__.<01> GROUP     Registered
     BILL FERGUSON <03> UNIQUE    Registered

C:\Documents and Settings\Bill Ferguson.XP1>
```

Hostname

A *host* is any computer that is on a TCP/IP network. A *hostname* is a unique designation for a computer on a TCP/IP network or internetwork. Hostnames exist in a hierarchy and must be unique only in their level of the hierarchy. This means that more than one computer can have the same hostname as long as it is part of a different domain or even a different domain level in the same hierarchy. For example, bobj.msft.com is a totally different hostname than bobj.sybex.com, even though they are both bobj. Computers are assigned only one hostname, which can be up to 255 characters in length. Most of the applications used today rely on hostnames to identify computers on the network. Some applications can use both hostnames and NetBIOS names. The simplest method of viewing just the hostname of a computer is by typing **hostname** on a command line, as shown in Figure 10.4.

FIGURE 10.4 A hostname command output showing just the hostname of a computer

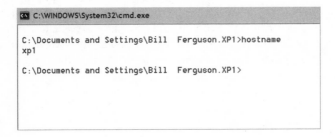

```
C:\WINDOWS\System32\cmd.exe

C:\Documents and Settings\Bill Ferguson.XP1>hostname
xp1

C:\Documents and Settings\Bill Ferguson.XP1>
```

Keep in mind that a computer's NetBIOS name and the hostname are separate designations, although for convenience's sake, they are frequently the same.

Types of Services and Files That Are Used to Resolve Names

Since computers use only MAC addresses, all of the other types of addresses are really just for people, applications, and network design. The addresses that people use have to be resolved back to a MAC address before a physical address of a computer can be determined so that the packets can be delivered to the correct location. Often, more than one name resolution method is involved in this process. For example, a hostname may be resolved to an IP address so that the IP address can then be resolved to a MAC address. Many types of files and services are used to provide this name resolution, including ARP, the Hosts file, the LMHOSTS file, WINS, and DNS. In the following sections, we will discuss each of these files and services in detail.

ARP

The Address Resolution Protocol (ARP), as discussed in Chapter 6, is the protocol that TCP/IP uses to resolve an IP address to a MAC address. ARP is actually used by computers and by routers. When ARP resolves an address, it caches the information for about 10 minutes so that the address can possibly be resolved faster the next time. ARP works by a two-step process. First, it checks the cache to see if it has resolved the address in the last 10 minutes, and then, if it hasn't, it broadcasts to resolve the address. In other words, it basically yells out into the network to ask the computer that is assigned that IP address to please tell ARP its MAC address. These broadcasts are typically limited to one subnet of one network because routers generally stop broadcasts. Network administrators are responsible for designing the logical network so that by the time ARP is used, the computer that ARP is looking for is in the subnet. You can view the ARP cache on a computer by typing **arp -a** on the command line, as shown in Figure 10.5.

FIGURE 10.5   The ARP cache

```
Command Prompt

C:\Documents and Settings\Bill  Ferguson.XP1>arp -a

Interface: 192.168.1.10 --- 0x10003
  Internet Address      Physical Address       Type
  192.168.1.105         00-02-a5-6e-72-65       dynamic

Interface: 68.190.17.158 --- 0x10004
  Internet Address      Physical Address       Type
  68.190.17.1           00-30-7b-f8-94-54       dynamic

C:\Documents and Settings\Bill  Ferguson.XP1>
```

> While you don't have to be an expert at ARP, you can obtain more information about it by typing **arp /?** on a command line.

The LMHOSTS file

The LMHOSTS file is a static text file that the computer uses to resolve NetBIOS names to IP addresses. The *LM* portion of the acronym stands for LAN Manager, which was one of the original network operating systems developed by Microsoft. The LMHOSTS file can also be used to preload important network addresses, such as those of domain controllers, into a NetBIOS name cache on the local computer. This has the effect of loading the entries into the computer's Net-BIOS name cache when the computer is initially started up so the computer already has these entries in its cache and does not have to broadcast out for them, resulting in faster name resolution. The LMHOSTS file is largely unused in today's networks since it has been replaced by the Microsoft WINS, except perhaps in smaller workgroup-sized networks. You can locate the sample LMHOSTS file on a Windows XP or Windows 2000 Professional client at `%systemroot%/system32/drivers/etc`. A sample LMHOSTS file is shown in Figure 10.6.

FIGURE 10.6   The sample LMHOSTS file in Windows XP

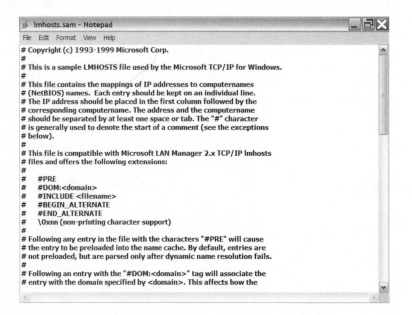

> While it is not necessary that you be an LMHOSTS file expert, you can obtain more information about the LMHOSTS file by reading the information in the sample file.

The Hosts File

The Hosts file is a static file that the computer uses to convert hostnames to IP addresses. Since it was originally designed for use with a wide variety of systems, as long as the system uses the TCP/IP protocol, it can be found on almost any computer, including Windows, Unix, and Linux computers. The Hosts file is rarely used in today's networks because it has been replaced by DNS. You can view a sample of a Hosts file on a Windows XP or Windows 2000 Professional client at `%systemroot%/system32/drivers/etc`. A sample Hosts file is shown in Figure 10.7.

FIGURE 10.7   The sample Hosts file in Windows XP

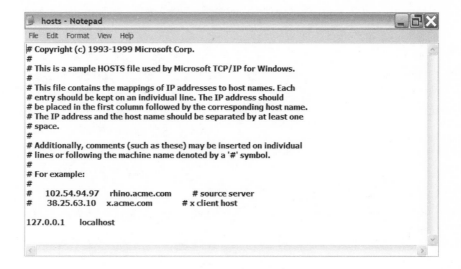

WINS

The Windows Internet Name Service (WINS) is a dynamic service that registers the NetBIOS names of computers on a network and then resolves the NetBIOS names to IP addresses. Some small networks may get by without using a WINS server, but in general, any network that has clients and/or applications that use NetBIOS name resolution should use a WINS server. These computers will chiefly be downward-level Microsoft clients, such as Windows 3.1/95/98/Me and NT. Since the network administrator is responsible for the WINS server, you do not have to be a WINS expert, but you should know how to determine whether a client is configured to use a WINS server. One method of determining whether a client is configured to use a WINS server is to check the network connection of the client. Exercise 10.1 walks you through the steps to check the network connections of a client to determine whether the client is configured to use a WINS server and change the server address if necessary.

EXERCISE 10.1

Using Network Connections for WINS Configuration in Windows XP

1. On the Windows XP Desktop, click Start and then choose Control Panel.

2. In Control Panel, choose Network Connections and then choose the network connection that you want to examine. (In this case, you want to look at the private network connection properties.)

3. On the Status dialog box of the connection that you want to examine, click the Properties button.

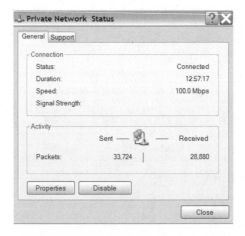

4. On the Properties dialog box for the connection, double-click Internet Protocol TCP/IP.

5. On the Internet Protocol (TCP/IP) Properties dialog box for the connection, click the Advanced button.

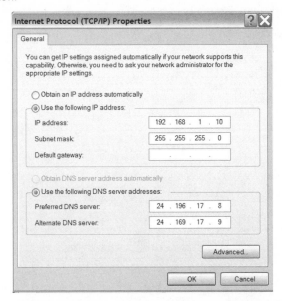

6. On the Advanced TCP/IP Settings dialog box, choose the WINS tab.

7. On the WINS tab, read the addresses in the box labeled WINS Addresses, in Order of Use. You can add or remove WINS servers or change the order of their use. You should consult with a network administrator before altering these settings on a client.

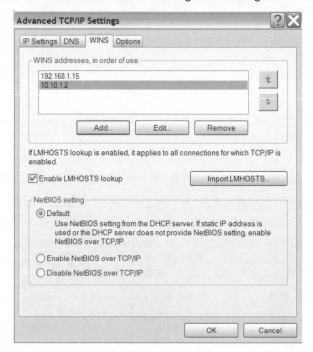

8. Click OK twice and then click Close to close the network connections properties and save any new settings.

If you only want to view the addresses and do not need to change them, you can also view the WINS addresses of the client in the `Ipconfig /all` output or in the Details section of the Support tab in the Status dialog box of the network connection.

DNS

The Domain Name System (DNS) is a dynamic database that resolves hostnames to IP addresses on any computer or network that uses the TCP/IP protocol suite. DNS can be used to resolve the hostnames of your clients and servers as well as the hostnames of computers across the world using the Internet. In fact, DNS is the primary service that makes the Internet possible. The DNS database encompasses all of the computers that are connected to the Internet, but the database is divided into thousands of servers that communicate with one another to make the name resolution possible. Network administrators are responsible for making sure that the DNS infrastructure is in place to provide the name resolution for clients and servers, but you should know how to examine the DNS configuration of a client and make changes when necessary. Exercise 10.2 walks you through the steps to examine and configure the DNS settings on a client.

EXERCISE 10.2

Using Network Connections for DNS Configuration in Windows XP

1. On the Windows XP Desktop, click Start and then choose Control Panel.

2. In Control Panel, choose Network Connections and then choose the network connection that you want to examine. (In this case, you want to look at the private network connections properties.)

3. On the Status dialog box of the connection that you want to examine, click the Properties button.

4. On the Properties dialog box for the connection, double-click Internet Protocol TCP/IP.

5. On the Internet Protocol (TCP/IP) Properties dialog box, examine the DNS settings. If Obtain DNS Server Address Automatically is selected, then you will have to type the `ipconfig /all` command at the command prompt to determine the address that the DHCP server has assigned to the client. If Use the Following DNS Server Addresses is selected, you can view the configured Preferred DNS Server address and Alternate DNS Server address. You can also change the DNS server addresses in this dialog box.

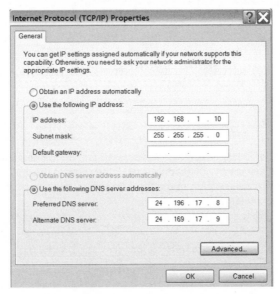

EXERCISE 10.2 *(continued)*

6. Click the Advanced button and then choose the DNS tab. If the client is assigned more than two DNS servers, you can view the configured DNS server addresses and their order of use. You can also add or remove server addresses or change the order of their use. You should consult with the network administrator before changing the DNS configuration of a client.

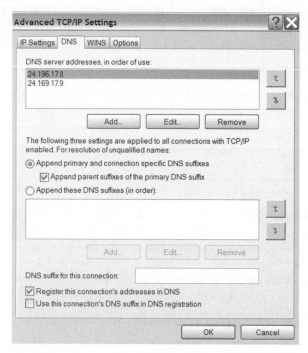

Advanced TCP/IP Settings

IP Settings | DNS | WINS | Options

DNS server addresses, in order of use:
```
24.196.17.8
24.169.17.9
```
[Add...] [Edit...] [Remove]

The following three settings are applied to all connections with TCP/IP enabled. For resolution of unqualified names:

◉ Append primary and connection specific DNS suffixes
  ☑ Append parent suffixes of the primary DNS suffix
○ Append these DNS suffixes (in order):

[Add...] [Edit...] [Remove]

DNS suffix for this connection:
☑ Register this connection's addresses in DNS
☐ Use this connection's DNS suffix in DNS registration

[OK] [Cancel]

7. Click OK twice and then click Close to close the network connections properties and save any new settings.

NOTE If you only want to view the addresses and do not need to change them, you can also view the DNS addresses of the client in the `ipconfig /all` output or in the Details section of the Support tab in the Status dialog box of the network connection.

Network Adapter Configuration

A network adapter card is like a little computer within the computer. Since it is a computer, it must be "programmed" correctly to function properly. Programming a network card includes installing the card and the drivers (as we discussed in Chapter 3, "Configuring and Trouble-shooting Hardware Devices and Drivers") and correctly configuring the IP address, subnet mask, and default gateway on the connection. If these are not configured properly, the computer will be unable to connect to the servers and resources that the user's applications require. You do not need to be a network connection expert, but you should be able to recognize the most common configuration errors in regard to network connections. These include an incorrect IP address, subnet mask, or default gateway. Since users can by default make changes to these settings, you should know how to examine the settings and make comparisons that you can use to troubleshoot the network card's configuration. In the following sections, we will discuss each of these settings in greater detail. You can view all three of these configuration addresses by typing **ipconfig** on the command line of a Windows XP, Windows 2000 Professional, or Windows NT Workstation client, as shown in Figure 10.8.

FIGURE 10.8   Sample output of an ipconfig command

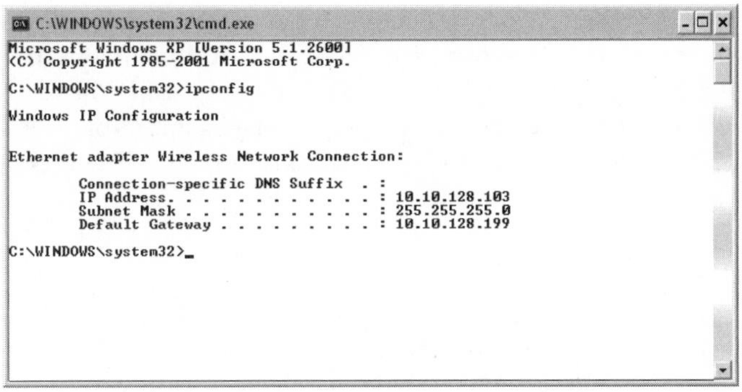

```
C:\WINDOWS\system32\cmd.exe
Microsoft Windows XP [Version 5.1.2600]
(C) Copyright 1985-2001 Microsoft Corp.

C:\WINDOWS\system32>ipconfig

Windows IP Configuration

Ethernet adapter Wireless Network Connection:

        Connection-specific DNS Suffix  . :
        IP Address. . . . . . . . . . . . : 10.10.128.103
        Subnet Mask . . . . . . . . . . . : 255.255.255.0
        Default Gateway . . . . . . . . . : 10.10.128.199

C:\WINDOWS\system32>_
```

IP Address

Networks in large organizations are generally divided into subnets to control and optimize network flow. Network designers and network administrators go to great lengths to make sure that host addresses are unique within each subnet. A proper IP address configuration is essential to allow applications such as Internet Explorer and Microsoft Outlook to provide a resource for the user. Most network administrators use a DHCP server to configure addresses automatically for clients. While you do not have to be an expert at network design, you should be able to recognize the addresses that belong in your network. You can compare the IP address of a client with the IP addresses of other clients in the same subnet to see if it is similar. If it is similar but it is still not working, you should check the subnet mask and default gateway as well. You may need to consult with the network administrator for the details on your IP addressing structure.

 You should use the winipcfg command on a Run line to view IP addressing information on a Windows 95/98 client.

Subnet Mask

The subnet mask of an IP address provides two functions. First, it divides the IP address into the network ID and the host ID. Second, it allows computers and routers to determine the network ID and host ID of an address. For example, if the IP address 192.168.100.45 has a default class C subnet mask of 255.255.255.0, this subnet mask tells you that the network portion of the IP address is 192.168.100. The clients on this particular network must all have this same network portion but will have a different host address. This is an easy example; however, keep in mind that subnetting can get to be a bit complex. Explaining the finer points of subnetting is outside the scope of this book. The subnet mask works by a binary process called *ANDing*. The IP address is ANDed to the subnet mask to determine the network ID and the host ID of a host on a TCP/IP network. As a desktop support technician, you do not need to be an expert at binary numbers or the ANDing process. You should know that the subnet mask is a very important part of the IP address and that it must be configured correctly in order for communication to take place.

Default Gateway

The default gateway is configured to allow a client to communicate outside its own subnet. When the traffic a computer is sending is not on the same subnet, it sends it to the default gateway so that the traffic can be routed to the correct address on another subnet. This is generally a router interface, but it could be the interface of a server or sometimes even a client with more than one network interface card. If the IP address and subnet mask are configured properly but the default gateway is not, the client will be able to communicate within its own subnet but will not be able to communicate with hosts outside its subnet. You can test the connection to the default gateway by simply pinging the default gateway from the client. As you may remember, we discussed using the ping command in Chapter 6.

LAN and Routing and Remote Access Configuration

In today's business world, people might work from just about anywhere! Some users will utilize only a desktop computer that is connected directly to the Internet or connected through a proxy server. Others might use a laptop from a remote location by dialing into the network with a modem. Both types of users ultimately just want to connect an application such as Internet Explorer to a server that contains the resources they need. As a desktop support technician, you should understand what is involved in each type of communication. You should also know how to configure the settings on Internet Explorer to provide access to a client through the LAN and through a remote access server. In the following sections, we will discuss each of these concepts in greater detail.

LAN Configuration

The local area network (LAN) of an organization is usually considered to be the internal collection of computers, servers, and other network devices that are connected with high-speed links, which the organization owns. Typically, clients are connected with cables or wireless connections to some type of *hub* or *switch*. Creating and maintaining this connectivity is essential so that the user can utilize an application such as Internet Explorer or Microsoft Outlook. Clients that use Internet Explorer may be directed to a proxy server to enhance the control of their Internet use. The Internet Explorer application provides a tool to configure LAN settings and proxy server settings for a client when needed. We will discuss each of these concepts in greater detail.

LAN Settings for the Client

The LAN settings for the client are primarily the settings that we have already discussed in this chapter and in Chapter 6. They are the configuration settings that allow the client to obtain an address, communicate on the network, and resolve names when necessary. As we discussed, many network administrators use a DHCP server to configure these settings by automatically assigning this information to a client when the client connects to the network. If the client is unable to communicate on the network, you should check the following configuration settings:

- The IP address of the client or the setting to obtain an IP address automatically
- The subnet mask (if not configured by the DHCP server)
- The default gateway (if not configured by the DHCP server)
- The address of the WINS server or servers (if not configured by the DHCP server)
- The address of the DNS server or servers (if not configured by the DHCP server)

Sometimes these settings, if configured manually, can be incorrect. Additionally, if they are manually configured, the network infrastructure may have changed since the last time these settings were checked and they may now be incorrect.

LAN Settings for Internet Explorer

Internet Explorer can be configured to connect directly to the Internet through an Internet service provider or to use the organization's proxy server to facilitate the connection. Some organizations use a proxy server to tightly control who is allowed access to what sites on the Internet and when they are allowed to access them. A proxy server also can be used to cache address requests to improve performance for users. The network administrator is responsible for configuring the proxy server, but you should know how to configure the clients to connect to the server. The two main tools that you can use to configure these settings are the Internet Options dialog box and the New Connection Wizard. We will discuss each of these tools in greater detail.

The Internet Options Dialog Box

Here we are, back to the Internet Options dialog box again! You probably thought that we had done just about everything that we could do with this box in Chapter 7, "Configuring and Troubleshooting Applications," and Chapter 8, "Resolving Usability Issues." Actually, we only briefly discussed the options available on the Connections tab, shown in Figure 10.9. To configure a client to use a proxy server for Internet Explorer and the applications that it controls, you should click the LAN Settings button. This will open the Local Area Network (LAN) Settings dialog box, as shown in Figure 10.10, which contains the following settings related to the proxy server:

- Automatically Detect Settings: This setting can be used with a proxy server that can be configured for automatic detection without the use of a script, such as Microsoft Proxy Server or its successors, Microsoft's Internet Security and Acceleration (ISA) Server 2000 or 2004.

- Use Automatic Configuration Script: This setting should be used when automatic detection of the proxy server requires a script. Your network administrator will provide the location of the script.

- Use a Proxy Server for Your LAN: This is a manual setting that configures the client to always use a proxy server at a specific location and port.

- Advanced: You should click the Advanced button only if you are directed by the network administrator to specify ports for an application or specify exceptions to the rules.

- Bypass Proxy Server for Local Addresses: This setting allows Internet Explorer to browse your organization's intranet as well. If this setting is not checked, the application will try to go out to the Internet through the proxy server to find locations that are in its own intranet.

WARNING   You should disable the Automatic Configuration settings when you manually set the configuration; otherwise, the Automatic Configuration settings may override the manual settings.

FIGURE 10.9   The Connections tab of the Internet Options dialog box.

FIGURE 10.10   The LAN Settings dialog box

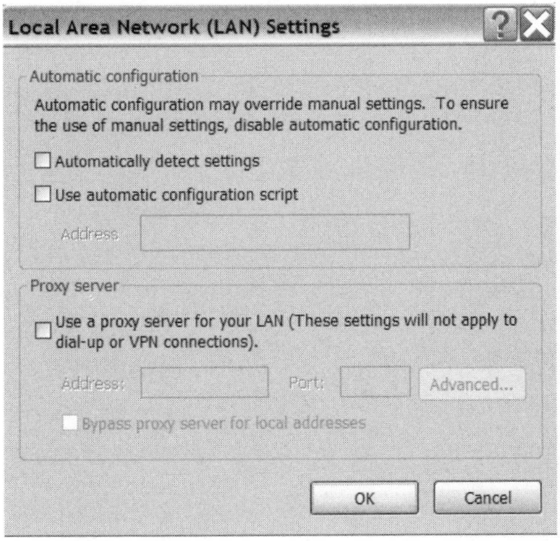

The New Connection Wizard

Some of your users may make connections directly to an ISP, while others will connect to other clients or servers that are connected to an ISP. The New Connection Wizard can assist you in creating the correct configuration. This is the same tool that we discussed in Chapter 6. You can access this tool through Network Connections in Control Panel, or you can simply click the Setup button on the Connections tab of the Internet Options dialog box in Internet Explorer. Click Next when the New Connection Wizard opens. This will open the Network Connection Type screen. Choose the first option, Connect to the Internet, as shown in Figure 10.11, and then click Next. This will open the Getting Ready screen, shown in Figure 10.12, which contains the following options in regard to LAN settings:

- Choose from a List of Internet Service Providers (ISPs): You should choose this option if you want to select from the list of ISPs that were installed with the Internet Explorer software.

- Set Up My Connection Manually: If you choose this option, you will need to know the address of the connection and you will need a valid username and password.

- Use the CD I Got from an ISP: You should use this option if you have obtained a CD from an ISP. Place the CD into the CD-ROM drive on your computer. The computer should automatically detect the presence of the CD. Follow the directions on the CD to complete the installation.

The New Connection Wizard can also be used for dial-up and VPN connections. We will discuss these options later in this chapter.

FIGURE 10.11   The Network Connection Type screen in the New Connections Wizard

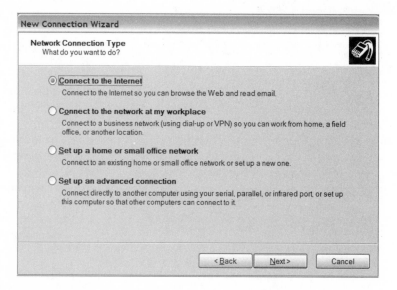

FIGURE 10.12   The Getting Ready screen in the New Connections Wizard

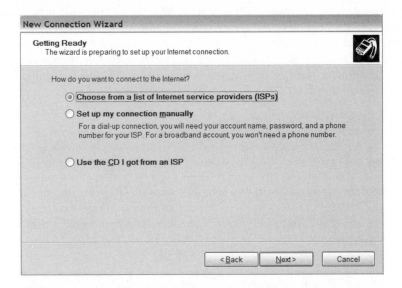

Remote Access Server Configuration for Clients

Since many users now work from their homes or from a laptop "on the road," businesses have had to adapt to the changes by allowing the users access to the organization's servers from remote locations. This began in the early 1990s with the installation of modems on both the users' computers and in the server rooms. This is referred to as *dial-up remote access*, in which one modem calls another modem using nothing but a regular telephone connection. This method soon presented two major drawbacks. First, the server rooms had to be equipped with multiple modems or special equipment that simulated multiple modems to handle the traffic from the users. Second, if the users were not in the same vicinity, long-distance charges were added to each call. Sometimes companies would install a toll-free number to help reduce long-distance phone charges, but this method of remote access was still cumbersome and slow at best.

With the growth of the Internet, businesses soon found that they could use the connections through the Internet to connect a client to their servers. The clients still used a modem to connect to the Internet through an ISP, but then they were "tunneled" straight to the servers in the organization. This offered a solution that could provide greater security and eliminate long-distance charges, provided that a local ISP was available to the user. The only remaining disadvantage of a VPN connection using a modem was that the modem was very slow when compared to a LAN connection. With the evolution of technology, broadband connections such as cable modems and digital subscriber lines (DSLs) make the connections from home almost as fast as those in the office. Many hotels now offer broadband connections at no charge or for a small fee.

The newest servers from Microsoft (Windows 2000 Server and Windows Server 2003) include a tool called Routing and Remote Access Server that enables a network administrator to configure dial-up connections and VPN connections for clients. Since the network administrator is responsible for configuring the connections on the server side, you do not need to know how to configure them. However, you should understand the advantages and disadvantages of each type of connection and know how to configure the connections on the client computer. In the following sections, we will discuss the configuration of each of these types of connections in greater detail.

Configuring Dial-up Connections

As we mentioned, dial-up connections are comparatively slow and should be used as a last resort, such as, for example, on a laptop from a hotel where no other faster method is available. You may also see dial-up connections used in very small businesses that do not have the resources for faster options. You should know how to use the tools built into Internet Explorer to configure dial-up connections for a client. Exercise 10.3 walks you through the steps to create a dial-up connection from within Internet Explorer. You may notice a marked similarity to the method that we used in Chapter 6 (from the Network Connections tool in Control Panel).

EXERCISE 10.3

Configuring Dial-up Connections from the Connections Tab of Internet Explorer

1. In Internet Explorer, choose the Connections tab and then choose Add under the Dial-up and Virtual Private Network settings.

2. Choose Dial-up to Private Network and then click Next.

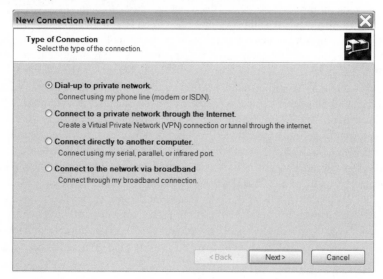

3. Type the phone number to dial, including any additional characters such as 1 for long dis-
    tance or 9 to get a local line at a hotel. Click Next.

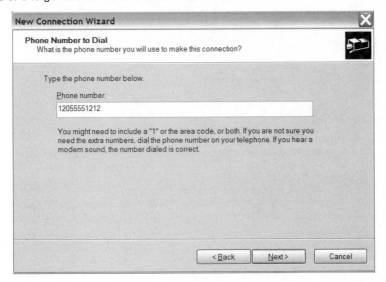

4. Type a name for your connection (any name will suffice) and then click Finish.

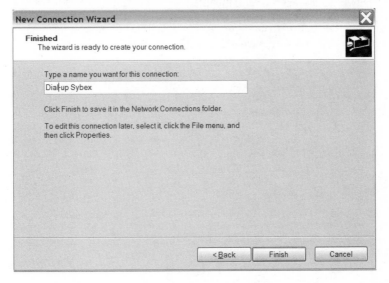

5. Clicking Finish creates the connection and exits the wizard. This will open the Settings dialog box for the connection.

6. Configure the proxy server and dial-up settings for the connection based on information from the network administrator and the ISP.

7. Click the Properties button to configure all of the settings of the connection just as you would configure them from the New Connections tool.

8. Click Advanced to change the default connection attempts, wait times, and idle time disconnects.

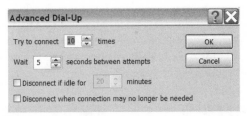

9. Click OK three times to exit the settings and close Internet Options. You can view and
manage the new connection in Network Connections within Control Panel.

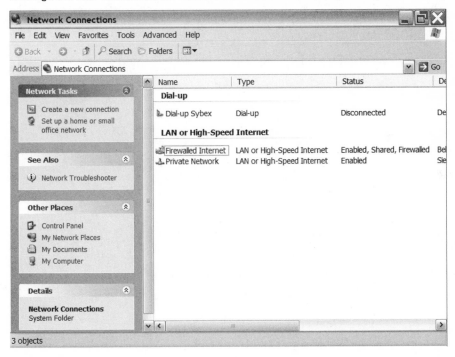

Configuring VPN Connections

VPN connections are not necessarily any faster than dial-up connections because you can establish a VPN connection using a regular modem and regular telephone lines to connect to an ISP. This will most likely be the case on laptops connecting from hotels, although many hotels are now installing broadband connections. Users who work from home and have a cable modem or DSL connection can establish a VPN connection that is almost as fast as their connection at the office. You should know how to use the tools built into Internet Explorer to create a new VPN connection for a client. Exercise 10.4 walks you through the steps to create a new VPN connection from Internet Explorer.

EXERCISE 10.4

Configuring VPN Connections from the Internet Options Tab of Internet Explorer

1. In Internet Explorer, choose the Connections tab and then choose Add under the Dial-up and Virtual Private Network settings.

2. Choose Connect to A Private Network through the Internet and click Next.

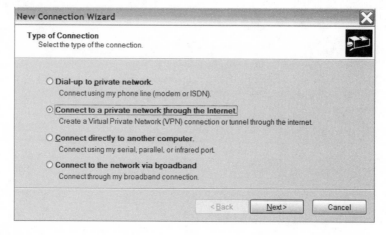

3. Type the hostname or IP address of the computer to which you are connecting, and then click Next.

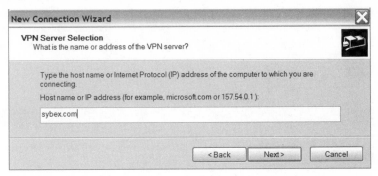

4. Type a name for your connection (any name will suffice) and then click Finish to create the connection. This will open the Settings dialog box for the connection.

5. Configure the proxy settings and dial-up settings for the connection based on information from the network administrator and the ISP.

6. Click the Properties button to configure all of the settings of the connection just as you would configure them from the New Connections tool.

7. Click Advanced to change the default connection attempts, wait times, and idle time disconnects.

8. Click OK three times to exit the settings and close Internet Options. You can view and manage the new connection in Network Connections within Control Panel.

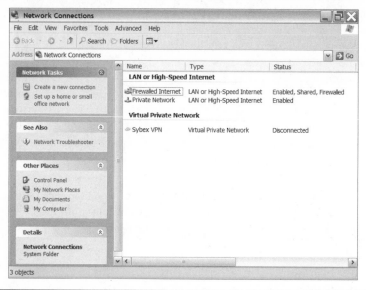

Firewall Configuration

Organizations often use corporate firewalls to filter traffic between two networks or between their private network and the Internet. Firewalls consist of a software program and/or a hardware device that is used to identify and "flag" different types of traffic. Traffic that is flagged by the firewall may not be allowed into the network at all, or it may be allowed in but with restrictions on where it can go in the network. Network administrators are responsible for configuring the corporate firewalls. Some firewall configurations can be very complex and can filter traffic by many different characteristics and even by combinations of characteristics. You should know that some user applications may fail to connect because they are inadvertently blocked by firewall settings when they meet the characteristics that the firewall is designed to block.

The following are examples of application or connection characteristics that a firewall may inadvertently filter or block:

- IP addresses: The firewall can block traffic from specific addresses, lists of addresses, specific network IDs, or even ranges of addresses.

- Domain names: The firewall can block access to specific domain names or even block access to all domains except for a specific domain name.

- Protocols: The firewall can be set to block traffic that is using a specific protocol or protocols, such as File Transfer Protocol (FTP) or User Datagram Protocol (UDP).

- Ports: Ports are specific logical addresses to which applications are assigned in a computer. Using ports, a computer can handle and process many types of data traffic at once. The firewall can be programmed to filter traffic that uses specific ports or even to permit only traffic that uses specific ports.

- Specific words or phrases: Some of the latest firewalls can fully examine, or "sniff," each packet to determine whether it can enter the network.

As you can see, a properly configured firewall can provide a tremendous barrier of security for an organization. You might also see that an improperly configured firewall can cause an interruption of communications. Since many firewalls do not send any type of message back to the user, the only real indicator that there is a problem is that the application has failed to connect. If a user can connect to other computers on a network or on the Internet using some applications but cannot connect using others, then you should suspect a firewall filter. You should, of course, contact your network administrator to confirm your suspicion and get the problem corrected.

WARNING If an application can't connect to the Internet, you could also check the configuration of the client's Internet Connection Firewall or Windows Firewall settings, as we discussed in Chapter 6, to make sure the client computer is not creating its own problem.

Locally Attached Devices

Modern computers can have many devices attached to them to perform functions related to the user's utilization of applications. Examples include printers, faxes, and scanners. Windows XP provides tools to install and configure these devices. Actually, most of the configuration these days happens through Plug and Play or through wizards built into the software, but you should know how to use the tools built into Windows XP to configure and troubleshoot devices when the automatic configuration does not work or has been changed. There are two main tools in Control Panel that you can use to configure these devices: one is Printers and Faxes, and the other is Scanners and Cameras. You should know how to use these tools to establish connectivity to the device so that the user can utilize the application associated with the device. In the following sections, we will discuss these two tools in greater detail.

Printers and Faxes

The Printers and Faxes tool allows you to manage the printers on a computer. Printers, contrary to popular belief, are actually software and not hardware. A printer is the software package, including the drivers, that controls the print device (the actual hardware) that actually creates the print job. The Printers and Faxes tool, shown in Figure 10.13, enables you and the users to manage the currently installed printers and to install an additional printer when necessary. We will discuss each of these concepts in greater detail.

FIGURE 10.13   The Printers and Faxes tool in Windows XP

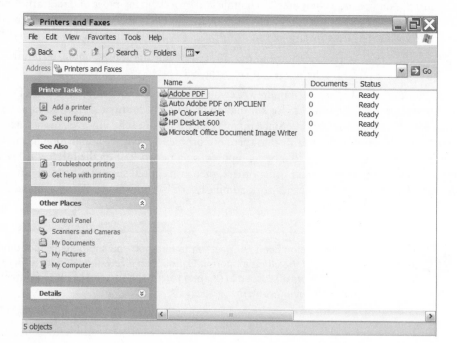

An Unintended Consequence

A colleague told us an interesting story about a company with which he worked. The company had just installed a corporate firewall with all of the latest filters. The network administrator went to great lengths to configure the firewall to block any dangerous or offensive content, including recognizing keywords within a document.

Shortly after the installation of the firewall, the human resource department began complaining that users could not get some of the forms from the FTP servers. They had been able to retrieve the forms with no problems before the installation. They said, "The forms are mostly just basic employee information and shouldn't contain anything offensive!"

The network administrator began by checking all of the IP address and port settings on these servers that contained the forms. When he found them to be configured correctly, the problem became even more curious. Why would certain forms transfer properly while others would not transfer it at all?

He continued to examine the firewall settings and found that the firewall was indicating that some of the forms that users had attempted to download from the HR department contained offensive content. As you may have guessed, the "offensive content" was discovered to be the word *sex*, which appeared on many forms to inquire of a person's gender. Changing the word *sex* to *gender* on the forms corrected the problem.

The moral of this story is that even the best intentions can sometimes have unintended consequences. Your network administrator will configure the corporate firewall to protect the organization and its users. It's your responsibility to make sure that the users can still use their applications normally after the firewall is configured.

FIGURE 10.14   Properties for an HP Color LaserJet printer

Managing Printers

You can simply right-click on any of the printers and then choose Properties to manage it. Figure 10.14 shows the properties of a printer used for an HP Color LaserJet print device. Most printers enable you to print a test page from the printer itself. If you can print the test page using the printer software but you cannot print from the application, then you have isolated the problem to the application. The other tools and settings for printers will vary by printer manufacturer and type of printer.

Adding a Local Printer

You can use the Printers and Faxes tool to add many types of printers, including local printers, network printers, and printers that just send output to other software, such as an Adobe Acrobat printer. In this section we will focus on adding a local printer to a computer. You should know that a *local printer* is printer software that is installed on a computer to which the associated print device is actually attached. Exercise 10.5 walks you through the steps to add a local printer to a user's computer.

EXERCISE 10.5

Adding a Local Printer

1. On the Windows XP Desktop, click Start and then choose Control Panel.

2. In Control Panel, choose Printers and Faxes.

3. In the Printers and Faxes tool, choose Add a Printer to open the Add Printer Wizard.

4. On the Welcome screen of the Add Printer Wizard, click Next.

5. Select Local Printer Attached to This Computer. You can also select the Automatically Detect and Install My Plug and Play Printer check box and then click Next to detect and install a printer that has been physically attached to the computer. If you choose not to automatically detect and install the printer, then proceed to step 6.

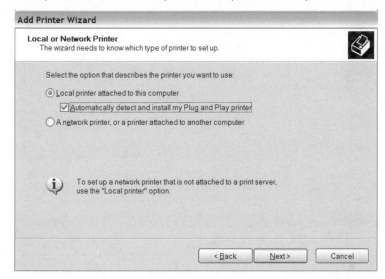

6. Click Next to open the Select a Printer Port screen.

7. On the Select a Printer Port screen, choose either Use the Following Port or Create a New Port and then use the drop-down arrow to select the port that you wish to use or create. Click Next to continue.

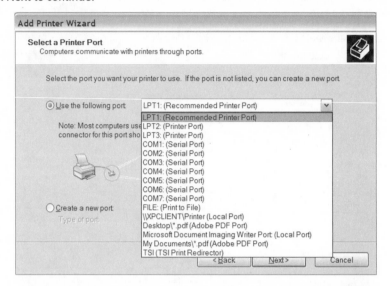

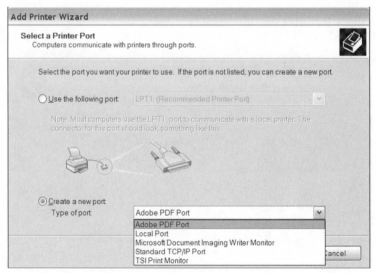

8. On the Install Printer Software screen, choose the printer manufacturer and specific printer model to obtain the drivers from the Windows XP driver cache, and then click Next. You can also choose Have Disk to install the drivers that came with the print device or Windows Update to search the Windows Update website for printer drivers.

9. On the Name Your Printer screen, type a name for your printer in the box below Printer Name or accept the default name for the printer, and then click Next. You can also choose whether you want the new printer to be the default printer for the user's computer.

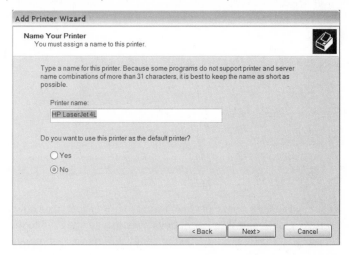

10. On the Printer Sharing screen, choose Do Not Share This Printer or choose Share Name and the type the share name for the printer. Click Next.

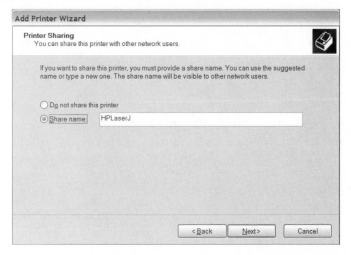

11. On the Location and Comment screen, enter the printer location and comments about the printer if you wish, and then click Next. Note that this is not a required step.

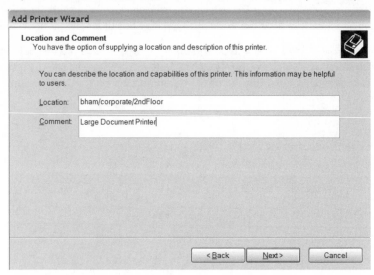

12. On the Print Test Page screen, select Yes if you want to print a test page now or No if you do not want to print a test page. If the print device is actually attached to the computer, then it is recommended that you print a test page. Click Next to continue.

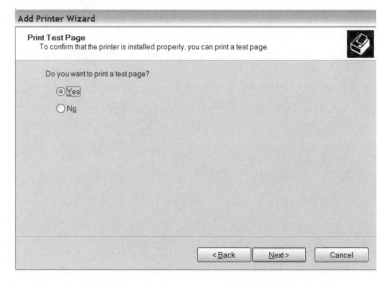

13. On the Completing the Add Printer Wizard screen, review your settings and then click Finish to create the printer and close the wizard.

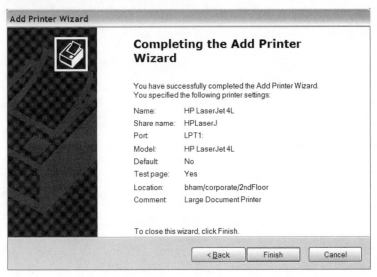

Scanners and Cameras

Users utilize a computer in many ways, including viewing and managing images that are produced by scanners, cameras, and other imaging devices. Windows XP has built-in tools to assist you and the user in managing the imaging devices that are connected to the computer. You can use the Scanners and Cameras tool, shown in Figure 10.15, to manage currently installed imaging devices and to install additional imaging devices. We will discuss each of these concepts in greater detail.

Managing Imaging Devices

You can install multiple imaging devices on a single Windows XP computer and manage them using the Scanners and Cameras tool located in Control Panel. As a desktop support technician, you should be familiar with the use of this tool so that you can assist users with managing their imaging devices. To manage a currently installed device, right-click on the device and choose Properties. The properties that you can manage will vary by the device, but most devices include a diagnostic tool, such as the device shown in Figure 10.16.

FIGURE 10.15   The Scanners and Cameras tool

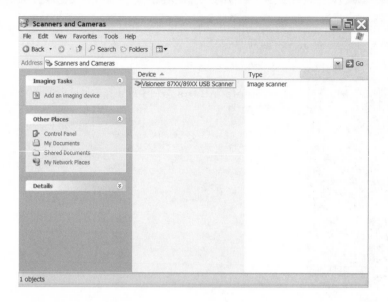

FIGURE 10.16   An imaging device with a diagnostic tool

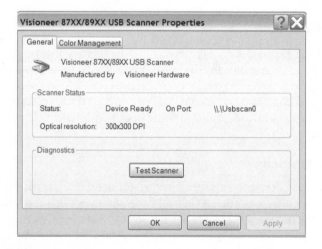

Adding an Imaging Device

You can also use the Scanners and Cameras tool to quickly add new imaging devices to a user's computer. The tool includes wizards to assist you in adding the devices. Exercise 10.6 walks you through the steps to add a new imaging device to a user's computer.

EXERCISE 10.6

Adding an Imaging Device Using the Scanners and Cameras Wizard

1. On the Windows XP Desktop, click Start and then choose Control Panel.

2. In Control Panel, choose Scanners and Cameras.

3. In the Scanners and Cameras tool, ensure that you do not have a device selected, and then select Add an Imaging Device to open the Scanner and Camera Installation Wizard. Click Next to close the Welcome screen of the Scanner and Camera Installation Wizard.

4. Choose the manufacturer and specific model of your imaging device. If you have software that was included with the device, you can click Have Disk and insert the CD/DVD in the appropriate drive. Click Next to continue.

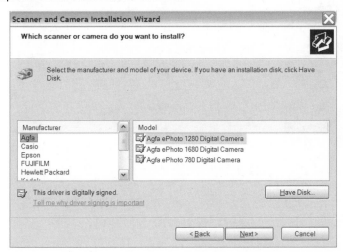

5. Select Automatic Port Detection or choose the port to which you want to install the device, and then click Next.

6. Accept the default name for the device or type the name that you wish to use, and then click Next.

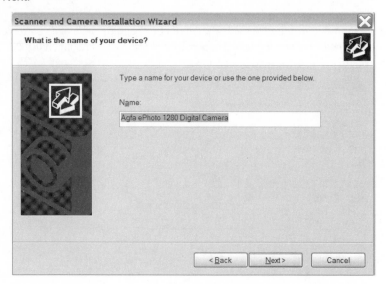

EXERCISE 10.6 *(continued)*

7. Click Finish to complete the installation. You may be required to restart your computer before using some devices.

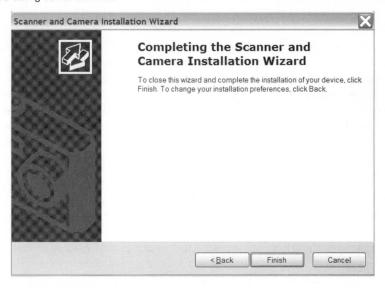

Case Study: Knowing How Applications and Networks Interact

Being a good desktop support technician means being well-rounded and knowing at least a little bit about everything. You definitely need to know how hardware, software, networking, and many other things work. Beyond that, however, you need to be able to figure out how all of these things work together or interact with each other.

For example, if you have customers who routinely connect to an MS SQL 2000 server from a client database application, you might need to know that the application probably talks to the SQL server on TCP port 1433 if you are experiencing connectivity issues with the database. All other network services may work, such as access to the Internet and email, but customers still may not be able to use the database. This might puzzle you and cause you to start looking at the application itself, perhaps restarting its services or even reinstalling the application. You may then find that for some reason the server itself is not listening on port 1433 or that a firewall or other network device is misconfigured and is dropping the packets. The point is that it is a very good idea to get to know the applications you work with every day and discover how they interact with other parts of your infrastructure.

Once I was troubleshooting a wireless network I had just installed for a customer. It was a small network with a file server running Windows Server 2003 and six client machines running Windows XP, all in a workgroup configuration. The computers were all wireless, connected to the Internet through a wireless access point and an external firewall to a dedicated T1 leased connection. When the computers were first powered up in the morning, most of the services, such Internet access through the firewall and email, worked fine. However, the client machines had two applications that were connected to a shared folder on the server and would not start up immediately, no matter what we did, and took several minutes to work correctly. First, I verified connectivity to the file server with the ping command and had no packet loss with a very fast reply. So network connectivity was not the issue. As I ran a continuous ping from one of the clients to the server, I also tried starting the application at the same time. It took about 10 minutes for it to start; all the while, the client was receiving an immediate good response to its pings. All the services that the applications required were started and working properly, so I decided to try the same troubleshooting steps on all the other computers, with the same results.

Just as I was about to begin reinstalling one of the applications, a thought occurred to me. Since this was a small network, it had no internal name resolution mechanisms (such as a DNS server), other than broadcasting out, to resolve names. Internet name resolution wasn't an issue due to an external DNS server at the ISP that all clients were pointed to. I didn't want to install an internal DNS server for the six clients and have to reconfigure the network, so I decide to test to see if name resolution was in fact the problem by trying the older method that clients used to use to resolve names: the Hosts and LMHOSTS files. I edited both of the files on one client to include the IP-address-to-server-name entry and restarted the client. When I immediately tried to access the application, as if by magic, it came up beautifully!

The moral of this story is that you have to know a little bit about how everything works on a network and hone your troubleshooting skills. Name resolution, as we covered earlier in the text, is a frequent problem with an application's network connectivity.

It will often happen that problems aren't always "cut and dry" and easy to narrow down to a single cause. If a client machine has no connectivity at all, it's fairly easy to narrow the problem down to a broken cable or one not plugged in. But if a problem either intermittently occurs or exhibits strange symptoms (such as some network services working and some not working when all should be either working or not) you will have to start thinking (sometimes literally) outside of the box!

Summary

There are many settings of a computer that must be configured correctly to provide connectivity for a user's applications. As a desktop support technician, you should be familiar with these options, including configuration and troubleshooting methods when a configuration is not correct. The settings that you should be familiar with include name resolution, network adapter configuration, LAN configuration, firewall configuration, and configuration of locally attached devices.

Computers actually use only one address to identify one another and facilitate communication: their MAC address. This address is burned into the network interface card installed on each computer in a network. People, on the other hand, use many names and addresses to manage computers and to design computer networks. The process of converting the names that people use to the MAC address that a computer can use is called name resolution. There are two basic types of name resolution: NetBIOS name resolution and hostname resolution. NetBIOS name resolution is accomplished using an LMHOSTS file or a WINS server or broadcasts if neither is available. Hostname resolution is accomplished using a Hosts file or, more commonly, DNS servers. In both cases, the name is resolved to an IP address, which is then resolved to a MAC address. Most newer applications use hostname resolution, but some of the older legacy applications still use NetBIOS name resolution. As a desktop support technician, it is important that you understand these concepts so you can assist the user with name resolution problems related to applications.

The network adapter card on a user's computer is like a little computer. Correct "programming" of the network adapter card requires a basic understanding of the TCP/IP protocol. It is essential that each computer's network adapter card be configured with a valid IP address, subnet mask, and default gateway. Since users can, by default, make changes to this configuration, a desktop support technician should be able to recognize and correct errant configurations for the user. The `ipconfig` command and the Network Connections tool in Control Panel are the tools most commonly used to analyze and correct these configurations.

Today's users are just as likely to be connecting to your network from a remote location as they are to be connecting from their own desktop computer. Many applications that the users utilize, such as Internet Explorer and Microsoft Outlook, require connectivity to the Internet. You can provide this connectivity with a direct connection to an ISP or require users to go through a proxy server to enhance the security of the network. The New Connection Wizard in Microsoft Internet Explorer has built-in tools to assist you in both types of LAN configuration. You can also configure and control remote access connections including dial-up and VPN connections.

Today's networks often incorporate corporate firewalls for the purpose of filtering traffic into and out of the network. These firewalls can be either your best friend or your worst enemy. They do protect the network from intruders who would harm it, but they might also inadvertently block regular application traffic and disrupt a user's communications. While it is unlikely that you will be able to manage the configuration of your corporate firewall, you should be familiar with the filters that the network administrator might have applied so that you can recognize a problem that is associated with the firewall. The types of filters that most firewalls use include IP addresses, domain names, protocols, ports, and sometimes even specific words or phrases. If most applications are working correctly but some applications cannot make a connection to a required resource, you should suspect firewall configuration as a possible problem.

Most of today's computers offer the ability to add locally attached devices for specific uses, such as printers, faxes, scanners, and cameras. These devices often work along with an application that assists users in some aspect of their job. Windows XP includes tools to manage currently installed devices and to install additional devices when necessary. The two main tools that you can use to manage locally attached devices are the Printers and Faxes tool and the Scanners and Cameras tool. Most often, installation of these types of devices is accomplished through

Plug and Play or through wizards included with the software that came with the device. You should be familiar with these tools so that you can assist the user in managing and installing these devices when the automatic installation does not work or when troubleshooting is required.

Exam Essentials

Know the name resolution methods.   You should understand the two main types of name resolution. You should know that most new applications use hostname resolution but that some older applications still use NetBIOS name resolution. You should understand that computers actually use only the MAC address and that all other names are to help people manage computers and design networks. You should also know the files and services that each type of name resolution uses. Finally, you should be able to recognize and correct application problems that are associated with name resolution.

Be able to configure network adapter cards.   You should know and understand the three main configurations on a network adapter card: the IP address, subnet mask, and default gateway. You should know how to examine the configuration of a user's network adapter card with the ipconfig tool on a command line. Finally, you should be able to use the Network Connections tool to further analyze and correct network adapter card configurations.

Understand LAN configuration.   You should know how to configure the essential LAN settings for a user's applications in the Windows XP operating system as well as in Internet Explorer. In addition, you should know how to configure proxy settings for client computers that are required to use a proxy. Finally, you should be able to configure the connection to bypass the proxy for addresses that are within your own intranet.

Be able to configure remote access.   You should know how to configure clients for remote access including dial-up and VPN connections. In addition, you should understand the differences between dial-up and VPN connections. Finally, you should be able to use the Network Connections tool in Control Panel and the tools built into Internet Explorer to configure both types of connections.

Be aware of how firewalls might affect applications.   You should know how firewalls can be used to protect the network. In addition, you should remember that firewalls can impede network communications and disrupt application traffic. Finally, you should know the various factors by which network administrators might filter traffic through a firewall so that you can recognize problems related to firewall configuration.

Know how to install and manage locally attached devices.   You should know how to manage locally attached devices using the tools provided by the Windows XP software. In addition, you should be able to use the tools in the Windows XP Control Panel to install additional devices. Finally, you should know how to locate the diagnostic tools in the properties of locally attached devices.

Review Questions

1. You are the network desktop support technician of your organization. Some users are utilizing legacy applications that use NetBIOS name resolution. Which of the following types of files and services might affect name resolution for these legacy applications? (Choose two.)

    A. WINS

    B. DNS

    C. LMHOSTS

    D. Hosts

2. You are the desktop support technician for a large organization. The network administrator has configured a server to automatically assign an IP address as well as the addresses of the servers that provide name resolution to each client computer when the computer is started on the network. Which type of server has the network administrator configured for this purpose?

    A. DNS

    B. WINS

    C. RRAS

    D. DHCP

3. You are the desktop support technician for a large organization. Some users complain that they can communicate within their own subnet but not outside their subnet. Which part of the IP configuration should you examine first?

    A. IP address

    B. Subnet mask

    C. Default gateway

    D. DNS server address

4. You are the desktop support technician for a large organization. A user has a connectivity issue with an application. You want to examine all of the IP settings of the user's network adapter from a command line, including the addresses of the name resolution servers for which it is configured. Which of the following commands should you type on the command line?

    A. `ipconfig`

    B. `nbtstat -a`

    C. `arp -a`

    D. `ipconfig /all`

5. You are the desktop support technician for a large organization. You have recently configured a client to use a proxy server. The user now complains that although she can access resources on the Internet, she can no longer access resources on her own intranet from her browser. Which of the following settings should you suspect first?

   A. Proxy server address

   B. Proxy server port

   C. Bypass proxy setting

   D. DNS server address

6. You are the desktop support technician for a large organization with many locations. You also have many users who utilize their laptops from hotels in remote locations. Since management is concerned about long-distance charges, you want to employ a technology that will reduce or eliminate long-distance charges for these users. Which of the following technologies should you employ?

   A. Dial-up

   B. Cable modems

   C. DSL

   D. VPN

7. You are the desktop support technician for a large organization. The network administrator has recently installed a corporate firewall. Now some of your users' applications will not function, while others function normally. The users still have general connectivity to all of the resources that they use. Which types of firewall filters should you suspect first? (Choose two.)

   A. IP addresses

   B. Domain names

   C. Protocols

   D. Ports

8. You are the desktop support technician for a large organization. You have recently installed a client computer onto the network. The computer can access some applications but cannot access others through the network. You suspect that the corporate firewall is causing the problem. You speak to the network administrator, but she insists that the corporate firewall could not be causing the problem because other clients in the same subnet as that client computer can access all applications properly. What configuration option should you suspect next?

   A. DNS

   B. WINS

   C. ICF

   D. DHCP

9. You are the desktop support technician for a graphics company. A user has obtained a new imaging device and attempted to install it on her Windows XP computer, but the automatic installation failed. Which Control Panel tool can you use to assist the user in completing and troubleshooting the installation?

   A. Printers and Faxes

   B. Sounds and Audio Devices

   C. System

   D. Scanners and Cameras

10. You are the desktop support technician for a large organization. Some users have personal printers directly attached to their client computers. A user complains that her personal printer will not print from one specific application. It seems to work fine with other applications, and she can print a test page from the Windows XP client software. Which of the following should you suspect first as the cause of this problem?

    A. Printer drivers

    B. The application

    C. The operating system

    D. The print device

11. How are logical addresses assigned to a computer's network interface? (Choose two.)

    A. Dynamically by a server

    B. Manually by a server

    C. By the manufacturer of the network interface

    D. Manually by the network administrator

12. Which one of the following is considered the computer's physical address?

    A. Logical address

    B. Network Node address

    C. NetBIOS address

    D. Media Access Control address

13. When a computer has traffic bound for an IP address not on its local subnet, where does it send this traffic?

    A. WINS server

    B. Default gateway

    C. DNS server

    D. Routing and Remote Access server

14. Which of the following items can a firewall block from entering your network?

A. IP address

B. Port

C. Protocol

D. All of the above

15. In the MAC address 00-05-1B-00-4B-F6, which bytes represent the hardware manufacturer's identification number?

A. 00-05-1B

B. 00-4B-F6

C. F6

D. None of the above

16. What are the two portions of an IP address called?

A. Network address and hardware address

B. Network address and host address

C. Logical address and physical address

D. Host address and MAC address

17. Which of the following is not an example of characteristics of a computer's NetBIOS name?

A. Can be up to 15 characters long

B. Must be unique

C. Can be up to 255 characters long

D. Can be viewed by running the `nbtstat -n` command

18. Which protocol does TCP/IP use to resolve IP addresses to MAC addresses?

A. DHCP

B. UDP

C. DNS

D. ARP

19. On a network containing hosts running both newer and older Windows operating system versions, which two services are critical for name resolution?

A. WINS and TCP

B. NetBIOS and DNS

C. WINS and DNS

D. DHCP and UDP

20. What are two most widely used methods of dynamic name resolution matched with their corresponding static resolution text files? (Choose two.)

   A. WINS and LMHOSTS file

   B. DNS and LMHOSTS file

   C. WINS and NAMES file

   D. DNS and Hosts file

Answers to Review Questions

1. A, C. NetBIOS name resolution can be accomplished using an LMHOSTS file or a Windows Internet Name Service (WINS) server. Domain Name System (DNS) and the Hosts file are used to perform hostname resolution.

2. D. The network administrator can configure the Dynamic Host Configuration Protocol (DHCP) server to automatically assign an IP address, the addresses of the name resolution servers, and other configuration information to a client. The DNS server is used for hostname resolution. WINS is used for NetBIOS name resolution. RRAS is used for routing and remote access.

3. C. If the default gateway is not correctly configured, users will not be able to communicate outside their own subnet. If the IP address and subnet mask were not configured properly, the users would not be able to communicate within their own subnet. The DNS server address is not a valid concern in this case.

4. D. The `ipconfig /all` command will display all of the IP settings related to each network adapter installed in a client. The `ipconfig` command will display only the IP address, subnet mask, and default gateway addresses assigned to the card. The `nbtstat -a` command will display the NetBIOS names assigned to a client. The `arp -a` command will display the ARP cache of a client.

5. C. You should suspect that the Bypass Proxy Server for Local Addresses setting is not selected. Selecting this setting will let the client gain access to local resources without using the proxy. The proxy server address and port address must be correct or the user would not be able to access the Internet. The DNS server address is not the issue in this case.

6. D. Virtual private network (VPN) connections will enable users to dial their ISP's local number wherever one is available. Once users are connected to the ISP, they can be tunneled through the Internet to your organization's servers. Dial-up connections will not eliminate long-distance charges. Cable modems and DSL might be used from the users' homes but cannot be relied upon at hotels.

7. C, D. Since some applications are functioning while others are not, you should suspect that the filter is specific to an application. The only two choices here that are specific to an application are protocols and ports. Since the users have general connectivity to their resources, you should not suspect IP address or domain name filtering to be the source of the problem.

8. C. The issue is probably related to a firewall, but in this case, it's not the corporate firewall but instead the Internet Connection Firewall (ICF) that is part of the Windows XP client software. You should access the advanced settings on the client's connection and examine the ICF configuration. The DNS, WINS, and DHCP servers are not part of this problem; otherwise, the client would not have access to any applications through the network.

9. D. The Scanners and Cameras tool in Windows XP enables you to manage currently installed imaging devices and install additional devices. The Printers and Faxes tool enables you to manage and install printers and faxes. The Sounds and Audio Devices and System tools are not appropriate in this scenario.

10. B. In this case, the specific application must be at fault. If there were a problem with the printer drivers, the operating system, or the print device, then none of the applications would work correctly with the printer and a test page would not print.

11. A, D. Logical addresses, such as IP addresses, are assigned to a network interface two ways: either dynamically by a DHCP server or manually (statically) by a network administrator. Servers don't assign logical addresses manually, and the manufacturer of a network card assigns its physical address (MAC address), not its logical one.

12. D. The physical address is also referred to as the computer's Media Access Control, or MAC, address. This address is physically "burned-in" to the network interface card when it is manufactured. A logical address is an address that can be dynamically or statically assigned by an administrator and may change over time. A Network Node address is an IPX logical address. There is no such thing as a NetBIOS address.

13. B. A computer uses a default gateway when it sends traffic intended for hosts that are not located on its own subnet. The other three choices are devices that perform services on the network but do not handle traffic in this manner.

14. D. A firewall can block traffic based upon a number of criteria, including IP address, port, protocol, and many other characteristics.

15. A. The first 3 bytes of the network interface's hardware address, or MAC, identifies the manufacturer of the interface. In this case, the first three bytes are 00-05-1B.

16. B. An IP address is divided into two portions: the network address and the host address. The network address portion indicates which network the computer is assigned to, and the host address uniquely identifies the computer on that network.

17. C. All of the options describe characteristics of a computer's NetBIOS name except for option C. NetBIOS names can only be 15 characters long, not 255.

18. D. IP addresses are resolved to MAC addresses by TCP/IP using the ARP protocol. UDP is a connectionless Transport layer protocol. DHCP is a protocol that dynamically assigns IP addressing information to network hosts, and DNS resolves IP addresses to hostnames.

19. C. Both WINS and DNS are critical services in a network comprising both older and newer Windows OS versions. WINS assists in dynamically resolving NetBIOS names used by older versions of Windows, and DNS is used for newer versions of Windows that do not rely on NetBIOS name resolution.

20. A, D. The WINS service corresponds with its older, static method of resolving NetBIOS names, the LMHOSTS file, and the DNS service was preceded by an older method of static hostname resolution using the Hosts file.

Chapter

11

Configuring Application Security

MICROSOFT EXAM OBJECTIVES COVERED IN THIS CHAPTER:

✓ **Identify and troubleshoot problems related to security permissions.**

- Answer end-user questions related to application security settings.
- Troubleshoot access to local resources.
- Troubleshoot access to network resources.
- Troubleshoot insufficient user permissions and rights.

✓ **Identify and respond to security incidents.**

- Answer end-user questions related to security incidents.
- Identify a virus attack.
- Apply critical updates.

✓ **Manage application security settings.**

Security on a computer or a network should be virtually transparent to users who are just doing their job. In other words, if users want access only to resources they have been allowed to use, they should be able to access those resources with their normal user logon and without providing additional credentials. On the other hand, security should become very apparent to users who attempt to use a resource for which they do not have permissions. In addition, your network and the computers that it contains should be continually updated to protect against attacks from intruders and viruses. Some applications provide tools and settings to enhance their own security.

As a desktop support technician, you should understand the elements of security that relate to a user's applications. In this chapter, we discuss security with a special focus on application security. The security of the user's applications relies on understanding and controlling the following three elements:

Problems related to permissions   Permissions either allow a user to utilize a resource or deny its use. There are many types of permissions that you can use to control access to a resource. The type of permission that you use will depend upon the type of resource and its location. The key is to make sure the user can utilize the resource transparently while at the same time blocking access to intruders. While the network administrator typically controls this, you should understand the problems that can result when permissions on the network and the computers that it contains are not controlled properly. You should also be able to recognize security issues related to applications so that you can bring them to the attention of the network administrator. Finally, you should be able to troubleshoot user permissions and rights to assure that users can remain productive.

Security incidents   Security incidents are not inherently the fault of the network administrator or the desktop support technician, but their success in causing a disruption could indicate a weakness in the security of a computer or a network. You should be able to quickly identify and troubleshoot a problem caused by a virus. In addition, you should ensure that you have installed the latest critical updates for your users' operating systems and applications. This should not be considered a one-time fix but rather a habit or ongoing procedure.

Application security settings   Some applications provide their own tools to enhance security for users and their documents. You should understand that these security measures are generally a trade-off for application flexibility and functionality. For example, when you enable macro security, you might limit the functionality of an application. We will discuss security settings that are built into the applications within Microsoft Office 2003. You should be familiar with these settings so that you can enhance a user's application security and troubleshoot issues related to these settings.

Problems Related to Permissions

There are many ways to use permissions to help secure your environment. One method is to control a user's access to an application that is installed on the user's computer. For example, only the users who have access to the executable files for each application will be able to utilize the application. This control is actually a side effect of the level of access to the Registry and file system. If a user cannot see the Registry entries used by an application, the user cannot open and use the application. Most applications that are used on today's computers have this level of "intelligence" built in. This means that they allow you to choose who can see and have access to the application and its files when you install it. You can see an example of this in Figure 11.1.

FIGURE 11.1   User-based installation options

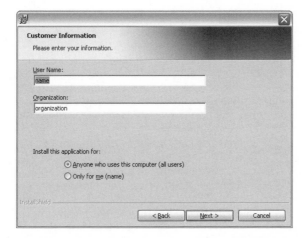

Primarily, you will rely on group membership for file and folder permissions related to data access on the network and local machine. In a workgroup environment, you will pay closest attention to local groups and user accounts. You can verify users and group membership by using the Computer Management Console, as seen in Exercise 11.1.

On a computer that is a member of a domain, the Domain Users group or another specialized group may be used for the purpose of configuring permissions. These groups will be maintained by the network administrator using the Active Directory Users and Computers tool. You will generally not be allowed to make changes to these groups, so you will need to forward your requests to the network administrator.

At this point, you may be wondering why it is so important to control a user's access to applications. After all, it's just an application, right? Well, applications are also doors into the operating system of the computer. Users generally don't have the technical know-how to make decisions on what software should be on their system and definitely shouldn't be able to configure it. With spyware and viruses running rampant on the Internet today, users with the privileges to install software can be very dangerous to your company.

EXERCISE 11.1

Examining Local Group Membership in Windows XP

1. On the Windows XP Desktop, right-click My Computer and choose Manage.

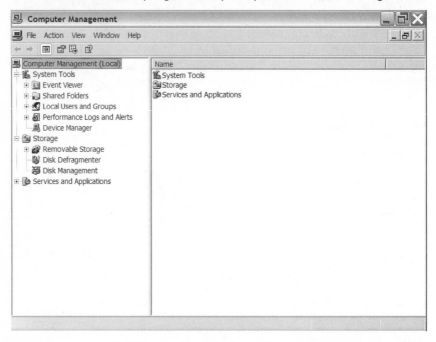

2. In the Computer Management Console, expand Local Users and Groups.

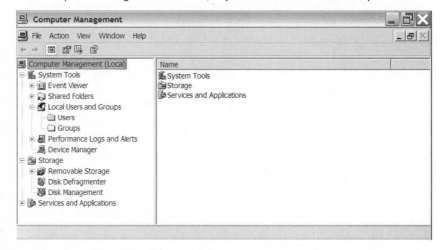

EXERCISE 11.1 *(continued)*

3.   In the console pane (on the left), choose Groups.

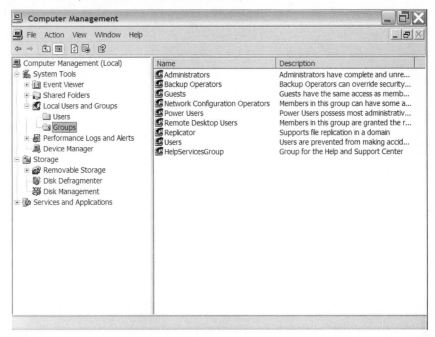

4.   In the details pane (on the right), right-click the group that you want to examine and then choose Properties.

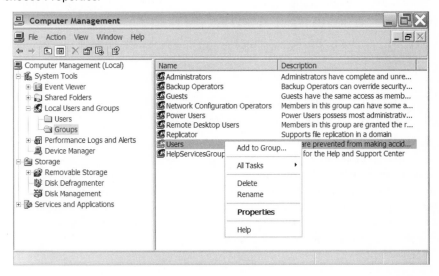

5. Examine the Members box to determine who is a member of this group.

6. To add a member to the group, click the Add button and then type the name of the new member. (You can also use the Advanced button to browse a list of users.)

7. When you have entered the name of the new member, click OK on the Users Properties dialog box to close.

The following is a partial list of security issues that can affect a user's productivity when installing an application locally as well as through the network:

Buffer overruns   A buffer is a special area of memory that is set aside to speed the execution of an application. Buffers are meant to improve productivity, but they can also become a potential security issue if permissions are not correctly configured. You should ensure that only the appropriate users have permissions for the executable files of applications and that the latest service packs are installed to reduce the possibility of an attacker's exploiting a buffer in a buffer overrun attack. You can refer to Microsoft Knowledge Base (KB) article 308035 for more information on buffer overrun attacks.

Registry access   The time during an installation or during a restart after an installation is an especially vulnerable period for the application from a security standpoint. This is because the application and the Local System account have been given access to the Registry. If an attacker has access at this point, or if a worm has been hidden in the computer, security could be breached at this time. For this reason, you should make sure that you know what software is being installed on the computers within your network.

Macros   Macros are designed to improve user productivity by allowing users and programmers to create command sets that automatically run a series of steps within the computer. You should know that an attacker can exploit macros and that the very resource that was designed to improve productivity can also be used to threaten security. We will discuss macro security in greater depth later in this chapter.

Viruses   Virus attacks threaten the security of computers and networks in all organizations. The only real way to protect your computers and networks from viruses is to install and maintain an antivirus program. We will discuss viruses and virus prevention in much greater depth later in this chapter. You can also refer to Microsoft KB article 129972 for more information on virus prevention.

You can often prevent these issues by simply being mindful of what level of local and network permissions you allow users to have. Generally, your applications should be installed either over the network or locally by someone with a good understanding of the hazards involved in application deployment.

Security Incidents

As a desktop support technician, you should understand the security procedures and policies of your organization. Most organizations use some type of antivirus software to protect the computers in their network from the harmful effects of viruses. This software prevents many viruses, but some might still slip through. You should be able to recognize the symptoms of a virus on a user's computer. In addition, most organizations require that computers be kept up-to-date with the latest critical patches. Although you may not be responsible for maintaining the security of the entire network, you are responsible for understanding the impact of the security policies on the individual computers in your network. In addition, you are responsible for understanding the methods that the network administrators might choose to deploy these updates. In the following sections, we discuss each of these topics in greater detail.

Viruses

Viruses are executable files that are designed to replicate themselves, thereby causing a disruption of service for the computer user. They're also designed to avoid detection by disguising themselves as legitimate programs. There are, as this book is being written, over 60,000 known viruses! In addition, even more viruses are being created on a daily basis. Most organizations use antivirus software on their networks and on the individual computers in their networks to combat the problem of viruses. You should recommend that your organization make use of an antivirus program that has an automatic update feature.

There are many different categories of malicious code, and even though a virus is actually one type of malicious code, all are commonly referred to as viruses. These types of viruses have specific characteristics that differentiate them from each other. Table 11.1 list the different types of malicious code.

TABLE 11.1   Malicious Code Types

Type	Function	Infection Method
Virus	A collection of code that infects legitimate files, such as executables and images	A legitimate, infected file is downloaded unintentionally by a user.
Worm	A self-contained piece of code that performs unwanted actions on a computer	A worm travels the Internet looking for vulnerable computers.
Trojan horse	A program that pretends to be a legitimate program but is, instead, a harmful file or set of files	A Trojan must be downloaded or executed by a user.
Macro	A script or Office file that uses the built-in macro engine of Microsoft Office	A macro is usually received in email and opened by an unsuspecting user.

There are many more classifications of malicious code. Table 11.1 lists only the most common types.

As the desktop support technician, you should be aware of how viruses might affect the computer. You should be able to recognize the effects of a virus such as a worm or a Trojan horse. In addition, you should know what steps to take to begin to recover the computer from a virus attack. Finally, you should be aware of procedures that can reduce the likelihood that another virus attack will succeed. We will discuss each of these concepts in greater detail.

The Effects of a Virus

The effects of a virus will vary depending on the type. Some viruses are just a minor nuisance, but others have been known to cause a considerable amount of damage to the user's data and to essential operating system files. You should be able to recognize problems that are most likely caused by a virus so that you can quickly troubleshoot a user's computer when it is infected. It's also important to quickly troubleshoot viruses because you want to make sure that you don't give them a chance to spread to other computers.

Users with Too Many Rights!

I recently did some consulting with a company that used a very advanced application deployment method. It had a program that ran on a server on the network and installed the applications automatically for the users. This meets part of the requirements for secure and intelligent handling of applications; it takes the responsibility of application installation out of the users' hands. The only problem with this is that the program required that the users be in the Administrators group on their local machine. This didn't seem like a big deal to the management at the time. Enter my role.

I receive a call from the IT manager. "Brad, our network has slowed to a crawl. It looks like our circuits and local network are overwhelmed with traffic." After arriving on-site, I performed some basic tests, and within an hour, I had an answer for them. After I talked with the IT manager and his staff for a few minutes, they realized that they had made a grave mistake giving users administrative privileges. Many users had installed peer-to-peer sharing software and were allowing people from all over the world to download music and movies from the corporate network! In addition, installing these P2P programs had brought a slew of viruses and spyware to the network, causing most innocent PCs to be overrun with malicious code at such a pace the desktop support group couldn't keep up. We immediately set to work removing the users' permissions. The problem is, the programs had already been installed, so removing the privileges only prevented them from installing more programs. They ended up taking over a month to remove all the file sharing software, worms, viruses, and spyware from their network. So what's the moral of the story? Users are just that, users of the computers, not administrators, so give them the permissions that fit their role!

The following is a list of symptoms that might be caused by a computer virus:

- The infected file makes copies of itself and ends up using much of the free space on a user's computer.

- The infected file is automatically sent to all or some of the addresses on the user's email address list.

- The user's hard drive is partially or completely formatted without any action from the user.

- Much of the user's hard drive is consumed, but the files and folders that contain the data are not recognizable or are not even visible.

- Security settings on the computer or the network are automatically changed without any action from the user or any other party.

- A user tells you that their computer hasn't been working well since they last checked email and opened some attachments.

- There are double extensions (such as `jpg.vbs`) on attachments that have been recently opened by users.

- The antivirus program on a computer is unexpectedly disabled and cannot be restarted.

- A new antivirus program cannot be installed on a computer or will not run properly.

- Messages or dialog boxes suddenly appear on the user's screen without any action from the user.

- A user tells you that they are receiving unusual email with attachments from people with whom they rarely have contact.

- Icons suddenly appear on a user's desktop that the user did not create and that are not associated with any application installed on the user's computer.

- Unexpected sounds are heard from the audio system of the computer.

- Programs that were previously installed and running on the computer have disappeared without any action from the user or any other party.

Recovering from a Virus Attack

While it would be nice to just prevent all virus attacks from affecting (and infecting) your users' computers, it's probably not a realistic goal. Chances are good that some viruses will sneak through onto some computers in your network. For this reason, you should know the steps to recover from a virus attack. While the details of each step will vary based on the virus, there is a method that will generally assist you in eradicating a virus from a user's computer.

To recover from a virus, you should take the following five steps in the order that they are listed:

1. Check the website of your antivirus software vendor to get the latest information about eradicating the virus. Follow any directions that are listed on the website. Often there will be detailed instructions that you can use to eradicate the virus while protecting most, if not all, of the user's data.

2. If your antivirus program is still working properly, then make sure you have the latest updates from your antivirus software vendor. When you are sure that you have the latest updates, scan the computer with the updated antivirus program.

3. If your antivirus program is damaged or is not working properly, reinstall the antivirus program with the latest updates. After the antivirus program is reinstalled, scan the entire computer to eradicate the virus.

4. After the virus has been eradicated according to the antivirus software, scan the entire computer once more to make sure that it is completely free of viruses.

5. In some cases, you may have to completely reformat the hard drive and reinstall the operating system and all of the applications. If the antivirus software states that it cannot eradicate the virus, the virus may have hidden itself in the master boot record or another operating system file. If the antivirus software will not clear the virus and the vendor's website does not have an adequate solution, you will have to reformat the user's hard drive to remove the virus. If possible, you should back up the user's data and configuration before reformatting the computer.

Be Careful about the Computers That You Connect to Your Network

A few years ago, a company with which I was associated brought a computer into their network from a user's home to install the latest security updates and antivirus programs. Shortly after they attached the computer to the network, they realized that they had made a mistake. Other computers that had the latest antivirus software began reporting the presence of the W32.FunLove.4099 virus. The FunLove virus has a cute name, but it is not a friendly virus. In fact, the FunLove virus has the ability to infiltrate the Windows NT security subsystem and cause degradation in performance and system instability on the computers that it infects. Unfortunately, before they could stop it, the virus had located network shares and replicated itself into the network and onto many computers. This was just the beginning of their FunLove problems.

They began by updating the antivirus software on the client computers and servers and installing antivirus software on any computers that did not currently have it. They ensured that all of the computers were aware of the FunLove virus signature. They then used the antivirus software and instructions from the vendor's website to quarantine and clean the FunLove virus from the network and its computers.

This process took approximately one week, but every time they thought they had seen the last of the virus, it managed to pop up in a few places again. By this time, most of the computers were protected against the effects of the virus, but it was still perplexing as to where the virus was hiding. They checked all of the drives of the computers on which it seemed to have surfaced again and found nothing.

Finally, when the virus appeared once more after over two weeks of absence, they determined where it had been hiding. Apparently, a user who did not know that his computer was infected had made a backup to a CD-R very early in the process. Whenever he decided to use the files that were on the CD-R, he unknowingly relaunched the virus onto his computer and into the network.

The moral of this story is "Be careful about connecting a computer to your network when you are not sure what it contains." Do not allow users to bring computers from home and connect them to your network. It may be tough to enforce strict rules at times, but it is much harder to track down a virus and eradicate it once it is released into an active network.

Preventing a Virus Attack

While it may be impossible to prevent every virus attack from succeeding, there are steps that you can take to protect your computers from viruses. Since you are responsible for the productivity of the users on your network, you should be familiar with the guidelines to prevent virus attacks from succeeding. Your ability to implement these measures will vary based on the policies of your organization. You should know that the more of these guidelines that are implemented, the safer the network and the computers that it contains will be.

The guidelines that are recommended by Microsoft to prevent virus attacks from succeeding are as follows:

- Install an antivirus program that includes an automatic update feature.

- Configure your antivirus program to automatically update virus signatures on a daily basis.

- Configure your antivirus program to automatically scan computers on at least a weekly basis.

- Install the latest security patches from the Microsoft Windows Update website at `windowsupdate.microsoft.com`.

- Configure Windows to download and install all critical updates. See Microsoft KB article 294871.

- Make sure the latest updates are installed for all email programs utilized by users.

- Disable Active Scripting in Outlook and Outlook Express.

- Enable and configure the Internet Connection Firewall (ICF) on users' computers or install a third-party personal firewall.

Security Updates and Patches

A security update is generally a new piece of software that is released by the software vendor to combat a known security weakness. Today's software vendors typically create and distribute security updates as soon as a weakness or flaw in an application's security is discovered. Microsoft's Windows Update website can help you keep a user's computer up-to-date with the latest security patches for the operating system. You should understand how to use the Windows Update website to enhance the security of applications on a user's computer by enhancing the security of the operating system. In addition, you should know how to use the Office Update website to check for any updates specific to Office applications. You should also know how network administrators might deploy security updates to a large group of computers using Group Policy and/or Systems Management Server (SMS). Finally, you should know the difference between critical updates and optional updates. In the following sections, we will discuss each of these concepts in greater detail.

The Windows Update Website

In Chapter 1, "Installing a Windows Desktop Operating System," we discussed the Windows Update feature of Windows XP and the Windows Update website as they apply to the operating system. You should know that the Windows Update website can also help you keep your computers up-to-date with the latest security patches for applications. When you access the Windows Update website, the site scans your computer and provides you with the selection of updates that apply only to the operating system and the applications on your computer that came with the operating system, such as Internet Explorer and Outlook Express. New content is added to the site on a regular basis, so you can always get the most recent updates to protect your users' computers and maintain their productivity. You should encourage users to access the Windows Update website on a regular basis. Exercise 11.2 illustrates how to access the Windows Update website and scan a user's computer for the latest updates.

EXERCISE 11.2

Accessing the Windows Update Website

1. In the address bar in your browser, type **windowsupdate.microsoft.com**. The system will convert the address to the latest Windows Update website. (As this book is being written, the site is v4.windowsupdate.microsoft.com/en/default.asp.)

2. Wait for the site to obtain the latest Windows Update software. (Depending on the speed of your connection, this might take a minute or two.)

3. When the Welcome to Windows Update page is displayed, choose Scan for Updates.

4. The system will scan your computer and then list the critical updates and other types of updates that are recommended for your computer and the applications installed on it.

5. When the Pick Updates to Install page is displayed, choose Review and Install Updates.

6. Read the information about each critical update and service pack first to determine whether to install it. (You should probably install all critical updates.) If you want to install an update, then simply leave it on the list. These updates are selected by default. If you do not want to install an update, choose Remove to delete it from the list of updates that will be installed.

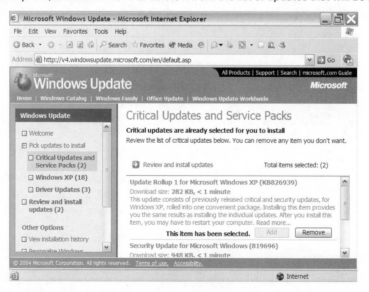

7. Next, read the information about the other updates. If you want to install any of them, you will need to click Add to put them on the install list. These updates are not selected by default.

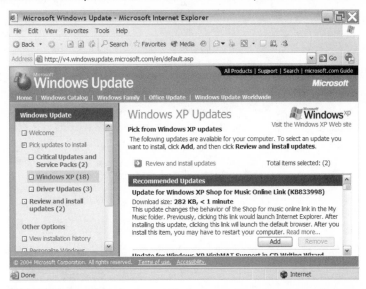

8. When you have finished selecting the updates to install, click Install Now to begin the installation of all selected updates.

9. The Windows Update dialog box will appear, indicating both the download progress and install progress of your selected updates. You may be required to restart your computer before some updates are effective.

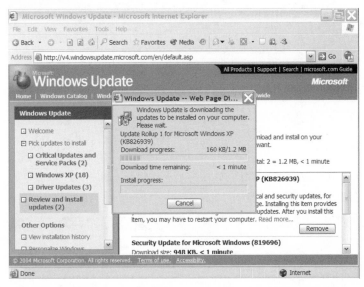

10. When you see the Installation Complete page, you have successfully installed your updates. (Restart the computer to make sure all updates become effective immediately.)

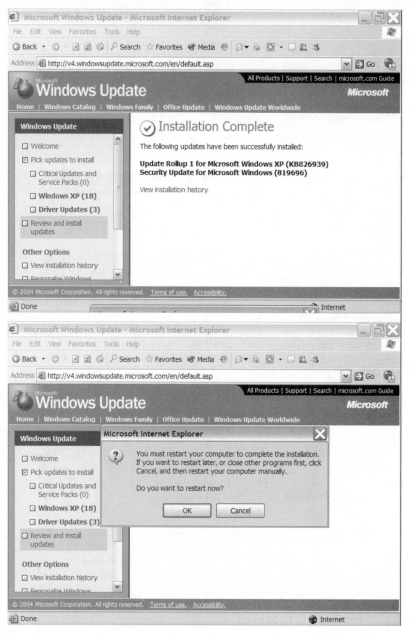

EXERCISE 11.2 *(continued)*

11. To view your installation history of this and other Windows Update software, choose View Installation History on the Installation Complete page.

The Office Update Website

The Office Update website contains information and tools for Office XP and Office 2003 applications. You can use the tools on the Office Update website to scan your computer to detect the applications that are installed and determine which critical updates, service packs, and other types of updates might be needed. You should know how to use this tool so you can help users and show them how to use the tool as well. Exercise 11.3 walks you through the steps to scan the applications on your computer using the tools on the Office Update website.

EXERCISE 11.3

Accessing the Office Update Website

1. In the address bar in your browser, type **officeupdate.microsoft.com**; or from any Office 2003 application, choose Help and then choose Check for Updates.

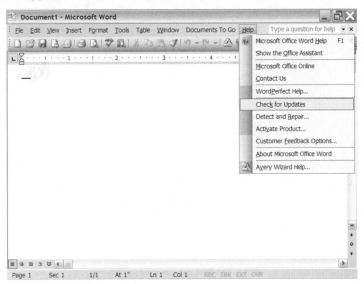

EXERCISE 11.3 *(continued)*

2. On the Office Update web page, choose Check for Updates. The system will examine your computer and make a list of critical updates, service packs, and other updates that are recommended specifically for your computer's Office 2003 applications.

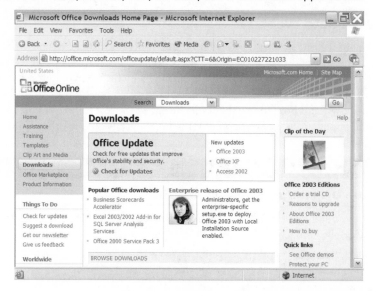

3. When the Microsoft Office Update page is displayed, you can browse the list of recommended updates and either select or deselect them based on your own needs. Note that the critical updates are selected by default and the other updates are not selected by default. To read more about each update, you can select More Information at the end of the general information for each update.

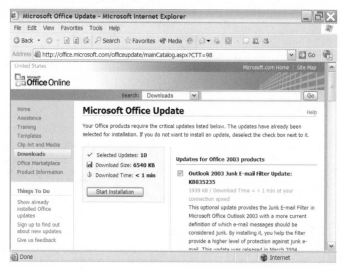

EXERCISE 11.3 *(continued)*

4. When you have made your choices, click Start Installation to begin to install the updates that you have chosen.

5. On the End-User License Agreement for Microsoft Software page, click Next (read it first if you want).

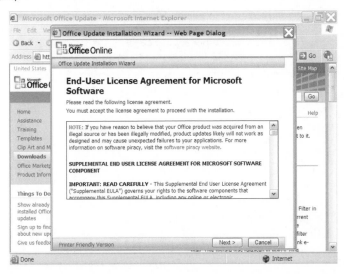

6. On the Please Confirm Your Selection page, click Next.

7. Depending upon the update, you may need to supply your Office product CD to complete the installation. Insert the CD and then click Next to begin downloading the updates.

8. When the updates are downloaded and installed, the system will display the Installation Result page and indicate which updates require rebooting the system.

9. Click Finish to close the Installation Result page, and restart your computer if necessary.

Methods of Deploying Updates

As a desktop support technician, you will probably use only the tools that we've discussed thus far; however, you should know that network administrators might use many other tools to deploy updates to multiple computers at the same time. While you don't have to be an expert on all of these tools, you should be familiar with them and understand how they may have affected the users' computers. The more familiarity you have with the tools that the network administrator might use, the more you can understand the big picture in regard to managing updates on users' computers.

The following is a partial list of the most common tools that network administrators use to deploy updates to users' computers:

- Systems Management Server (SMS): SMS is a Microsoft server application that helps network administrators automate the management of their networks. With SMS, administrators can install, execute, and access network resources. They can also strengthen network accountability and maintainability. Network administrators sometimes use SMS to install security patches in a mandatory fashion without giving the client computers any choice. At other times, SMS is used to provide the security patch and make the client computers and the users aware of its availability; then the users can install the security patch if they so choose.

- Active Directory: Windows 2000 Server and Windows Server 2003 servers employ Active Directory as a means of identifying and managing all of the objects in all of the domains of an organization. Active Directory has tremendous power to control objects. With Active Directory and group policies, administrators can install security patches on computers within their organizations.

- Group Policy: Group Policy consists of groups, or combinations, of policies that are used to control sites, domains, and organizational units within Active Directory. Group Policy provides granular control of all installations of software, including security patches.

- Executable patch: Sometimes the patches themselves provide an executable file or a wizard to assist the network administrator or even the user in the installation.

Application Security

Historically, most of the security of applications has been delegated to the operating system. Due to increases in technology and the constant need for greater security and more layers of security, the latest Microsoft applications now have their own built-in security features. These should be used in addition to, not instead of, operating system-based security methods such as NTFS permissions. In this section, we will focus on the application security built into Microsoft Word 2003. You should know that the same security features are now available on all of the latest applications in Microsoft Office 2003. Figure 11.2 shows the Security tab within the Options dialog box (Tools ➤ Options) in Microsoft Word 2003.

FIGURE 11.2 The Security tab of the Options dialog box in Word 2003

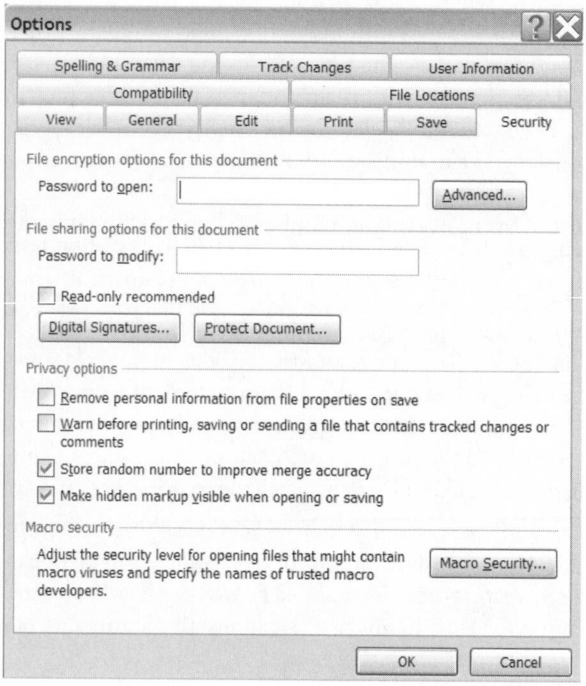

It contains the following security settings:

- File Encryption Options for This Document:

  - Password to Open: Users can password-protect individual documents and files to prevent others from seeing or changing them. Users can enter a password in the Password to Open text box to secure a document. Users should realize that they must remember this password; otherwise, they will be locked out of their document until they can remember it. The administrator and desktop support technician cannot override this security to assist the user.

  - Advanced: You should click the Advanced button to apply specific encryption when your organization requires it.

- File Sharing Options for This Document:

  - Password to Modify: This is actually not as much of a security feature as a feature to prevent a user from unintentionally modifying a document. Users can enter a password in the Password to Modify text box. This feature can also be used to stop users from changing a file and saving it with the same name, but it does not stop them from saving the file with a different name and then modifying it.

  - Read-Only Recommended: This is the recommended setting when a password is used. This will also prevent another user from modifying a document and saving it with the same name unless they have the Password to Modify credentials. It is not a strong security feature.

- Digital Signatures: Users who have a digital signature from your organization's certificate authority or a third-party certificate authority can apply the digital signature to a document. This may not be considered as a legally binding signature.

- Protect Document: Users should click the Protect Document button to apply granular restrictions to their documents. These include formatting and editing restrictions.

- Privacy Options:

  - Remove Personal Information from File Properties on Save: This option removes the Author, Manager, and Company entries from the document properties. The author's name is also removed from comments, tracked changes, and macros. This option does not remove fields in headers and footers that may contain the same information.

  - Warn Before Printing, Saving or Sending a File That Contains Tracked Changes or Comments: This option should be used only if the information regarding those who created and modified a document is sensitive.

  - Store Random Number to Improve Merge Accuracy: This option should be used to get the best results when merging changes with multiple reviewers. It is selected by default.

  - Make Hidden Markup Visible When Opening or Saving: This option should be used when the hidden markup in a document is not of a sensitive nature.

- Macro Security: Macros are lists of commands that can be used to control a computer. You can adjust the degree to which the application will respond to macros to prevent attackers from using them as part of their attack. Figure 11.3 shows the Security Level options that are available, which include the following:

  - Low: This option is generally not recommended because it does not protect the user from unsafe macros. Users should use this option only if they are also using third-party software that protects them from unsafe macros.

  - Medium: This option allows the user to choose whether to run a potentially unsafe macro.

  - High: This option allows only signed macros from trusted sources to run. Unsigned macros are automatically disabled.

  - Very High: This option allows only specific macros installed in trusted locations to run. All other signed and unsigned macros will automatically be disabled.

- Trusted Publishers: This tab includes a list of the entities that users have specifically added as a trusted source:

  - Trust All Installed Add-ins and Templates: To provide for the greatest security, this box should not be checked.

  - Trust Access to Visual Basic Project: This option should be selected for specific access to Microsoft Visual Basic.

- Prior Trusted Sources: This tab includes a list of trusted sources that was created by a prior version of Office. You cannot add new sources to this list.

FIGURE 11.3   Macro Security Level settings in Word 2003

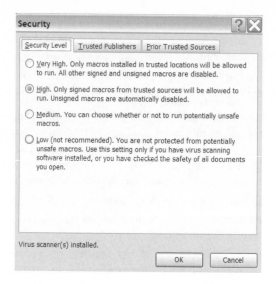

Case Study: ABC Group Security Concerns

ABC has been a financial consulting group for many years. It has struggled with many technical and security-related issues over the years. The latest threat the company faces is not an
attacker, a lawsuit, or anything it has dealt with before. This time it's compliance. ABC's
mother company, CBA Firms Inc., has been audited and is forced to be sure that all child companies, such as ABC, are compliant with new government regulations. Because you are a part
of the help desk support team, you will be required to configure many of the client-based
security changes that are requested. You have been given the following vague objectives:

- Configure each client computer to be protected against macro-based malicious code.

- Configure each client workstation to automatically download and install Microsoft Windows updates.

- Configure each client machine to be protected against viruses.

Your first objective is going to be specific to Microsoft Office. Based on what you have
learned, there are many options available. Because your users probably use some level of
macros in their day-to-day activities, you can't totally block all macros. So you will most likely
choose a setting that will allow users to choose whether or not they want to allow macros.
Part of meeting this objective will be educating users to block macros they aren't expecting.

Your second objective is a very simple one to complete. You can simply configure each work-station to automatically download and install critical updates at a certain time.

Your final objective is also fairly simple to meet. You will have to purchase third-party antivirus scanning software. Once the software has been deployed, you will most likely configure it to automatically download virus definition files.

Although most of these solutions seem very easy, the strategy behind this case study is to show you that no single security mechanism can seal the deal for any company. Security is always an uphill battle and cannot be mastered overnight.

Summary

Our constantly changing world creates a continual supply of security challenges for desktop support technicians and network administrators. Experience tells us that the best type of security is a system that includes multiple layers. Because of improvements in technology, we now have applications that can be used as security tools. In addition, we have security settings built into the latest Microsoft Office applications. As a desktop support technician, you should be familiar with the security problems that are related to improperly configured permissions. In addition, you should know how to recognize and respond to security incidents on your network and on the computers within your network. Finally, you should know how to configure security for the latest Microsoft Office applications.

As a general rule, permissions are controlled by the operating systems in a network, including those that are on the clients as well as the servers. The purpose of permissions is to provide transparent access to resources that a user utilizes. At the same time, permissions should deny access to users who have no need to use a resource. In addition, permissions should be controlled to prevent an attacker from manipulating the operating systems or applications in a network. When permissions are not controlled properly, the result is a weakness in the network or the computers that it contains. These weaknesses can take the form of buffer overruns, unauthorized Registry access, installation issues, macros, and viruses. Buffer overruns and unauthorized Registry access are generally exploitations of the system that an attacker executes after waiting for the opportune time. Macros and viruses are a more automated type of attack that can be loaded into a system to be executed at a later date. You should be familiar with each type of attack so that you can recognize it and respond accordingly. Your response will most likely include involving the network administrator.

Security incidents are attacks upon the computers within your network. An attack itself is not the fault of the network administrator or the desktop support technician; however, its ability to succeed may well indicate a weakness in your network or the computers that it contains. Typically, a successful attack indicates that your network does not have either virus protection or the latest critical updates for operating systems and applications or both. You should be able to identify a problem caused by a security incident and take the steps to assure that the network remains safe in the future. This should include recognizing viruses and understanding the methods used to deploy critical updates in your organization.

Some of the latest applications developed by Microsoft and other third-party companies have security features built into them. These include the capability to password-protect individual documents created by the application. You should know the security settings that are available in Microsoft Office 2003 applications. In particular, you should know about password protection, digital signatures, and macro security. You should understand that, while security is a must in all networks and in the computers that they contain, some of the security features represent a trade-off between security and the flexibility and functionality of an application.

Exam Essentials

Understand security issues.   You should understand the security issues that can result from improper configuration of permissions. In addition, you should be able to recognize computer and network problems created by security issues, such as buffer overruns, Registry access, installation issues, macros, and viruses. Finally, you should understand that tightening security usually includes a trade-off with functionality and flexibility.

Know how to prevent security incidents.   You should understand that security incidents are caused by an attacker or a virus but can often be prevented by solid network administration. In addition, you should know how to make the most effective use of antivirus software to protect your network and the computers that it contains. Finally, you should know the various methods that your organization might employ to distribute and install critical updates and other updates.

Be able to implement application security.   You should understand that application security is an additional layer of protection that can be used to secure documents. In addition, you should know that the latest Microsoft Office applications include security features to protect documents. Finally, you should know how to configure security settings such as password protection, digital signatures, and macro security.

Review Questions

1. You are the desktop support technician for your organization. A user complains that her Microsoft Word application has recently developed a "mind of its own." It seems to execute steps that she has not ordered or programmed it to do. Which of the following is probably configured improperly on her application?

    A. Viruses

    B. Registry access

    C. Macro security

    D. Buffers

2. You are the desktop support technician of your organization. A user complains that her computer has not worked properly since the last time that she checked her email. You ask her if there were any unusual messages in her email the last time that she checked it. She responds that there was one message that had an unusual title and a weird file attached to it, but that she deleted the email as soon as she saw what was in the attachment. What is the most likely cause of the user's problem?

    A. An unsafe macro

    B. A virus

    C. A buffer overrun

    D. Improperly configured Registry access

3. You are the desktop support technician for your organization. A user complains that one of his applications has been performing very slowly as of late. Now, all of a sudden, it's performing well again, but he does not have access to some of the files that he needs and it seems as if permissions have been altered. What type of an attack should you suspect?

    A. Buffer overrun

    B. Registry access

    C. Virus

    D. Unsafe macro

4. You are the desktop support technician for your company. A user has recently installed a new application but now finds that she is having multiple problems with many existing applications. Which type of attack should you suspect?

    A. Virus

    B. Unsafe macros

    C. Buffer overrun

    D. Unauthorized Registry access

5. You are the desktop support technician for your organization. A user's computer has become infected with a virus. The virus was able to shut down and disable the antivirus software installed on the user's computer. You install the antivirus software with the latest updates from the Web, but the antivirus software indicates that it cannot eradicate the virus from the user's computer. What should you do next?

   A. Reinstall the antivirus software and try again.

   B. Reinstall the operating system on the user's computer.

   C. Back up the user's data and configuration, if possible, and reformat the hard drive of the user's computer.

   D. Ignore the virus as long as it doesn't affect the user's productivity.

6. You are the desktop support technician for your organization. You are assisting a user who utilizes a Windows XP desktop from her home. She has recently experienced several problems that seem to be related to application security. As a first step, you want to make sure that she has all of the latest critical updates for the Windows XP operating system. Which of the following should you do? (Choose two. Each answer is part of the solution.)

   A. Direct the user to the Windows Update website.

   B. Direct the user to the Office Update website.

   C. Tell her to check for updates and then select all of the suggested updates.

   D. Tell her to check for updates and then accept all of the updates that the system selects.

7. You are the desktop support technician for your company. You are assisting a user with setting automatic updates on his computer. On the Automatic Updates tab, the settings are configured but they are grayed out and you cannot access them. Which of the following should you suspect?

   A. A virus

   B. An unsafe macro

   C. A buffer overrun attack

   D. Group policies

8. You are the desktop support technician for your organization. A user asks you how she can get the latest updates for her Word 2003 application. Which of the following should you tell her? (Choose two. Each answer is a complete solution.)

   A. In her browser, type `www.windowsupdate.microsoft.com`, and then choose Office Updates.

   B. In her browser, type `www.officeupdate.microsoft.com`, and then choose Check for Updates.

   C. In her Word 2003 application, choose Help ➢ Check for Updates, and then choose Check for Updates again on the web page that opens.

   D. On the Windows XP Desktop, choose Help ➢ Check for Updates.

9. You are the desktop support technician for your organization. A user has password-protected an important document using the security features built into Word 2003. Unfortunately, he cannot remember the password that he used. He did not write it down and did not tell anyone else. He wants you to override the system so that he can obtain his document. Which of the following should you tell him?

A. You are not authorized to override the system; he will have to talk to the network administrator.

B. There is nothing that anyone can do; he will have to either remember the password or re-create the document.

C. He can override the security simply by creating a document with the same name as the one that is password protected.

D. Overriding the security will mean that he will have to change his username and password on the network as well.

10. You are the desktop support technician for your organization. Management wants you to make sure that only signed macros from trusted sources are allowed to run on the Office 2003 applications installed in client computers. Which macro security option should you choose?

A. Very High

B. Medium

C. Low

D. High

11. You are the senior help desk support technician at your company. Your organization uses Microsoft Windows XP as its mainstream operating system and Microsoft Office 2003 as its desktop production software. You have been called in because the CEO's computer seems to have been infected by malicious code. She said that she hasn't downloaded any files, opened any new emails, or browsed the Internet for weeks. The computer's virus protection just popped up with a message saying it was infected. She has no idea how the virus got on her system. You have been asked what type of malicious code could have made its way onto her system.

A. A virus

B. A worm

C. A Trojan horse

D. A macro virus

12. You are the senior help desk support technician at your company. Your organization uses Microsoft Windows XP as its mainstream operating system and Microsoft Office 2003 as its desktop production software. A user is trying to find a Microsoft Word file on a network share. Each time the user tries to browse to the file's location, he gets an "Access denied" message. The user was able to access the file a few weeks ago. You must ensure that the user has access to his file. What has most likely happened?

    A. The user has lost the file and is looking in the wrong place.

    B. The permissions of the directory containing the Microsoft Word file have changed.

    C. The user's account has been locked for several days.

    D. Someone else is using the file.

13. You are the senior help desk support technician at your company. Your organization uses Microsoft Windows XP as its mainstream operating system and Microsoft Office 2003 as its desktop production software. Your company has many traveling users that require Internet access when away from work. These users generally use the Internet in hotels and at their home. You have been tasked with determining a way to protect users from Internet-based attacks when they're not on the company network. Which of the following solutions would provide the *most* protection against Internet attacks?

    A. Configure antivirus software on the laptops.

    B. Turn off the Client for Microsoft Networks feature of the network interfaces.

    C. Turn off macro capabilities on the laptops.

    D. Enable the Internet Connection Firewall.

14. You are the senior help desk support technician at your organization company. Your organization uses Microsoft Windows XP as its mainstream operating system and Microsoft Office 2003 as its desktop production software. Your company uses many intranet applications that are hosted on servers internal to your network. A user calls the help desk and states that when she attempts to access the intranet sites, she gets an error saying that her security settings are too restrictive. The user doesn't want to change the settings for fear of enabling a malicious code attack. What should you tell her?

    A. Turn off the security features while accessing the intranet.

    B. Enable more relaxed security in Internet Explorer only for intranet sites.

    C. Use an alternate browser when accessing intranet sites with dangerous content.

    D. Refrain from using intranet sites because they are dangerous.

15. You are the senior help desk support technician at your company. Your organization uses Microsoft Windows XP as its mainstream operating system and Microsoft Office 2003 as its desktop production software. Your CIO calls the help desk and informs you that he is writing year-end performance reviews for many of his upper management. These reviews will be very sensitive and he should be the only one able to view them until they are printed just before the meeting. How can you ensure that the CIO can protect his sensitive information? (Choose all that apply.)

    A. Use EFS to encrypt his information.

    B. Store the information on the public file servers.

    C. Store the information unprotected on his personal system at home.

    D. Use Microsoft Office protection to enable a password for the file.

16. You are the senior help desk support technician at your company. Your organization uses Microsoft Windows XP as its mainstream operating system and Microsoft Office 2003 as its desktop production software. A user reports that his Microsoft Excel spreadsheet is not working properly. You discover that he receives a message stating that his security settings prevent him from running macros when he opens the Excel file. What should you do to ensure that the user can open the Excel file and run the macros?

    A. Add the user to the computer's Power Users group.

    B. Add the user to the computer's Administrators group.

    C. In Excel, choose Tools ➢ Macro ➢ Macros.

    D. In Excel, change the macro security settings to medium and enable macros if prompted.

17. You are the senior help desk support technician at your company. Your organization uses Microsoft Windows XP as its mainstream operating system and Microsoft Office 2003 as its desktop production software. Your users have a popular antivirus program installed to protect them from viruses. One of your users has called the help desk to report that after downloading and installing a program from the internet, he is receiving emails from people he does not know. The people say that they have received emails from him. The user has since uninstalled the application but the emails are still coming from other people. You need to identify the source of these emails. What should you do?

    A. Connect to the Microsoft Windows Update website and scan his computer.

    B. Download the most recent version of the virus definition files to his computer and scan for viruses.

    C. Run the Microsoft Baseline Security Analyzer on his computer to scan for security updates.

    D. Run the Security Configuration and Analysis tool to analyze his computer.

18. You are the senior help desk support technician at your company. Your organization uses Microsoft Windows XP as its mainstream operating system and Microsoft Office 2003 as its desktop production software. A user reports the she wants to be sure that her computer files are not damaged by viruses. She works from home three days a week. She uses a laptop computer with a high-speed Internet connection at home. You need to be sure that the user's laptop computer is always kept up-to-date with the most current Windows security updates. What should you instruct the user to do? (Choose two. Each answer represents part of the total solution.)

   A. Log onto the system using an account with administrative privileges.

   B. Log onto the system using her regular user account.

   C. Go to the Microsoft Update website and scan her computer.

   D. Configure automatic updates to automatically download the updates and install them on a specified schedule.

19. You are the senior help desk support technician at your company. Your organization uses Microsoft Windows XP as its mainstream operating system and Microsoft Office 2003 as its desktop production software. A user in the marketing department has recently received a virus on his system. He calls the help desk to inform them of the incident. He says the virus name that showed up in his scanning utility was winword.exe. He is puzzled because he manually updates his computer via the Windows Update website each day. He also updates his antivirus signatures on a weekly basis. The user wants to know how this virus was able to infect his system. What do you tell him?

   A. The virus infected the operating system itself, resulting in bypassing your security features.

   B. The antivirus software you use is apparently inferior to others.

   C. You have been a victim of a bad joke by a coworker.

   D. Microsoft Office is updated separately from your operating system. You should visit the Office Update website as well.

20. You are the senior help desk support technician at your company. Your organization uses Microsoft Windows XP as its mainstream operating system and Microsoft Office 2003 as its desktop production software. A user calls into the help desk and is concerned that his computer is not receiving the most recent updates available from Microsoft. He states that his automatic update feature is disabled on his system and he does not have permissions to install updates manually. What are the possible methods of update delivery that your company could be using? (Choose all that apply.)

   A. Systems Management Server

   B. Active Directory Administrators group

   C. Group Policy

   D. Manual install by users

Answers to Review Questions

1. C. The most likely cause of her problem is improperly configured macro security. The problem could also be caused by a virus, but the question specifically asks about configuration and viruses would not be configured. The problem is not caused by improperly configured Registry access or improperly configured buffers.

2. B. The most likely cause of the user's problem is that her computer has been infected with a virus. The fact that she opened the attachment is the key to the answer. Closing and deleting the message does not eradicate the virus after the computer has been infected. Since the symptoms are affecting the entire computer, they are most likely not caused by an unsafe macro. This would not be caused by a buffer overrun or improperly configured Registry access.

3. A. The most probable explanation is a buffer overrun attack. The attacker used the buffers built into the application to gain access to the application and its properties. He then changed the permissions, giving himself permissions to control the application. This is probably not related to a Registry access attack because it did not happen during the installation of additional software. This attack does not have the symptoms of a virus or an unsafe macro.

4. D. The type of attack that would most likely cause this problem is an unauthorized Registry access attack. Since the problem occurred immediately after installing additional software, you should consider this option first and inform the network administrator. Since the user is having problems with applications but not the operating system, a virus would not be the first suspect. Since the problem exists on many applications, it is not likely just unsafe macros. Since the problem happened after installation and the user did not report a problem with the applications prior to the new installation, it is probably not related to a buffer overrun.

5. C. In this case, you will need to reformat the user's hard drive to completely rid the computer of the virus. You should attempt to back up as much of the user's data and configuration as possible before you reformat his hard drive. Reinstalling the antivirus software will probably have no effect. Reinstalling the operating system will not eradicate the virus from the computer. You should never ignore a virus because it can spread to other areas of the computer and to other computers within your network.

6. A, D. You should direct the user to the Windows Update website to get the latest critical updates for Windows XP. The critical updates will be automatically selected for the user when she checks for updates. She should accept the defaults to obtain only the critical updates that are not already installed on her computer. The Office Update website does not contain critical updates for Windows XP operating system software. She does not need to select the suggested updates to obtain the critical updates because the critical updates are automatically selected by the system.

7. D. The most likely suspect in this case is group policies configured by the network administrator. These can be configured for an organizational unit, a domain, or even a geographical site. Group policies will override the local security configuration of a computer. These symptoms do not indicate the presence of a virus, an unsafe macro, or a buffer overrun attack.

8. B, C. She should either use her browser and type **www.officeupdate.microsoft.com** and then choose Check for Updates on the Office Update Downloads page on the Web or choose Help from the Word 2003 application, choose Check for Updates from the Help menu, and then choose Check for Updates from the Office Update Downloads page on the Web. The Windows Update website does not contain the updates that she needs. She cannot access the correct Help menu from her Desktop.

9. B. Unfortunately, in this case, there is nothing that you or the network administrator can do. If the user cannot remember the password, then he will have to re-create the document. You should not direct the user to the network administrator because there is nothing that the network administrator can do about the password protection of a local file. He cannot override the local password protection of the application by creating another file with the same name. Local password protection at the application level is completely separate from user credentials, such as username and password, at the network level.

10. D. You should choose the High setting on the Security Level tab to allow only signed macros from trusted sources to run. Unsigned macros will then be automatically disabled. The Very High option will allow only specific macros installed in trusted locations to run. The Medium setting will allow the user to choose whether to run the macro or not. The Low setting does not provide for macro security and should be used only in a situation in which other third-party software is protecting against unsafe macros.

11. B. Because she hadn't really performed any activities that could be considered dangerous, such as opening emails or browsing the Internet, this infection most likely came from a self-replicating source. The only type of malicious code that moves and infects on its own is a worm. Worms travel the Internet looking for victims by searching for vulnerable systems. The only real protection from worms is to keep your system up-to-date and use virus protection.

12. B. This is a common scenario for users who access network resources. In order for the user to have access to a network resource, such as a file share, he has to be in a group that has been granted appropriate permissions to the resource. Losing the file would not produce an "Access denied" message. If the user's account was locked, he would not have been able to log onto the network. Had someone else been accessing the file, it would have still opened and the user would have received a read-only copy of the document.

13. D. Antivirus software would protect against only viruses, not all Internet-based attacks. Disabling Client for Microsoft Networks would keep the laptops from working on the corporate network. Macros are just one of many Internet-based attacks and would not be a complete solution. Enabling the ICF would block all attacks from the Internet that are not explicitly allowed.

14. B. Inside of Internet Explorer, you can adjust security settings for only the Internet, for allowed sites, for restricted sites, and for the intranet. Have her configure more relaxed settings for the intranet.

15. A, D. Encrypting File System (EFS) will allow protection through encryption, allowing only his user account to access the file. Microsoft Office protection will allow his to password-protect his document so it cannot be read by anyone else. The information's storage location is irrelevant.

16. D. The user's group membership will not enable macros in the Excel application. You have to change the default macro settings so that the user can run the macros inside the Excel spreadsheet.

17. B. Most likely, this user has downloaded a program that was either a Trojan horse or infected with a virus. Simply uninstalling the software will not get rid of a virus. You will have to perform a virus scan. You always want to be sure you have the most recent virus definition files before scanning for viruses.

18. A, D. You will need administrative privileges in order to configure automatic updates. Option C would only provide the current security patches. It would not protect her in the long term.

19. D. Although updating your operating system and antivirus software is great step in the right direction, each piece of installed software will also require updates to produce an overall secure computer.

20. A, B, C. There are many methods of installing Microsoft patches. Generally, you will automatically handle patch delivery and take that ability from the user so that you get to choose what patches and updates they get.

Glossary

A

accessibility features   Tools located in the Accessories menu that can be used to magnify elements on the screen, read text, and provide other assistance for users with physical disabilities.

accessibility options   Settings in Control Panel that control the keyboard, display, and sounds that a computer generates when keys are pressed. These can be configured to assist a user who has a physical disability.

access token   A virtual list created for a user at logon based on permissions that are assigned to the user and to groups of which the user is a member. This list is used to gain access to resources in a computer or a domain.

activate   See Windows Product Activation (WPA).

Active Directory   A proprietary name given to Microsoft's X.500-compliant directory structure hosted by domain controllers. Active Directory is a distributed yet hierarchical database used to host user, computer, and group accounts as well as domain, application, and object configuration information.

active partition   The partition that contains the files that are required to boot a computer and find the operating system. This partition must always be on the first disk in the computer.

Address Resolution Protocol (ARP)   A name resolution protocol that is part of the TCP/IP protocol suite. ARP resolves an IP address to a MAC address by first checking a cache and then broadcasting when necessary.

Advanced Configuration and Power Interface (ACPI)   An open industry specification that defines a flexible method of controlling power to components on a system board.

ANDing   A binary calculation whereby 1 and 1 equals 1 but anything else equals 0. This process is used by IP in routers to determine whether a packet's destination address exists on the local subnet or on a remote subnet.

answer files   Files that contain configuration information that is common to a group of computers that are being installed using an unattended installation. These files can be used to automate the installation process and answer the questions asked by the installation program.

attended installation   A type of software installation that requires a person to monitor the entire installation and occasionally choose options or enter additional information.

auditing   The process of recording a sequence of events on servers, workstations, and other networking devices. Audited events are recorded in one or more logs.

Automated System Recovery (ASR)   A last-resort, floppy-disk-based recovery method used to reinstall and recover the previous settings of the Windows XP operating system when every other option has failed.

authentication   The process of verifying the identity of a user. For example, a user might be authenticated by providing the username and password combination.

AutoCorrect   A feature of applications in Office software that automatically corrects common typing errors or replaces text based on configuration by the user.

Automatic Private IP Address (APIPA)   An automatic addressing system that can configure each client computer with a unique IP address in the 169.254.0.0 subnet. This type of addressing is typically seen when a DHCP server has failed and a client is configured to obtain an address automatically.

B

basic disks   Disks that follow the rules and standards of the earliest operating systems. Basic disks can contain a maximum of only four partitions, but they can contain one extended partition that can be divided into multiple logical drives.

basic input/output system (BIOS)   A set of software or firmware contained in a computer that tests the hardware at startup, starts the operating system, and supports data transfer among the hardware devices within and attached to the computer. The BIOS also keeps track of the date and the time.

boot partition   The partition in a computer that contains the Windows system files that are required to run the operating system after a successful boot.

boot sequence   A component of the basic input/output system (BIOS) configuration on a computer that determines which drives a computer will address at startup and in what order they will be addressed.

C

cached credentials   Permissions and rights that were used on the last successful logon and stored in the system for later use. These are sometimes used when a user cannot gain access to a domain controller due to a network problem.

cathode ray tube (CRT)   The earliest method of creating a display from computer-generated output. Consists of an electron gun that fires a series of electrons through a vacuum tube onto a phosphorous screen that is very much like a television screen. This is still the most common type of display used on computers today.

certificate   An electronic piece of identification received from a certificate authority. The certificate contains information about the certificate holder, including the public keys used for signatures and encryption.

certificate authority (CA)   A certificate server that has authority to issue certificates for security purposes. Some CAs are considered root CAs, while others, called subordinate servers, derive their authority from a root CA.

computer name   A generic term used to describe a computer in a network. This is usually also the NetBIOS name and the hostname of a computer on a network using TCP/IP.

Content Advisor   A tool in Internet Explorer that is used to prevent users from accessing websites that contain material that could be considered offensive.

control set   A copy of configuration settings stored in the Registry that is used to configure the drivers and other software to work with the hardware of a computer.

cookies   Small files that contain a user's personal information and can be used to automatically log on to websites and provide information. Cookies can also be abused by other entities and should be controlled carefully.

Creator Owner   The user who originates a document. The Creator Owner has default permissions assigned by the system.

D

Data-Link layer   Layer 2 of the Open Systems Interconnection (OSI) model. The Data-Link layer is responsible for the physical addressing of a computer. It contains two sublayers: the logical link control layer and the media access control layer. The MAC address derives its name from the second sublayer.

data recovery field (DRF)   Used in EFS encryption to store the symmetric key used to encrypt and decrypt a file stored with the encryption attribute enabled. The DRF contains the file encryption key used to encrypt a file and is encrypted using the recovery agent's public key. Only the recovery agent can then decrypt the DRF and retrieve the file encryption key and decrypt the file.

decryption   The process of taking an encrypted file and decoding the encryption so that it can be read in its original format.

default gateway   The interface that can give a computer access outside of its own subnet. This is usually an interface on a router, but it could also be a network interface card on a server or another client computer.

dial-up   A remote connection that is formed using two modems. One modem is used to dial in to a network, and the other modem answers the first modem.

digital certificate   See certificate.

digital signature   Certificates used to prove the identity of the user or company. Often used for signing email or for code signing. Provides nonrepudiation, which means that a user cannot later say that they didn't say something or send something. Digital signatures are sometimes even considered legally binding.

disk 0   The first physical disk in a computer. This is the disk that must always contain the active partition.

display device   A device that produces visual output that a user can see and interpret.

drivers   Software that allows the hardware to communicate with the operating system. Each driver is designed specially for a hardware device and a specific operating system.

DNS servers   Domain Name System (DNS) servers are network-based servers that are used to provide hostname resolution for clients.

dynamic disks   A new type of disk management that allows a disk a tremendous amount of flexibility over that of a basic disk. Dynamic disks can contain as many volumes as needed.

Dynamic Host Configuration Protocol (DHCP) servers   Network-based servers that can automatically assign and configure an IP address and many other network configuration parameters onto a client computer when the client computer is started up on the network.

E

Effective Permissions tool   A GUI-based tool in the NTFS advanced permissions that assists administrators in determining the effective NTFS permissions for a resource, especially when a user is a member of multiple groups.

Encrypting File System (EFS)   EFS is unique to Windows products and is a core technology of Windows. It is used to store files in an encrypted format on an NTFS file system.

encryption   Encryption is the process of changing data from its native format to a ciphered format that cannot be read by unauthorized users.

error message   Text output from a computer system that indicates that a problem has occurred.

Ethernet   The most common method of putting data onto wires using the Carrier Sense Multiple Access with Collision Detection (CSMA/CD) method.

extranet   An extension of the internal network or intranet that allows access for remote clients or partner networks. Usually involves connections over the Internet.

F

Fast User Switching   A new feature in Windows XP that allows more than one user to log on to a computer at the same time. This enables a user to let another user log on to their computer without having to close all of the applications first. This feature is available only if the computer is not joined to a domain.

fdisk tool   An MS-DOS-based tool that you can use to view partition information about a disk, partition the disk, and delete partitions from the disk.

File and Settings Transfer Wizard   A GUI-based tool included with Windows XP that can be used to transfer files and settings on computers that are not a member of a domain.

File Signature Verification tool   A GUI-based tool in Windows XP and Windows 2000 Professional that assists you in determining which drivers in your computer are signed.

file system   A set of rules or standards that determines how data is stored and accessed on a partition. Examples of file systems include FAT, FAT32, and NTFS.

fixed storage device   A common term used to describe a hard drive that is permanently mounted in a computer, although hard drives can be easily removed from most of today's computers.

firewall   A system with special security configurations used to protect the company network from untrusted traffic from networks such as the Internet. A firewall is used to filter out undesirable network traffic.

flash   The process of updating the BIOS of a computer. This was at one time performed with light, but now it is done electronically.

flat-panel monitor   A display device that consists of a liquid crystal display (LCD) or plasma gas display. The display has many levels, which are used to produce all needed colors. Flat-panel displays are not as bulky as CRTs and they do not produce heat.

format   The process of applying a file system to a partition on a disk. The file system will be used to control how data will be stored and accessed.

format tool   An MS-DOS-based tool that can be used to place a FAT or FAT32 file system on a partition.

G

gpresult   A command-line tool that you can use to determine the Resultant Set of Policy (RSoP) of a computer and the currently logged-on user.

graphical user interface (GUI)   A control system for a computer that hides the commands that are actually being used, allowing the user to simply point and click with a mouse or another pointing device.

H

hardware profiles   Settings that can be added to a computer to control the devices that are enabled when the computer is started. The default profile provides for all devices to be enabled when the computer is started. You can copy the default profile and then create a new hardware profile that disables some of the devices in the computer as needed.

Help and Support   Special tools built into Windows XP that assist the administrator and the user in ongoing management and maintenance of the computer and the Windows XP operating system. You can access these tools by pressing F1 while on the Windows XP Desktop.

host   A computer that is on a TCP/IP network.

Hosts file   A static file that is sometimes used for hostname resolution instead of, or as a backup for, DNS.

hostname   A hierarchical computer name that can be used within a network or between networks. The hostname must be unique within its own hierarchy.

hub   A device that works at Layer 1 of the Open Systems Interconnection (OSI) model and connects devices to each other without any intelligence or filtering.

I

identity   A term used with Outlook Express to identify each person when more than one user utilizes the same computer. Each identity can have one or multiple accounts.

IEEE 1394   A standard of very fast data transfer that was developed specifically for use with digital cameras and other graphics peripherals. Also referred to as FireWire.

Internet Message Protocol (IMAP)   A method of storing and retrieving messages that allows users to search through messages on a server and download only the items that they choose.

input/output (I/O) device   Any device that can send and receive data to and from a computer.

infrared (IR)   Communication or control using light that people cannot see because it is below the frequency of red light. Requires line-of-sight communication to work correctly.

Internet Connection Firewall   A new feature in Windows XP that includes a firewall that can be configured for each connection. You can configure the firewall in the advanced settings of the connection.

Internet Control Message Protocol (ICMP)   A protocol that works at the Internet layer of the TCP/IP suite and provides information to higher-layer protocols about the status of the network and the packets that are flowing through it. ICMP responds when an administrator uses the ping tool.

Internet service provider (ISP)   An organization that provides connections to the Internet for its clients.

IP address   A unique address assigned to each computer and interface within a network to allow the routing and delivery of messages throughout the network using the TCP/IP protocol.

ipconfig   A command-line tool that can be used to determine the IP address, subnet mask, and default gateway of a computer's connection. You can also add switches to this command for other functions.

issuing CA   A certificate authority that issues certificates to users and computers on the network.

J

junk email   Unrequested and unwanted email that is sent to a user. This type of email can be filtered by Outlook 2003.

K

key   A parameter used in an answer file for unattended installations. Also can be a string of numbers used for encryption and decryption.

L

Last Known Good Configuration   The control set that is stored in the Registry and was used the last time the computer was successfully booted and logged onto. You can revert to this control set using the tools in the advanced startup options by pressing F8 at startup.

LMHOSTS file   A static file that is sometimes used for NetBIOS name resolution instead of or as a backup to WINS.

loadstate   The User State Migration Tool component that is used to configure other computers with the configuration captured using `scanstate`.

local printer   The software that is used to control a print device that is physically attached to the computer on which the software is installed.

Localization   Refers to the language that is displayed by the operating system itself. This includes the Start menu, Taskbar, and help screens. There are 24 Localizations of Windows XP, including the English version.

Local User Accounts and Groups   A GUI-based tool within Computer Management that allows an administrator to create and manage users and groups that are being given access to the local computer.

Local Security Authority (LSA)   A system that operates on a local computer, providing the logon screen and communicating with the domain controller when necessary.

low-level format   The factory formatting of a hard drive that creates the sectors that will later be used to store data.

log   A file that holds records of noteworthy events.

M

Media Access Control (MAC) address   A hexadecimal address that is encoded on most network devices and consists of an assigned number that identifies the manufacturer and a serial number assigned by the manufacturer.

Microsoft client   Software built into all Microsoft operating systems since Windows 95. This software provides the method of networking computers using a common client.

Microsoft Office   A suite of applications designed to assist users in performing business-related tasks.

Microsoft Windows Installer   A group of programs and services that are used to assist in the installation of Windows software.

mirrored volume   A fault-tolerant disk configuration that duplicates data on two separate hard disks.

modem   A device used to transfer information through regular telephone lines by converting digital information into analog information in the form of sounds. The term stands for *modulator/demodulator*.

multiboot installation   An operating system software installation that includes two or more operating systems installed on the same computer within different partitions.

Multilanguage User Interface (MUI)   A special version of Windows XP operating system software that includes all 24 Localizations of the software.

N

name resolution   The process of converting one type of computer name to another to facilitate communication. Some names, such as hostnames and NetBIOS names, are used by people but not by computers. Name resolution is the process of converting the names that people use into names and addresses that computers and network devices can use.

nbtstat   A command-line tool that you can use to manage NetBIOS name information and display statistics and details regarding current IP connections.

NetBIOS name   A name (or names) that is unique to a computer and defines the computer and/or services that it can provide for the network. NetBIOS names must all be unique within a network. They can be a maximum of 15 characters in length. The system automatically adds the 16th character to create additional NetBIOS names associated with services that the computer can perform for the network.

Network Address Translation (NAT)   An Internet standard process that allows the user to use one set of IP addresses internally for a company and completely different IP addresses for the perimeter devices exposed to the Internet. All internal addresses are converted to an external address before any information or requests are sent out of the network.

net   A command-line tool that is used primarily to view network settings on a computer.

network printer   Software that is used to control a print device that is not attached to the computer on which the software is installed.

nslookup   A command-line tool that you can use to test hostname resolution and to verify that a computer is registered in the DNS server(s) of a network.

O

Office 2003 Proofing Tools   Software that includes tools such as a spelling and grammar checker that are used for checking documents and that are available in English as well as many other languages.

offline files and folders   Local copies of network resources stored on local hard drives. While offline (off the network), users can open, modify, delete, and create new files that can then be synchronized with the network resource once the client computer is reconnected to the network.

original equipment manufacturer (OEM)   A computer vendor that installs software into the computers as part of their production.

Outlook Express   A simple messaging program tool for email and newsgroups that comes bundled with the Windows operating system.

P

packets   Communication that is delivered and guaranteed using acknowledgments at the transport layer of the TCP/IP protocol.

paging   The process of moving memory from a hard disk into RAM to be used by an application. Memory on the hard disk is referred to as virtual memory.

page file   The area of a hard disk that is set aside for virtual memory.

parallel communication   The exchanging of information between computers and peripherals using multiple data bits and control bits simultaneously over parallel wires.

parent folder   The folder above another folder in a folder hierarchy. The parent folder is said to contain the child folder.

parity data   Fault-tolerant records that are spread across all of the disks in a RAID configuration.

partition   A specific portion of a disk that is set aside from the rest of the disk and can then be formatted with a file system. You can also treat an entire disk as one partition.

permissions   Rules and settings that define a user's access to files, folders, printers, computers, and other components in a network. The two most common permissions in Windows-based networks are share permissions and NTFS file and folder permissions.

power scheme   A collection of settings that can be configured in the Power Options properties of Control Panel. These include the ability to turn off the monitor, hard drives, and other components after a set period of time. Power schemes are part of Advanced Configuration and Power Interface (ACPI).

Plug and Play   The capability of the Windows operating system to recognize a new device and automatically assign it the resources that it needs to operate within the computer.

POP3   Post Office Protocol, version 3 (POP3) is used to store messages in a user's mailbox and to assist the user in retrieving the messages when the user is logged on.

printers   Software that is used to control a print device.

print device   A hardware peripheral device that attaches to a computer or a network cable for the purpose of creating a hard copy of documents and graphics, generally on paper.

print job   The data that is transferred to the print spool that will be used to create the hard copy of a document, picture, and so on.

printer driver   Software that is specifically designed to allow a printer to communicate with the operating system.

printer permissions   Rules and settings that control a user's ability to use and manage a printer and the print device(s) to which it is attached. These include Print, Manage Documents, and Manage Printers.

private key   Half of the public-private key pair issued with most certificates. The private key is held and protected by the user of the key. It is not published or made available to others.

profile   A storage location for many configuration settings for a user account. It contains many folders and files specifying how the computer desktop should be configured on a client computer.

public key   Half of the public-private key pair issued with most certificates. The public key is made available to everyone to verify the user or computer.

public key cryptography   The use of private-public key pairs to provide encryption and decryption as well as authentication by breaking the key into two pieces that work together. The public key is published and made available to everyone, while the private key is held and kept secret. To be completed, actions taken with the public key require other actions to be taken with the private key.

Public Key Infrastructure (PKI)   Consists of protocols, services, and standards that support public key cryptography. A PKI consists of applications and services that use public-private key pairs provided by certificates issued by either public or private certificate authorities.

R

radio frequency (RF)   Communication and control using radio waves in a specified frequency. Does not require line-of-sight communications.

recovery agent   Used to recover EFS-encrypted files when the user is not available to decrypt the files.

Recovery Console   A command line interface that will allow you to perform advanced configuration on a system that won't even allow you to boot into Safe Mode.

regional settings   Configuration in Regional and Language Options that defines the method of displaying dates, times, currency, and so on based on a country and region.

Regional and Language Options   A setting in Control Panel that allows an administrator to add new languages that the computer can understand and that can be used to create documents. This might also require a special keyboard or a keyboard overlay.

Remote Assistance   A new tool in Windows XP that allows a user to request assistance from a more-experienced user and allows the more-experienced user to take control of a less-experienced user's computer remotely to attempt to fix a problem.

Remote Desktop   A tool built into Windows XP that enables a user to connect to and control a remote computer provided that the remote computer is configured to allow the connection and that the user can log on to the remote computer.

Remote Installation Server (RIS)   A network server that is configured by the network administrator to be used for automated installation of client operating systems and applications.

removable storage devices   All types of devices that are used to store data with the exception of hard drives.

Resultant Set of Policy (RSoP)   The combination of Group Policy settings that determines the effective settings when more than one group policy is applied to the same object.

Roll Back Driver   A new feature on Windows XP that allows you to easily return to a previous driver for a device when a driver upgrade fails.

Routing and Remote Access Services (RRAS)   A Windows service that provides access to LAN resources to remote users through dial-up or VPN connections.

Redundant Array of Inexpensive Disks (RAID-5) volume   A special type of stripe configuration that creates fault tolerance as it stripes the data across all of the disks. With a RAID-5 configuration, you can lose any one of the disks in the configuration and still rebuild the array from the fault-tolerant data spread across the other disks.

remote connections   Computer connections into a network from the outside using dial-up or virtual private networking (VPN).

routers   Devices that work at Layer 3 of the Open Systems Interconnection (OSI) model and transfer packets from one subnet to another.

S

safe mode   A setting that you can use to load Windows for troubleshooting while disabling many features to further isolate the cause of a failure and affect a repair.

scanstate   The User State Migration Tool component that is used to capture the configuration settings of a computer.

section title   A category of settings in an answer file.

Secure Sockets Layer (SSL)   Also called Transport Layer Security, SSL is used to encrypt data at the Transport layer when that data flows between a web server and a web client.

serial communication   The sequential exchange of information between computers and peripheral devices one bit at a time over a single channel.

Setup Manager Wizard   A tool that administrators can use to create answer files and uniqueness database files for unattended installations of Windows operating system software.

shared folders   Folders on a computer that have been made available to other computers and users who can access the folders through the computer network.

share permissions   Rules and settings on a folder or printer that control a user's access to that resource through the network. These settings include Read, Change, and Full Control.

simple file sharing   A permission system whereby files are only shared by placing them into the Shared Files folder. NTFS permissions are not controlled and remain in their default position. Simple file sharing is enabled by default in Windows XP Home Edition and can be selected in Windows XP Professional.

simple volume   A single region on a hard disk or multiple regions that are linked together on the same hard disk. Simple volumes are not fault tolerant.

single sign-on   The process of logging on one time and being able to access resources throughout the network, including resources on different operating systems.

Software Update Services (SUS)   Free software from Microsoft that is designed to download updates and hotfixes from Microsoft and then internally distribute them to all your Windows 2000–based (and later) servers and workstations.

spanned volume   A region of disk space that exists on more than one hard disk. The size of a spanned volume is increased by extending it onto additional dynamic disks.

special permissions   NTFS permissions that are not standard but instead are customized. Special permissions display as Special in the advanced settings of NTFS permissions.

startup error   An error that occurs when a computer is in the processes of booting or accessing the operating system.

stop error   An error that occurs in the text mode of a Windows installation and causes the computer to stop installing software and to stop responding to all user input.

storage device   Any device that is installed on or connected to a computer for the purpose of storing data.

striped volume   Regions of hard disk space that are composed of "stripes" of equal size data that are written across all of the disks in the volume.

symmetric   Processes that utilize a single key. Unlike asymmetric processes that require two different keys, a symmetric process requires only a single key to encrypt and decrypt a file. Many symmetric keys are simple passwords.

synchronization   The process of ensuring that shared folders and offline copies of the folders have the same content. This can be accomplished manually or with some automation.

system access control list (SACL)   That portion of the access control list that contains entries specifying what actions and user, group, or computer accounts will be audited.

system partition   In a computer, the partition that contains the files that are required to successfully boot the computer and locate the operating system.

systemroot   The folder on the boot partition in which the Windows system files are stored. On most client computers, this is either the `C:\WINNT\System32` or `C:\Windows\System32` folder.

switch   A programmable device that works at Layer 2 of the Open Systems Interconnection (OSI) model and filters traffic based on the MAC addresses of hosts.

T

Take Ownership   A special permission that is granted to users to allow them to control permissions on an object and assign other users permissions for the object. The Take Ownership permission is included by default with Full Control permissions and can be assigned through special permissions.

Task Manager   A GUI-based tool that can assist a user or administrator in troubleshooting and managing applications on the computer. You can access this tool by right-clicking an empty area of the Taskbar and choosing Task Manager.

text editor   A tool such as Notepad or WordPad that an administrator can use to view, change, and create text-based files.

Transmission Control Protocol/Internet Protocol (TCP/IP)   A suite of protocols that represent the most prevalent communication standard used for network communication on today's networks, including the Internet.

U

unattended installation   An automatic installation that makes use of answer files and uniqueness database files to choose options and enter information previously programmed by an administrator.

Unicode enabled   Term that means a document follows a standard of character mapping that is universal in nature and applies to all Localizations.

Uniform Resource Locator (URL) Address   A user-friendly web address that includes the DNS address of a computer and the complete path to the resource located on the computer.

uniqueness database files   Files that contain information that is specific to a computer. These files can be used to override the settings of an answer file during an unattended installation.

Universal Serial Bus (USB)   One of the newest methods of transferring data from a computer to a peripheral device. Devices can be daisy chained and can be attached and unattached without shutting down the computer or the peripheral device.

Upgrade Advisor   Software built into Windows XP that checks the hardware and software of a computer for compatibility with Windows XP and creates a report prior to installing the software.

upgrade installation   A software installation of an operating system or an application that is performed on a computer that already has a previous version of the same software.

user accounts   Security principles that identify a user and allow an administrator to assign permissions and audit the user activity within a computer or a network. An individual must have a user account to log on to a computer or a network.

User State Migration Tool   Software included on the Windows XP CD that can be used to capture the configuration settings of a computer and load those settings into other computers. It consists of two components: `scanstate` and `loadstate`.

V

value   A configuration setting that corresponds to a key used in an answer file.

virtual private network (VPN)   A connection to an existing network from a remote location through private or public IP networks using encapsulated packets that are encrypted and difficult to decrypt by unauthorized users. These are often used to improve security and avoid long-distance charges.

virus   A piece of self-replicating code attached to some other piece of code. This code can be harmless or harmful, depending on what the developer wrote the code to do. The virus searches a user's files for an uninfected executable program for which the user has security write privileges. The virus infects the file by putting a piece of code in the selected program file. When a program that is infected with a virus is executed, the virus immediately takes command, finding and infecting other programs and files.

virtual DOS machine (NTVDM)   See Windows NT Virtual DOS Machine (NTVDM).

volume   An area of space on one disk or multiple disks that can be used to store data. Volumes can contain multiple partitions.

W

Windows 9x   A term used to refer to the Windows client operating systems of the 1990s and early 2000, including Windows 95, Windows 98, and Windows Millennium Edition (Me).

Windows Internet Name Service (WINS) server   Network-based server that dynamically registers IP addresses and NetBIOS names of computers on a network and then provides name resolution to clients.

Windows NT virtual DOS machine (NTVDM)   A special application environment that a newer operating system creates to simulate the environment that a DOS application expects.

Windows Performance Tool   An administrative tool that consists of two components: System Monitor and Performance Logs and Alerts. This tool can be used to collect and monitor real-time data as well as to create logs for later review.

Windows Product Activation (WPA)   The process of electronically pairing up a scan of hardware components in a computer with the software license. The result is an activation key, which allows the software to continue operating. This process is designed to prevent casual copying of Windows software.

Windows Update   A feature included in the Windows XP operating system that allows the computer to automatically download the latest security updates from Microsoft's website. These can also be installed automatically based on a schedule set by the user.

Windows Update website   A site that is maintained by Microsoft to provide the latest critical updates and other security updates for operating systems and built-in applications.

Index

Note to the Reader: Throughout this index **boldfaced** page numbers indicate primary discussions of a topic. *Italicized* page numbers indicate illustrations.

J

K

The Best MCDST Book/CD Package on the Market!

Get ready for the 70-271: Supporting Users and Troubleshooting a Microsoft Windows XP Operating System and 70-272: Supporting Users and Troubleshooting Desktop Applications on a Microsoft Windows XP Operating System exams with the most comprehensive and challenging sample tests anywhere! The Sybex Test Engine includes the following features:

- Chapter-by-chapter exam coverage of all the review questions from the book

- Challenging questions representative of those you'll find on the real exams

- Deluxe Edition's **four** bonus exams, available only on the CD—twice as many as in the standard Sybex study guide

Use the Deluxe Edition's 350—twice as many as in the standard Sybex study guide—Electronic Flashcards for PCs or Palm devices to jog your memory and prep for the exam at the last minute!

- Reinforce your understanding of key concepts with these hardcore flashcard-style questions.

- Download the Flashcards to your Palm device, and go on the road. Now you can study anywhere, anytime.

Search through the complete book in PDF!

- Access the entire *MCDST: Microsoft Certified Desktop Support Technician Study Guide, Deluxe Edition*, complete with figures and tables, in electronic format.

- Search the *MCDST: Microsoft Certified Desktop Support Technician Study Guide, Deluxe Edition* chapters to find information on any topic in seconds.

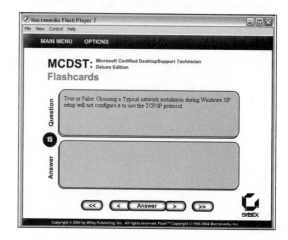